D1422756

The Working Class in Modern British History

The Working Class in Modern British History

Essays in Honour of Henry Pelling

Edited by
JAY WINTER

CAMBRIDGE UNIVERSITY PRESS

Cambridge
London   New York   New Rochelle
Melbourne   Sydney

Published by the Press Syndicate of the University of Cambridge
The Pitt Building, Trumpington Street, Cambridge CB2 1RP
32 East 57th Street, New York, NY 10022, USA
296 Beaconsfield Parade, Middle Park, Melbourne 3206, Australia

First published 1983

Printed in Great Britain at
the Pitman Press, Bath

Library of Congress catalogue card number: 82–9424

British Library Cataloguing in Publication Data
The working class in modern British history: essays
in honour of Henry Pelling
1. Pelling, Henry   2. Labor and laboring
classes—Great Britain—History—Addresses, essays,
lectures
I. Winter, Jay   II. Pelling, Henry
335'.1'0941   HD8395
ISBN 0 521 23444 1

PP

Contents

v

Introduction: labour history and labour historians

JAY WINTER

Labour history in Britain has changed substantially since its emergence as an academic discipline in the years following the Second World War. Against the background of the defeat of fascism and the sweeping victory of the Labour party in the 1945 general election, the first generation of labour historians aimed to reconstruct the evolution of labour movements. This they did through a painstaking retrieval and reconstruction of the record of the institutions of labour – trade unions, political parties and sects, cooperatives, and educational and religious societies. In terms of this aim, their achievement is undeniable. The question remained, however, as many of them would admit, as to how representative of the history of labouring men and women as a whole is the record of organized struggle? Of course, without institutional history, this question simply cannot be answered. But while admitting that in aggregate terms the labour movement has never recruited more than a minority of the working class, labour historians until recently shared a consensus that the record of its struggles expresses, and indeed embodies, both the aspiration of ordinary people to have a better life and their commitment to change the world in which they live and work.

In contrast, recent developments in labour history reflect a different approach to the question of the relation between movement and class. The aim is to complement (rather than supersede) earlier research by defining labour history as the social history of the working class and not primarily as the political history of militants and militancy. The claim of some earlier historians that labour movements reflect the progressive ideas and commitments of the rank-and-file of the working class has been challenged. This is not because labour historians now subscribe to the view of G. M. Trevelyan that social history is history with the politics left out. It is rather that these historians believe that the true political character of the labour movement in modern Britain, and its limitations in outlook and organization in the past, can be identified only when set in the context of the social history of stable working-class communities which by and large have accepted their subordination in the capitalist social order. If the commotion of struggle gave to the earlier studies of labour history their particular tone, it is the silence of political submission which later labour historians have asked us to hear. In the first phase of labour history, the customs and traditions of labouring men were shown to be sources of revolt. In the second phase, other aspects of working-class culture and community become the sources of passivity. There is truth, of course, in both camps. And it would be wrong to exaggerate the extent to which the study of apathy has displaced the study of activism as the dominant theme in recent labour history. Still, it is apparent that a change of emphasis has taken place.

This historiographical development reflects more than a change in transient academic fashions. Its sources partly lie in the disappointment of hopes that fundamental social change would follow the election of Labour governments in the years since the Second World War. There are also more particular generational differences at work. The first phase of the development of labour history in Britain was dominated by the work of a remarkable cohort of historians whose outlook reflected a number of shared experiences. Most were educated at Oxford and Cambridge in the 1930s and 1940s and thereafter began to teach in provincial universities or in adult education. Most saw military service in the Second World War. Most passed through the Communist party in the 1930s and 1940s, and most left after 1956. Most retained the following belief.

> The atomized and predatory logic of capitalism (which persists even within static forms) can only be displaced by the alternative intentions and aspirations of a social consciousness which can (as empirically-given historical fact) be shown to find partial and fragmented embodiment in the actual working-class movement. British history, over 150 years, has shown this alternative possibility to be waxing and waning and waxing again – not as *exactly the same* possibility, but the same in terms of an alternative, socialist logic.[1]

This view had been voiced even earlier by the socialist historian and economist, G. D. H. Cole, whose teaching, encouragement and inspiration were instrumental in launching the post-war generation. Evidence of Cole's influence can be found in *Essays in Labour History*, the *Festschrift* published shortly after his death in 1960, in which some important aspects of the work of the first phase of labour history may be surveyed.[2] In addition, when a professional organization of labour historians was founded, consideration was given to naming it the 'G. D. H. Cole Society'. A more descriptive title was adopted, and it has been through the 'Society for the Study of Labour History' and its *Bulletin* that the subject has developed in the last two decades.[3]

The achievement of this group of historians has been to transform the way history is studied in Britain. Undergraduate and post-graduate courses in labour history have multiplied. Conferences and publications have proliferated. In the early 1960s, it probably would have taken an afternoon for a student of labour history to catch up on what had appeared recently in the field. Twenty years later, reading the literature (not to mention adding to it) has taken on the character of a full-time job.

The influence of labour history extends well beyond the parochial boundaries of a sub-discipline. The work of Asa Briggs, J. F. C. Harrison, Royden Harrison, Eric Hobsbawm, Sidney Pollard, John Saville and E. P. Thompson,[4] among many others, has made it virtually impossible for general historians to relegate discussion of working people and their lives to the background chapters of political histories or to describe them as quaint examples of local colour. Furthermore, the élitist assumptions that workers propose but propertied people dispose (and that this has always been the case) have been banished from the pages of serious historical writing in Britain.

Given the passage of time, the failure of the student revolts of 1968, the fate of the Prague 'spring' of the same year, the onset of an international economic crisis and in Britain the recrudescence of mass unemployment in the 1970s and 1980s, it was perhaps inevitable that a change in direction among labour historians would take place. Some drew on the writings of Antonio Gramsci to explore aspects of cultural history and to investigate the nature of the working-class community as both a realm apart *and* an area where the 'dominance the employers exerted' was manifested in 'the ordinary business of people's lives, inside and outside the factory'.[5] The explanation of political attitudes was still the objective of many of these studies, but others forsook the political realm entirely in order to concentrate on aspects of working-class social history.[6] In recent years, some have sought in the work of historians of France ways to escape from the primacy of political activism. The example of historians wedded to both the concept of *histoire totale* and the resurrection of the unchanging mentality of the masses was of particular importance in this regard. Other scholars have also proved willing to apply to their own work independent advances in historical demography, family history and the history of ritual and religion.[7] In addition, an older suspicion that quantitative techniques and economic theory in general were in some way intrinsically right-wing tools of analysis has largely faded away. Consequently, statistical studies of aspects of working-class life and analyses of business behaviour and entrepreneurial strategies have become a recognized part of the study of labour history.[8] It has recently been claimed that the trend in historical study is to move away from analysis and back to the narrative.[9] Whatever the truth of this claim in general terms, labour history, it appears, is moving in precisely the opposite direction.

Among the pioneers of the subject in Britain, Henry Pelling has had a distinguished and influential career. His first publications were concerned with the emergence of independent labour politics and the 'socialist revival' of the

1880s and 1890s. His edition of writings from Tom Paine to Richard Crossman entitled *The Challenge of Socialism* (1953) set these phenomena in a long-term perspective and provided a sympathetic introduction to the 'richness of debate and controversy on distinctly socialist lines that has been an invigorating influence throughout the political life of this country'.[10] One year later his *Origins of the Labour Party* was published. It was the first major work of scholarship on the subject which was not written by a party activist, past or present. In place of what may be called the 'sixty years' march syndrome' of labour history, Pelling quietly and authoritatively provided in this, as in later work, a rigorous and accurate account of the evolution of the institutions of the modern labour movement. In subsequent studies on trade-unionism, the Labour party and the Communist party in Britain, as well as in writings on the American labour movement,[11] he has shown that it is possible to write about the past of organized labour without adopting a plebeian version of the Whig interpretation of history through which we see the struggles of the past moving inexorably to the victories of the present. In a sense, his political histories have helped to fulfil the classic aim of historical scholarship: the replacement of mythology or vague memory by painstakingly-researched and documented historical analysis. In the process he has produced books which are still indispensable introductions to the subject a generation later.

He has devoted his later work to more general aspects of the social and political history of modern Britain. In his book of collected essays, *Popular Politics and Society in Late Victorian Britain* (1968), he developed incisive and provocative interpretations of key problems in the history of the British working class. In this studies of the labour aristocracy, the 'labour unrest' of 1911–14 and of popular attitudes to welfare and to empire, he has offered challenging reappraisals of the relation between political and industrial activism and the class structure of modern Britain. A similar concern to deepen the social historical content of political history marks his *Social Geography of British Elections 1885–1910* (1967). This book is a meticulously-researched unique guide to the study of regional and local politics, an area in which much more work still needs to be done.

In more recent years, his interests have centred on the period of the 1940s, when his own historical work began. In both his *Britain and the Second World War* (1970) and his biography of Winston Churchill (1974), which naturally covers a much longer period, we see further examples of Pelling's considerable skill in reducing an enormous literature to economical proportions and in writing history that both scholars and general readers will understand and appreciate. His latest research on the Attlee government of 1945–51 is informed by the same concern to place the history of labour in the context of the wider political and social history of Britain which is the hallmark of all his historical scholarship.

In a sense, Pelling's work spans the historiographical divide described above. His major studies chronicle the history of activism and struggle but do so in a way which makes us take full account of the coexistence of 'profound class consciousness' and popular conservatism and apathy.[12] Even those whose interpretations differ from his recognize that his work has contributed to a better understanding of the multiple political and social meanings of the experience of class in modern Britain.

The essays in this book are intended as further explorations of this complex historical problem. They reflect as well the dual character of much recent writing about the history of the British working class. The first section focuses on the outlook, organization and policies of the Labour movement. Three essays deal with political choices; three with political achievements. The first three chapters describe the major forms of left–liberal politics which have emerged over the last three generations. The labourism of Keir Hardie (and others) created the Labour party and remains in it to this day. It displaced liberal paternalism, like that of Churchill, which made the running in working-class politics before 1914 but faded rapidly after the First World War. Whether or not both will be superseded by 'social democracy', in the shape of a party separated from the trade union movement but representing traditional Labour commitments to equality and social justice, remains to be seen. But as the essays of Peter Clarke, Fred Reid and Paul Addison show, each of these options has a history which contemporary observers ignore at their peril. Chapters 4–6 focus on the vicissitudes of Labour politics in the period between 1920 and 1950. The image of the shaky local foundations on which the Labour party rested in the 1920s, presented by Christopher Howard, contrasts sharply with the record of the Attlee government, examined by Partha Gupta in terms of Imperial policy and by Kenneth Morgan in terms of post-war reconstruction in Wales. Perhaps the Labour party did not fully realize the hopes of its founders in this period, but under the circumstances its record was not inconsiderable, as these essays demonstrate.

The second section is concerned with central aspects of the social history of the British working class. Ross McKibbin's study of work and hobbies and Paul Johnson's essay on credit and thrift tell us much about the nature of working-class culture and the working-class domestic economy. Alastair Reid contributes to the discussion of the labour aristocracy with a close examination of the ideas of Thomas Wright, a Victorian metal worker and social commentator often taken to be the exemplar of that problematic social formation. Chushichi Tsuzuki's account of the National Council of Labour Colleges in the period 1920 to 1950 raises intriguing questions about the nature of British Marxism and the meaning of socialist education. José Harris furthers the debate on the working class and social policy by an analysis of the findings of G. D. H. Cole's 1942 survey of popular attitudes to welfare. Arthur Marwick's essay challenges the view that since the 1930s the distinction between working class and non-working class has faded and emphasizes the centrality of cultural and economic, rather than political, manifestations of class sentiment. The stubborn persistence of the trend towards improving health among the working population in the period of the interwar depression and during the Second World War is the theme of the editor's contribution, which is the final essay of the book.

Taken together, these studies provide striking evidence of two central points. First, they document the ways in which the experience of class has pervaded virtually every corner of this nation's public life. Secondly, they show that the mixed political record of organized Labour, its hesitations and failures as well as its struggles and successes, cannot be understood without a full appreciation of the collective and individual lives of working people outside the political arena.

This book does not claim to provide a complete or comprehensive history of the working class in modern British history. No single volume could even begin to approach that task. If space permitted, there would be a separate section in this book, entitled 'The Working Class in British Industry', which would reflect new approaches to the study of trade-unionism and the labour process.[13] Many historians working on these themes are as indebted as the authors of this book to the work of Henry Pelling. In a way, anyone working in labour history today is informally one of his students. It is appropriate, therefore, that to mark his retirement from his Readership in History in the University of Cambridge we collectively dedicate this volume to him.

Pembroke College, Cambridge   December 1981

I

The working class in British politics

1

The social democratic theory of the class struggle

PETER CLARKE

I

There can hardly be a topic in the whole field of British labour history which has attracted less attention than the social democratic theory of the class struggle.* Nor is this neglect at all surprising. It may even be disputable whether such a theory (understanding this as a scheme or system of ideas held as an explanation or account) in fact exists. In the course of the first section of this essay, I acknowledge that the theory may not constitute much of an answer. What does exist, I maintain, and what cannot be wished away, is the problem to which it is addressed. In developing my theme, therefore, the starting-point must be a definition of terms.

The social democratic label became fashionable in British politics during the 1970s, chiefly as a pejorative description of the section of the Labour party which could not display either left-wing or trade-union credentials. Even the apostles of revisionism in the party have been uneasy with the term. Anthony Crosland's reported definition that a social democrat was 'somebody about to join the Tory Party',[1] shows that we are dealing with masked words. The force of his allusion to the procession of right-wing renegades in the late 1970s is undeniable. Yet if Crosland himself was not a social democrat, who was? There is no getting away from the fact that, historically, social democracy has not been easily adopted into the language of British politics.

Part of this historical uncertainty lies in the fact that in Britain, unlike most continental countries, the major party of the left did not call itself Social Democrat. This may be another way of saying that the Marxist Social Democratic Federation (SDF), led by H. M. Hyndman, did not succeed in becoming the major party of the left. The SDF (or SDP from 1908) certainly tried to establish itself under the name in the years 1884–1911 with the result that

* The foundation of the Social Democratic party during 1981 has lent to my subject some current connotations which could hardly have been intended. My title was agreed with the editor in June 1979. A first draft of the paper was given to the Open University History Seminar in London, convened by Christopher Harvie, on 1 February 1980, and I benefited considerably from this discussion. The present version was written in September 1980 and, following helpful criticism from John Thompson, Stefan Collini and Jay Winter, it underwent a final revision in April 1981.

3

'Social Democrat' was gradually appropriated as a term of art designating Hyndman's followers. In the early publications of the Fabian Society there was no such impediment to a more ecumenical usage, though in *Fabian Essays* (1889) Bernard Shaw talked of the socialists having 'fallen into line as a Social Democratic party'. On the other hand, we also find Graham Wallas proposing a 'tentative and limited Social Democracy', and in 'The Impossibilities of Anarchism' (1891) Shaw likewise refers to 'State Socialism, which, for the sake of precision, had better be called Social-Democracy'. By the time Shaw came to reissue this lecture sixteen years later, however, he had been forced to justify using the term.[2]

> The word Social-Democrat is used in these pages in its proper sense, to denote a Socialist who is also a Democrat. In England it has come to be used in a narrower sense, to denote doctrinaire Marxism and the characteristic propaganda of the Social-Democratic Federation. Whilst this transient misunderstanding lasts, my readers will have to allow for it by remembering that all Socialists who postulate democracy as the political basis of Socialism, including, of course, the members of the Fabian Society, are entitled to describe themselves as Social-Democrats.

Thus in the Edwardian period the connotations were often Marxist, even when Social Democratic was not being used as a formal title. 'In Germany,' Winston Churchill argued in October 1906, 'there exists exactly the condition of affairs in a party sense, that Mr Keir Hardie and his friends are so anxious to introduce here. A great social democratic party on the one hand, are [*sic*] bluntly and squarely face to face with a capitalist and military confederation on the other.' This sort of reference was plainly reinforced by the continental example. An explicit attempt at definition in an anti-socialist handbook sponsored by the Conservative party stated that 'the terms "Socialism" and "Social Democracy"' were 'in practice to-day convertible terms'. It suggested, however, that Social Democracy, owing to its more recent introduction and its German origin, was the less commonly used and linked its currency with the activities of the SDP.[3]

Before the First World War a reference to Social Democracy would normally have carried the 'narrower sense' against which Shaw's protest was directed. Its flavour would have been revolutionary, and it would not, therefore, have been associated with the reformist ideology of 'Labourism' for which recent social democrats have been arraigned by Marxist critics. The historical development of Labourism may be taken, in John Saville's useful formulation, as 'a theory and practice which accepted the possibility of social change within the existing framework of society; which rejected the revolutionary violence and action implicit in Chartist ideas of physical force; and which increasingly recognized the working of political democracy of the parliamentary variety as the practicable means of achieving its own aims and objectives'. When the young G. D. H. Cole wanted to describe contending forces in the Labour movement during the labour unrest, he naturally wrote: 'Syndicalism, in the widest sense, and the old Unionism confront each other in the industrial field just as Social Democracy and Labourism are opposed in the sphere of politics.'[4]

It may appear, therefore, that modern social democrats lack historical rights in their very name which was merely misappropriated on their behalf after 1917. Even so, there would still be some point in applying the term historically if a recognizable and continuous tradition could be identified, albeit one which only later became known as social democratic. This would cut through a quibble over copyright (Shaw's 'transient misunderstanding') with a freshly-honed analytical concept.

The social democratic tradition, on this reading, has been distinctively collectivist, seeking to use the state as the direct agent of social amelioration. It has been socialist chiefly in this rather restricted definition. It has been committed to parliamentary methods as the means of securing the agency of the state for these purposes. It has been reformist, in Lenin's sense, stopping short of revolutionary changes which were seen as neither desirable nor necessary. The social democratic slogan has therefore been social justice, with the dual implication that market forces will not produce it but that it is a feasible goal within 'the mixed economy' (as social democrats generally now term it, that is, what their opponents on the right usually characterize as 'socialism', and what their critics on the left persist in describing as 'capitalism'). This was surely the 'Gaitskellite' position in the 1950s and 1960s. Its key text in this period was Crosland's *The Future of Socialism* (1956) which owed a considerable debt to Evan Durbin's *The Politics of Democratic Socialism* (1940).[5] The writings of R. H. Tawney, especially *Equality* (1931), lay, in turn, behind the restatements of the Gaitskellite generation, and Tawney was himself influenced by the early Fabians. But not just by the Fabians. The theorists of the new Liberalism, especially J. A. Hobson and L. T. Hobhouse, also have strong claims for being regarded as among the progenitors of British social democracy. This is true regardless of the language of political argument which sentiment, prudence, fashion or polemical advantage dictated at the time.

There is, however, evidence in contemporary usage, especially by Hobhouse, which establishes the origins of the term more directly. In May 1907, for instance, Hobhouse was urging the Liberal government to take up social and economic issues as the means of mobilizing the forces necessary to confront the veto power of the House of Lords. He could thus argue: 'the road to political democracy in England lies through what, in a broader sense than is usually given to the term, we may call social democracy'. He clearly wanted to employ this vocabulary but was inhibited from doing so more readily by the recognition that another sense held the field. Thus in *Liberalism* (1911) he loosely acknowledged contemporary usage in referring to the awkward position of Liberalism at the close of the nineteenth century as being 'between two very active and energetically moving grindstones – the upper grindstone of pluto-cratic imperialism, and the nether grindstone of social democracy'. Even here the word collectivism could probably be substituted without violating Hob-house's meaning. A further reference in a passage written at much the same time suggests why Hobhouse kept toying with the term despite the risk of confusing his readers.[6]

> Political changes, then, which have given us constitutional democracy, have paved the way for what, if the term were not limited to a rather narrow theory, we might call a social democracy, what we at any rate call a democracy seek-ing, by the organised expression of the collective will, to remodel society in accordance with humanitarian sentiment.

Hobhouse's essential point was to connect the case for collectivism, about which Liberals might well be dubious, with the case for democracy, on which it was safer to appeal. This was a shrewd polemical strategy but it also reflected Hobhouse's own values. As he once put it, 'the extension of public responsi-bility under a representative system is one thing; under any other system it is open to quite another set of objections'. This was, in short, a distinctively liberal case for collectivism and one which implied, despite initial appear-ances, a fundamental congruity between the old Liberalism of *laissez-faire* and the new Liberalism of state intervention. On Hobhouse's view of the nine-teenth century, 'the doctrine of popular liberty, which enshrined a social truth of permanent value, became identified with doctrines restricting collective action, which were of merely temporary value'. So when the people 'could look upon the Government as their servant and the acts of the Government as their acts, it followed necessarily that the antagonism between democracy and governmental action fell to the ground'.[7] If the characteristic achievement of the old Liberalism had been political democracy, what the new Liberalism sought was, given this connotation and cue, social democracy.

The logic of this approach was that social democrats claimed a prior commit-ment as democrats as a constraint upon their social measures. Since for them 'the system' was democracy, their analysis might well be at odds with that of socialists for whom 'the system' was capitalism. This raises, then, the second problem in my title. The socialist theory of the class struggle is well understood and may be quickly summarized. The system is capitalism, which comprises the ownership of the means of production by a privileged class. As the system works, it is necessarily exploitative, hence antagonism is the essence of rela-tions between classes. The class struggle is not only inevitable; it is also desir-able in that it is the only way of changing the system and thus remedying its inequities and malfunctions. Class *in itself* manifests the problem to which class *for itself* provides the solution. These propositions constitute both an internally consistent theory and one which is ideologically effective in explaining and justifying conflict.

Social democrats, by contrast, seem to be committed to two incompatible positions. In the first place they deny the desirability or necessity of class conflict. Their leaders spoke of 'rejecting the class war' in 1980, whereas a quarter of a century previously Crosland had written: 'Nobody now rationally believes in a theory of irreconcilable conflict, or that anything which helps the management must *ipso facto* hurt the workers . . .' Durbin gave emphasis (literally) to the following proposition. 'The economic life of an advanced society is peculiarly the sphere of the most complex and successful kinds of co-operation.' Earlier references by Hobson to the rationale of the industrial system as 'a great co-operative society of consumers', and to the recognition of 'a harmony of interests' between capital and labour (at least over the division of the 'productive' surplus) suggest the same perspective.[8]

How far Tawney subscribed to these views is admittedly more open to question. In *The Acquisitive Society* (1921), his most radical book, there is a caustic reprimand implying that he did not. 'To deplore "ill-feeling", or to advocate "harmony", between "labour and capital" is as rational as to lament the bitterness between carpenters and hammers or to promote a mission for restoring amity between mankind and its boots.' No doubt. Yet there are similar passages in Hobson, which may only indicate that it is the appeal for harmony as a means of propping up the *status quo* which is scouted. Conversely, we can find Tawney in 1917 asking why 'the unity of the nation [should be] marred by ever-recurring conflicts between the two partners in the business on which, as they know when both sides stop to think, the future of the country depends?' Though it might fairly be said that this is the voice of the patriot in wartime, of the wounded soldier succoured on the goodwill of promises for reconstruction, it nonetheless seems a better representation of Tawney's considered view. It is part of his indictment of economic and social inequalities in 1938 that they produce 'a perpetual class-struggle, which, though not always obtrusive, is always active below the surface and which is fatal to the mobilization of co-operative effort'.[9] Despite the undeniable changes of tone, Tawney can be considered consistent in his view of the fundamental issue. He saw class conflict as the destructive and internecine result of existing injustice in society, not as the effectual means of its redress. Class for itself would not emancipate society from the chains of class in itself.

I hope that I have established the existence of a distinctive British political tradition prominently represented by the early Fabians, the new Liberals, Tawney, Durbin and the Gaitskellites; and that there are inescapable historical and semantic reasons for calling it social democratic. I hope that I have also shown that one of its foundation stones has been a rejection of the Marxist concept of the class war and an appeal instead to the interests of the community as a whole, to a model of economic cooperation and social harmony, immanent if not yet fulfilled. But we are heading here for an awkward corner, because social democrats have simultaneously held a second view. A question arises to which (historically) the social democratic theory of the class struggle has been the answer.[10] As an answer it may be dismissed (politically or philosophically) as a lacuna, as fantasy, as hypocrisy, or at best as a paradox. For the question is, how have social democrats squared their language of unity and consensus with their commitment to *class* parties? After the First World War the Labour party was their political home. Moreover, those like Hobson who had previously been Liberals had given their strongest and clearest support to the Liberal party in 1910, exactly at the moment when it acquired its sharpest image as a class party. How, therefore, could the belief that class conflict was a bad thing be reconciled with the knowledge that it was what democracy was really all about?

II

Social democrats characteristically argued the case for equality by reference to social justice. An important objective was thus the redistribution of wealth from rich to poor. As Hobhouse put it, 'let us consider the remedy, and admit, once for all, that whatever be the character of that remedy, it must fulfil this first condition of distributing the products of industry with more regard to the welfare of the masses than is paid by the blind and sometimes blindly adored forces of competition'. It was also generally assumed that the poor could be identified with the working class and more specifically with organized labour. Hobhouse again: 'the organised workmen are in a way the leaders of the working class as a whole'.[11] It may be felt, therefore, that there existed a simple way of resolving the whole problem, viz. that the efforts of the labour movement were motivated by self-interest but deserved support because of the justice of labour's claims. There is something in this. But the logic of this resolution prises apart the 'social' and 'democratic' ascriptions in a way that was resisted by the thinkers considered here, perhaps because their view of progress was 'moral' rather than 'mechanical'.[12] The engine of change, so they professed, properly lay in the social purchase of ideas, as norms and motives, rather than in the expedient implementation of prescriptive programmes and policies.

As the heir of political liberalism social democracy took over a view of politics which was already familiar. 'To those of us who were brought up in the liberal and democratic traditions of British political life,' Durbin contended, 'a certain form of utilitarianism is bred in our bones, and will not pass from us until we are dead.'[13] When he made out the case for democracy, he spoke, like Bentham and Mill, of making representative government responsible to the popular will as the only means of promoting the greatest happiness of the greatest number. The reality of this agency was not questioned. Such a pure and explicit avowal of intellectual pedigree may be unusual. Nonetheless, the foremost strand in the social democratic theory of politics has undoubtedly been the rational utilitarian view.

Benthamite man was a creature of solipsism. Self-interest was his invariable motive and his infallible guide. The greatest happiness of the greatest number was a legitimate sanction for public policy. Since the working class composed the greatest number of persons, and ultimately of electors, their collective self-interest might be expected to prevail through their parliamentary representatives. None saw this more clearly than utilitarian opponents of democracy, who rode hard on an argument which the Benthamites themselves tried to restrain. To the future Lord Salisbury it was evident that the struggle for power lay 'between the classes who have property and the classes who have none', which was a good reason to resist electoral reform in the 1860s. 'Wherever democracy has prevailed,' he warned, 'the power of the state has been used in some form or other to plunder the well-to-do classes for the benefit of the poor.'[14] From their own point of view social democrats readily accepted the class dimension of this fundamentally utilitarian conception of democracy. The rationale of the whole process was (positively) the maximization of happiness, and therefore (negatively) the redress of the grievances of a majority. This was rational insofar as the desired ends were self-interested and the chosen means appropriate. Since the insight of socialism was that the majority had rational grievances as an exploited class, it followed that socialism was the economic obverse of democracy.[15] The Fabian preference for parliamentary methods initially rested on this sort of reasoning.

The more the Liberal party took up issues of social reform, the closer it came to acknowledging that the people's cause really rested on class interest, at least in a certain sense. Winston Churchill, speaking in 1908, offered to tell the wealthy and powerful the secret of their security of life and property in Britain. It arose

> from the continuation of that very class struggle which they lament and of which they complain, which goes on ceaselessly in our country, which goes on tirelessly, with perpetual friction, a struggle between class and class in this country which never sinks into lethargy, and never breaks into violence, but which from year to year makes a steady and constant advance.

This was a rationalistic view of class interest in politics, the direct ancestor of the social democratic position, assuming that melioristic proposals naturally command majority support. Its commendation of the class struggle should be taken in conjunction with a slightly later comment. In July 1909 Churchill stressed the urgency of adopting welfare policies by arguing that otherwise the gap between rich and poor, in both wealth and outlook, would widen, in which case 'I think there is nothing before us but savage strife between class and class'.[16] The implication was that the domesticated class struggle of democratic politics was the alternative to the real thing.

Put in this way, the argument was primarily directed as a warning to the class in possession against the dangers of a die-hard policy. But the virtue of liberal methods has been more positively urged by social democrats and firmly associated with the parliamentary road. They sought to set the processes of rational deliberation and decision-making in a social context which acknowledged their class aspect. It was Hobson's contention that every instalment of economic reform involved an attack upon vested interests. It was not so much a symmetrical class struggle as the opposition between the sectional interests of the possessing classes and the general principles of economic justice. 'The man who is surrounded by riches', according to Hobhouse, 'sees the world as through a glass darkly. He hears its cries as through a blanket . . .' Hobson was ready to admit that the parliamentary game had been deftly turned into a defence of the *status quo*. But the fact that, with the growth of political liberties, class ascendancy was increasingly preserved by ideological control rather than open menace, was in itself a sign of progress. It gave better ground to fight on. 'When the struggle is on the plane of brute force, numbers and justice may indeed be overborne, but every elevation of the struggle raises their power.' Ideas were the strongest weapons in the people's hands. Likewise Tawney's later assessment that 'unequal as the struggle is in the political field, it is less one-sided there than it would be in any other'.[17]

The case against a revolutionary alternative was double-barrelled, and shot at anything that moved. The first target was a spontaneous insurrection, of the sort generally envisaged before the First World War. This was shot down because it would enjoy no chance of success, Hobson seeing it as 'a conflict between the armed trained forces of the State defending the interests of capital and an unarmed, untrained rabble'. But a disciplined seizure of power by a dictatorship of the left, on the Bolshevik model, met the charge from the other barrel that it negated the very ends of social democracy. Durbin's case against it was that the minimum content of the idea of social justice was the combination of political liberty with economic equality. While 'a dictatorship of the Left might achieve a greater equality in the distribution of wealth', it could not achieve justice, 'because it cannot give freedom to those who do not like inequality, and dare not put to the test its claim that the great majority of mankind really want equality at all'. It was not just that bourgeois ideas of liberty would have to be subordinated to the general welfare: without liberty there would be no subjective test of the general welfare.[18] The interests of the working class were therefore just as keenly at risk from authoritarianism, as they well recognized. Tawney argued that the existence of a strong liberal tradition in Britain meant that there was widespread and deep-rooted support for notions of fair play, with which he specifically identified parliamentary government. It had to be realized, he contended, 'that the class which is the victim of economic exploitation, instead of merely reading about it, is precisely the class which attaches most importance to these elementary decencies'. So socialists 'must face the fact that, if the public, and particularly the working-class public, is confronted with the choice between capitalist democracy, with all its nauseous insincerities, and undemocratic socialism, it will choose the former every time'. To Tawney, with social democratic priorities, this was 'a proof, not of stupidity, but of intelligence'.[19] Although couched in the language of utilitarian rationalism, this approbation of the wisdom of the working class verges on populism, of which more must be said later.

If the first strand in the social democratic theory of politics was utilitarian rationalism, it was often intertwined with a second, that of progressive élitism. It was in the Edwardian period that an incisive challenge was mounted to the conventional Benthamite assumptions about democracy, with important contributions from two Fabian essayists, Bernard Shaw and Graham Wallas. According to Shaw, it was the hard experience of what he called 'proletarian democracy' that damned it. 'Only under depotisms and oligarchies has the Radical faith in "universal suffrage" as a political panacea arisen.' The flaw in representative government was not the exclusion of certain interests, as Bentham had supposed, but the inclusion of such poor human material in a mass electorate, merely changing the conditions under which the older wisdom of Machiavelli had to be applied. Instead of flattering kings, the politician now had 'to learn how to fascinate, amuse, coax, humbug, frighten, or otherwise strike the fancy of the electorate', as the courtier had been superseded by the demagogue. A far-seeing statesman was left with 'no chance unless he happens by accident to have the specific artistic talent of the mountebank as well, in which case it is as mountebank that he catches votes, and not as a meliorist'. This was the justification for the growing Fabian preoccupation with the manipulation of the political system at an élite level. Social amelioration was to come despite democracy, no longer because of it. Shaw's candid and amoral avowal of these views in *Man and Superman* helped to provoke Wallas into formulating a more dispassionate response. In *Human Nature in Politics* (1908) we have a classic exposure of the 'intellectualist fallacy' on which liberal democrats had been accustomed to rely. We move, with a compelling sense of immediacy, into the real world of democracy where Wallas had fought his many local electoral campaigns. No ideal citizen here, only the tired householder, whose political opinions were neither rational nor well-informed, but the results of half-conscious inference fixed by habit. How could such a figure be relied upon to perceive the true nature of his grievances, still less to bend the state to his will in effecting a remedy? This is the question which Wallas's work left hanging over the social democratic prospectus.[20]

The third strand which merits examination can be termed moral populism, within which two notions were spliced together. One of these was another piece of old rope left over from the Liberal era, imputing an almost mystical wisdom to the common people. Gladstone's belief in the virtues of the Christian poor was enhanced in old age by his growing disillusionment with the Christian rich (or their disillusionment with him). Though his career was founded upon keeping class conflict out of politics, he was nonetheless to make his famous declaration in Liverpool in 1886: 'All the world over, I will back the masses against the classes.' It is important to note the difference between this sort of vapid romanticism and a utilitarian acknowledgement of the concrete grievances of the working class. It was to their disinterested judgement and to their unselfishness that Gladstone appealed. The popular verdict thus carried an authority which overrode all the special interests and biases fostered by wordly possessions.

The other form of populism rested more directly upon a sense of the organic nature of society. In part this may have been no more than a recognition of the sociology of opinion-forming, with special reference to the 'collectivist' norms of the working class. Hobson at various times staked out both the weak and the strong forms of this conception. In the weak (or sociological) form it expediently fused one social democratic nostrum about social harmony with another about political rationalism. 'Modern industrialism,' Hobson held, 'cannot proceed without increasing cooperation and solidarity of the masses as workers and as citizens: these processes of formal integration cannot fail to generate and feed a fuller and more intelligent popular consciousness.' This was really Marx and water, with capitalism unwittingly calling forth its own critique. Hobson's analysis of the results of the 1910 elections was largely in this pattern. The division between Progressives and Conservatives, he concluded, was 'organised labour against the possessing and educated classes, on the one hand, against the public house and unorganised labour on the other'. He was not disconcerted by the class character of this cleavage; it showed that the good seed of rational argument had been broadcast but had occasionally fallen on stony ground (in the Home Counties, for example). Intellectuals who find themselves sympathizing with a tide of popular opinion no doubt often exaggerate its closeness to their own views, and tend to interpret it in their own terms.[21]

The strong form of the populist case, however, swept Hobson appreciably further as he succumbed to its temptations in deep draughts. Not only did he conclude that working-class life provided 'the best conditions for the emergence and the operation' of the sort of 'sane collective will and judgement' of which he approved, but he also discounted 'mere individual self-interest, or more intimate acquaintance with the facts of trade and industry', as the rational grounding for such political opinions and allegiances. Well into his cups by now, he ventured instead a more far-reaching speculation:

There is, I feel sure, a half-instinctive, half-conscious drive of collective wisdom, set up by the associated working class life which the needs of modern capitalistic production have established, a genuine spirit of the people, however incomplete in its expression, which makes for political righteousness.

We encounter here a sort of superior collective mind, a version of the general will, which guarantees social progress through its capacity to defeat the unpredictable impulses latent in all individuals. This provided a means of escaping from the problem of irrationality, as unmasked by the social psychologists, without ostensibly resorting to the élitist solutions of Shaw, to which the political objection is obvious. This heady version of populism boosts confidence in a rational outcome without requiring the victory of rationalism as the means of bringing it about. Such notions, it must be said, have provided social democrats not only with grains of comfort but also with seeds of delusion.

III

It would be wrong to identify a preference for moral rather than mechanical change as distinctively social democratic. This would be to ignore a prevalent strain of reformist priggishness and a Fabian fascination with institutional manipulation on the one side, and to discount the sort of socialist humanism of which E. P. Thompson, both as historian and as polemicist, stands as a good exponent on the other. Entrenched in the tradition of William Morris, socialist humanism has affirmed the moral agency of men in making their own history as against Marxist and Fabian attempts to impose socialism from above in the name of science. Thompson has claimed voluntarism as the vocabulary of 'authentic liberalism'. He has denounced 'the mechanical theory of human consciousness' as an imposture on Marxism and instead defended 'moralism' against its Marxist assailants.[22] It seems to me that moral revolutionists of this kind and moral reformists in the social democratic tradition share an intellectual affinity, whether it be called liberal or humanist, which sets them apart from their Stalinist or Fabian bedfellows. In short, the irreducibility of the distinction between moral or mechanical methods of change resists the attempt to conflate it with the degree of change (reform or revolution) which is desired.[23]

A commitment to the moral method of change elevates the values of spontaneity and free will. Social democrats have often ambitiously linked these with the workings of the representative system, without, however, adequately acknowledging the institutional constraints to which they are subject. After all, the approved democratic method in fact relies on elaborate mediation between the popular will and its execution: by party, by the electoral system, by parliament, by cabinet government and by the civil service. Hobhouse, for one, was tireless (some would say tiresome) in his criticisms of the actual working of these institutions. Yet he still spoke of 'the people', looking upon collectivist measures as 'their acts' as though no such distortion or alienation had intervened.

Conversely, there is a standing temptation for manipulation of the transmission procedures. Hard-headed strategists of power – the Webbs virtually all the time, Beveridge most of the time, Keynes some of the time and even Cole at one particular time – have calculated how to get their hands on the right levers in order to give effect to their deeply-held convictions about policy. They have been dubbed wirepullers, technocrats, operators and dictators accordingly. Yet are not reform proposals merely utopian affirmations unless there is some practicable means of achieving them? Behind the polemical taunts there lurks a problem which social democrats cannot be said to have faced, or even acknowledged.

Social democrats have usually denounced the exploitation of the institutional possibilities of an intricate representative system, whether it turned on control of the party machinery or abridgement of parliamentary government. A good example can be found in the following notably clear and emphatic statement by Hobson and Lloyd.

> There are indeed some social reformers who appear to think that it is their duty to get themselves elected into office by electors who do not know how 'advanced' they are, in order that they may use their legislative power to put on the statute book laws which express, not the actual will of the people, but what 'ought' to be their will if they were as wise as their representatives. Now of this mode of forcing the pace of legislation it may be said that it is not democracy and it is not progress. No law is good *per se*, and true progress is not secured, but is actually retarded, by getting on to the statute book measures not acceptable to the people.

This argument justifies the principle of the referendum as a pragmatic test of the workability and acceptability of legislation. Although it sits more easily with an organic view of social arrangements than with a mechanistic conception of legislative change, it does not rest on a presupposition about the creative role of an organic general will, whatever may be said elsewhere in Hobson's writings. Such a test, Hobson and Lloyd maintained, 'imputes no superstitious wisdom to the man in the street'. His lack of legislative expertise was acknowledged; but nonetheless 'he knows his needs and those of his neighbours, and he and they know when they are "suited" with a law'. At this point rational utilitarianism and moral populism are at one against progressive élitism.[24]

One might expect, therefore, that social democrats would have shown more enthusiasm for the referendum as a means of obviating the features of the representative system which they claimed to dislike. But they have not generally given this problem sustained attention. They have stood by the parliamentary method, showing little interest in more direct applications of democracy, while denouncing as opportunism any effort to cut the corners in order to implement policy. Their own opportunism has lain in a willingness to trim their proposals in order to win democratic assent. Tawney took some trouble to insist that 'a socialism which is to exercise a wide appeal must be adapted to the psychology, not of men in general, nor of workers in general, but of the workers of a particular country at a particular period. It must wear a local garb.' But how far should declarations of faith be tailored to suit the popular taste? The legendary politician's claim ('these are my principles, and if you don't like them I can change them') has not usually been taken as a vindication of his democratic ardour. When, in the 1950s, revisionists asserted that Labour's image needed modernization before the party could hope to recapture power, they met with a scornful response from the left wing. Their suggestion was, so Bevan claimed, to 'find out why a majority of the electorate voted Conservative and then adjust our policies accordingly'.[25] Moral reformists who saw themselves as making an attempt to voice the inarticulate aspirations of Labour's natural constituency might thus appear to others as being ready to jettison political principles in favour of market research.

This dilemma is most acute if human nature, or social consciousness, or political opinion, is thought of as static. In that case the existing deadweight of social conservatism, in all classes, seems to preclude radical change by democratic means. The truism that history is nothing if not a dynamic process serves to spring this trap. Moral revolutionists have thus been able to argue that 'human nature is potentially revolutionary' and that the project of socialism (though guaranteed *by nothing*) can find its own guarantees 'by *reason* and through an open *choice of values*'.[26] What Morris spoke of as the education of desire unlocks this potential force for change. And moral reformists, though usually more sceptical in temperament and more incremental in strategy, have likewise pinned their hopes on education.

Better schools for everyone, and more access to formal teaching at all levels, have been prominent goals, signalled strongly in the work of Wallas, Hobson, Tawney and Crosland. As citizens and as workers, moreover, people are forever learning in other ways; and work experience, trade unions, political organizations and the business of democratic government, have all been commended as means of fostering this process. Hobhouse's early study of the Labour movement shows with what promise its development was invested. He asseverated that 'the spread of moral and economic education among workmen' would enable trade-unionism 'to extend and perfect itself as a moral, educational, and economic movement'. Glossing self-interest as incipient altruism, he defended the fact that trade-unionism began with the solidarity of the workshop in teaching 'the doctrine of fellowship and brotherhood', for the principle was then capable of extension. Deeply impressed, Hobhouse practically wrote these passages in pokerwork: 'He who is faithful in small things will be faithful also in great, and he who loves and will serve his brother whom he hath seen will learn to aid his brother whom he hath not seen.' Embellishing this text later, he pointed to the 'many channels through which Trade Unions become penetrated by wider, more unselfish, and more enlightened views of their duties and their interests'. They were necessarily led, therefore, from a merely sectional outlook to seek more theoretical 'principles of remuneration' which were fair to all.[27] The Labour movement's potential role as bearer of ideas of social justice was thus marked out. Its ostensible receptiveness to their ideas gave social democrats a sense of challenge and opportunity. The logic of their position, founded on an ambitious notion of democratic change, thus demanded a commitment to educative participation, not least in their own party. In this respect, however, theory and practice have diverged.

The high point of social democratic influence in the Labour party was during the leadership of Hugh Gaitskell. By the time of his death in 1963, the revisionist outlook for which he stood, formulated in the works of Tawney, Durbin and Crosland, seemed to be widely accepted in the party. Its subsequent course, however, suggests that the conversion was at best skin-deep, and that the superficial appearance temporarily belied the underlying nature of the party. To be sure, Gaitskell himself fully exemplified the characteristic traits of the moral reformist. His faith in the efficacy of reasoned argument was ineradicable. 'I still tend to assume that people are rational and that if you go on telling the truth as you see it you convince them,' he admitted privately in 1960. His appeal, moreover, was couched in the liberal language of conscience and reform. He was, by the more mechanistic standards of Crossman, 'someone who takes a moralizing and reactionary attitude, which is, in my opinion, almost instinctively wrong on every subject outside economics'. Shaw's denunciations of the pro-Boers had pointed to the same characteristic debility.[28] It is hardly surprising, therefore, that the Gaitskellites' struggle against the Bevanites was conducted as a crusade, enlisting an emotional as well as an intellectual response.

It would, however, be an 'intellectualist fallacy' to attribute Gaitskell's ascendancy in the party to the ideas which he espoused. His decisive rise, after all, dated from the 1952 Morecambe conference and his anti-communist speech at Stalybridge which followed. After this, Michael Foot has commented, Arthur Deakin 'knew he had found his man'; and Foot subsequently refers to 'the Gaitskellites or the Deakinites, which ever they properly be designated'.[29] This points to an important truth. For Deakin can hardly be designated a social democrat. As leader of the Transport and General

Workers' Union, he had a stolid conception of Labourism which drew upon trade-unionist norms of solidarity. Through these spectacles, the activities of the Left looked merely factious. He berated the Bevanites at Morecambe 'for their disregard of those principles and loyalties to which our Movement has held so strongly throughout the whole course of its existence'.[30] Deakin naturally saw it as his task, charged with the responsibility of the largest block vote in the Labour conference, to work with like-minded trade-union leaders for the defeat of the Left.

Gaitskell was carried to the treasurership of the party with such support, a crucial step towards the leadership. And he in turn was prepared to do their 'dirty work' (as he acknowledged), notably in the extraordinarily illiberal attempt to expel Bevan from the party in 1955. As Crossman warned him at the time, Gaitskell 'seemed to be playing the role of merely being a stooge for big forces outside'. Gaitskell's leadership, moreover, was sustained by the same means. When he tackled the fundamental doctrinal declaration of Clause IV in 1959–60, his social democratic prognosis was brushed aside by the unions. No wonder he confided that they now lacked 'a really formidable figure, like Deakin, to give a lead on policy'. The Gaitskellites had been wrong, Crosland commented, 'to go for *doctrine*; we should have gone for *power*'.[31] When Gaitskell recovered his footing in 1960–61, the big unions rallied to his side over defence for quite different reasons: because of familiarity with the issue, loyalty to the leadership, anti-communism, and a lot of business in smoke-filled rooms. Deakin was dead; but Deakinism had triumphed. So had Gaitskell; but had Gaitskellism?

Even in the Gaitskell era, therefore, the foundations of the social democratic position were less secure than they seemed. Furthermore, two flaws that had been latent in its historic assumptions now became manifest. First, its devoted adherence to parliamentary methods came to look rather facile as a solution to the problem of reconciling democracy with collectivism. Second, the identification of the poor with the working class and the recognition of the trade unions as their champion no longer seemed axiomatic. The trade-union propensity to serve the brother whom he hath seen tended to push the rest of the brothers not only out of sight but also out of mind. Both these difficulties were exacerbated by a third failing. The social democrats had in fact lived more by institutional manipulation than by educative participation. If their rhetoric derived from the new Liberalism, their practice was Fabian.

Progressive élitism, far from being suppressed, had merely run underground as a subterranean current, more readily recognized by their opponents than by social democrats themselves. They rarely acknowledged a gap between their rational reformism and the sort of spontaneous Labourism, economist in character, which it paralleled. The dissonance was concealed, especially within the Labour organization itself. When the block votes went the right way, no questions were asked. Ideally, social democracy aimed at winning the hearts and minds of the working class. But as long as trade-union leaders showed that their hearts were in the right place, the fact that their members' minds were on other matters was tacitly condoned.

There are three overlapping reasons why this was so. The first is obviously self-interest. This has doubtless taken many forms, of a more or less unflattering character, from careerism and hypocrisy to pragmatism and the expediency of letting sleeping dogs lie. Secondly, though, self-interest has bred self-deception, particularly about the inscrutable ways of the working class. Crossman records Gaitskell's confidence to him: 'We, as middle-class Socialists, have got to have a profound humility. Though it's a funny way of putting it, we've got to know that we lead them because they can't do it without us, without abilities, and yet we must feel humble to working people.'[32] If this humility was the price of leadership, it meant also an exercise of will to respect attitudes that were incomprehensible and condone practices that were alien to middle-class minds. Practical analysis was again superseded by pokerwork: God moves in a mysterious way and the Labour movement likewise. Thirdly, self-deception was buoyed up by the nostrums of moral populism which predisposed intellectuals towards systematic complacency whenever events turned out well. The man in the howdah may suffer from all sorts of delusions of grandeur, but the most insidious is the belief that he has a unique empathy with the mind of the elephant.

Social democrats have been prey to these temptations because they wanted to get things done. The moral reformist view, that true progress cannot outrun the growth of the social consciousness needed to validate and vivify it, is not conducive to quick results. Its failings in this respect as a theory of power are obvious. Its key word has been 'unless'. It specified that unless prior conditions are satisfied, institutional changes imposed from above will prove as unsatisfying as the Dead Sea fruit. The cutting edge of this critique has been largely monitory, a prescient warning against both authoritarian solutions and bureaucratic corporatism. But if there is no substitute for winning popular approval, there is no easy way of doing so either. The clash of material interest in society is an educative force of uncertain impact and tendency; it is one of the terms of the problem, not the force making for its solution. With the growing complexity of competitive sectional claims, it has become less plausible to postulate a practical congruence of trade-union self-interest and social justice. This proposition, however, has been crucial to the social democratic case in favour of the Labour party. The social democratic theory of the class struggle, in the form surveyed in this essay, was what was needed to make out this case. Perhaps historically it never met this need very adequately, and perhaps now this version will be consigned to the dustbin of history.

2

Keir Hardie and the *Labour Leader*, 1893–1903

FRED REID

There is no church, sayest thou? The voice of Prophecy has gone dumb? This is even what I dispute: but in any case, hast thou not still Preaching enough? A Preaching Friar settles himself in every village; and builds a pulpit, which he calls Newspaper. Therefrom he preaches what most momentous doctrine is in him, for man's salvation; and dost not thou listen, and believe? Look well, thou seest everywhere a new Clergy of the Mendicant Orders, some bare-footed, some almost bare-backed, fashion itself into shape, and teach and preach, zealously enough, for copper alms and the love of God. These break in pieces the ancient idols; and, though themselves too often reprobate, as idol-breakers are wont to be, mark-out the sites of new Churches, where the true God-ordained, that are to follow, may find audience, and minister. Said I not, Before the old skin was shed, the new had formed itself beneath it?

Thomas Carlyle, *Sartor Resartus* (1831), p. 201.

I

Henry Pelling accorded the labour press an important place in the origins of the Labour party.[1] The pioneers of socialism and independent labourism were fully alive to the significance of the printed word, both as a means of disseminating their message and as a means of winning converts. Yet the labour press in the late nineteenth and early twentieth centuries has received little attention from historians. Compared to the 'pauper press' of the earlier nineteenth century,[2] the liberal press of the mid-Victorian period or the 'new journalism' of the turn of the century,[3] the socialist and labour press stands virtually neglected. Important questions such as the journalistic outlooks of its editors, its sources of finance and its circulation figures have received little more than casual attention from labour historians.

Keir Hardie's *Labour Leader* has shared in this neglect. Given his importance as the leading propagandist for the 'labour alliance', it seems a pity that his journalistic endeavours have usually been treated as marginal. More attention has been given to the colourful *Clarion*, though its political

19

importance is scarcely so great, and Blatchford's commercial success has tended to put Hardie's corresponding failure in a bad light.[4] Hardie is simply dismissed as lacking talent in this field. More recently, scholars have pointed to the apparent paradox whereby Hardie described the *Labour Leader* as the 'organ of the Independent Labour Party', yet insisted on keeping it under his personal control,[5] but no attention has been paid to his reasons for doing this.

Hardie saw himself as the hero-editor depicted by Thomas Carlyle in *Sartor Resartus*,[6] winning his readership by the inspiration of his word and its truth for the times. He wished to be neither a commercial editor of the age of 'new journalism', nor the servant of the party, loyally supporting its official line and holding the ring between its conflicting tendencies. The *Labour Leader* was not a party paper like *Justice* or *Vorwärts*. It was a paper for a party that was yet to be, whose glory could only be seen as a promise of tomorrow through the mists of today. It was the 'organ of the Independent Labour party', which was in a state of becoming, not of full existence. This makes Hardie somewhat special in the history of the press. Comparisons with editors like Blatchford and W. T. Stead are only helpful if we bear in mind Hardie's special distinction. The tensions in his editorship of the *Labour Leader* spring from his claim to be independent. But independence could have been enjoyed only by a commercial owner or editor. Hardie consciously rejected the commercial role, and placed himself at the service of socialism.

This essay attempts to examine Hardie's approach to journalism in the *Labour Leader* from this point of view. As an editor appealing directly to his readers he is compared with W. T. Stead. In his relation to the Independent Labour party (ILP) he is compared with Robert Blatchford. Throughout, the context of the 'new journalism' of the 1880s and 1890s is borne in mind. In this way it is hoped to make sense of stages in his career which may otherwise seem bewilderingly paradoxical or inconsistent. At any rate, it may help us to understand Hardie's mind and his interpretation of himself to himself.

II

The *Labour Leader* began to appear as a monthly in January 1889, as a successor to Hardie's first publication, the *Miner*.[7] After running for less than a year, it folded and was merged with H. H. Champion's *Labour Elector*. Hardie revived the *Labour Leader* in February 1893, and undertook weekly publication in March 1894.

From this new beginning, it displayed close affinities with the 'new journalism' of the period. One aspect of this was the way in which the paper magnified the personality of its editor. It kept his deeds before the public and provided a platform for his opinions. Its cartoons frequently depicted him in the political fray, and his name appeared on almost every page. Like W. T.

Stead, he sought to use his paper to form an intimate personal link between himself and his readership.

For this purpose, the most important instrument was his personal column, 'Between Ourselves'. It usually covered more than one column, appeared on the first inside page and was signed 'Keir'. Its style was directly personal, purporting to give the reader direct access to Hardie's thoughts about anything of immediate concern to himself or the movement. The reader who turned to it could expect to discover what 'Keir' was thinking about the name of the party, the future of socialism, the present state of civilization, the latest play or the state of his health. The personal effect was heightened by apparent self-revelation. It is from 'Between Ourselves' that the biographer learns much of the colourful detail about Hardie's early life: his childhood in the dark city streets and his country boyhood in the mining villages of Lanarkshire. It was from 'Between Ourselves' that readers learned of the deaths of his mother and father, the illness of his wife and his frequent bouts of melancholy.[8]

In addition to 'Between Ourselves', Hardie usually wrote at least one of the leading articles, and frequently contributed signed feature articles on matters of political moment. Since the 'staff' usually contributed their copy over *noms-de-plume*,[9] the articles heightened the impression that the paper consisted of Hardie's personal statements.

The paper also devoted much space to Hardie's political deeds. During the years 1892–95, when he was the only independent Labour member in parliament, such reports were naturally concerned with his guerilla warfare against the Liberal government on the floor of the House of Commons. His various motions and amendments on the unemployed, his speech on the 'royal baby', and his revelations concerning the dismissed government workman, William Pluck, all received ample coverage in the pages of the *Leader*. All this may have seemed natural enough in the years when Hardie was the ILP's only representative in parliament, but the years between his defeat in 1895 and his re-election in 1900 saw the same use of the paper to keep his name before the party and the public.

To this end, Hardie turned to 'exposure journalism', some of which is directly reminiscent of W. T. Stead's use of the *Pall Mall Gazette* in the mid-1880s. Both men appealed, as hero-editors, to the righteous against the forces of Mammon. Yet, however close the similarities of technique, Hardie's 'exposure journalism' had a political purpose never present in Stead's. Hardie wanted to make Christian Socialists rather than merely Christians. His socialism was idealist, though it had an economic content. He believed that the rise of commercialism had spread a corrupting spirit of selfishness throughout society. Britain had become a nation ruled by greedy capitalists and landlords who had crushed the spirit of independence and cooperation at every level. Craftsmanship, community life and family morality had all succumbed.

Government had been reduced to the corrupt instrument of commercial policy. But this reality was masked by a sanctimonious pall of pharisaical religion cast by the churches. Living in Britain in the 1890s and early 1900s was like living in the heyday of the Roman Empire. Rich and poor alike were corrupted by wealth and power. Consequently, socialists had to play the part of the primitive Christians, and through the *Labour Leader* inspire fierce denunciation of Mammon-worship and its tyrannical oppression of the toiling masses.

In this spirit, Hardie conducted a series of exposure campaigns whose inter-linking themes have not yet been fully explored. All sought to expose the decadence, corruption and tyranny of 'those latter days'.

The 'West End scandal'

Glasgow's 'West End scandal' was his first major exercise in exposure jour-nalism. Early in 1896, a widely-publicized case of brothel-keeping was heard in the Glasgow magistrates court. It was stated in evidence that Mrs Pollock, a woman charged with running a brothel in the fashionable West End of the city, had introduced several factory girls to rich clients for purposes of prostitution. The girls appeared in court to give evidence against her, and their names were published with their evidence in the press. But the names of an 'old gentleman' and several other clients were withheld from publication.[10] The double stand-ard involved in publishing the names of the girls whilst safeguarding the ano-nymity of the clients was the starting-point from which Hardie embarked on a series of exposures, entitled 'The West End Scandal', which are reminiscent of Stead's 'Maiden Tribute to Modern Babylon'.[11] Commenting on the court reports in the Glasgow press, Hardie demanded: 'Why are these spaces left blank? Why is not the name of the rich seducer given the same prominence as that of the victim, whom he lures by his gold to her ruin?'[12] It was, he said, 'a palpable case of class distinction'.[13] The rich went scot-free. The girls, who were all reported to be 'redeemed' prostitutes, had suffered badly from the publicity, being ostracized by neighbours and workmates. Hardie wanted to know why the clients had not been subpoenaed to give evidence against the brothel-keeper, and alleged that there was a conspiracy among the whole legal establishment to protect a fashionable vice-ring. 'Baillies, religious phil-anthropists who hold their heads high in society, lawyers, businessmen, great employers of labour, clergymen and men of title, are known to the authorities as being among those who would have been dragged through the mire, and because of this, the matter was hushed up.'[14] Hardie promised to track down the 'old gentleman' and as many of the other clients as he could and print their names in the *Leader*.

During the next five weeks, a series of articles by a 'secret commissioner' appeared, in which names were promised 'next week', but were never fully revealed. Hardie's treatment of the subject was as sensationalist as Stead's had been. 'Astounding revelations' shouted the *Leader's* headlines, bill boards and newsboys. Prurient detail was piled on prurient detail. The brothel-keeper was said to have been the mistress of a deceased Church of Scotland clergyman and to have had an illegitimate child by him.[15] She had then taken to procuring respectable girls for rich debauchees. A Sunday-school teacher had been seduced and made pregnant.[16] Another daughter of the church had been kept in a milliner's business by one of her rich clients.[17] Mrs Pollock had even thrown a Christmas party for the whole choir of Burnbank United Presbyterian Church.[18] Occasionally, the 'revelations' seem so tangential to the purpose of the articles that they must be judged to be pure sensationalism. 'In Chicago recently,' ran one of the statements, 'a millionaire's daughter was delivered of a coloured child after a visit to a similar establishment.'[19]

The identity of the rich clients was never satisfactorily cleared up. They were said to include a Port Glasgow shipowner, a young minister named 'Mr W.', an Edinburgh advocate named 'Maxwell' and a man nicknamed 'the Elephant'. Hardie claimed that the 'old gentleman' mentioned in court was a Mr M. A. or D. A. Campbell. No positive identification was provided, although Hardie promised 'It may be next week, or it may be the week following. It may be later.'[20] At this point the story was abruptly killed. It had become an embarrassment. The *Leader's* printer, fearing libel actions, refused to take responsibility for further identifications. Bribes and private detectives were being employed against the paper's 'special commissioners' and the weekly articles were being used to anticipate their movements. Besides, Hardie blandly claimed, 'it was no part of our intention to pander to the public taste for prurient and filthy detail'.[21] He had to admit that innocent men were suffering because of allegations that they were characters possessing the names hinted at by the *Labour Leader*. A hasty charge that the police had shielded Mrs Pollock's rich clients by using the girls as witnesses had to be withdrawn without reservation.[22]

W. T. Stead's more famous 'Maiden Tribute' articles showed similarly unpleasant qualities of sensationalism. Stead had the excuse that he wanted to shock parliament into passing an important measure of legal reform, the raising of the age of consent. Hardie had no such aim in view. His initial criticism of the case had been that the press applied a double standard by printing the names of the prostitutes but withholding those of their clients. He offered little discussion, however, of the legal aspects of the case beyond declaring flatly that the newspapers could not be subjected to libel actions for publishing statements made by witnesses in court. Whether it was right to publish the names of any of the witnesses or other people mentioned, apart from the person accused, was, he said, 'an open question'.[23]

There must be serious doubt as to whether Hardie's real target was either 'the old gentleman' or the law of libel. There is, however, evidence which suggests that his real target was the exposure of what he regarded as the hypocrisy and pharisaism of the evangelical workers for 'social purity' in Glasgow, who were closely allied with Scottish liberalism. The girls who gave evidence were 'redeemed' prostitutes, and several workers in the field of rescuing prostitutes were present in court to give the girls (as they claimed) moral support. One of them was in fact the minister of Burnbank Presbyterian Church, whose choir was said to have been entertained by Mrs Pollock. Hardie wrote to him and asked him to supply the *Labour Leader* with the names mentioned in court. He declined, but promised to comply once he had verified his suspicions if 'at liberty' to do so.[24] The real object of the 'West End scandal' exposures was to show up these self-styled friends of the poor as timid time-servers to Mammon. Official Christianity was failing the people while socialists fought for righteousness.

The case of Boggarthole Clough

The same themes run through the attack on Manchester City Council for trying to prevent the ILP from holding meetings in Boggarthole Clough during the summer of 1896. The Boggarthole Clough affair has been seen too narrowly as an issue of free speech. It was also, for the *Labour Leader*, an opportunity to attack both sabbatarianism and a corrupt petty tyrant of unsavoury reputation.

Boggarthole Clough was a natural park belonging to Manchester City Council. The district surrounding it was of mixed social composition, containing the respectable lower-middle-class areas of Mosston and Blacklie as well as the slum of Harpurhey. It was a wild place, of some natural beauty. A visitor, turning off the Rochdale road, would have strolled up a narrow path, beside a tinkling brook. On the far side of the brook stood a belt of trees, and on the other side of the path a grass slope rose steeply. At the top of the path, the visitor would have entered the Clough, a cup-shaped hollow or cleft which formed a natural amphitheatre in the hillside, the grass slopes rising in terraces on either side. It was an ideal open-air meeting place, big enough to hold forty or fifty thousand people in attractive surroundings. Beyond the Clough stretched sixty acres of rough grass, sandy sloped and natural woods. Another eight acres or thereabouts were farmed by a tenant of Manchester City Council.[25]

The Council had purchased the land from a private owner in 1892 for the purpose of turning it into a public park. Public parks in England were largely the creation of the mid-Victorian era. They were modelled on, if not simply purchased as, the private parks of stately homes. As such, they were artificially laid out with lawns, flower beds, groves and stretches of water. The public were expected to behave in them as their superiors were supposed to behave in private parks, decorously and respectably. A park was not thought of as a place for people to let off steam, but as a garden to which people could go for peace and quiet and the polite society of their peers. They were expected to wear their best clothes, stroll on the paths, sit on the benches, and keep off the grass.

Manchester, as a crowded industrial city, was short of large parks. It had just missed the opportunity of purchasing Trafford Park and negotiations were still going on for the purchase of Heaton Park.[26] But Boggarthole Clough had never been a park in the private sense. Prior to its acquisition by the City Council, it had consisted of unfenced common pasture and enclosed farm land.[27] It had been open and accessible to the people of the surrounding district for generations. They did not go there to be decorous or sedate. They went to roam about freely. It was possible to bag rabbits for the pot in the Clough. There were no park constables to preserve order and decorum. People could behave in the Clough as they pleased.

This was not the kind of behaviour which the Manchester parks committee and its chairman, Mr George Needham, wished to encourage. Needham, a Conservative, had a reputation as a churchman and sabbatarian. To him and many of his colleagues, the Clough had an unsavoury reputation as a haunt for sex offenders and other miscreants.[28] When they acquired it, at a cost of £8,000, the parks committee proceeded to spend a further £15,000 on its 'improvement', laying out paths and planting neat rows of shrubs and flower beds. This won the approval of many of the respectable residents of Mosston and Blacklie, whose letters to the press show that they regarded the Clough as a wild, sinister place infested by low people without regard for property or common decency. As one of them complained to the *Manchester Guardian*:

> There are a few wild rabbits in the Clough, and the parks committee have encouraged them thinking the public would be pleased to see them, and in this they have not been disappointed. A man one day went down into the Clough with gun and dog and, when asked by one of the watches what he was going to do, replied that he was a ratepayer and that he should shoot the rabbits when he liked.[29]

It was, therefore, peculiarly distasteful to Needham and the representatives of decency and order that the Manchester ILP should desecrate the sabbath in Boggarthole Clough by holding public meetings among the strolling nursemaids and courting couples. The new park constables were instructed to stop the meetings. The ILP refused to desist, and its speaker was arrested and fined ten shillings.[30] This began both a series of defiances by the local ILP on successive Sundays and a series of arrests, which culminated in the imprisonment of Leonard Hall and Fred Brocklehurst, who refused to pay their fines. Audiences at the meetings rose from two hundred to ten thousand by the middle of June 1896.[31]

The *Labour Leader* became involved in a campaign which stretched well beyond the confines of 1896 and went deeper than the fight for 'free speech'. Hardie seized the opportunity to attack sabbatarianism and pharisaism generally. The *Leader's* reports of the campaign's meetings exploited all the techniques of 'the new journalism'. The personalities of the leading speakers – Hall, Brocklehurst, Mrs Pankhurst and Hardie himself – were prominently built up. The scene was vividly described and there was even an illustration of the Clough. Needham's motives and personal character were impugned.

The trial of Hardie and Mrs Pankhurst, which took place on 14 and 15 July 1896, received special prominence in the *Labour Leader*. Hardie attempted, with not a little success, to turn it into a trial of Mr Needham and the City Council. He began by requesting an adjournment of the hearing in order that he might serve subpoenas on the Lord Mayor of Manchester, the town clerk, the chief constable, the chairman of the watch committee and the parks committee and the chief detective-inspector. The magistrate, Mr Headlam, refused and, when Hardie persistently repeated his request, lost his patience and rapped out 'This is nonsense'. 'Allow us to conduct our case in our own way', Hardie retorted. 'Don't describe my conduct as nonsense.'[32] After the prosecution called witnesses to prove that there had been 'rough characters' at the meetings, Hardie cross-examined a constable, and asked him how he defined a 'rough character'. The constable replied that a 'rough character' was a person who preferred to stand at street corners without working for his living or who lived on the earnings of others. 'Do you describe the Prince of Wales as a rough character?' asked Hardie. 'Did you ever hear of him doing any work?'[33] Another witness who stated that he considered the ILP meetings to be a desecration of the sabbath was asked whether he was aware that Christ had held open-air meetings on the sabbath, two thousand years before, in Palestine. The witness said he was aware of the fact, but could not say what attitude he would have taken up towards those meetings had he been alive and present at the time.[34]

Speaking in his own defence, Hardie alleged that Needham had brought the prosecutions against the ILP maliciously, out of concern to suppress the meetings of political opponents. When the magistrate ruled this line of defence inadmissible, Hardie put Jesse Butler, an ILP member of the parks committee, into the witness box and tried to question him as to the discussions held in the parks committee concerning the prosecutions. There were further exchanges between Hardie and the magistrate until Hardie dramatically interrupted the proceedings by announcing that he had just received a telegram from his London solicitor saying that the Queen's Bench division had issued subpoenas. Mr Headlam still refused to adjourn the proceedings, whereupon Hardie blandly announced that he thought an adjournment would be helpful to the court because he still had 473 witnesses to call to prove that the meetings were orderly. After hearing twenty of them, Mr Headlam adjourned the hearing.

Hardie's intransigence had succeeded in transferring the dispute from the courtroom to the council chamber. The magistrate twice postponed resumption of the hearing while the Council debated what to do. A majority on the parks committee was for standing firm. They drafted a new by-law which would have forbidden meetings in the parks altogether and confined them to a specified list of open spaces.[35] It soon became apparent that some of these spaces were quite unsuitable for public meetings. The Conservative leader on the Council, Sir John Harwood, intervened and proposed that public meetings should be allowed in any park, provided application was made beforehand and meetings which were 'hostile . . . or offensive to any established institution' or 'absolutely partisan or political' should be prohibited.[36] Not surprisingly, this failed to satisfy the ILP which had already been refused permission to hold its May Day demonstration in the parks.[37] A combination of trade union, Irish, radical and ILP councillors passed an amendment to make part of Boggarthole Clough available for public meetings. In this they were unsuccessful, but they succeeded in preventing adoption of the new by-law by rendering the meeting inquorate.

An impasse had thus been reached once again. Harwood brought pressure to bear on Needham to withdraw all proceedings. This immediately reduced Liberal support for the ILP demand for the right to meet in the Clough, and Harwood's by-law was adopted.[38]

However, this was far from being the end of the affair. In implementing the new by-law, the Council refused, by a majority of one vote, to permit any political meetings in any park on Sundays.[39] Unfortunately for Needham, this renewed conflict with the ILP coincided with the conviction of a high-ranking Manchester policeman, Inspector Bannister, for corrupt involvement in a vice racket. Needham had strongly supported Bannister against demands for his dismissal and was strongly attacked in the *Labour Leader* as a pharisee and a hypocrite. In April 1897, Jesse Butler succeeded in obtaining withdrawal of the hated Sunday prohibition.[40] By the autumn of 1897, after another series of ILP summer meetings in the Clough, the *Labour Leader* was calling on the electors of Manchester to turn out every member of the council who had supported Needham and Bannister.[41]

The *Labour Leader's* interest in the Boggarthole Clough affair was directed only in part to the vindication of the right of public meeting. This right was under attack from many quarters at the time. The National Administrative Council of the ILP had received a number of reports during the 1890s to this effect, notably from London and Liverpool.[42] Manchester was singled out because Hardie saw its potential for rallying a broad spectrum of socialist, Christian and radical support for a crusade against a corrupt establishment which was denying the people their God-given birthright. Hardie knew by the time he joined Mrs Pankhurst in speaking at the Clough that a broad coalition of support existed around the ILP. This support rested to a marked extent on dislike of the officious, sabbatarian policy of Needham. Hardie's Christian socialism enabled him to exploit the situation to the full, and Manchester became one of the urban centres in which a 'labour alliance' of trade-unionists, socialists and radicals was foreshadowed after 1897.

The case of Lord Overtoun

The party-political character of Hardie's exposure journalism can be finally illustrated from the circumstances surrounding the well-known Overtoun exposure of 1899. J. C. White, part-owner of Shawfield chemical works at Rutherglen, Glasgow, was a well-known evangelical and supporter of the Liberal party. He had devoted much of his considerable fortune to the Free Church of Scotland and to the Scottish Liberal party during the difficult years after the Home Rule split of 1886. Gladstone had made him Lord Overtoun for his services. In 1899 he took a prominent part in preparing a religious revival known as the 'Glasgow evangelical campaign'.

It was at this point that the *Labour Leader* launched a series of articles intended to expose the idol's feet of clay. It accused him of devoting his life to the pursuit of wealth and title while exploiting men at his Shawfield chemical factory under conditions worse than any others in Scotland. Wages were threepence or fourpence an hour. Shifts lasted twelve hours. Horrible diseases of the nose and skin affected the men. Sanitary conditions were intolerable.

Week after week, the *Labour Leader* flayed Overtoun as either a pharisee or a 'Holy Willie'.[43] Hardie published his articles as a series of pamphlets, *The Overtoun Horrors*, which he sent to the many Christian organizations with which Overtoun was connected. The result was a general scandal. Overtoun was attacked on the committee of the evangelical campaign,[44] and at a general meeting of the Young Men's Christian Association (YMCA).[45] The Church of Scotland took up the cudgels against this celebrated pillar of its rival, the Free Church.[46] Learned doctors of divinity debated the social gospel in the press and the *Glasgow Evening Times* joined in the 'holy crusade', as Hardie called it.[47]

What caught the imagination of all those critics was the charge of unnecessary Sunday labour. Overtoun was a strong supporter of the Lord's Day Observance Society and had recently led a deputation of the Society to obtain the Sunday closure of the People's Palace, much to the annoyance of a majority of Glasgow Trades Council.[48] He was on record as objecting to all unnecessary Sunday labour, and found it difficult to convince some of his religious associates that Sunday labour on the production of chrome was necessary in the biblical sense. His claim that it was necessary for chemical processing also fell flat when he suddenly abolished most Sunday labour at Shawfield in response to the outcry.[49]

Overtoun's defenders pointed out that he was not personally responsible for the conduct of the Shawfield works, which were under the direct supervision of his partner. Overtoun claimed that his firm had a good record of research into ways of reducing Sunday work in chemical factories and that competition from other firms prevented speedier progress. But an independent medical investigation commissioned by the Glasgow Trades Council supported the substance of Hardie's charges. Overtoun stood condemned as the worst type of modern capitalist, remote from the scene of operations, shunning personal responsibility and indifferent to both human suffering and the devastation of the environment. With him also stood condemned those churchmen who had rallied to his defence. There was once again a hint of sexual irregularities behind the evangelical campaign. One of the Overtoun pamphlets contained a warning that 'clergymen living separated from their wives should be very chary in their references to scandal'.[50] This sentence had to be deleted under threat of libel action by the minister concerned.

Hardie was able to muster a wide range of Christian support in the name of the social gospel against this builder of temples and manufacturer of widows and orphans. His campaign unleashed a latent stream of anti-evangelical criticism in such circles as the Church of Scotland and the YMCA. Like Manchester, Glasgow was rapidly becoming a forcing house for a local labour alliance.

III

How far was Hardie consciously in debt to W. T. Stead for his type of exposure journalism? It is not possible to be certain about the answer to this question. Complimentary references to Stead often appeared in the *Labour Leader*,[51] and Hardie's treatment of the 'West End scandal' bears a close resemblance to Stead's most famous campaign. Hardie also used Stead's device of republishing his articles in pamphlet form. But before rushing too quickly to the conclusion that he copied Stead, we should remember that Hardie had his own roots in the Christian tradition and that the exposure of bad conditions in chemical works was a speciality, not of Stead, but of H. H. Champion, Hardie's ally of the late 1880s.

Stead apart, Hardie was in tune with other aspects of the 'new journalism'.[52] He was concerned from the outset to give the paper a bright image by emancipating the reader from the labour of scanning long blocks of reported speech and weighty feature articles. Within the limits of finance he strove to avoid a dull appearance. Three-decker headlines, subheadings and cross-heads broke up the layout. Illustrations were expensive, but the front page often carried a full-page cartoon by some socialist artist. Mrs Pankhurst was shown speaking at Boggarthole Clough and readers were provided with a drawing of a muzzle worn by workmen in chemical works.[53] Interviews were also a technique which Hardie borrowed from the 'new journalism'.[54]

The 'new journalism', as has often been stressed, was not simply a matter of typographical innovation or even of personal editorial comment. What was to ensure the commercial viability of newspaper publishing in the 1890s and beyond was the combination of political and apolitical features. Robert Blatchford founded the commercial viability of the *Clarion* on this approach, including, besides political comment, columns on sport and features for amusement rather than instruction. This was the aspect of the 'new journalism' which the evangelical Hardie firmly rejected. The *Labour Leader*, to be sure, had its women's column and its children's page, but the content of Mrs Bream Pearce's 'Matrons and Maidens' was fully charged with discussion of the social and political position of women, while even the children were enrolled as 'Crusaders' for Hardie's war against Mammon. We can, if we like, describe the *Labour Leader* as more 'puritan' than the *Clarion*, but only so long as we are careful to define exactly what we mean. Both papers disclaimed any interest in prurient news. The proceedings of the divorce court and the police court were banned by both editors, unless some political point had to be made. The tone of Blatchford's political comment was just as serious and moral as Hardie's. The difference was that Hardie could not admit gratuitous fun in his newspaper. Blatchford's readers, like Northcliffe's, were left to skip over the political copy if they wished, to enjoy a good joke with the 'Bounder' or an innocent review of a good night at the theatre. Hardie banned sport from the *Labour Leader*, reviewed fiction only if it had a strong moral content, and his idea of a good serial was that it should have 'plenty of greetin' scenes with a real, genuine unexpected tragedy at the end to attract the womenfolk'.[55] Jokes were a rare find in the *Labour Leader*. The following account of a conversation between two Scots gossips on the occasion of the Diamond Jubilee is worth rescuing from its oblivion, since it demonstrates that even jokes had to have their political point.

> 'Can ye tell me, woman, what it is they ca' the jubilee?'
> 'Well, it's this,' said her neighbour. 'When folk has [sic] been married twenty-five years, that's a silver wedding. An' when they've been married fifty years, that's a golden wedding. But if the man's dead, then it's a jubilee.'[56]

Hardie was well aware that the rejection of the commercial approach of the 'new journalism' restricted the *Leader*'s chances of building up a viable circulation: 'Times out of number, friendly advisers have urged that the *Leader* should be more of a general newspaper than a special organ. There is no doubt that way lay success . . .'[57] But he replied to such comments that his object was to serve the independent labour movement and that the success of the paper was the mark of the movement's staying power.

These high aims were not crowned with success. Although reliable circulation figures are as hard to come by for the *Labour Leader* as for most nineteenth-century newspapers, it seems clear that Hardie launched the new paper in 1893 and expanded it into a weekly in 1894 in a mood of extravagant optimism. This was engendered, no doubt, by the rapid growth of the ILP movement and the failure of Joseph Burgess's *Workman's Times* after the appearance of the *Leader*. Hardie's claim of a circulation of 15,000 in 1893[58] was probably not much wide of the truth, and the weekly edition was launched on the expectation of doubling this figure. For some months the auguries seemed promising. An increase in size from twelve to sixteen pages in mid-1894 was made conditional on the circulation reaching 50,000. We cannot be certain that its increased size proves that the circulation had actually increased, but a figure approaching 50,000 is not implausible for a short period in 1894.[59]

Much of the readership, however, was probably shared with the *Clarion*. As open rivalry developed between Blatchford and Hardie in 1895 and thereafter, it was the *Clarion* which proved to have the greater staying-power. *Labour Leader* circulation fell back and even dropped below the starting-point. The size of the paper had to be reduced back to twelve pages in 1895 and further reduced to eight pages in 1896. Hardie managed to keep it at this size for the rest of his time as editor, but the underlying circulation pattern was unsteady and seems to have slumped badly after about 1900. In 1898 he was calling for a doubling of circulation in order to restore the paper to its larger size,[60] but such appeals had little effect. When the ILP took over the *Labour Leader* in 1904, Bruce Glasier, Hardie's successor as editor, found the circulation to be only about 11,500.[61]

This downward trend could not be arrested by Hardie's type of journalism. Exposures, as Stead found, gave only very temporary boosts to circulation. Hardie made the best of any fair wind that offered itself. Extra copies were printed for great occasions, such as May Day. Special issues were produced for unique events like the international socialist congress of 1896. There was a *Hardie's Herald* for the East Bradford by-election in 1897 and a special *Leader* for the London County Council elections of 1898. Additional income could be obtained from occasional series of pamphlets such as the *West End Scandal* or the *Overtoun Horrors*. But they probably produced little more than windfalls. The *Labour Leader* simply could not make way against the *Clarion* without adopting the latter's methods. Hardie kept hoping that some revival of the Christian conscience would bring readership to him from the Sunday papers for working men, but he could see in 1899 that his appeal was too narrow. As he told his assistant editor David Lowe, in reference to his column 'Between Ourselves' 'I think, perhaps, that page lends itself to the lighter vein as well as any. At least I mean to give it a try, for I am certain we keep right out of reach of all save those intensely in earnest and they, at this stage, are not numerous enough.'[62]

The decline in circulation in 1895 affected the *Leader*'s position by causing an abrupt withdrawal of advertising. The advertising columns show that, between March 1894 and July 1896, the number of advertisements placed by commercial firms seriously declined, to be replaced by advertisements by ILP branches and sympathetic labour organizations. Thus, in the first number of the weekly edition, the whole of the back page and more than half of page four was taken up with commercial advertisements.[63] By January 1895, the space devoted to advertising had shrunk to two-and-a-half columns, and some of the advertisements were for socialist lectures and cooperative concerns.[64] By the beginning of 1896, the advertising space had spread to four columns, but most of the advertisements were placed by labour organizations and specialized booksellers. In addition, the back page was now completely given up to an ILP 'directory' in which branches of the party advertised. The commercial splendour of the early numbers was never recaptured and the picture throughout the remainder of Hardie's editorship is one of increasing dependence on the ILP, both as a source of advertising revenue and as a volunteer labour force to push the paper against the icy winds of newsagents' boycotting. Branches of the ILP were exhorted to display *Labour Leader* posters not only in their clubrooms but also on public hoardings at their own expense.[65] By 1895, Hardie was asking branches to make up the paper's loss of advertising revenue and to work for a doubling of circulation. Each member was urged to order more than one copy.[66]

IV

It is against this background of falling circulation, declining revenue from advertisers other than labour organizations and increasing dependence on rank-and-file party support that we should consider Hardie's attitudes to ownership and control of the *Labour Leader*.

Announcing the launching of the paper at the Scottish Labour party conference of 1893, Hardie declared that it would 'belong to and be under the control of the Scottish Labour Party. He was certain it could be made to pay its way and would be invaluable in keeping the members in touch with each other.'[67]

From the outset, however, Hardie's concept of party ownership was an indirect one. He was already negotiating to set up a company to be known as the Scottish Labour Party Trading Society.[68] This was to be a reconstruction of a small cooperative printing society known as the Glasgow Labour Literature Society. The latter, formed in 1891, was heavily in debt by the end of 1892.

Hardie secured for it a loan of £195 from the Scottish Labour party (SLP) seeing in the Society a valuable labour force of committed and enthusiastic printers.[69] He then sought to combine this labour force with the resources of capital available to him through C. W. Bream Pearce, a wine merchant and leading member of the SLP.[70] The new SLP Trading Society was to be run by a committee of trustees, three appointed by the Glasgow Labour Literature Society and three by the SLP. The SLP Trading Society was contracted to print the enlarged *Labour Leader* of 1894 and, in return, obtained £400 worth of printing machinery and an office in the premises of the SLP.[71]

The marriage proved far from happy. The members of the Glasgow Labour Literature Society held very different political views from Hardie. They were in fact a very mixed crew. Some, like George Mitchell, were Glasgow trades council men, suspicious of Hardie's independent politics. A few were advocates of 'one socialist party' and looked to the new SLP Trading Society (with its fresh capital) to publish a wide range of socialist literature. Notable in this section were three ex-members of William Morris's Socialist League, Glasier, Rae and Shaw. Glasier had been taken on by Hardie as subeditor of the *Leader*, but Hardie replaced him by David Lowe in 1894, declaring somewhat slightingly that nature had never intended Bruce for the work. Glasier was in fact quite a competent journalist and we may suspect political disagreement to have existed.

Given these political divisions and tensions, it is hardly surprising that the members of the Glasgow Labour Literature Society began to complain that the enlarged *Labour Leader* of 1894 was swallowing up all the resources of the new trading society, leaving nothing for the expansion of the book-publishing side of the business. Hardie, they alleged, was incompetent and autocratic. The committee of trustees never met during the first six months of his chairmanship, in spite of repeated requests from the Literature Society that it should do so. David Lowe confirmed in retrospect the catalogue of miseries that these complaints reflect. Hardie was absent most of the time, in parliament or on speaking tours: '. . . money was being spent lavishly without adequate results and it was much in need of concentrated attention . . .' He found 'faulty, second-hand machinery, inadequate equipment, loose arrangements, a squalid office, trade opposition, garrulous correspondents, financial chaos'.[72]

The men of the Glasgow Labour Literature Society had other grounds for complaint. Hardie was in arrears with payments to the SLP Trading Society for printing the *Leader*, even though this was done at less than the nominal commercial rates. They could see that the *Labour Leader*, far from being the salvation of their venture, was rapidly becoming a deadweight, threatening to drag them into bankruptcy.

Hardie's response to this crisis was to ask his friends in the SLP to sink yet more capital into the Trading Society, but they would only do this, he stated, if the members of the Literature Society were prepared to give up their democratic control. The Literature Society had been run on cooperative principles, each member possessing one vote regardless of the number of shares which he held. In mid-1894, it was discovered that the 1893 articles of amalgamation were invalid, and their renegotiation had to be commenced in an atmosphere of distrust. The Literature Society men wanted to reimpose democratic control over the committee of trustees. Hardie, Bream Pearce and the two other SLP trustees demanded cumulative voting, each member possessing the same number of votes as shares. Since more than half the share capital of the SLP Trading Society belonged to four members and the rest to forty, the effect of the latter proposal would have been to concentrate control in the hands of Hardie and his sympathizers. Matters came to a head at a general meeting of the Trading Society on 22 December 1894. A motion calling for equal voting was proposed and Hardie walked out, along with two of his supporters. The rest of the people at the meeting, including Bruce Glasier and David Lowe, stayed behind and voted for the motion, which was carried unanimously.

Nothing but damage to the SLP came out of the ensuing long and bitter quarrel between Hardie and the Glasgow Labour Literature Society. Hardie evicted the Literature Society from the *Leader's* premises, claiming payment of rent for their occupation, and demanding that they return to the SLP the £195 loaned to them in 1892. The Literature Society counter-claimed that Hardie owed them far more in arrears for printing than they owed him and refused to hand over the *Leader's* printing machinery, retaining it as security against settlement of the debt. Hardie tried to take action in the courts, but lost. After a great deal of wrangling, he agreed to submit the question to professional arbitration. He was found to owe the Literature Society, after settlement of all claims and counter-claims, £25.[73]

Many of the details of this complicated dispute are impossible to verify, but one point stands out clearly enough. The members of the Literature Society wanted democratic control of all funds contributed by the SLP to the SLP Trading Society and control over the management of the paper. Hardie, on the other hand, was determined, at least after renewal of negotiations in 1894, to keep control of the *Labour Leader* out of the hands of the members of the Literature Society. In October 1894, he twice urged the principle of cumulative voting on the grounds that it would lead to 'the securing of considerable sums'.[74] 'Friends of the socialist movement', he wrote later, 'had offered funds for a Society under ILP control *conditional* on the committee of management being elected by those who found the money.'[75] 'I wanted', he added, 'to see the Society managed by responsible men, and not left to the scratch team who then had charge.' That is to say, Hardie wanted the paper to be controlled by a committee of relatively wealthy men who sympathized with his own political standpoint. He wanted to use the *Labour Leader* to propagate his own views of socialism and independent labourism. Some at least of the Literature Society men wanted to use the SLP Trading Society to publish educational works on socialism and trade-unionism. Hardie was afraid that the *Leader* would fall foul of the faction-fighting that developed during 1894 and 1895 over socialist strategy in the ILP. When the Trading Society plan fell through, he decided to keep the *Labour Leader* under his own personal ownership.

> The paper will be my property . . . I must be free to speak and act the truth at all costs. To secure this, I have declined office in the ILP and to preserve it, I will keep the paper in my own hands. Whatever the cantankerous individual may say, the rank-and-file will agree with me.[76]

V

Hardie's confidence was misplaced. Without commercial viability, he could not be independent of the ILP. Furthermore the rank-and-file members proved unwilling to give blind support to an editor as committed as Hardie was to the pursuit of a particular party strategy. To some extent, Hardie could rely on subventions from wealthy sympathizers. T. D. Benson contributed some £400 to the *Labour Leader* between 1898 and 1903.[77] But offerings of the faithful were never enough to make a crucial difference. The *Leader* had to be an ILP paper or it was nothing.

Hardie used the *Labour Leader* to advance his own strategy of alliance with the trade unions and public hostility to the Liberal party. This earned him the opposition of those who supported the alternatives, either union with the Social Democratic Federation (SDF) or alliance with the Liberals. Hardie did not keep criticism of his strategy entirely out of the columns of the *Labour Leader*, but he certainly did not maintain a fair balance of views. Overwhelming preponderance was given to letters which supported his strategy. There was no correspondence column in the strict sense and Hardie took it upon himself to cut and edit letters as he pleased. He used his personal column to try to influence the selection of delegates for, and voting at, the ILP annual conferences.

Hardie saw himself as the pioneer of independent labourism and socialism. He thought that there would one day emerge in Britain a socialist Labour party, that is, an alliance of socialists and trade-unionists in which the ILP worked continuously to raise the consciousness of the trade-unionists until they too were committed to a socialist conception of society. He saw control over the *Labour Leader* as his means of ensuring that the ILP would continue to fulfil this vanguard role. His vision was that such a party would replace the Liberal party as the party of the workers in Britain. He was well aware that this could not happen without striking bargains, both with the trade unions and with the Liberal party, but he was determined that the labour alliance would never be absorbed into the broad stream of Liberal progressivism or reduced merely to the status of a pressure group in a broad coalition of radical forces.

I have argued elsewhere for the consistency of Hardie's political strategy from 1887 onwards.[78] Both the SLP and the ILP were originally conceived in his mind as broad alliances of trade unions, socialist societies and groups of social reformers. But the strength of the 'socialist revival' and of 'new unionism' in the early 1890s led him to hope that the Trades Union Congress (TUC) could be won over to a simultaneous commitment to independence and socialism. These hopes were dashed by his own defeat in the election for the secretaryship of the TUC in 1894, and by the change of TUC standing orders, which precluded him from membership of Congress in 1895. In 1894 and 1895, therefore, Hardie devoted himself to building up the ILP as a vanguard party, committed to independence and a broad, undogmatic socialism, which could appeal to a wide range of people in sympathy with social reform.

In 1895, the ILP was far from united around this strategy. Its annual conferences instructed the National Administrative Council (NAC) to pursue a policy of 'fusion' with the SDF. Hardie had never liked the Federation and became convinced that it wanted to force its own intransigent opposition to trade-unionism and radicalism on the ILP.

Hardie had his own peculiar view of the British road to socialism. He wanted organized labour to use its electoral strength to get the capitalist parties to provide work for the unemployed. He saw the removal of the unemployed from the labour market into specially-organized colonies as a kind of holy crusade around which Christians and other radical social reformers could coalesce. The Liberal party could never be the permanent vehicle for carrying this through. The great landlords and employers who funded it would never consent to the use of the land for such non-profitable purposes. Hence the pressure by the trade unions for work for the unemployed must in the end lead to the division of politics between a party of labour and a party of capitalism. Thus freed, the party of labour could proceed to establish an organized society in which land and the other means of production would be nationally owned and democratically controlled through parliament, municipalities and cooperative institutions.

The authoritarian implications of this version of socialism have recently been emphasized. Here I am simply concerned to show that socialism meant something serious to Hardie. Whatever electoral arrangements the Liberal party might offer the Labour party and however the Liberals might trim their sails to the wind of social reform, there could be no permanent understanding between the two parties. Radicals had to be wooed for their support in the righteous crusade against Mammon. In the end, though, they would have to choose between labour and socialism on the one hand, and capitalism and imperialism on the other.

Hardie used the *Labour Leader* to keep this vision before the ILP after 1894. His trip to the United States in that year was publicized as an exercise in bringing trade unions and socialist bodies into united action.[79] Back home in 1896, he worked to get the parliamentary committee of the TUC invited to the unity negotiations with the SDF. At the ILP conference in 1896, he suggested a conference between trade unions and socialist bodies,[80] and published in the *Leader* a model resolution advocating independent labour representation for members of the ILP to move at their trade-union branches.[81] In 1897, he used his column 'Between Ourselves' to make clear his opposition to 'fusion' and his preference for a federation of socialist societies into which the trade unions could be accommodated. He demanded both a ballot vote of the ILP membership and a two-thirds majority for 'fusion' and, as a condition of his personal agreement, insisted that the SDF should give up attacking trade unions and recognize them as part of the 'great evolutionary movement making for industrial peace'.[82]

All this was perfectly consistent with the strategy which he had been pursuing since the late 1880s. 'It must be evident to everyone that no labour movement can ever hope to succeed in this country without the cooperation of the trade unions . . . Some of us have held the opinion from the beginning that it was possible to make trade unionism and ILP'ism interchangeable terms for electoral purposes.'[83]

Hardie's confidence in the future of the unions was based on a socialist analysis which pointed to a widespread conflict between large-scale, monopolistic companies and organized workers. This analysis had been a commonplace of socialist commentary since the late 1880s. Hardie gave space in the *Labour Leader* to the conflicts between American trade-unionists and giant trusts like the United States Steel Company and the Gould railways. During his tour of the United States in 1895, he publicized the work of Eugene V. Debs in organizing American railway unions, and stressed that the use of court injunctions and troops against American strikers had contemporary parallels in Britain. At home in 1896, he expounded the theme that British industrial relations were developing along lines already manifest in the United States. As early as 1896, he was pointing to the role of large-scale shipbuilding and armaments companies behind the Federation of Engineering Employers. He also condemned the London and North-Eastern Railway Company for dismissal of trade-unionists and made it a major charge against Lord Overtoun that he had no personal responsibility for the supervision of his works.[84]

Hardie found another parallel with developments in the United States in the stream of anti-trade union decisions beginning to flow from the English law courts. 'We have repeatedly of late drawn attention to the hitherto unchallenged and presumably legal rights of trade unionists. . . . If the law be as the judges have laid down in several cases of late, not only picketing, but the act of going on strike will be made illegal . . .'[85]

The *Labour Leader* urged that Britain was not free from the world-wide tendency of capitalism to concentrate into monopolies and cartels. A coal mining ring in South Wales, an iron bedstead association in the Midlands, the amalgamation of cotton thread manufacturers and the federation of engineering employers were taken to be harbingers of an era of British trusts and combines.[86] In any case, British industry felt the effects of world-wide concentration, because trusts in America and Germany competed more efficiently in Britain's markets. 'Whether we like it or not, Germany, Japan, India and America are competing with us and ousting us from the markets of the world. Capital is growing in volume, and as it grows, so does its power increase.'[87]

It has been argued that Hardie derived this kind of analysis from radical and progressive writers like J. A. Hobson and H. B. Lloyd.[88] It would be more accurate to say that all three commentators derived their interest in trusts from the earlier socialist emphasis on the tendency towards capital concentration. Hardie read and reviewed Hobson and Lloyd in the *Labour Leader*,[89] but he treated Hobson's work as supporting evidence for a socialist analysis which Hardie did not hesitate to push to its conclusions. To stop short at social reform was to appeal to the selfish side of human nature. 'Socialists demand no Bismarckian policy of social reform. They demand an end to private ownership.'[90] Socialism stood for production for use: capitalism for profit. Hardie sometimes used Hobson's well-known argument about under-consumption, but he always insisted that setting the unemployed to work in home colonies was the dividing line between mere social reform and socialist reformism. Hardie's view was that as the unemployed were progressively removed from the labour market, so the strength of trade-unionism would become irresistible. Its agitations would be strengthened for a legal minimum wage, a legal eight-hour day and ultimately the nationalization of industry.

The *Labour Leader* held this vision before trade-unionists by teaching the lessons of the concentration of industry and increasing international competition. The workers could never be emancipated merely by the voluntary action of trade unions. Only the power of the state, common ownership of the means of production and international cooperation between national labour movements could bring complete freedom. ILP members should agitate in their trade unions to convert the rank-and-file to this view and to overthrow the advice of their officials. The mining industry was singled out for particular attention partly because Hardie knew it better than any other and partly because many local factors combined to reduce earnings to a level below the wage-rates fixed by agreement with the union.[91] Hardie urged the Miners' Federation of Great Britain to see the solution to miners' poverty in socialism, and republished his scheme of 1895 for the nationalization of coal mines.[92]

Other industries were not neglected. The election of George Barnes to the secretaryship of the Amalgamated Society of Engineers and the sacking of

Lib–Lab officials from the Amalgamated Society of Railway Servants were hailed as the fruits of ILP propaganda, which in part they were. Nevertheless, it was perfectly apparent that the creation of the Labour Representation Committee (LRC) in 1900, and its subsequent development, did not mean the capture of the trade unions by the socialists. For many of the trade union leaders, it represented, not a turning towards the paths of the *Labour Leader*, but simply a strengthening of trade union pressure to obtain repeal of the Taff Vale decision.[93]

Hardie was willing enough to join an alliance with the trade unions even on these terms. He did not insist on their prior acceptance of socialism because he envisaged that agitation would continue on issues as they arose. He did not view the LRC simply as a pressure group or as a constituent in a broad progressive movement for social reform. The work of the ILP vanguard would go on. Answering a correspondent in the *Labour Leader*, he commented:

> It may be that some day the need for an Independent Labour Party apart from the trade unions will not exist, but that time is not yet. Nor will it be until the trade union movement consciously feels that militant socialism is an integral part of its working policy. How far we are from that may be discovered by anyone who will take the trouble to open his eyes. In the new organisation [the LRC] the ILP will be what steam is to machinery, the motive power which keeps all going.[94]

By the same token, the ILP could never allow the Labour movement to come to any understanding with the Liberals about a programme of social reform. To do so would be to accept that there was a stopping-point short of socialism. Hardie used the *Labour Leader* to oppose all attempts to formulate such a programme. He criticized Tom Mann's Workers' Union,[95] A. M. Thompson's campaign in the *Clarion* for a 'new party',[96] and the efforts of London radicals and labour men to form a national democratic league around a programme of political and social reforms.[97] To acquiesce in such tendencies would simply be to slip back into Lib–labism.

On the other hand, Hardie had never been against tactics aimed at wresting electoral concessions from the Liberal 'wirepullers'. He often seemed grossly inconsistent in denouncing those who wanted agreement around a common programme while he himself was wooing radical support for the ILP at elections. The essential difference between his strategy and that of the programme-makers, however, remains clear.

Hardie was like a wily fowler decoying radical birds away from the Liberal flock. But this was a tactic for electoral purposes, an opportunist device to get independent labour men into parliament where they would have a much stronger voice when agitating for socialism. His decoy trick was not intended to divert socialist propagandists into progressivism, but to put them in a position to criticize progressivism from a socialist standpoint. It was the task of the

Labour Leader to support every radical cause compatible with socialism, while insisting that there could never be permanent harmony between the Liberal and Labour parties.

This apparent inconsistency is easy to understand if we remember Hardie's own underlying premises. Labour's chief short-term aim was to obtain work for the unemployed. Liberalism, he believed, could never provide it on a scale that would strengthen the workers' social position since this would undermine the principles of the 'plutocrats' who ran it. Therefore any concessions offered by the Liberals to Labour would be tactical only, and must never be viewed in the light of alliances or understandings. Thus during the 1895 general election campaign, Hardie championed extreme independence, but signalled willingness to negotiate with the Liberal party managers.[98] The same was true in the London County Council elections in 1898[99] and again in the run-up to the general election of 1900.[100] But in each case, these signals were accompanied by forthright declarations that the ILP could never give up its socialist strategy.[101]

It is in this context that we can understand his attitude to J. Ramsay Mac-Donald's electoral bargain with the Liberals in 1904. MacDonald may have taken a very different view, but for Hardie, the arrangement about seats was a concession wrung from the Liberals by the organized strength of the LRC. Previous approaches had failed because the ILP had been too weak to pose a major threat to the Liberal party. But in 1903, the Liberal managers (who could not, after all, foresee the landslide victory of 1906) genuinely feared the wrecking-power of organized labour. Hardie may not have been aware of the extent to which MacDonald was prepared to compromise the independence of Labour in these negotiations, but he used the *Labour Leader* to make it clear that his own view of labour's aims remained unchanged.[102]

VI

If we take Hardie's socialism seriously, his attitude to control of the *Labour Leader* becomes easier to understand. The ILP was never under his personal domination. Personalities and groups threatened to pull it now towards socialist unity, now towards alliance with the Liberals. Hardie believed that he, almost alone, stood firm for socialism and independent labourism. *Vox populi vox dei* was a Latin tag he was fond of quoting and he might also have said that the voice of the *Labour Leader* was the voice of socialism speaking through him to the party. In this sense the paper was 'the organ of the Independent Labour Party', the organ of a party coming into existence. To have placed it under party control would have robbed it of this character and would have placed it at the mercy of the factions and turned it into something different. Like Carlyle, he believed that the editor should be a latter-day hero, free to lead his readers, and not in bondage to them.

There was an unresolved tension in this view of the situation. By renouncing any ambition to achieve editorial independence by the commercial techniques of the 'new journalism', he condemned himself to increasing dependence on the support of the ILP. This was already very evident by 1898, but Hardie struggled to resist the inevitable as long as the trade union strategy remained unfulfilled. Thus in 1898 he proposed to set up a new company and asked the ILP to take shares in it. He offered the party one or more seats on the board of directors and an allocation of space in the paper for party matters, to be under the control of a person appointed by the NAC. He himself was to remain editor. Glasier, no doubt recalling the conflicts with Hardie in 1894, strongly resisted the idea of 'making the *Labour Leader* or the *Clarion* or any other privately-owned paper the official medium between the council and the members'.[103] The proposal was shelved, and Hardie went on to form a company with David Lowe, his brother, T. D. Benson and other sympathizers.[104]

The background to this move seems to have been not dissimilar to the launching of the enlarged *Labour Leader* in 1894: a temporary upward trend in circulation at the opening of the Boer War and fresh resources of capital from Benson's trade in slum properties. Once again the venture was not a success. The underlying problems were also similar to those of 1894. Socialist unity continued to rumble on in the ILP, fuelled by the good SDF poll in the Dewesbury by-election. Hardie's willingness to work with radicals in resisting the war was not as enthusiastically taken up by the ILP as he would have wished, and there was underlying suspicion that the party was being led by MacDonald and the trade unions into an alliance with the Liberals. In these circumstances, the paper could not prosper. Circulation slumped and advertising by ILP branches fell away. Hardie's personal finances were in some disarray, and David Lowe was proving unequal to the task of editing the paper while Hardie was absent on parliamentary business.

By 1902, therefore, Hardie was negotiating with the ILP for the purchase of the paper. He hesitated, however, for more than a year.[105] The NAC insisted that he give up the editorship as well as ownership. Glasier continued to object that the rank-and-file would never rally round a 'Hardie paper'.[106] MacDonald backed up Glasier because he found Hardie's consistent independence an obstacle to friendly relations with the Liberal party managers.[107] At last, Hardie reached the conclusion that the cause of independence could best be served by allowing the party to take over the control of the paper. Glasier had impressed him for some time as a sturdy champion of his own independent socialist strategy and his succession as editor no longer seemed the affront to nature that it had constituted in 1893. Hardie, moreover, feared that the ILP would be dragged by MacDonald, the LRC and the pro-Liberal trade-unionists from the course of socialism and independence. As he told Glasier: 'Recent political events especially inside have very much strengthened your argument for the new paper being in a position to give an independent support to those of us who are trying to go straight'.[108] By October 1903, agreement had been reached in principle for the ILP to form a company to purchase the *Labour Leader* at a price of £1,000. Hardie was to receive £250 in cash and the rest as shares in the new company. As part of the agreement, Hardie insisted on the right to contribute regular articles to the new *Labour Leader*, but waived all other claims.[109]

It was to be another nine months before the paper was transferred. In the meantime, Hardie had an operation for the removal of his appendix. This and other personal expenses compelled him to ask for an increase in the purchase price, which Glasier, MacDonald and Snowden resisted, to Hardie's intense chagrin.[110]

Recent biographical research has brought these transactions to light in a way that tends to reflect little credit on Hardie. His readiness to hand the paper over to the ILP in 1903 seems surprising and the whole episode suggests more than a little mercenariness on Hardie's part. The present study, however, emphasizes the underlying consistency of Hardie's actions, which seem less paradoxical when his approach to the problem of building a labour alliance is understood. He had always believed in winning the trade unions over to the support of a Labour party and saw the *Labour Leader* as an indispensable instrument for their conversion. That is why he struggled, against great financial odds, to prevent it from becoming either an ILP sheet or another commercial newspaper. With the formation of the LRC in 1900, however, the victory against rival strategies was won and the ILP was committed to his own course. Furthermore, as the financial position of the paper worsened, it became imperative to surrender the paper to the party. But the questions still stood: would the ILP remain faithful to its task? Would it use the paper to struggle against the backsliding elements in the trade unions and in its own ranks? Hardie read the auguries with little confidence. His inspiration would be as necessary in the future as it had been in the past. Merely to serve as the editor of the party's sheet, upholding agreed policy and maintaining neutrality between different factions could have no attractions for a man who cast himself in the heroic mould. Accordingly, his objectives came to be to secure the succession of his most reliable disciple, Glasier, in the editorial chair, and to survive the crisis in his personal affairs so as to be able to resume the fight for independence and socialism.

3

Winston Churchill and the working class, 1900–14

PAUL ADDISON

Winston Churchill's career before 1914 depended in many respects on his relations with the urban working class. When he was first returned to parliament, in 1900, he owed his election to the cotton workers of Oldham, where he took his stand on his father's old platform of Tory Democracy. Churchill was then only twenty-five, a political novice with an unquenchable thirst for recognition and an intense drive to keep ahead of political events. As he grew and changed, Tory Democracy proved to be the first of his many roles, and the first of the four faces that Churchill presented to the world of labour before the First World War.

The second face was that of Free Trade. In 1903 Joseph Chamberlain split the Unionist party (or the Conservatives as they will be called here) with his campaign for tariff reform. Churchill rejected not only Chamberlain's programme but, more crucially, the compromise position cobbled together by Arthur Balfour in the hope of minimizing the divisions within the party. Taking the pure free-trade line, he crossed to the Liberal benches in 1904 and was adopted as the candidate for the prosperous commercial constituency of Manchester North-West. In the run-up to the general election of 1905, Churchill was second only to Asquith in advertising the merits of free trade to the electorate, and was suitably rewarded when Campbell-Bannerman appointed him Under-Secretary at the Colonial Office (in December 1905). It was during this period as a junior minister that Churchill transformed himself into an advocate of collectivist social reform, and when Asquith became Prime Minister (in March 1908) he gave Churchill the opportunity to translate his rhetoric into practice by raising him to cabinet rank as President of the Board of Trade. One consequence of this, required by the constitutional convention of the day, was a by-election. Defeated in Manchester, Churchill was returned instead for the predominantly working-class constituency of Dundee, which depended mainly on the jute trade and shipbuilding. At the same time Churchill seized the initiative in cabinet, successfully launching a number of major innovations in social policy: the regulation of wages in the 'sweated trades',

43

compulsory unemployment insurance and labour exchanges. It was in pursuit of an advanced social programme that Churchill campaigned in 1909 for the proposals of 'the People's Budget'. Finally, Churchill received at the Board of Trade an education in the rapidly-growing practice of government intervention and conciliation in industrial disputes.

Churchill's promotion from the Board of Trade to a term at the Home Office (January 1910 to October 1911) necessitated another change of role. At the Home Office Churchill dealt with various measures, including the Shops Bill and the Coal Mines Bill, designed to improve working conditions. But the Home Office also bore the responsibility for public order, and Churchill's arrival there coincided with the onset of a period of intense labour unrest punctuated by riots. On more than one occasion he authorized the use of troops to assist the police in keeping order, and this brought him into sharp conflict with sections of the labour movement for the first time. Shadows of social reaction and militarism began to gather around Churchill's head, at least in the minds of radicals and socialists. As if to confirm these suspicions, Churchill moved to the Admiralty in October 1911 and became immersed in warlike preparations.

The record of events poses a biographical problem. There are some historical figures we take seriously as social statesmen: Lord Salisbury and Lord Milner for the coherence of their ideas, Lloyd George for his early radicalism and later *finesse*, Joseph Chamberlain as a pragmatic social engineer and Clement Attlee, perhaps, as a public-school socialist. But does Churchill belong to this company, and if so, how is he to be characterized? Naturally, the point has been mulled over by historians with various results. There is general agreement, unsurprisingly, that Churchill was a man of phenomenal push and go, a great rhetorician and a decisive influence in propelling the Asquith Cabinet towards social reform. But here the consensus ends, with Churchill's attitude to social policy as the touchstone. Some commentators argue that Churchill's involvement with social reform was transitory and superficial. Churchill, it is said, was an inherently rootless and unstable character who picked up the language and policies of radicalism in a blaze of opportunism, and forgot all about them again when his ambition turned in other directions. Reinforcing such scepticism is the conviction that if Churchill was anything, he was, as Charles Masterman wrote, 'an aboriginal and unchangeable Tory'.[1]

But if Masterman was right, there must have been rather more substance and continuity to Churchill than some of his critics have recognized. The point is made by Robert Rhodes James when he stresses the conservative rationale of Churchill's experiments in social policy. 'Improvement and reform were desirable and necessary in Churchill's eyes not to transform society but to preserve it more effectively.'[2] Ronald Hyam argues along similar lines: 'Social reform to him was not an end in itself . . . All Churchill's speeches upon social reform were full of concern for the stability of society, of anxiety about state resources of "inestimable advantage running thriftlessly to waste".'[3] A second continuity is detected by writers who find in Churchill an underlying sympathy for the underdog. Both Randolph Churchill and Martin Gilbert have woven this assumption into the official biography of Churchill. The scholar to whom these essays are dedicated, Henry Pelling, concludes that Churchill was 'instinctively on the side of the man or woman in the street'.[4]

In seeking a language to describe Churchill it is always wise to bear in mind Attlee's verdict that he was 'the most protean person I ever came into contact with'.[5] Attlee did not mean that Churchill was a random dance of molecules, without form or pattern. He did mean that Churchill was a many-sided personality in constant motion, or (to vary the metaphor) a man living on a number of different levels at once. At one level Churchill has to be understood as a creative opportunist, a professional politician who excelled in the capacity to respond to each new situation with a fresh strategy: inventiveness was his forte. But one cannot read through the long narrative of Churchill's life without recognizing a strong bias of inspiration. He never sank his identity in that of any particular group, nor did he acquire a set of principles to govern his activities. But if he lacked the social discipline to keep him on a straight course, he possessed instead a vision of the world to inspire the roles he might play. A sense of class, a sense of authority and a sense of history can all be said to have contributed to a romantic consciousness of a world fit for heroes to live in.

Churchill's class loyalties transcended party and were attached instead to the plutocratic network of the Court, the great country houses and the City of London. In this world there were in effect only two classes: the upper crust and their dependents, young Winston and Mrs Everest, officers and other ranks. Churchill believed in his own class and its paternal relationship with 'the people', but knowledge of the middle classes was a gap in his education. In an abstract way he was all for capitalist industry, but he lacked practical rapport with manufacturers or suburban ratepayers. Middle-class instincts were missing from Churchill's consciousness and it was no accident that he collided with Joseph, and later with Neville Chamberlain. Another hallmark of Churchill's style was the coexistence in his outlook of tough- and tender-minded attitudes, the Tory sense of the need for repression and physical force, and the Liberal sense of the need for conciliation and moral force. Churchill sought to run the two in harness. As he was to say in 1919 in connection with the peace terms to be imposed on Germany: 'The finest combination in the world is power and mercy. The worst combination in the world is weakness and strife.'[6] As for Churchill's sense of history, his Whig assertion of the uniquely progressive character of the British constitution and the British Empire would have been commonplace but for the fact that he treated the past as the key to his own destiny: a destiny to be traced through the Churchill family tree.

Churchill's first notion of the working class was appropriated from his father, Lord Randolph. The relationship of father and son was highly fraught, and after Lord Randolph's death in 1895 Winston preserved an ambivalent attitude to his memory. He idealized him as a great man, celebrating him first as the hero of a work of fiction, *Savrola* (1900), and soon afterwards in a marmoreal biography, *Lord Randolph Churchill* (1906). To the end of his life the ghost of Lord Randolph haunted his thoughts. On the other hand, Churchill also made calculated use of his father's record. What better way of establishing himself in politics than to exploit the network of his father's friends and contacts, to pick up his slogans and imitate his tactics? 'No doubt', Churchill told the electors of Oldham, 'the Radicals will say I am trading on my father's name. Well, and why should I not?'[7] Lord Randolph, in other words, served his son both as myth and strategy, and the same applies to the idea of 'Tory Democracy'.

The main proposition of Tory Democracy, as expounded by Lord Randolph, was that the Conservative party could broaden its electoral base by appealing to the working classes of the cities and industrial towns. Historians with twentieth-century assumptions have searched in vain for a programme of collectivist social reform in Lord Randolph's speeches. They forget that in the 1880s radicalism rather than collectivism was still the main form of class politics. Lord Randolph assumed that the industrial working classes were Gladstonians or Chamberlainites, and his Dartford programme of 1886 spoke of local government reform, temperance, elementary education and the reduction of public expenditure. Tory Democracy, as Lord Rosebery wrote, was 'the wolf of Radicalism in the sheepskin of Toryism'.[8] In the twilight of his career, after his fall from power, Lord Randolph took a deeper interest in labour questions and expressed sympathy for minimum-wage legislation, but his collectivism remained tentative. When, in a letter to his mother, the young Winston Churchill tried to sketch out a programme of Tory Democracy he still thought mainly in terms of peace, retrenchment and reform. Under the heading of domestic policy he listed as his objectives: 'Extension of the franchise to every male. Universal Education. Equal establishment of all religions. Wide measures of local self-government. Eight hours. Payment of members (on request). A progressive Income Tax.'[9]

Though Churchill rehearsed ideas like this in private, he never formulated a public agenda of Tory Democracy. In his first election campaign he told the electors of Oldham: 'I regard the improvement of the condition of the British people as the main end of modern government.'[10] But when it came to detail he confined himself to applauding one measure already passed, the Workmen's Compensation Act, and recommending another for which there was widespread support in the party: old-age pensions. Apart from these, a search through his early writings and speeches produces only suggestive fragments. In a despatch from South Africa to the *Morning Post* he spoke of the need of a scheme of state-aided emigration to relieve the congestion and poverty of the cities.[11] For a time he attached himself hopefully to his father's old friend Lord Rosebery in the belief that the latter would form a new political combination devoted to the current vogue for 'national efficiency'. In private correspondence he advocated 'a well-balanced policy midway between the Hotel Cecil and Exeter Hall, something that will co-ordinate development and expansion with the progress of social comfort and health'.[12] But although concerned about poverty, Churchill was uncertain what to say about it. In 1901 he read and evidently assimilated Seebohm Rowntree's study of poverty in York, and wrote an unpublished article arguing that the recruitment of healthy soldiers to the army depended on a well-fed population.[13] How they should be fed was not explained. In a contribution to a volume of essays on physical fitness, published in 1904, he discussed the merits of school meals but would not commit himself on the issue of whether they should be compulsory.[14]

The main reason why Churchill handled social reform so gingerly is that he attached overriding importance to the cause of economy and laissez-faire economics. It was in protest against increased public expenditure that Lord Randolph Churchill had resigned in 1886. Winston took up his father's mission, seizing on St John Brodrick's scheme of army expansion as the butt for a campaign against government extravagance. 'Trade is vital', he explained to readers of the *Daily Mail*. 'All taxation is a drag on trade. Long before the comfort of the people would be touched their competing power would be diminished. Therefore, the amount of money we can safely raise annually by taxation is limited.'[15] Churchill's belief in minimal government can only have been strengthened by his defence of free trade between 1903 and 1906, for his chief adviser on the problem was Sir Francis Mowatt, a senior Treasury official who had once been Gladstone's private secretary. Churchill recorded of Mowatt: 'He represented the complete triumphant Victorian view of economics and finance . . . Let the Government reduce itself and its demands upon the public to a minimum; let the nation live of its own; let social and industrial organisation take whatever course it pleased, subject to the laws of the land and the Ten Commandments.'[16]

Tory Democracy equipped the young Churchill with a parliamentary and electoral strategy, and served him well as a stepping-stone to fame and fortune. But, unlike his father, Churchill did not live by hard politics alone. Already he was formulating a romantic myth of English history in which Tory Democracy took on a second dimension as an explanation of the past and an inspiration for the future. Though *Savrola*, his only novel, is a work of Ruritanian fantasy, and *Lord Randolph Churchill* is a closely-documented biography, a single vision inspired them both. The context in each case is 'the rise of democracy'. In *Savrola*, a popular movement closely resembling the Liberal party, with a left wing of labour representatives, breaks into revolt against a dictatorship. In *Lord Randolph Churchill*, the two parties face the challenge of a growing labour consciousness.

> Not merely the decay of a Government or the natural overripeness of a party produced the agitations of 1885 and 1886. It was the end of an epoch. The long dominion of the middle classes which had begun in 1832 had come to its close and with it the almost equal reign of Liberalism. The great victories had been won. All sorts of lumbering tyrannies had been toppled over. Authority was everywhere broken. Slaves were free. Conscience was free. Trade was free. But hunger and squalor and cold were also free; and the people demanded something more than liberty.[17]

In Britain, as in the imaginary state of Laurania, the age of popular politics throws up a new type of hero, the orator-statesman who can stir up, and at the same time control, the emotions of a mass audience. A chapter of *Savrola* describes with obvious excitement the rhetorical techniques used by the hero to convert a hostile meeting to a state of passionate enthusiasm. *Lord Randolph Churchill* records 'the spectacle, repeatedly presented, of multitudes of working men hanging upon the words of a young aristocrat'.[18]

The moral that Churchill drew from all this is a simple but powerful one. The privileged classes could rely neither upon resistance to constitutional reform nor upon the purely negative support of vested interests fearful of change. The only way to maintain political stability was to carry on active propaganda among the masses, and respond to grievances with a measure of reform. Or as Lord Randolph put it in a public letter to Arnold White:

> If under the Constitution as it now exists, and as we wish to see it preserved, the Labour interest finds that it can obtain its objects and secure its own advantage, then that interest will be reconciled with the Constitution, will find faith in it and will maintain it. But if it should unfortunately occur that the Constitutional party, to which you and I belong, are deaf to hear and slow to meet the demands of Labour . . . the result may be that the Labour interest will identify what it will take to be defects in the Constitutional party with the Constitution itself, and in a moment of undiscriminating impulse may use its power to sweep both away.[19]

Beginnings are important, but Churchill's period as a young Tory was brief. If he went to school with the Conservative party, the Liberals provided his university. It was as a Liberal that he learnt to master major areas of controversy, and as a Liberal that he obtained his first experience of administration and the conduct of parliamentary business. Churchill was still young and open to new ideas, anxious to read the books recommended to him by more educated colleagues and ready to fall under the spell of new father-figures like David Lloyd George and Sir John Fisher. In spite of the continuities between the MP for Oldham and the president of the Budget League, Churchill's career as a Liberal collectivist represented a far more ambitious stage of development.

Churchill's move to the Liberal party naturally produced a shift in his rhetoric. His speeches between 1904 and 1906 included many references to unemployment and social distress together with injunctions to the Labour party to throw in their lot with Liberals rather than socialists. But as yet he couched his analysis in terms of radicalism rather than collectivism. Free trade, the issue on which he had abandoned the Conservatives, was of course his main theme, with appropriate tributes to Cobden. Chamberlain's tariff reform proposals were condemned on the grounds that they would enable capitalists and militarists to convert the state into an engine for taxing and exploiting the people. Economic recession was attributed to excessive public expenditure and high taxation.

> A period of enormous expenditure, of the lavish casting about of public money for unprofitable objects has affected alike the credit and consuming power of the people . . . After the riot of extravagance comes the pinch of want. An undue percentage of unemployment, a hampering lack of ready money throughout the country, a restricted credit in business circles, a considerable increase in pauperism – all follow in the track of the storm.[20]

Emphasizing that as an ex-Tory reformer he wanted to see the Liberal party tackle the problem of poverty, Churchill was not yet ready to respond to the promptings of the Webbs. In June 1904 Beatrice noted in her diary: 'I tried the National Minimum on him but he was evidently unaware of the most elementary objections to unrestricted competition and was still in the stage of "infant school economics".'[21] When Churchill was challenged at election meetings to say what the government would do about unemployment, he could only waffle hopefully:

> The Liberals have got some men together who might be able to do something. In Mr. Asquith, Sir Edward Grey, Mr. John Burns, and Mr. Lloyd George I see many men not only of great intellectual ability but men in close and intimate touch with the real needs of the people, and I think the Government has a right to ask the electors to give them the power and as good a chance as they so freely gave to the late Administration to grapple with the questions which are occupying the people.[22]

The immediate cause of Churchill's conversion to the New Liberalism seems to have been apprehension that the Lib–Lab alliance was unstable. In the general election of 1906, twenty-nine Labour MPs were elected mainly in straight contests against Conservative candidates, the Liberals having stood aside. The Liberal party underwrote this electoral alliance in the belief that in constituencies where there was no Labour candidate, Labour supporters would vote Liberal. However, the durability of this understanding was always in doubt since sections of the Labour party were determined to oppose the Liberals. In August 1906, Churchill's cousin and personal crony F. E. Guest was defeated in the Cockermouth by-election through the intervention of a Labour candidate, the seat going to the Conservative. Churchill condemned Labour for dividing the progressive vote, and his first reaction was to call for electoral reform in the shape of the second ballot.[23] By this time Churchill was in close touch with Lloyd George, and it may well be that they thought out a combined initiative. A speech by Lloyd George on 25 September 1906 warned that the Independent Labour party would sweep Liberalism away unless the government addressed itself to social conditions and the presence of widespread poverty 'in a land glittering with wealth'.[24] The point was reiterated by Churchill at Glasgow on 11 October. It was being argued, he said, that there could be no progress until the Liberal party had been destroyed by Labour. But in this event the result would be, as in Germany, the triumph of a reactionary anti-socialist movement. The best hope for Labour, and the only guarantee of social progress, lay in the continued cooperation of the Labour and Liberal parties. To demonstrate his sincerity, Churchill decided for the first time to put the case for collectivism and the 'universal establishment of minimum standards of life and labour'.[25] With the passage of time this early emphasis on the danger from an independent socialist party was replaced by a concentration on the Conservative enemy. Between 1908 and 1910 Churchill was mainly concerned to present social reform as the alternative to protection.

The view that Churchill's initiative was dictated by a desire to win or keep working-class votes has been questioned by Henry Pelling. He points out that Churchill defined the beneficiaries of Liberal social policy as the 'rearguard', a minority of the population stranded in poverty after the majority had moved on to a secure and comfortable existence. Evidently, Pelling maintains, the electoral advantage of courting this minority would be marginal, and Churchill himself admitted in May 1908 that social reform was liable to make the government unpopular. The implication seems to be that Churchill took up collectivism for purely non-electoral purposes.[26]

Questions of ultimate motivation are wisely avoided by historians, but the strategic grounds on which Churchill sought to justify social reform are clear from his letters and speeches. As a statesman he argued that social reform would stabilize society and fortify the authority of the state, and in this respect he was confident that in the long run history would prove him right. As a politician he treated social reform as the spearhead of the Liberal party's appeal to the electorate. We have only to glance at any of the great platform orations given by Churchill between 1908 and 1910 to see the huge investment of his persuasive powers in expounding social insurance or the 'People's

Budget'. Sometimes Churchill doubted whether social reform would prove to be popular even with the working class. But his entire effort was based on the assumption that social reform could be sold if it were advertised boldly and persistently. Churchill distinguished between the poor and the more fortunate members of the working class, but he did not think of the 'rearguard' as numerically insignificant. 'Liberalism', he declared, 'is the cause of the left-out millions.'[27] The two main parties, he told the House of Commons in 1907, were increasingly the parties of the rich and the poor. The danger was that owing to the intransigence of the House of Lords, with its power to block popular measures, about a quarter of the population would be left 'to rot and fester'.[28] As the scope of social policy widened, Churchill began to claim that the various measures proposed 'are part of a concerted, interdependent system for giving a better, a fairer social organisation to the masses of the people of our country'.[29] Churchill's speeches were peppered with references to the 'millions', the 'masses' and the 'labouring classes', and the wide-ranging effects of social policy were emphasized in passages like the following.

> Look at them for yourselves – the old-age pensions which have been given already on a scale unexampled in any other country, the legislation which has practically passed through Parliament to deal with the evils of sweating where they are found to exist, the attempt to multiply smallholdings, which we have not done with yet, the improved methods of finding work through a system of labour exchanges, the system soon to be introduced of insurance against unemployment, the State-aided insurance against invalidity, against sickness, and for a provision for women and orphans. The main object and result of each and all of these is to give a greater measure of security to the family and the home of the sober and industrious worker.[30]

Nor was Churchill indifferent to the 'aristocracy of labour'. He recognized that all workers were affected by the trade cycle and as the winter of 1908–9 approached, he urged the First Lord of the Admiralty, Reginald McKenna, to relieve unemployment by placing new naval contracts.

> The situation in the Shipbuilding and Engineering trades is most unsatisfactory; more than one third of the engineers are out of work irrespective of those affected by the strike. The distress on the Tyne and the Clyde cannot fail to be exceptionally acute during the whole of the coming winter and will produce a grave unrest among the artisan classes greatly to the prejudice of all the most essential interests of the government.[31]

Churchill, then, did define the major aim of Liberal policy as the alleviation of poverty, but he treated poverty as a common incident and prominent feature of working-class existence.

Social policy also needs to be understood in the context of a coherent rhetoric designed to comprehend working-class interests as a whole and identify them with the Liberal party. Ever since 1903 Churchill had stressed the class implications of the Conservative party's love-affair with tariff reform, and naturally he continued to do so. When speaking to Scottish miners at Perth in July 1908, he argued that protection was a deliberate attempt to alter the balance of class interests 'sensibly to the disadvantage of the labour classes'.[32] In the same speech there is a reference to temperance, the cause least associated with Churchill apart from communism. His many eloquent passages on the Licensing Bill were not exactly humbug, for Churchill had inherited an interest in temperance reform from Lord Randolph and had been 'brought up and trained to have the utmost contempt for people who got drunk'.[33] Other motifs of Churchill's speeches were his praise for trade unions as responsible bodies antithetical to socialism and his celebration of the Trade Disputes Act of 1906 as the Liberals' charter for organized labour.[34] As President of the Board of Trade, Churchill's influence ensured the passage of the Eight Hours' Act for the coal industry, a measure once championed by Lord Randolph, and by which means Churchill cultivated the goodwill of the miners. Invited to address the 1908 miners' gala in the Rhondda Valley, he coupled the Eight Hours' Act with the cause of temperance and received, according to the Rhondda District minutes, 'thrice-prolonged applause'.[35] As President of the Board of Trade, Churchill accelerated the incorporation of trade union officials in government by appointing them to newly-created posts. David Shackleton and Richard Bell, for example, became Labour Advisers to the Home Office.[36] The situation can be summed up by saying that Churchill was attempting to base the Liberal party on a renewed alliance with the trade unions and a wide-ranging appeal to the poor. Nothing better epitomized his politics than the double-member constituency of Dundee where, from January 1910, Churchill shared the representation of the seat with the Labour party's nominee, Alexander Wilkie. Wilkie was general secretary of the Ship Constructive and Shipwright's Association, an anti-socialist and later a fervent supporter of the First World War and the Lloyd George coalition. With allies like Wilkie, Churchill could well imagine that the Liberals had a healthy future ahead of them as the natural party of labour.

As a social reformer, Churchill was both an agent for the ideas of other people and a great patrician working to a Whig design. In Churchill's brain, as can be seen from his speeches, the inspirations were all mixed up together; but for the purposes of analysis some sorting out can be done. In recent years, political, administrative and intellectual historians have been excavating the foundations of Edwardian social policy, and incidentally setting Churchill's activities in a fresh context. As a result of the work of Peter Clarke, Roger Davidson, Michael Freeden, Bentley B. Gilbert, José Harris and others, the extent to which Churchill fed off the ideas of intellectuals and civil servants is now apparent.[37]

From the 1880s onwards the more advanced Liberal academics and publicists had been attempting to redefine the Liberal creed to encompass economic and social, as well as political rights. It was argued both that society was evolutionary and that institutions ought to be modified to express the collective aspect of man's nature. There was a practical force to these high thoughts, for a measure of collectivism would enable the Liberal party to counter the challenge of Labour and the socialists. But the 1906 general election was fought on traditional issues and at first the progressive wing of the party felt frustrated by the Campbell-Bannerman government. Churchill was the first major politician in the party to give voice to the ideas of Hobson, Hobhouse and the other New Liberals. Not only the general notion that Liberals should now apply themselves to 'the social question', but also particular arguments such as the distinction between the collective and the individualistic elements in society, or the case for the taxation of unearned increment on land, were borrowed by Churchill from the New Liberals and built into his speeches.[38] Lloyd George, born and bred in the language of Victorian radicalism, was slower to pick up the new idiom and happier to attack peers, publicans and landlords in the traditional vein.[39]

When Churchill first met Beatrice Webb he confided that he never did any brain-work that he could get somebody else to do for him. This made him fair game for the Fabian strategy of permeating influential minds, and the Webbs did succeed in capturing his attention for a while. It was to the Webbs that he owed the phrase 'the national minimum', and in March 1908 Beatrice noted that Churchill had 'swallowed whole Sidney's scheme for boy labour and unemployment, had even dished it up in an article in *The Nation* the week before'.[40] These words, however, were written while Churchill was still Under-Secretary at the Colonial Office. The following month Churchill took office as President of the Board of Trade. In his new department Churchill came to rely heavily on the guidance of the Permanent Secretary, Sir Hubert Llewellyn Smith, who gradually weaned him away from the thoroughgoing philosophy of the Webbs to a more piecemeal approach. The Webbs may have hoped that at the Board of Trade Churchill would frame a unified programme for the replacement of the poor law. Churchill had sketched out a comprehensive Webbian approach in his article for *The Nation*, 'The Untrodden Field in Politics', and again in a letter to Asquith.[41] But Llewellyn Smith aimed to bypass the Webbs and tackle in a piecemeal fashion only those aspects of poverty with which the Board of Trade was equipped to deal. And, as Roger Davidson has pointed out, the provisions drafted by Llewellyn Smith and Beveridge were not to the liking of the Webbs. 'The Webbs favoured a system of compulsory labour exchanges, subsidised voluntary insurance and maintenance under disciplinary training of uninsured men in distress. The official draftsmen opted instead for compulsory insurance and voluntary labour exchanges. They rejected compulsory exchanges and penal reformatories as unacceptable to all but "Chairmen of Schools of Sociology".'[42]

There can be little doubt that, having escaped the tutelage of Sidney and Beatrice Webb, Churchill fell under the tutelage of this Permanent Secretary. As head of the Labour Department of the Board of Trade from 1893 to 1907, Llewellyn Smith was an expert on the workings of the labour market, the unruly sea across which all social reformers had to chart a course. Churchill, knowing practically nothing about the subject to begin with, learnt fast, mastering his briefs for the Cabinet and the House of Commons. The three great measures with which he came to be associated at the Board of Trade – the Trade Boards Act, the Labour Exchanges Act and the first draft of the scheme for unemployment insurance – were devised by civil servants and not very much amended by the minister. In 1909, following a discussion of the point in Cabinet, Llewellyn Smith drafted penalty clauses to deprive 'malingerers' of the right to benefit during the first six weeks of unemployment. Churchill argued vehemently that a worker's record of contributions ought to serve as the only qualification necessary for benefit. 'I do not like mixing up moralities and mathematics.' But Llewellyn Smith's proposals carried the day.[43] True to his visionary egotism, Churchill also became excited by the idea of building up the Board of Trade as a kind of civil Committee of Imperial Defence coordinating government expenditure to counteract the trade cycle. 'Understandably', Roger Davidson writes, 'Llewellyn Smith restrained his chief . . .'[44]

For obvious reasons, intellectual and administrative historians tend either to minimize the influence of politicians on public policy or to present them as actors rehearsing a script written by somebody else. But without Churchill much less would have been done. It was he (with Lloyd George) who supplied the political imperative, and in his own mind the ideas of the experts took their place as components of a Churchillian grand strategy. Historians often discover that a drive for innovation is linked to an equally powerful drive for stability and order, and so it was in Churchill's case. Ronald Hyam has argued that his attitudes to social reform were rooted and grounded in paternalist desire to strengthen the authority of the state.[45] This emphasis may irritate some of Churchill's admirers who insist, fairly enough, on the importance of his sympathy for the suffering and the defeated. A protective instinct for those under his care is certainly the mark of the authentic paternalist. Paternalism, however, depends upon the authority of the ruler over the ruled. Mercy is the prerogative of power, but power is the primary requirement.

Churchill argued that social reform would strengthen the state both at home and abroad. At home the function of the Liberal party was to prevent the polarization of Britain between the extremes of wealth and poverty. Why, Churchill asked, was property so secure in Britain? It was not because Britain had repressive laws, nor because the constitution provided legal checks against popular movements.

> I will tell those wealthy and powerful people what the secret of the security of life and property in Britain is. The security arises from the continuation of that very class struggle which they lament and of which they complain, which goes on ceaselessly in our country . . . which never sinks into lethargy, and never breaks into violence, but which from year to year makes a steady and constant advance.[46]

Disconcerting though it is to hear the language of class struggle from Churchill's lips, the intent is plain: reform binds workers to the social structure and the state. Or, as he put it on another occasion: 'The Government of a State is like a pyramid, and I have told you before that the function of Liberalism is to broaden the base of the pyramid and so increase the stability of the whole.'[47]

Between 1900 and the Agadir crisis of 1911, Churchill appeared confident that peace would prevail between Britain and Germany, and his belief in social reform cannot be traced specifically to the expectation of war. What Churchill did absorb was the general sense, expressed by so many politicians and publicists around the turn of the century, that competition between the great powers was increasing, and that Britain must improve its 'national efficiency' in order to remain a world power. As an embryo Tory, Churchill had declared in 1898: 'To keep our Empire we must have a free people, an educated and well fed people. That is why we are in favour of social reform. That is why we long for Old Age pensions and the like.'[48] This is how he put the point to a Liberal audience at the beginning of 1908:

> If the British people will have a great Empire, if any ray of true glory is to fall upon it, they will need an Imperial race to support the burden. They will never erect that great fabric upon the shoulders of stinted millions crowded together in the slums of cities, trampled in the slush of dismal streets. Not that way lies the future of the British race, and any neglect of these considerations will lead not merely to the destruction of our material dominion but of the moral forces upon which that material dominion is based.[49]

Churchill's credentials as a paternalist were tested out in the spring of 1909 by Lloyd George's budget proposals, introduced to the Cabinet in March and revealed to the House of Commons on 29 April. Since the budget was designed to finance a social programme of which he and Lloyd George were the joint promoters, Churchill had a strong vested interest in its success. But the budget also raised in a sharp and controversial form the principle of the redistribution of wealth. Lloyd George's fiscal strategy singled out the rich, and especially the landowning class, to bear the main weight of direct taxation. For this reason it is sometimes thought that Churchill disliked and attempted to dilute Lloyd George's proposals. Lloyd George alleged this in August 1909, though he had said the opposite in May of that year.[50] In fact there is no need to suppose that Churchill was concerned about the fate of the agricultural estate. Private letters to Lloyd George and to Clementine Churchill show him looking forward to the break-up of the great estates, and celebrating the thriving peasant agriculture of Germany.[51] As for the rich, it may be that Churchill was familiar enough with the luxury and extravagance of Edwardian plutocrats to conclude that they could well afford a modest contribution to social welfare. In public he argued as before that the best security for property in Britain was to be found in the willingness of men of wealth and position to embrace the popular cause. Even after the budget, the wealthy would still find Britain the best country in the world to live in.[52]

As president of the Budget League, Churchill attacked the privileges of landlords and peers with force and precision. No doubt he convinced himself, as he sought to convince his audiences, that the social order would be all the stronger for a slight flattening at the top. But it required unusual sleight of hand to attack the top without alienating the middle. The aim of the exercise was to subsume working-class discontent in an alliance of the industrious classes against passive property-owners and the super-rich. But the consequence might have been to accelerate the polarization of politics between capital and labour. Cameron Hazlehurst has suggested that by encouraging a spirit of social antagonism, Churchill 'undermined the foundations of the political system which he strove to preserve. The more sharply focussed the wealthy Conservative enemy became, the greater was the drift away from the sanity of Liberalism into the extremes of class antagonism.'[53] In effect, Churchill stood for a non-socialist and non-militant labour movement under the patronage of property-owners. But after 1910 this position was challenged as industrial conflict superseded debates over the budget and the House of Lords. Churchill began to figure as the victim instead of the beneficiary of class feeling: Labour politicians, by attacking Churchill, implied that he was an enemy of the working class.

In January 1910, Asquith promoted Churchill to the Home Office. Churchill no doubt aimed to go down in history as a great reforming Home Secretary but his efforts were interrupted by his other duties as the minister responsible for public order. As has already been mentioned, Churchill had attempted, while at the Board of Trade, to build up a relationship with the miners, the Gurkhas of the Liberal army. But in November 1910 the understanding was ruptured at Tonypandy. The Eight Hours' Act, coupled with a new current of class resentment, triggered off a series of disputes in the coalfields, and by 1 November 1910 strike action affected all the collieries belonging to the Cambrian Combine in the Rhondda Valley.[54] On 7 November, as miners visited each pit in turn to expel officials and close down machinery, violent clashes occurred between police and strikers outside the Glamorgan colliery at Llwynypia, a quarter of a mile from Tonypandy. Fearing that the police would be over-powered, the Chief Constable of Glamorgan requisitioned two companies of infantry and 200 cavalry from the military authorities, informing the Home Office of his action the next morning. Meanwhile advanced warning of the troop movements reached William Abraham, Lib–Lab MP for the Rhondda, president of the South Wales Miners' Federation and better known as 'Mabon'. Mabon appeared at the Home Office on the morning of 6 November to plead with Churchill to withhold the troops.[55] After a conference with Haldane, the Secretary for War, Churchill wired the Chief Constable to inform him that metropolitan police were to be substituted for soldiers. The cavalry were to go no further than Cardiff while the infantry were to halt at Swindon. To the men on strike Churchill sent a personal message that was read out to them at a mass meeting on the afternoon of 8 November.

> Their best friends here are greatly distressed at the trouble which has broken out and will do their best to help them to get fair treatment. Askwith, Board of Trade, wishes to see Mr. Watts Morgan with six or eight local representatives at Board of Trade, 2 o'clock tomorrow. But rioting must cease at once so that the enquiry shall not be prejudicial and to prevent the credit of the Rhondda valley being impaired.[56]

But rioting did not cease. With the metropolitan police still on their way from London, fighting broke out again outside the Glamorgan colliery and spread to the main square of Tonypandy. One man, Samuel Rays, received a fatal injury to the skull. Later in the evening rioters rampaged through Tonypandy looting or damaging some sixty-three shops. With ominous news filtering through from the Rhondda, Churchill had already lifted his ban on troop movements, which did not, therefore, outlive the day on which it was promulgated. On the following day, General Nevile Macready, whom Churchill had arranged to command the troops in the valley, reported that a detachment of Lancashire fusiliers was on duty at Llwynypia.

As we now know, there was to be more than one legend of Tonypandy. Keir Hardie led off with the pious theory that the people of Tonypandy had never rioted at all: the trouble was all caused by 'a small body of under one hundred, few of whom were resident in the place, who had been drinking most of the day, and who had been turned out of the public houses . . .'[57] Then came the oral tradition to the effect that Churchill had sent in troops to shoot down strikers. Overreacting against this falsehood, Randolph Churchill asserted in the second volume of his father's life that troops were never sent into the Rhondda Valley at all, a thesis that has since led others astray. It would be interesting to speculate why the spectre of military force in the streets of Britain should lead to so much distortion of the facts, but assuming that the misunderstandings are removed, what was the significance of Tonypandy for the politics of Winston Churchill?

Tonypandy was a test of Churchill's faith in the viability of Lib–Lab politics. His first reaction was that of a Liberal Home Secretary on his best behaviour just before a general election, and looking perhaps for a timely personal triumph. Not only did he wish to avoid enraging the miners by the use of troops, Asquith's mistake at Featherstone in 1893, but he was hopeful that the Lib–Lab conspiracy would lift him clear of embarrassment. His message to the miners was intended as a very plain reminder that under the provisions of the old pals' act there was a clause declaring that one good turn deserved another. Peaceful conduct would be rewarded by sympathetic arbitration. When riots continued and the use of troops became inevitable, Churchill made strenuous efforts to avoid direct confrontation between the people and the military. As Macready reported:

> In accordance with the verbal instructions of the Home Secretary, the general line of policy pursued throughout the strike was that in no case should soldiers come in direct contact with rioters unless and until action had been taken by the police. In the event of the police being overpowered . . . the military force would come into play, but even then each body of military should be accompanied by at any rate a small body of police to emphasise the fact that the armed forces act merely as the support of the civil power . . .[58]

Churchill's restraint, by preventing bloodshed, also prevented a political disaster for Liberalism. In spite of Tonypandy some life remained in the old Lib–Lab relationship. In the general election of December 1910 'Mabon' was once again returned as MP for the Rhondda. He at least refused to join in the condemnation of Churchill, and Churchill, whose exact thoughts we do not know, may well have assumed that the majority of miners resembled 'Mabon' rather than Keir Hardie. If so, the situation looked very different from the Labour side of the fence. Mabon's vote in December 1910 was down by more than three thousand, a loss of nearly a quarter of the support he had won in the previous general election in January. Though he remained president of the South Wales Miners' Federation, the Cambrian Colliery dispute destroyed his influence in the union. As every labour historian knows, the initiative in the coalfields was passing to a younger generation of militants, inspired, if only in part, by syndicalism. Churchill's restraint, therefore, availed him little in the eyes of his class antagonists. Soldiers did not kill anyone, but they remained in the Rhondda until the end of the strike in October 1911 and as David Smith comments, their presence 'ensured that the miners' demands would be utterly rejected'.[59] Nor were the police likely to be regarded as neutral. Keir Hardie in the House of Commons quoted several allegations of police brutality, and on a number of occasions demanded that Churchill institute an inquiry. Indeed the conduct of the metropolitan and other police imported from outside the district quickly superseded the question of the use of troops as the major source of embarrassment to Churchill.[60]

In the debates over Tonypandy, Churchill figured for the first time as a public enemy in Labour rhetoric and, as though to oblige his critics, he at once responded with an exercise in self-parody. In January 1911 Churchill hastened to the scene of a drama in the East End of London, where a group of revolutionaries were trapped inside a house by police and soldiers. As Henry Pelling has remarked, the boyish excitement displayed by Churchill at the 'siege of Sidney Street' contributed to the notion of him as a lover of military force, an idea reinforced by recollections of his well-publicized career as a soldier.[61]

Churchill's fascination with all things military should not be allowed to obscure the contrast between his behaviour over Tonypandy and his actions during the national rail strike the following year. In South Wales Churchill was dealing with a localized industrial dispute which did not endanger the economy as a whole. Law and order might benefit the colliery owners but neither Churchill nor the Liberal party had a vested interest in the defeat of the miners. But when in June 1911 transport workers at the ports began to come out on strike, the government faced a different situation. A prolonged stoppage carried on simultaneously in a number of major ports would cut off the supply of food to the cities and sever the main arteries of the economy. As railway workers too began to join in, there arose the spectre of economic collapse accompanied by social disorder. Even if they had not been kept up to date on the point by G. R. Askwith, ministers could hardly have failed to appreciate the changed temper of the world of labour. They had only to read the newspapers to learn that a new generation of union organizers was employing the rhetoric of syndicalism and class conflict. For the first time since the 1840s, industrial action could be equated with a challenge to the authority of the state. The temptation therefore was to throw the weight of authority into the scales in order to intimidate strikers or directly break a strike.

In June Churchill authorized the despatch of extra police to Hull. In July, responding to an appeal from the Lord Mayor of Manchester, he moved a detachment of the Scots Greys to Salford. In the first week of August a general strike of transport workers in Liverpool precipitated riots on a scale approaching that of a local civil war. Acting once more on the request of the local authority, by 14 August Churchill had given orders to bring the strength of forces in the city up to a complete brigade of infantry and two regiments of cavalry. The following day one man was shot dead by troops when a crowd attempted to prevent the movement of a prison van escorted by soldiers. As a further precautionary measure, Churchill arranged with the Admiralty for the cruiser *Antrim* to be despatched to the Mersey to assist in the protection of the docks.[62]

In all this, Churchill preserved a semblance of neutrality on the part of the government, and did not exceed the requirements of public order. Nor did he neglect the processes of conciliation with which he was familiar from the Board of Trade. In late July he urged an inquiry headed by the Prime Minister, or a committee representing the employers, the unions and the government, to investigate the causes of the unrest and propose remedies. At the same time Churchill argued that events were coming to a head and that the decisive issues would soon have to be faced.

> Serious crises have been in recent years, and very often lately, surmounted only by a narrow margin of safety and now specially a new force has arisen in trades unionism, whereby the power of the old leaders has proved quite ineffective, and the sympathetic strike on a wide scale is prominent. Shipping, coal, railways, dockers etc. etc. are all uniting and breaking out at once. The 'general strike' policy is a factor which must be dealt with.
>
> While control can probably be maintained, even in a dozen or simultaneous Tonypandys or Manchesters, control would be more difficult if the railways went, and adequate control must mean great uncertainty, destruction of property, and probably loss of life.[63]

The first critical moment occurred early in August when the London docks were brought to a standstill. Pressure built up on Churchill from various quarters to send in the troops to unload the ships and convoy food supplies through the city. On 11 August he informed the King that twenty-five thousand soldiers were being held in readiness outside the capital.[64] But whether it was from innate caution, or because he was influenced by the pleas of Ben Tillett, Churchill decided to allow time for mediation by Askwith. The dispute was finally settled by a meeting at the Home Office on 18 August and Tillett subsequently recorded his gratitude to the Home Secretary. 'He refused to listen to the clamour of class-hatred, he saved the country from a national transport stoppage becoming a riot and incipient revolution.'[65] Churchill himself drew a slightly different conclusion, arguing in a letter to the King that the intention of the government

> to use very large bodies of troops to maintain order & the food supply if the strike was not settled promptly had a potent influence on the men's decision. They knew that they had reached the psychological moment to make their bargain, & that to go on was to risk all that they had within their grasp.[66]

During the national railway strike of 18 and 19 August, Churchill for the first time employed the army in a public display of force calculated to make the strikers back down. In preparation for the strike troops were marched into London and twenty-three other towns in England and Wales.[67] Previously the use of troops had been governed by two principles: firstly they were only provided at the request of the local authority concerned, and secondly it was understood that such requests were only to be made after a breakdown of order had occurred. But on the eve of the strike Churchill swept these conventions aside and suspended the Army Regulation which required a requisition from a civil authority.[68] The purpose of the troops, apart from the protection of the rail network from sabotage, was to enable the companies to continue as best they could with non-union labour. This led directly to the incident at Llanelli on the second day of the dispute. A train driven by blackleg labour was halted by strikers, soldiers of the Worcestershire regiment intervened to clear the tracks. After the reading of the Riot Act, troops fired into a crowd killing two men.[69]

It is most unlikely that Churchill acted without the support of Asquith and the majority of the Cabinet. Both the Prime Minister and his colleagues were, so Crewe recorded, 'full of fight against these dangerous elements': Lloyd George was unrepresentative in his conciliatory approach.[70] After a summer of discontent the unprecedented challenge of a simultaneous national stoppage by all four railway unions must have convinced respectable opinion that the world was being turned upside-down. The conjunction of the crisis at home with persistent tension abroad in the aftermath of the Agadir incident contributed to a spasm of acute insecurity. *The Times* commented on 16 August: 'These trade unionists in their crazy fanaticism or diseased vanity are prepared to starve the whole population, including of course their own families and all the ranks of "Labour" to ruin the country and leave it defenceless to the world.'[71] This was precisely Churchill's line. As he told the House of Commons later on, he feared that the halting of the trains would in a short time 'produce total unemployment followed by absolute starvation'. If the machinery for distributing food and raw materials were broken,

> catastrophe would follow; if once things went too far it might not be possible to recover in time, even if all classes worked together. The trains might run again, the ships might pour their cargoes on to the quays, food might flow into some great starved-out district – daily bread would be there again only a week too late. That week would satisfy even Mr. Keir Hardie himself.[72]

Churchill was too confident of the moral and physical sway of the governing classes to imagine a successful British revolution. But for a moment he was Savrola holding chaos at bay, and his apprehension was connected with fear of subversion inspired from Germany. Guy Granet, the general manager of Midland Railways, had been passing to Churchill allegations that labour leaders were receiving payments from a German agent called Bebel. And on 18 August the clerk of the Privy Council, Sir Almeric Fitzroy, noted in his diary: 'Winston Churchill is said to be convinced that the whole trouble is fomented by German gold, and claims to have proof of it, which others regard as midsummer madness.'[73]

In the event, the rail strike was rapidly ended by the intervention of Lloyd George, the atmosphere of crisis dissolved, and the Labour party collected another snapshot of Churchill in a Napoleonic pose. In the House of Commons he was singled out for attack by Ramsay MacDonald and Keir Hardie, who must have been grateful for a providential escape from embarrassment. Whoever had organized and represented the strike movement over the previous three months, it had not been the leaders of the Labour party. Nor could they honestly condone the physical-force tactics of intimidation and riot. By focusing indignation on Churchill they could divert the class war back into the House of Commons, and subtly shift the onus of responsibility for extremism on to a Liberal Cabinet. Their sincerity is not in question: like most politicians they emphasized only the convenient truths. They enjoyed the added advantage of exploiting the radical tradition against a Liberal minister. Churchill himself in the past had conjured up the fear of militarism and 'Prussianism'; now he stood accused of imposing the army on local authorities against their will, and introducing troops into peaceful and law-abiding districts. Keir Hardie went further by accusing Asquith and Churchill of deliberately sending soldiers to shoot and kill strikers, an allegation repeated in his pamphlet *Killing No Murder*.[74]

We have it on the authority of Charles Masterman that when Lloyd George settled the rail strike Churchill immediately telephoned him to say that he was sorry to hear it. '"It would have been better to have gone on and given these men a good thrashing."'[75] The remark suggests a hardening of attitudes against trade unions and the grievances of industrial workers. Can it then be argued that Churchill's period as Home Secretary marked a turning-point, a moment when he abandoned social reform in favour of social resistance? The idea has some initial plausibility. If Hardie and MacDonald turned against Churchill it would seem to follow that Churchill 'turned against the working classes'. His move to the Admiralty in October 1911, after which his radical alliance with Lloyd George began to disintegrate, can be seen as a return to his main path of development as a man of military and imperial affairs. But all this strains the evidence too much. Churchill would have been just as much opposed to a general strike in 1906 as he was in 1911. At no time was he likely to befriend the socialism of Hardie and MacDonald. Churchill was always in favour of resistance in the sense that he opposed syndicalism and socialism, and always in favour of reform in a Tory Democratic or Lib–Lab sense. In other words, resistance and reform were the two sides of a constant Churchillian coin.

In spite of his encounter with industrial unrest Churchill continued to assume that Lib–Labbery could be made to work. He did not despair of his or the government's reputation among the miners, but sought to restore their goodwill through energetic action to implement the improvements in pit safety recommended by the Royal Commission on the Mines.[76] When the national coal strike began in March 1912, his warning of its consequences was couched in supremely tactful terms. 'The miners are a great community . . . We owe them much and they owe us much.'[77] In his diagnosis of the industrial troubles of 1911 he was careful to avoid a purely negative conclusion. While defending his use of troops he went on to say that

> law and order and its maintenance are only half the question that is before us. Our experience of history – our knowledge of our fellow-countrymen and of their character – teaches us this important fact, that where there is a keen discontent in any large body of British people there is sure to be some very real and very good cause for it . . . Now there is one obvious cause, an obvious and unmistakable cause, of discontent among the wage-earners. The prices of food and necessaries have risen in the last fifteen years more than wages. That is an undoubted fact which every employer who is a worthy citizen and wishes to be a good captain of industry is bound to face and do justice to.[78]

Churchill's vision of a benign but hierarchical society did not fade away. But it is true to say that after his term at the Board of Trade the theme of working-class improvement gradually tapered off to become one strand among many. The Home Office provided some scope, but less than before. Apart from the miners Churchill attempted to aid shop assistants, but the Shops Bill was thoroughly emasculated before it reached the statute book. The introduction of a Trade Union Bill to enable trade union members to contribute to political funds gave him the chance to express his sympathy with organized labour:

> I consider that every workman is well advised to join a trade union. I cannot conceive how any man standing undefended against the powers that be in this world could be so foolish, if he could possibly spare the money from the maintenance of his family, not to associate himself with an organisation to protect the rights and interests of labour.[79]

At the Admiralty Churchill was not quite removed from responsibility for social welfare, and it would be hard to imagine a more perfect example of paternalism than the reforms he introduced to improve conditions on the lower deck.[80] Liberal party gatherings and his constituents in Dundee were still treated to disquisitions on the sufferings of the poor, the merits of social insurance and even the virtues of land reform. But something had changed. Naval policy and Ireland now occupied the strategic heights of his rhetoric and absorbed his political and administrative energies. And while Churchill sometimes struck out in the old way against the Conservatives, he was beginning to think and speak much more in terms of a 'national' approach appropriate to a country facing an external threat. In short, domestic politics were receding to the back of his mind. Churchill did not abandon reform for resistance. He simply relegated the social question to a lower level of priority. Only when the First World War was over did Churchill not only actively revive his commitment to working-class improvement but also his opposition to socialism and the general strike.

Early in this discussion the question was raised as to whether or not Churchill should be taken seriously as a social statesman. The answer proposed here is that he should be. Intellectuals are concerned with theory and Churchill was no intellectual in spite of his remarkable brain. Civil servants are concerned with administrative mechanisms and Churchill, for all his bright ideas, was never a bureaucratic engineer. He has to be judged as a politician mediating between the governors and the governed and confronted with the perennial problem of modern British politics: what to do about the working class. His response was fundamentally ideological rather than opportunist. Out of his early experience as an aristocrat, an officer and a naïve Tory Democrat, there arose in his mind a picture of a patriotic working class dominated by a paternal élite. In Edwardian Liberalism, interpreted along Bismarckian lines, he discovered the prescription for a harmonious society, an orderly state, and a strong Empire. For others the Liberalism of the 'People's Budget' was a point of departure, but for Churchill it was the terminus of his social thought. Far from abandoning his Edwardian outlook in later years, Churchill maintained it with great tenacity throughout the 1920s and in patches thereafter, whenever social questions came to his attention. But the First World War destroyed the conditions in which paternalism could flourish, and in trying to revive it after 1918, Churchill was to find himself at war with Labour on the left, and constrained by the hard facts of capitalism on the right. No contrast need be drawn between the politician who spoke of the 'left-out millions' in 1906, and the politician who condemned Labour as 'unfit to govern' in 1920. The first of these statements might have come from a guilt-ridden liberal confessing the sins of the wealthy. But in fact it came from a full-blooded Whig assured of his right to rule and equally confident of the benefits that his rule would confer on the less fortunate. The second statement, therefore, follows on logically from the first: in peacetime politics, Churchill made his main contribution as a statesman of order.

4

Expectations born to death: local Labour party expansion in the 1920s

CHRISTOPHER HOWARD

I

'The Labour Party knocks the heart out of me', Ramsay MacDonald wrote in 1921, 'and expectations are like babies born to death and should not be created'.[1] This characteristically self-indulgent complaint was more perceptive than MacDonald may have realized. By the end of 1921, Labour's leaders had created expectations of political and social advance which they could not realistically hope to fulfil except by abandoning the unrestrained idealism which had won converts and stirred enthusiasm during the last year or so of war and the first years of peace. This article will examine the fading of expectations within local Labour parties during the first post-war decade.

The senior midwife of the 'babies born to death' was Arthur Henderson. In 1918 he and Sidney Webb had created more than the Labour party constitution; they had given official approval, through the National Executive Committee (NEC), to the notion that a Labour government was an imminent possibility. Such hopes were obviously raised after the Russian revolutions and may have been partly justified early in 1918.[2] The failure of the alternative vote clause of the Franchise Bill[3] 'immensely worsened'[4] Labour's chances, though, and the Ludendorff Offensive on the western front in the spring of 1918 almost killed them altogether.[5] However, at the party conference of June 1918, when Labour still hoped to gain credit for a negotiated peace, Henderson and Webb showed the delegates an electoral Canaan and by so doing engineered the approval, almost without thought,[6] of an extremely broad party programme. This was deliberately designed to be a 'forest of Christmas trees with presents for everyone',[7] particularly everyone disenchanted with Lloyd George's conduct of the war.

Hopes of an immediate Labour advance were crushed by the success of the Foch Offensive, Germany's unconditional surrender and the climate of the 'coupon' election.[8] By the spring of 1919, however, J. H. Thomas was writing *When Labour Rules*, enthusiastic converts like Leonard Woolf were convinced that the party had 'ideals and principles which were real and alive'[9] and most activists assumed that the party was on the verge of creating a new social order. They were also easily able to persuade the uncommitted that Labour would soon be in power and would make major changes to the fabric of British life.[10] After a series of by-election successes in late 1919, culminating in victory at Spen Valley in 1920, the other parties also accepted that Labour was a major force in the land.[11] It then became essential for party leaders to maintain the somewhat illusory image of an all-conquering 'party of attack'.[12] Having come so far so quickly, the Labour establishment then began to talk of consolidation and responsibility. This tended to exaggerate the party's failure to expand its base and only contributed to the frustration of expectations among both leaders and led.

Despite the gains of the early post-war years, Labour's leaders remained riddled with doubt and insecurity and began to lay more and more stress on the need for 'a great mass organisation'[13] which would 'get down to the brass tacks of scientific electioneering'.[14] What was naturally assumed was that the party would continue to grow (as it had done during the war and the first years of peace) owing to the growth of trade union membership and the attraction of particular pressure groups within the party's orbit. Trade union membership continued to expand, but Labour never fully built on the foundations laid during the war.[15]

II

As a result of a network of contacts established between 1914 and 1918, especially with Christian pacifists (Lord Parmoor and Joseph King), progressive Anglicans (R. H. Tawney, Albert Mansbridge and William Temple), supporters of the League of Nations (Bertrand Russell and Lord Ponsonby) and even 'enlightened' or disgruntled generals (C. B. Thomson), the post-war Labour party was more than ever seen as a moral crusade. In 1918 and 1919 Henderson and the NEC had encouraged this idea by building links with other pressure groups opposed to the Lloyd George coalition. They had approved of the use of class-conscious and collectivist rhetoric designed both to gain the support of the broad left and to facilitate the building of a national party.[16] Rank-and-file leaders were also trying to broaden the party's base by working with other groups whose own leaders often related their particular grievances to the failings of an unrestrained capitalist economy. The attraction of such groups was vital to the building of the national party which Henderson had envisaged in 1917–18. As it happened, the party failed to make use of such connections, partly because of the hesitant attitude of the leadership, and local parties were thus denied support in several important fringe areas. The formation of the British Communist party in August 1920 probably began this process: certainly the party leadership's attitude to both 'direct action' and cooperation with outside bodies hardened after that date, as is well illustrated by reactions to the Labour Councils of Action and, later, to the groups of unemployed workers organized by Communists like Wal Hannington.[17] Henderson, Mac-Donald, Snowden and others were shaken by what they erroneously believed to be Communist infiltration of the Councils of Action and many prejudices were confirmed in the winter of 1920–21.[18] 'Black Friday', in the following April, set the seal on this and, as a result, the NEC began to withdraw from contact with other non-party groups to which it had looked for support in the latter stages of the war. The result, as has frequently been noted, was a some-times bitter dispute within the party over Communist membership, a dispute which touched most local parties before it was finally settled in the mid-1920s.

Other local initiatives also met with mixed results. For example, after 1918 attempts were made, at both local and national level, to win the Irish vote, which had been left in a vacuum by the collapse of the Liberals and the Irish Nationalists. Irish troubles had occasionally elicited a favourable response from British Labour, but emotion was cheap and action rarely followed.[19] After 1918, constituency pressure forced the NEC into action with positive results for the localities.[20]

The intervention of the Irish at the Stockport by-election in March 1920 caused Labour to lose a winnable seat and appeared to be the thin end of a broad Irish wedge.[21] Late in 1919 James Connolly's daughter had begun lectur-ing for the *Herald* League in London, and early in 1920 Irish workers on the Clyde began to organize branches of the Irish Labour party in Britain, with some encouragement from the Dublin executive.[22] In April 1920 the newly-formed Irish Labour party in Britain precociously held its first annual con-ference at Gateshead.[23] Independent Labour party (ILP) propagandists like Tom Myers and Tom Snowden, together with members of the Manchester Labour party, were among the speakers at a meeting of some one thousand Irishmen at Manchester in May 1920, and calls for Council of Action interven-tion in the Irish troubles stemmed from the Tyneside area, where the new Irish Labour organization seems to have been well-established.[24] The secretary of the Irish Labour party saw the 'making of a very powerful movement' and set his mind to aiding the establishment of similar Irish organizations in South Wales and Lancashire.[25]

The NEC ignored such developments but found it impossible to resist further pressure after the formation of the Council of Action and the sub-sequent escalation of the violence in Ireland.[26] A Commission of Inquiry was sent to investigate the problem and it produced a commendably intelligent report which was scathingly critical of government policy.[27] Backed by a con-certed national campaign, which was thought to be reminiscent of Gladstone's Bulgarian agitation, it achieved all the NEC could have hoped of it before being overtaken by the coal crisis in April 1921.[28] It did much to win the support of liberal-minded middle-class Englishmen and it cemented local ties between Labour and the Irish. In Glasgow, Irishmen who had formerly been United Irish League ward bosses resurfaced as Labour councillors.[29] In Blackburn the Irish were seen to be working with the ILP, and in Leeds they had publicly identified themselves with the local Labour party.[30] Irishmen 'now formed a most valuable element' in the Stepney Labour party and there were many in the Liverpool party who were 'closely related to Ireland by blood and sympathy'.[31] MacDonald took pains to win over the Irish vote in Port Talbot and, despite opposition from the ailing John Dillon, T. P. O'Connor pledged the Irish vote to Labour candidates at Spen Valley and Ashton-under-Lyne. O'Connor himself refused an offer of a Labour peerage but did accept a privy councillorship from the 1924 government.[32]

Labour won its Irish bride, and in many industrial constituencies after 1918 Labour successes owed much to the capture of the Irish vote. Similar connections between the Highland Land League and Labour in the Scottish highlands and between the Clydesiders and Erskine's national committee in the Scottish lowlands stole the thunder of the political separatist movement in Scotland and gave a further boost to the Labour vote there.[33] Not for another fifty years were these ties seriously questioned; had it not been for constituency pressure, they might not have been established at all.

Other links established between 1914 and 1918 were not so productive. Towards the end of the war, more and more Anglican churchmen were moving to support the Labour party. Post-war links between the Labour movement and the Church of England revolved around the Life and Liberty Movement founded by William Temple, Albert Mansbridge, H. R. L. Shepherd and other Anglicans many of whom were 'shell-shocked padres' who had served as chaplains in the forces. Its guiding lights were Tawney and Temple who by 1918 were both committed to the Labour party as the political instrument of social and moral reform. The Movement gathered strength in the early 1920s, supported the concept of a legally-established minimum wage in 1920 and peaked at the interdenominational Conference on Christian Politics, Economics and Citizenship (Copec) at Birmingham in April 1924.[34] In essence it represented a coalescence of Christian socialist, adult educationalist and ecumenical thought; in the long run it altered the character of mainstream opinion in the Church of England but gave the Labour party no more than a small thread of additional rationalism and idealism.

However, these links were of some use in constituency politics. The Bishop of Peterborough was able to claim in 1919 that a 'large proportion of the clergy . . . in the towns voted Labour . . . I have heard of one or two towns where it is said they did so almost to a man'.[35] His public support of Labour may have been unique among the higher clergy of the East Midlands,[36] but there were other examples of Labour activists working with the established church as well as the nonconformist churches, their more traditional reservoir of support. In Bradford, the trades council attended the cathedral in September 1920 to hear a special sermon by the Bishop of Bradford. Later it was decided to inaugurate an 'industrial Sunday'.[37] A similar event was held annually at Gloucester in the 1920s although here, in 1928, the local Labour organization declined to participate after the Dean of Gloucester refused to allow the Labour sympathizer Canon F. L. Donaldson to preach one of the sermons.[38] At Cardiff one of the most important features of Labour activity in 1921 was a well-attended conference from which emerged a Church and Labour committee chaired by the vicar of Cardiff, while at Leeds in 1922 the election manifesto of the Anglo-Catholic, Henry Slesser, was endorsed by a prominent Anglican priest, much to the annoyance of the latter's colleagues.[39] And there is the egregious example of Conrad Noel, the vicar of Thaxted (a living in the gift of the socialist Countess of Warwick) and Chaplain-General of the 'Catholic Crusade' whose 'sixpenny sermons' drew parallels between Christ and Lenin.[40] Most important, however, because of the otherwise undocumented volume of support which it demonstrates, was the petition offering all legitimate aid to the Labour party from over 500 clergymen in the Church of England and its sister churches in Scotland and Wales.[41] It marked, thought Archbishop Lang, 'one of the most significant events in post-war history'.[42]

The support of the Church was probably of most use in rural areas where the local party might try to use a sympathetic parish priest to overcome the 'loving feudalism' of the countryside. Certainly, Labour candidates in rural areas took care to stress their affinity with the Christian ethic.[43] It is doubtful whether the national leaders paid any attention to such developments. Parmoor, a leading lay Anglican, found a place in MacDonald's first Cabinet, but the Church appointments made by MacDonald in 1924 were undiplomatic to say the least.[44] The Labour government's failure to acknowledge Bolshevik persecution of Russian Christians also lost Labour some Church votes in 1924.[45] The events of May 1926 finally brought an end to this awkward flirtation between Labour and the Anglicans: its legacy can perhaps be seen either in the anti-war campaign associated with Parmoor's son, Stafford Cripps, in the 1930s, or in the unilateralist campaign of the 1950s.

Even this experience marks a triumph when compared to Labour's attempt to win the countryside. As a result of the growth of the farm workers' unions during the war, Labour had made considerable progress in 1918 in constituencies usually thought to be unwinnable.[46] This progress was repeated in the next two elections. Labour won its first seats in rural Britain, and by attracting the support of Josiah Wedgwood and Noel Buxton, acquired leading members of the pre-war Liberal land campaign. Hopes of Labour gains in the countryside thus rose in the immediate post-war period. The challenge, however, was eventually contained, as the experience of that rural heartland, East Anglia, clearly shows (Table 1).[47]

Table 1. *The Labour vote in rural East England 1918–29[a]*

	1918	1922	1923	1924	1929
Cambridgeshire (with Isle of Ely)	29.8[b]	25.9	22.9	27.9	27.4
Lincolnshire	35.1	32.8	37.0	34.1	30.0
Norfolk	32.3	34.2	35.2	34.2	34.9
Suffolk	32.1	36.0	26.1	25.8	22.1
N. and E. Essex	35.4	29.7	37.9	24.7	31.2

[a] Figures express the average percentage Labour share of the vote in contested divisions.
[b] The Labour candidate in Cambridgeshire had not received NEC endorsement at the time of the poll but his votes have been included in the calculation.
Source: F. W. S. Craig, *British Parliamentary Election Results 1918–1949* (Glasgow, 1969).

There was one outstanding reason for this failure: the farm labourers' unions suffered more than most from the coming of the depression in 1921 and were in no position to lead a Labour assault on the countryside.[48] Larger industrial unions sometimes gave assistance to the rural areas: the National Union of Railwaymen gave aid to the Agricultural Labourers; James Read fought Gainsborough with aid from the Engineers in 1923; and the Boot and Shoe Operatives continually tried to strengthen the rural unions in order to stamp out sources of cheap alternative labour available to shoe manufacturers in Norwich and Northamptonshire.[49] But the industrial unions were usually loathe to invest in rural organization and policy formulation[50] and the Labour party executive paid little real attention to the needs of the rural parties. By the time it had been shaken from its complacency, the opportunity had been lost. Local Labour parties in the countryside had good reason to feel aggrieved.

In the counties Labour relied very heavily on a small group of activists and a meagre party membership bore little resemblance to the size of the Labour vote. In the Cambridgeshire constituency the newly-established party decided to fight the 1918 election at the very last moment but secured a highly respectable 6,686 votes. Just before the 1922 election the constituency party was on the point of winding up its activities, but it campaigned on £171 and came within 671 votes of winning the seat: one of its better performances to date.[51] But although rural workers were prepared to vote Labour after 1921, few were prepared to be active within the movement. The day-to-day activities of these local parties therefore bore no little resemblance to the labours of Sisyphus. Isolated members of the industrial unions often provided the pioneering spirit for the rural parties (railwaymen, especially signalmen, were the 'backbone of the Labour Party in the outposts')[52] but, for the most part, working-class representatives relied heavily on middle-class support. Students and dons from Oxford helped to organize many constituencies in the Midlands between the wars, and in Cambridge the party was greatly helped by the activity and ability of dons' wives like Clara Rackham and Agnes Ramsay (the mother of Frank, the mathematician and Michael, the Archbishop) while Dr Alex Wood, a physics lecturer and Fellow of Emmanuel, was one of the leading figures in the city party throughout the interwar period.[53] In the cathedral city and market centre of Peterborough where a small local party tried to organize a mixed farming and urban constituency, the sympathetic attitude of Anglican clergymen like Canon F. L. Donaldson and G. M. Davidson must have been invaluable in the surrounding farming villages.[54]

In Cambridgeshire the officials' expenses at the 1923 election were paid by T. H. Langan, a fruit merchant from the Fens, and the campaign was financed by Herbert Titmarsh, a local printer, together with Michael Pease (the son of the first secretary of the Fabians) and Helen Pease (the daughter of Josiah Wedgwood).[55] In Lincolnshire professional men from the locality probably financed their own campaigns at Brigg, Lincoln and Rutland-and-Stamford in 1922 and 1923, while Holland-with-Boston and North Norfolk were in the pockets of an apostate Tory businessman, W. S. Royce, and a renegade Liberal aristocrat, Noel Buxton.[56] In Cambridgeshire, Gloucestershire and Peterborough during the 1920s, the ability of a candidate to pay the salary of his agent was a major condition of selection.[57]

Despite such support, propaganda in the countryside was limited by financial stringency, especially as it was so expensive. It was thought to cost between £500 and £600 to run a reasonable election campaign. Few local parties could hope to raise this kind of money by their own efforts. They turned to Head Office for support, but Eccleston Square was slow to respond. Some local officials despaired of ever receiving backing from London. As the Suffolk parties pointed out, where help was given by the regional organizers, it was given inefficiently.[58] After 1922 national propagandists like J. W. Kneeshaw were 'engaged almost solely on work in the county divisions',[59] but what most county parties wanted was a permanent agent whose salary would be met largely from central funds. The NEC stubbornly refused to bale the county parties out, however, and it was slow to formulate a farming policy which would both meet the needs of British farming and distinguish Labour from the Liberals. After two years of internal haggling, Sidney Webb at last produced a programme which contrived to please all sections of the party, and Labour finally announced a comprehensive rural policy.[60] 'At present they have no competitors' observed one Tory in December 1921.[61] The Liberals also were incensed that their thunder had been stolen by a policy designed to snatch votes rather than solve problems.[62]

By November 1922, however, Labour's policy had been outdated by the slump. After 1921 heavily-mortgaged farmers found themselves facing rising labour costs, falling land values and the problems inherent in an under-capitalized industry.[63] Their troubles were passed on to the labourers, especially in over-manned East Anglia where wage reductions, unrest and victimization reached a peak. In December 1922 wages had fallen to the twenty-five shillings a week minimum established by the then-defunct Wages Boards in 1917.[64] In 1923 even full-time labourers in Norfolk were said to be in receipt of poor relief.[65] The class tension engendered by the depression was to hinder Labour's attempt to gain broad-based rural support for a programme which included land nationalization and a marked improvement in the labourers' social and economic wage as its cardinal points.

The national leadership only slowly came to terms with the fact that more effort was now needed on its part if Labour was to hope to win the countryside. Yet not until 1926 was a revised programme launched.[66] One reason for the delay was that only the left laid any emphasis on policy deficiencies, mainstream opinion believing Labour's rural failure to be a simple communications problem. Only the ILP produced a full analysis of the crisis in the countryside, outlining the links between urban under-consumption and rural distress and attempting to meet the problems of the industry rather than one section of it.[67] At the ILP stronghold of Keighley in 1924 the local party produced a leaflet specifically intended for farmers, and ILP propagandists gave emphasis to their intention to give security of tenure to efficient farmers after the abolition of landlordism.[68]

By the time such ideas had been considered by the NEC and the programme had been revised, the initiative had been lost. The Liberals, in a parlous state in the shire counties in the early 1920s, recovered lost ground and realized that they could again win at least those seats they had once taken in years of average fortune.[69] In 1925 the ILP propagandist Minnie Pallister warned that if socialists did not seize the opportunity presented in the farming districts, 'other seed may be sown'.[70] Three years later it was, with the Liberal land programme completely overshadowing Labour's similar effort and Lloyd George once again working his populist magic as its main proponent. Labour land policy had developed little since the better days at the very beginning of the decade. In the meantime much of the countryside had been alienated and many rural Labour parties felt that they had been left in the lurch by an unsympathetic executive.

By the mid-1920s, therefore, important sections of possible support were beginning to slip away from Labour and the reservoir of votes which Henderson had tried to tap at the end of the war was beginning to run dry. The far left were gradually excluded after the formation of the British Communist party in 1920, though, as in Battersea, there were many little local difficulties between 1920 and 1925; ties with the Anglican church grew weaker and many were cut altogether after the General Strike; mismanagement of the farm vote allowed the older parties to contain Labour. It may be argued that rural support was of little value to a socialist party. It cannot be denied, though, that the party was poorer for losing it at this time, since it also lost whatever chance it had of gaining a parliamentary majority. Middle-class support for the new 'people's party' did not expand, and Labour's industrial base was not so strong that it could afford to neglect the peripheral areas of socialist politics. Even in the industrial areas, Labour's immediate post-war expectations were not fully realized.

What were the aspirations and activities of local parties in the industrial belt? MacDonald's own constituency at Aberavon, an essentially working-class area based on the colliery villages of the Afan valley and the tinplate areas around Port Talbot, provides a convenient starting-point. When Mac-Donald accepted Aberavon's invitation in 1920, it seemed as secure a seat as he could wish to find after his unenviable experience during the war.[71] There was a local Labour party in each district and the constituency possessed one of the most flourishing ILP branches in the country at Briton Ferry, an added attraction for MacDonald.[72] The trade union and ILP vote was well-organized and local officials did not neglect the grievances of the Irish or ex-servicemen.[73] Some of MacDonald's meetings were extraordinary. 'Scenes reminiscent of the great religious revival' were witnessed daily during the 1922 campaign. James Griffiths, then the Llanelli party agent, recalled a similar reception being given to MacDonald across the Carmarthenshire border in 1924.[74] 'It was like a fervour, a religious fervour'; 'he was like a god', one of his constituents recalled years later.[75] In some parts of the South Wales coalfield, Labour seats could still be threatened by real or tacit alliances between the anti-socialist parties, but the Labour tide was flowing and most of the coalfields were safe Labour territory after 1922.

In local politics too these were 'years of attack' when the 'edge in involvement of meetings was sharpening as elections were being won' and when it was relatively simple to organize large public meetings and to find an ample supply of speakers.[76] Local party activists were prepared to give large amounts of their time to the party as the diary of a typical month's activity in Aberavon demonstrates (Table 2).[77] Activity on such a scale was perhaps exceptional and would not have been found outside the coalfields, the West Riding or the Clyde, in all of which the ILP held large open-air meetings every week.[78] Some constituencies like Coventry were able to build up a large membership relatively quickly. But even in areas of solid Labour support it was often difficult to build up mass support. By the middle of the decade it was becoming increasingly important for MacDonald to nurse Aberavon to such an extent that the demands on both his time and his purse became intolerable.[79] An Aberavon constituent reported in 1926 that, with unemployment rising and short-time working now widespread, rank-and-file criticism of the leadership was growing. The future was no longer assured, and at the next election 'J.R.M. will have to work very hard otherwise the seat is lost'. MacDonald was no doubt relieved to leave all this behind and move to the safer and cheaper seat of Seaham Harbour in 1928.[80] MacDonald may well have said that Aberavon finally asked too much of him, but it might be as well to ask whether the leadership expected too much of the local parties. Despite the heady success of the immediate post-war period, the academic insistence of Barry Hindess and the nostalgic testimony of many who battled through the period, the picture gained from local party records does not suggest that this was a golden age of working-class politics.[81]

Table 2. *Diary of Aberavon Constituency Labour party (CLP) activity, January 1926*

2 Jan.	CLP Executive meeting
5 Jan.	Meeting at Kenfig Hill
6 Jan.	Meeting at Cefn; entertainment at Pontrhydyfen
8 Jan.	Port Talbot Labour Group meeting
9 Jan.	A. J. Cook at Glyncorrwg
10 Jan.	A. J. Cook at Kenfig Hill, Blaengwynfi & Port Talbot
	George Hall at Briton Ferry; Councillor Thomas at Cwmavon
12 Jan.	Alderman Davies at Kenfig Hill
13 Jan.	Social evening at Cymmer; Dan Griffiths at Pontrhydyfen
14 Jan.	Supper with South Ward Womens' Section
17 Jan.	Rev. J. C. Jenkins at Port Talbot; Dan Griffiths at Cwmavon
19 Jan.	J. W. Kneeshaw at Kenfig Hill
20 Jan.	James Dixon at Cymmer; J. W. Kneeshaw at Cefn
21 Jan.	Morgan Jones, J. W. Kneeshaw at Glyncorrwg
	Aberavon Women's Section dance
22 Jan.	Morgan Jones, J. W. Kneeshaw at Abergwynfi & Cwmavon
26 Jan.	Morgan Jones at Briton Ferry; T. C. Morris at Bryn; Councillor Woods at Kenfig Hill
27 Jan.	Port Talbot Labour Association Annual Meeting; J. Brown at Pontrhydyfen; eisteddfod at Pontrhydyfen.
30 Jan.	Dance with Aberavon ILP branch; Emanuel Shinwell at Pontrhydyfen & Glyncorrwg
31 Jan.	Emanuel Shinwell at Kenfig Hill & Port Talbot

Source: See note 77.

The reconstruction programme of 1918 certainly asked for a great deal of commitment from party members. Labour was to be all things to all men. Constituency party activity, as Webb later put it, was to be 'stratified', and was to appeal to each sectional group in 'the language which [it] understood' and 'substitut[ing] for the greyness of mass propaganda the warmer and more individualised colours of each man's speciality'.[82] In keeping with this grandiose notion, Labour's organizers made a conscious effort after the war to integrate each local party within the local community and 'mix politics with the social life of the people'.[83] The attempt to broaden the party's base by winning sectional support played a vital role within this strategy. Another key element in the scheme was the building of a Labour press.

In the 1920s the provincial Labour press was considered to be a more useful propaganda vehicle than the *Herald*, which was regarded with increasing scepticism by Eccleston Square after Edgar Lansbury and Francis Meynell had blundered into the 'Russian gold' controversy in 1920. The NEC therefore contemplated the publication of a monthly inset which could be included in existing local Labour publications. The *Labour News* service was consequently established at Head Office. In 1921 the organizer Herbert Drinkwater told the party agent that the local press was 'the greatest force we have, or can handle, or can build up'. Will Henderson gave the official seal of approval to this in the following year when he predicted that the *Herald* would go the way of the defunct *Daily Citizen* and that 'the local weekly papers wield a far greater influence than the dailies'.[84] Party organizers like Egerton Wake, Samuel Higgenbottam and Herbert Drinkwater were all pioneer members of the ILP and must have absorbed the traditions of the ILP press; they tried to persuade local parties to set up their own journals.

Initially, results were encouraging and in some areas there was immense enthusiasm.[85] One of the more ambitious schemes was based in the Midlands where several partly-syndicated papers (such as the Birmingham *Town Crier*, *Nottingham Tribune* and Derbyshire *Worker*) were produced at the press of the Leicester *Pioneer*, one of the great ILP journals. Syndication helped the Midlands group to produce a high-quality paper that could compete with Fleet Street.[86] But there were objections that syndicated material clogged the papers and destroyed their local character; by 1924 only thirteen local parties were using the *Labour News* inset.[87] On the other hand, very few parties could afford to build up a substantial newspaper without such help from Head Office, though Herbert Morrison's *London Labour Chronicle* was expanded without *News Service* help in 1921. In Llanelli the local party was only too grateful for syndicated material, for without it the establishment of its weekly would have been impossible.[88] This was true of most parties outside the larger towns: if they wished to publish a viable newspaper, they had to accept syndication and some dilution of local flavour.

Even so, as the slump progressed it became increasingly difficult for such papers to compete and survive. As Labour was forming its first government, some of the 'oldest and best established [Labour] papers in the country' were going under, including such aces in the pack as the Woolwich and Merthyr *Pioneers*.[89] In 1925, prospects revived slightly owing to rank-and-file resentment of press hostility during the 'Zinoviev' election. Several fresh newspapers appeared. The most notable was the *Newport Labour Searchlight* which sold 3,500 copies a week in Monmouthshire and paid for itself after only four issues.[90] A survey of the local Labour press reveals that although there were certainly more local party newspapers in the late 1920s, they were of inferior quality and were, for the most part, simply constituency party bulletins serving artificially-created electoral districts and not, as originally planned, a truly homogeneous community of readers.[91] Only the local Co-operative press and a few of the Labour periodicals (for example, the Birmingham *Town Crier*, Glasgow *Forward* and *Labour's Northern Voice*) managed to approach the ideal. Will Henderson, in charge of the *News Service*, emphasized the need to produce papers of varied appeal, but his own output saturated the newspapers with pure propaganda.[92] And as long as the periodicals confined themselves to target audiences defined by the boundary commissioners, as many did by the mid-1920s, they were doomed to failure. Arthur Henderson and the NEC admitted this when they discontinued the *News Service* in 1926, and the party had to wait for the revival of the *Herald* in the 1930s to obtain favourable mass treatment of its policies and actions.

Other ventures to mix people and politics fared little better. In Labour's best areas such attempts inevitably revolved around the needs of its working-class members. In many provincial centres Labour football, darts, tennis and other recreational or sports leagues were established. In Cardiff East the local agent reprinted the fixture lists of both the rugby and association football clubs in the city with Labour propaganda, in suitably appropriate form, on the reverse. This was a useful initiative in a year when the soccer club was one of the most powerful in the English League and reached the final of the FA Cup.[93] Labour brass bands, orchestras and choirs were popular; in 1926 there were ninety-four Labour choirs in existence, mainly in the South and Midlands, and in 1925 the NEC contemplated the formation of a Labour Choral Union.[94] In Hertfordshire in the early 1930s, the County Labour Federation ran a successful choral union of its own while one of the principal events in its calendar was the annual eisteddfod, an eloquent testimony to the prodigious number of Welsh exiles in the Home Counties.[95] The national party's Young People's Sections, launched in the mid-1920s, were not intended to produce a 'superior crowd' of intellectuals (like the summer schools!) but were to provide a 'mass organization . . . so divided in activity that committees for sport, education, art and social events may be fully and usefully engaged'.[96] It was hoped that such schemes would fare better than the Labour clubs which, in certain areas (and probably most), had 'degenerat[ed] in the direction of drinking', much to the despair of more earnest party workers. Such chapel morality, however, obscures the fact that the clubs often doubled as both bar and party headquarters and provided a convenient means of acquiring revenue before many of them passed out of direct party control.[97] Moreover, the clubs were at least catering for proven demand and were not attempting to impose any bourgeois cultural ideal. One Glamorgan miners' agent who attempted to stage midsummer performances of Bernard Shaw with union money found that miners' families preferred seaside outings and his lodge colleagues preferred him to play a more realistic part in the real-enough drama of coalfield politics.[98]

Most of these projects now appear to be naïve and quaint, but party workers evidently attached great importance to them. Idealized and utopian as they were, they held their place in the 'new social order'. Nearly all of them collapsed in the interwar period. None of them expressed community or group feeling as impressively as the marching bands, choirs and glee clubs which defiantly appeared in the coalfields during the 1926 lock-out. None of them could match the village choirs of South Wales or the brass bands of the industrial north in providing a natural focal point for community feeling. And none of them could match the 'participation in a community of interests' and *Zahlabend* (contributions evening) of the German SDP.[99]

A major cause of this failure lay in the fact that the slump prevented local parties from matching up to Henderson's earlier aspirations: a mass membership never materialized in the 1920s. Woolwich CLP, whose individual membership fluctuated between 3,000 and 5,000 in the years 1923–25, was the best supported in the country, while Westhoughton CLP's attraction of 3,000 individual members in the two years prior to 1925 represented an 'exceptional achievement'. Colchester CLP's individual membership of 1,921 could be equalled by few parties in a similar type of constituency.[100] In the 1930s the rapid rise in individual membership began to fulfil earlier hopes, but there was some reasoning behind Webb's famous condemnation of the local parties as 'little unrepresentative groups of nonentities'.[101] Of course, one can no more accept the validity of this generalization than one can accept the frequently-asserted propositions that most local parties were 'militant' (which was what Webb was really complaining about) or that many local parties were undemocratic. Clearly the character of each local party was determined by relationships between differing social and political groups, and so each organization necessarily possessed a certain individuality.[102] Nevertheless some observations can reasonably be made about local party attitudes.

The unions, generally seen as conservative forces, certainly provided the money for most local parties since individual membership was so low.[103] Consequently the unions controlled certain districts as they did at Leicester and Coventry, to give two examples outside the more obvious cotton, coal and steel belts.[104] But this was not the case for all local parties, especially those in the rural areas, and, besides, socialist penetration of the unions had broken down the old pre-war distinctions between socialist and unionist mentalities.[105] There were many union leaders who lay firmly within the traditions of Labour party socialism, just as there were socialists whose erstwhile zeal had disappeared with maturity of years. Simple generalizations about militancy or control are therefore impossible to make.

The one common factor in most party records in the 1920s is the sense of frustration lying behind the simple faith in the inevitability of eventual triumph. Labour was winning municipal seats and magistrateships in most areas, had taken control of County Durham and a few smaller municipalities and urban districts and, in the late 1920s, was taking power in some cities, most notably Sheffield, and some of the London boroughs. Widespread electoral success bore little resemblance to restricted party membership, however, and disappointments were common. MacDonald's agent, for one, found them too much to bear and retired to keep a pub.[106] It was these headaches, resulting from slow growth and lack of legislative progress at Westminster, which were exhibited annually at conference.

The other result of this failure to expand the base in line with the visions of 1918 was that many parties were dominated by a small hierarchy. There were two reasons for this. Firstly, limited membership and non-involvement in the vital post-war period of expansion created the conditions in which controlling cadres could be created. Younger members, willing to devote time and energy to organization, could often acquire the secretaryship of the local party and build a dominating position around that, particularly if they had a trade union position and union support. As many parties realized, without a secretary there was no effective organization, and trade union officials were often the only people available for party work during the day. This enabled them to play a large part in local party affairs even as young men, particularly if they were, by nature, more energetic, or perhaps more ambitious, than others. James Griffiths at Llanelli, Jack Mansfield at Peterborough, George Hodgkinson at Coventry and H. B. Taylor at Mansfield provide examples of young union or party organizers who built key positions within their constituencies in the post-war period.[107] Similar pressures arising from either the workplace or the necessity of looking for work, together with intimidation by employers, meant that there was also difficulty in finding local representatives. Housewives often filled the bill where this occurred. Surviving activists, like Lord Taylor of Mansfield, recollect a 'united cooperative effort to propagate socialist ideals & to organize to take control of the local authorities'. Of course, party activity did retain the characteristics of a cooperative crusade, but the net effect of such pressures was to allow small groups to dominate local party activity.[108] Although contemporaries would no doubt deny that there was any sinister implication, a handful of activists controlled Barnsley Labour politics for a generation after the war. Similar observations can be made about the Labour parties in Llanelli, Doncaster, Coventry, Cambridge, Cambridgeshire, Wolverhampton, the Rhondda and presumably many others besides.[109] Sir Oswald Mosley, admittedly a special case, 'literally bought up' Smethwick.[110]

Secondly, as Labour's assault on town and county halls was mounted, so the local leadership became aware of the fundamental problems faced by reforming councillors, especially in times of slump. In some areas of Morrison's London, such as Bermondsey, and in Sheffield, where significant municipal improvement schemes were carried through between the wars, these problems were partially solved.[111] But the realities of local government imposed the restraints of orthodoxy upon local bodies in a manner unprecedented in Labour's propagandist past. Morrison, for example, deplored the deleterious effects of the Poplar Guardians' attempts to mitigate the disaster of the outdated poor law.[112] Pontypridd Labour councillors solved a similar though less critical dilemma by deciding to make themselves 'abnoxious [*sic*] in a respectable manner' in protest against the holding of daytime council meetings.[113] Generally, as a Labour group evolved on a local council, it would acquire a hierarchy, disciplinary structure and orthodoxy of its own, bringing it into conflict with party activists. At Pontypridd and Gloucester there were complaints that Labour councillors were staying away from party meetings while at Wolverhampton relations between the party and its councillors were severely disrupted in the early 1920s and continued to be strained for the rest of the decade.[114] There were also areas where loyalty to the Labour group was strictly demanded and usually received. The following extract from the 'Catholic Socialist Notes' in the Glasgow *Forward*, almost certainly inspired by John Wheatley, is extremely revealing:

> an excited raving mob will never be trusted. Our movement must display fitness for the task which is offered . . . the ruling of a country requires great power of self-control and mental balance . . . Until now we have been mainly critics of the great [governing] class . . . We are now about to brush this class aside and take their [*sic*] place.[115]

Wheatley, 'a thorough Tammany type',[116] who led the excited and raving Clydesiders in the 1923 Parliament, knew the time and place for propagandist ranting. The time and place was not Glasgow in the 1920s. By the time of the General Strike new local Labour oligarchies had developed, some undoubtedly based on the ILP 'cells' active in most local parties before the war. Wheatley controlled one of them: he and his brother Patrick could make or break a career on Clydeside. There were probably others in similar positions of authority in areas dominated by Labour.[117]

The pursuit of power prompted such concern for discipline and control. Unemployment only exaggerated the trend because it forced a limited number of active members to shoulder an increasing amount of routine work. Long hours of activity demonstrated a genuine dedication to democracy, but democracy does not flourish among the over-zealous, particularly if they have a world to lose. As one of the great Lib–Lab journals of the coalfields remarked, 'much may be forgiven men who, after long years of toil in the wilderness, are tasting the first fruits of victory'.[118] The post-war Labour establishment took full advantage of such feeling.

Labour councillors clung to the power bases that they had built and, with few exceptions, waited for a trade revival or a genuinely reformist majority Labour government to bale them out of their administrative difficulties: 'some of those Councils stewed in their own juice so long they became rancid', Aneurin Bevan commented bitterly some time later.[119] Labour's young bucks did what little they could to displace them. Only a man of Bevan's own conspiratorial cunning could succeed. Even then, the tightly-knit 'Query Club' run by Bevan and Archie Lush in Tredegar was just another caucus in the making, however democratic its rhetoric.[120] In the years after 1918, as Bevan himself found, the Labour party provided opportunities for self-advancement unknown to all but a few of its pioneers.

Too many Labour politicians were thus content with the formula adopted in 1918. Lacking any Marxist foundation, Labour's aims had always been ill-defined: it was expedient to let them remain so. The radicals did not help their cause by poorly presenting their case, since the economic solutions proposed by J. A. Hobson, E. F. Wise and (less relevantly in this context) Maynard Keynes represented a journey into the unknown which had to be promoted with patience and skill.[121] The militants charged in like bulls chasing red coat-tails. By delineating a specific course of action they were forcing issues which the 1918 conferences had happily avoided. That is why they were ignored in the 1920s when few Labour politicians wished to reopen the party's wartime debate on reconstruction; that is why others chose to support them in the more desperate decade which followed.

Labour's opportunism after 1917 had carried the party too far too fast, and it was structurally unprepared for the role it was now destined to play. There was no real basis for expansion, no real basis for confidence, only a recipe for disappointment and bitterness. The Gloucester party was beset by difficulties throughout the 1920s because it relied on its candidates to finance a full-time agent and as candidates came and went, so did agents. Additional problems caused by personality clashes in 1928 turned the vibrant optimism of the early 1920s into general despair.[122] The Suffolk Labour parties, which in 1920 had expected to make both Ipswich and rural Suffolk into safe Labour territory, were simply 'marking time' a year later owing to the 'economic storm' while 1922 was spent in 'suspended animation'.[123] These examples are typical of many others. Because the depression placed such severe limits on party activity, Labour could not expand its predominantly working-class base. On the other hand its taste for power and a sense of its own weakness generated a pusillanimity of thought and action which was disseminated through many of the agents, organizers and elected representatives to all levels of the party. The defeats of 1926 and 1931 rubbed home the fact that there would be no gradual road to power and no easy return to the relatively tolerant and euphoric consensus of the immediate post-war period. The image of a vibrant, expanding new party was an illusion. Labour was fortunate that its opponents were deceived.

5

Post-war reconstruction in Wales, 1918 and 1945

KENNETH O. MORGAN

When I was appointed to succeed Henry Pelling as Fellow and Praelector in Modern History and Politics at the Queen's College, Oxford, in 1966, my first reaction was one of some apprehension at having to follow a scholar of such eminence who had served at Queen's for the previous seventeen years. However, I was fortified by the thought that, then, as now, one of my major research interests was the history of Wales, including its labour history, in the recent period. For Dr Pelling has always been distinguished for seeing the history of the labour movement and other aspects of late nineteenth- and twentieth-century history in a British, and not merely an English, context. Indeed, in a famous review of A. J. P. Taylor's *English History 1914–1945*, he showed how misleading it was to examine British political developments since the First World War without relating them centrally to the Welsh and Scottish dimension.[1] Dr Pelling has written in the *Welsh History Review* on more than one occasion.[2] His *Social Geography of British Elections* contains excellent sections on the electoral history of both Wales and of Scotland between 1885 and 1910.[3] His essays on *Popular Politics and Society* include many incidental observations on the importance of political and industrial developments in the Celtic nations, for instance on the impact of the Welsh miners upon the outlook of the Miners' Federation of Great Britain between 1906 and 1910.[4] It is, therefore, highly appropriate in a volume in honour of Dr Pelling to include a contribution specifically related to the history of Wales. To examine, as it is proposed to do here, the comparative experience in Wales in 1918 and 1945, after the two world wars, in many ways raises issues that have been prominent throughout Dr Pelling's long and distinguished career as a working historian.

In twentieth-century Wales, as in Britain as a whole, the experience of total war has been powerful in shaping the political, social, economic and intellectual development of the nation. But, for Wales, as for Britain generally, the emphasis by historians has too often centred, somewhat misleadingly, upon the actual years of wartime themselves. In many respects, this is inappropriate. Developments during 1914–18 and 1939–45 respectively had often only an indirect effect on subsequent history. They generated some false or abortive starts, as in the apparatus of wartime controls introduced in 1914–16, or gave transient and misleading prominence to temporary prophets (for example, Milner in 1916 and Beaverbrook in 1941) whose influence promptly diminished sharply as soon as peace returned. Lloyd George, so transcendent a figure as Wales's national hero in 1916, was a supreme war casualty in 1922. In any case, to concentrate upon the events of wartime seems peculiarly inappropriate for a radical nation such as Wales, where peace movements, whether Liberal, socialist or nationalist, have been so powerful in the present century, as the present writer has argued elsewhere.[5]

It is the post-war years, the periods immediately after 1918 and 1945, that were the real crucibles of modern Wales, both for the ways in which they continued or rejected innovations of the war years and for.the new themes thrown up as soon as peace was restored. The continuities and contrasts between the two Welsh post-war experiences, especially during the years 1918–22 and 1945–51, are crucial to the understanding of the nation's evolution. In fact, the two post-war phases are usually seen in stark contrast with one another, as in Britain generally. The period of the Lloyd George coalition of 1918–22 is seen as a time of betrayal when pledges given during the war of building up a land fit for heroes were wantonly neglected. Conversely, the years of the Attlee government of 1945–51 are viewed as a period of fulfilment when faith was kept with the working-class electors who had returned Labour to power with such a massive landslide majority. The contrast seems stark indeed between Black Friday in 1921 and the Miners' Charter in 1946, between the Geddes Axe and the National Health Service (NHS), between deflation after one war and full employment after another, between the treatment of Ireland in 1920 and of India in 1947.

This view was popularized, for Welsh and other readers, in Aneurin Bevan's powerful tract, *Why not Trust the Tories?* It was published under the pseudonym 'Celticus' in 1944 and in many ways is his most effective political publication, certainly more so than *In Place of Fear* (1952), a compilation of fragmentary writings, many of them brilliant, but put together at different times and with no dominant theme. In *Why not Trust the Tories?* Bevan linked modern social democracy with an ancient libertarian socialist tradition in Britain, going back to the Levellers and Tom Paine. But the main thrust of the argument underlines the contrast between the consequences of 1918, the legacy of deceit and betrayal left by a Tory-dominated coalition in 1918–22, and the politics of hope opening up as the Second World War came to its close. Bevan spelt out, with furious passion, the record of mass unemployment, housing failures and disastrous labour relations that had been the miserable outcome of pledges in 1918 to build a 'land fit for heroes'. In Bevan's view, the conclusion to be drawn was the basic incompatibility between the Tory ethic and political democracy itself.[6] He ended with a call to all electors and especially to the working class to make certain that in the post-war election shortly to follow in 1945 or 1946 no such betrayal of popular aspirations occurred again. After six years of Labour government ending in 1951, Bevan continued to insist that faith had indeed been kept. Despite the bitterness that was to surround his resignation from the government in April 1951 over charges on the NHS and the wider scale of rearmament during the Korean war, despite the internecine quarrelling associated with the rise of 'Bevanism' between 1951 and 1955, Bevan, like his Gaitskellite opponents, continued to emphasize that the contrast between post-war Britain after 1918 and after 1945 was overwhelming and complete. Whatever dissensions marked the later period of the Attlee government, the general record of the administration in which Bevan himself had served for almost six years stood in total contrast to the years of 'Tory rule' after 1918.

How far is this picture correct? And, in particular, how accurate an account does it provide of the experience of Bevan's native Wales? Is Bevan's account of capitalist reaction after one world war and of progressive social revolution after another to be dismissed as the over-simplified version of the facts provided by an angry, embittered partisan? Does a more sober historical reflection upon the two post-war periods suggest continuities as well as contrasts? These are the questions that I now propose to examine in greater detail.

In some ways, in fact, there were broad similarities between the two post-war periods in Wales, between the régime of Lloyd George's coalition and the society presided over by Attlee's peaceful revolutionaries. Certainly, both post-war phases in Wales were marked by dramatic and convulsive change. In each case, the established social order was radically transformed and the values associated with it emphatically overturned. After 1918, Wales experienced a pronounced change of mood. The remnants of the old ascendancy of both the Anglican Church and the squirearchy, against which radicals had crusaded since the 1840s, were swept aside. There was disestablishment of the Church in 1920, and a more subtle disestablishment of the gentry, too, as many great estates were dissolved for ever. Conversely, the old Liberal quasi-nationalist nonconformist ethic, which had dominated Welsh life at least since the general election of 1868, proved to be a casualty of total war. The position of the chapels, and the puritanical sabbatarian ethic that they embodied, was henceforth to be in steady decline. There was a persistent loss of membership, and a wider diminution of influence, of which the erosion of the 1881 Welsh Sunday Closing Act in successive local polls from 1961 onwards was one landmark. The vibrant Welsh culture associated with the heyday of such writers and scholars as Sir John Morris-Jones and Sir Owen M. Edwards before the war was henceforth defensive. A new sense of the vulnerability of Welsh culture in the face of new pressures promoting anglicization was widespread from the early 1920s. It did not help that literary patriots like Morris-Jones and Edwards had somewhat tarnished their reputations in radical circles with their rampant jingoism in Welsh-language journals such as *Y Beirniad* and *Cymru* in 1914–16.[7] The new and heightened nationalism associated with Saunders Lewis and the founding of Plaid Genedlaethol Cymru in 1925 was a very different force from the national movement of the pre-war era, though manifestly the creed of a minority.

After 1945, too, there were mighty changes. The surviving heirs of private capitalism, the position of mining capitalists such as Sir Evan Williams and Sir David Llewellyn and the traditional techniques of treasury finance as maintained during the 'special areas' policy of the 1930s could not survive the massive state intervention in the economy and the new regional policies instituted during the wartime years. New developments such as the steel works and hot strip-mill to be located at Port Talbot, announced by Hugh Dalton while a member in the Churchill government in early 1945, together with the combination of steel firms that led to the formation of the Steel Company of Wales in 1947, owed everything to state intervention. Conversely, the trade unions, pariahs in the social order that prevailed after 1918, were vital to the new planning policies operating under Labour after 1945. Arthur Horner, the tribune of Maerdy, 'little Moscow', who was imprisoned in 1919 for refusal to serve in the armed forces, was, as secretary of the National Union of Miners, a major architect of post-war economic recovery and the dramatic surge of industrial production after 1945. The old Welsh poacher narrowly avoided turning gamekeeper, since he seriously considered appointment to the National Coal Board after nationalization,[8] truly a sign of the times.

Just as Wales showed some common features in the social, economic and intellectual changes that engulfed it after each world war, so, too, its governmental structures were not necessarily as divergent as popular left-wing legend would have us believe. Both after 1918 and after 1945, the land was governed by what appeared at first to be the most progressive reforming administration that was available at the time. Both post-war governments, that of Lloyd George in 1918 and that of Attlee in 1945, drew inspiration from the sweeping new social blueprints drawn up during wartime. There were the programmes of the Ministry of Reconstruction in 1917–18 and of the Beveridge, Uthwatt and other reports that emerged between 1940 and 1945. Nor was there as great a disparity between the general elections that followed each world war as has often been claimed. Lloyd George in the 'coupon election' of November to December 1918, like Attlee and his Labour colleagues in June to July 1945, campaigned largely as a social reformer.[9] Housing, health, insurance, pensions, agriculture and industrial relations were more characteristic themes in the rhetoric of coalition ministers in 1918, even Tory ones, than chauvinistic cries for 'hanging the Kaiser' or squeezing the Germans until the pips squeaked, for all Keynes's subsequent avowals to the contrary.

And yet, it is evident that there was, in the immediate aftermath of war a crucial contrast between the two periods, especially in Wales. Indeed, in some ways, the post-war phases illustrate yet again (1910–14 is another example) the ways in which Wales has tended to diverge from the English experience at critical times in our political and economic history. A case could be made out for there being many similarities in the policy pursued by the Lloyd George coalition and by the Attlee government in industrial policy, in finance, in colonial policy and in foreign affairs. But the case cannot be reasonably sustained in Wales. In his native land above all, Bevan's diagnosis, however extreme or exaggerated in its language, is broadly correct. After 1945, in Wales as in other older industrial areas, the social and economic reforms of wartime became permanently enshrined in the new social order that was created. There was no hint of betrayal now. Indeed, the Attlee government was very much aware of the way in which popular disillusionment had been created after the previous world war. In the 1945–51 Cabinet, to remind them of these past events, there was the septuagenarian Lord Addison, who had resigned from Lloyd George's government in 1921 in disgust at the betrayal of his housing programme then. In Wales, the 1920s brought disillusion, despair and the crushing weight of mass unemployment and stagnation as the legacy of wartime. The later 1940s, by contrast, brought a clear sense of renewal, of economic growth unknown since 1918 and of community pride. By the mid-1920s, association with the Lloyd George coalition was a badge of shame for many in Wales, especially the remnants of his old Coalition Liberals, even in such rural areas as Cardiganshire where the Wee Frees gained ultimate revenge. E. W. Evans, publisher of the *Cymro* weekly newspaper, wrote to Sir Herbert Lewis, MP for the University of Wales, that 'the Labour Party is going to sweep the board. A great number of our ministers are silently joining the Labour Party, not because they like it, but because it is the best choice they can make.'[10]

The Attlee government's reputation, on the other hand, was further enhanced even after the government itself fell from power in October 1951. Indeed, it has been plausibly argued[11] that Attlee initiated a new social consensus that broadly dictated British domestic policy until the advent of the Thatcher government, committed as it was to monetarism and a reversal of Keynesian-style management, in 1979. Welsh politics for three decades after 1945 tended to be a commentary upon the consequences, and the active Keynesian-style regional policies, of the 1945 Labour government.

In three areas, then, the divergence between the post-war experiences of Wales after 1918 and 1945 is transcendently clear – in party politics, in social policy and, above all, in the handling of organized labour. In the sphere of post-war politics in each case, the differences between the two periods is very marked indeed. As has been noted above, the Lloyd George coalition so triumphantly elected in 1918 (its 'couponed' supporters carried twenty-five Welsh seats out of thirty-six) did not seem necessarily illiberal. All Labour MPs elected for Welsh constituencies – William Brace in Abertillery, Mabon in Rhondda West, John Williams in Gower and even Vernon Hartshorn in Ogmore – claimed to be supporters of the domestic and foreign policies of the coalition government. John Williams, in the confusion typical of the time, even claimed to be a possessor of the precious 'coupon' himself![12] The charisma of Lloyd George, hero in peace and war, 'the greatest Welshman yet born', surrounded by a kind of Welsh Mafia in Downing Street, was more potent than ever. But nemesis came very rapidly. By the summer of 1919 the fundamental characteristics of the government were coming through, and meeting with a powerful popular reaction.

The revulsion against the government was more evident in Wales than in any other region of Britain, with Lloyd George's Coalition Liberals the usual victims of it. In 1919 Labour gained control of the county councils of Glamorgan and Monmouth, which apart from a brief interlude in the 1920s were to remain continuously in Labour hands until the counties were abolished and transformed into 'Gwent' and other novelties in 1973. Urban district councils in Aberdare, Maesteg and Llanelli followed this pattern. By-elections in South Wales showed a massive shift towards the Labour party, beginning with Swansea East in July 1919 which the Coalition Liberals narrowly retained at the height of the furore surrounding the Sankey Commission on the coal industry. There were further swings to Labour in other by-elections in Welsh mining seats, such as Abertillery (December 1920), Caerphilly (August 1921), where Morgan Jones, imprisoned during the war as a conscientious objector (and therefore unable to vote), was victorious; and in Gower and Pontypridd in July 1922, in both of which Labour gained seats from a Lloyd George Liberal. In the 1922 general election, the revulsion against both the outgoing Lloyd George coalition and its leader, was very pronounced in Wales. Only the rural constituencies of the west and north, and not all of them, stayed faithful to him. There were eight further Labour gains, six in the South Wales coalfield, one in Wrexham, another industrial seat, in the north-east, and, most startling of all, one in Caernarfonshire. Here, in Lloyd George's own bailiwick, the secretary of the North Wales Quarrymen's Union, R. T. Jones, was returned.[13] In Aberdare, there was a symbolic defeat for C. B. Stanton, the very embodiment of the bellicose jingoism of wartime, at the hands of the miners' agent, George Hall. For the proto-fascist Stanton, the war was finally over. Dick Wallhead, another wartime conscientious objector and an old lieutenant of Keir Hardie, captured Merthyr Tydfil from the Coalition Liberals. With Labour now holding eighteen Welsh seats, half the total, it was clear that the 'khaki election' of

1918, with its patriotic euphoria, had been totally unrepresentative of the underlying changes in Welsh political culture.

On the other hand, Welsh politics after 1945, if anything, merely confirmed the election results. At the polls, Labour had made seven gains and now held twenty-five seats out of thirty-six. But the leftward tide continued to flow strongly, in local government elections in 1945–46, and in by-elections at Ogmore, Aberdare and Pontypool, where only Plaid Cymru mounted any sort of challenge. Labour remained buoyant and expansionist during the Attlee years in Wales. The period from 1945 saw it making new inroads in north and mid-Wales as well, both traditional Liberal territory. The statistics are evocative of the change. In 1945, Labour won twenty-five seats, with 58 per cent of the vote. In 1950, after the redistribution of constituencies, it claimed twenty-seven seats, and 58.1 per cent of the vote. In 1951, the election that saw the downfall of Labour in government, the Labour party retained twenty-seven Welsh seats, with gains in Anglesey and Merioneth in the far north to compensate for losses at Barry and Conway. Labour's percentage of the poll, 60.5 per cent, was the highest ever, higher even than in the *annus mirabilis* of 1945, while the very high turn-out of well over 80 per cent in most Welsh constituencies confirmed the enthusiasm that the Labour government aroused amongst its natural supporters despite the Bevanite controversies. All the evidence points to continuing enthusiasm in Wales for the Attlee administration's policies, for nationalization, social welfare, 'fair shares', colonial freedom and above all full employment through vigorous regional policies. In 1951 in Wales, as in Britain generally, Labour gained the highest poll ever obtained by a British political party. Converts continued: the famous Liberal name of Lloyd George appeared as a Labour MP in 1957. The pattern endured until 1966 when Labour reached its high-water-mark of achievement with thirty-two seats out of thirty-six.

Apart from these somewhat mundane statistics of electoral performance, one can detect more subtle changes in the intellectual bases of politics if one compares the two post-war periods. After 1922, Welsh intellectuals moved sharply to the left, to socialism or even to pacifism. The victory of George Maitland Lloyd Davies in the 1923 general election for the University of Wales seat, even if it owed much to a split between two Liberal candidates, spoke volumes for the changing mood in the Welsh intelligentsia in this old stronghold of *Cymru Fydd*. A literary journal like *Y Llenor*, founded by W. J. Gruffydd in 1922, owed much of its impetus and distinction to anti-war or neo-pacifist writers.[14] It afforded a platform, too, for the new kind of nationalists such as Saunders Lewis or Ambrose Bebb, who were destined to form the tiny Plaid Cymru in 1925. Beyond the cloistered world of the Welsh-language *literati*, the Central Labour College in Regent's Park, London, provided a powerful stimulus to socialist activists. Young students at the college between

1918 and 1926 like Aneurin Bevan, James Griffiths, Morgan Phillips and Ness Edwards, all miners, were to create a new generation of political and industrial leaders for the Welsh labour movement.[15] The intellectual energy of Wales was as Labour (or sometimes nationalist) in character after 1922 as it had been overwhelmingly Liberal before 1914. In total contrast though, the intellectual developments within Wales after 1945 confirmed the electoral victory of the Labour party at the polls. From then onwards, perhaps until the 1970s, all the major debates leading up to the arguments over governmental devolution during the Crowther Commission, were in large measure debates within the Labour ranks. Until Plaid Cymru experienced a resurgence in 1966 and thereafter, there was no significant challenge to the political and intellectual dominance of Labour, the product of the war years and their aftermath. The difference from the experience of Lloyd George and his contemporaries after 1918 was overwhelmingly apparent.

A second area in which a clear contrast can be noted is the realm of social policy and administration. The Lloyd George government in 1918–19 began with a blaze of reformist activity. It looked as if the new Liberalism of pre-war was being re-enacted, notably by such Liberal ministers as Addison at the new Ministry of Health.[16] There were new state-subsidized council houses, new schools, a new provision for public health, increased pensions and a comprehensive system for unemployment insurance. The Addison housing programme, above all, largely carried out the main lines advocated by the Tudor Walters committee at the end of the war. But these measures were limited in scope: the Addison Housing Acts, for instance, gave only limited assistance to working-class occupants and made little impact on the massive housing shortage in industrial areas. It tended instead to favour well-planned open estates and semi-detached cottages in suburban districts such as Rhiwbina in Cardiff, Townhill in Swansea, Barry garden suburb or the Acton Park estate in Wrexham, originally intended for miners from the Gresford colliery. The entire social programme of the government was in any event being fatally undermined by the Treasury. Austen Chamberlain, the Chancellor, and his successor, Robert Horne, were reinforced by Warren Fisher within the bureaucracy long before the downfall of the government. The deflation that presaged a return to the gold standard made matters worse by inflicting high interest rates on local authorities trying to launch public housing programmes. The housing drive was completely wound up after Addison's resignation in 1921, while much of the rest of the social policy, including education, in spite of Fisher's strenuous resistance at the Ministry, was undermined by the Geddes Axe in 1922. The Welsh elementary and 'county' schools, proud creations of the national movement before 1914, were struggling throughout the 1920s. The 'anti-waste' business tycoons, over whom Eric Geddes presided, reduced Lloyd George's social programme to shreds. In any case, it could be argued that some of the government's legislation had been aimed at social control rather than social improvement, and had been counter to the interest of the working class in Wales. The revised National Health Insurance scheme, for instance, had curbed the miners' own union-sponsored medical schemes and had helped whittle away voluntary provision.[17] By the mid-1920s, as Bevan angrily wrote, the social prospectus of the coalition government of 1918 was a mockery.[18] Accounts of the state of housing and health in the 1930s, notably the annual reports of the Welsh Housing and Development Association prepared by Edgar Chappell and others, gave alarming details of the extent of slum housing and urban and environmental decay in Wales. The parliamentary committee on the anti-tuberculosis (TB) services, chaired by Clement Davies, painted a quite appalling picture of the extent of the 'white scourge' of TB in rural and urban Wales alike, largely because of damp, insanitary housing and other social inadequacies.[19]

The findings of that committee also illustrated a significant divergence between industrial and rural Wales by the 1930s. Cost-conscious local authorities in north and mid-Wales were far less anxious to expend money raised by the rates on health, housing and other social services than were Labour authorities in Carmarthenshire, Glamorgan and Monmouthshire in the south and Wrexham in the north-east. In short, it is clear that by the 1930s, the wartime pledges of sweeping social reforms, betrayed by central government from 1920 onwards, were only being honoured, if at all, by the local endeavours of county and municipal councils under Labour control. In the 1930s, in the worst years of depression and unemployment, Labour local authorities kept up public spending in South Wales on social services as best they could. Local resources were remarkably fully deployed on behalf of slum clearance, health provision, free midday meals and free school milk for children, parks, libraries, baths and other public amenities. The Labour local authorities were also most active in such places as Newport, Cardiff, Aberdare, the Rhondda, Llanelli and Swansea in campaigning against the means test and attempts by the central government to curb local social expenditure. Particularly strong resistance was mustered against both restrictions upon unemployment assistance, and Circular 170 of September 1932, which sought to cut down the number of free places in secondary schools and to impose a new means test on fee payments.[20] In addition, many local authorities were remarkably enterprising in trying to enlist aid from the Nuffield Trust and other bodies in order to introduce new industries into the depressed mining valleys. In short, social policy in Wales from the mid-1920s onwards is largely a tale of the Labour-run local councils (and also the trade unions, notably through the Miners' Welfare Fund, set up in 1920, and the miners' own medical aid provision)[21] trying to repair the damage wrought by the abdication of responsibility by central government.

After 1945 it was all very different. Central and local government were largely united in the creation of the welfare state. Labour-run local authorities now played a less conspicuous role. In many respects, indeed, the social programme now enacted went distinctly beyond the blueprints of the wartime years. Certainly it is an error to see the Attlee government as merely reproducing the schemes of planners such as Beveridge. James Griffiths' National Insurance Act of 1946 was more comprehensive and included more generous scales of payment than Beveridge's report had proposed. This was partly the result of intervention by backbenchers such as Sidney Silverman. Aneurin Bevan's National Health Service was more radical than Willink's wartime compromise scheme, especially in the nationalization of the hospitals and the abolition of the sale of private practices. Throughout the post-war years, the impact of the new welfare measures on the social and economic fabric of Wales, as on that of many older industrial areas, was immense. Indeed, the popularity of such literary works as *How Green was my Valley* and A. J. Cronin's *The Citadel* during the war years had helped to make South Wales a key point of reference in the entire debate about launching a welfare state. From 1946 onwards, there were rising standards of health, housing and nutrition amongst children and old people. Bevan's housing programmes, so often criticized (frequently without regard to the wider economic picture or to such technical problems as the shortage of imported soft wood for building), had a powerful effect in many Welsh towns. Swansea, ravaged by the blitz, engaged in a programme of building six thousand council houses between 1946 and 1952.[22] Elsewhere, in mid- and north Wales, such towns as Aberystwyth, Caernarfon, Newtown and Holyhead were much revived by a progressive policy of public housing aided by low interest rates. The NHS was from the start very popular in Wales where such diseases as tuberculosis and silicosis had been scourges in the recent past. Environmental conditions in long-depressed areas like the slate-quarrying districts of Caernarfon and Merioneth were revolutionized. *Lancet* reports indicated a greater enthusiasm for the NHS amongst general practitioners in Wales than in other parts of Britain. Aneurin Bevan's own personal experience of health provision in the mining communities, such as in his own Tredegar Medical Aid Society, also played its part in launching the new service. Nor was this simply a case of action by central government alone. Voluntary activity also played its part, notably in Arthur Horner's prolonged campaign against lung disease among miners, and in the National Union of Mineworkers' efforts on behalf of the rehabilitation of disabled mineworkers.

The outstanding difference in the social history of Wales after 1945, compared with the years after 1918, was that the momentum of wartime was kept up. This time the Treasury maintained a generally benevolent attitude towards social spending. This was obviously so under Dalton, but also during the more austere régime of Cripps in 1947–50 when a high level of welfare expenditure was maintained despite balance of payments difficulties. Even during the balance of payments troubles of 1949 that led to devaluation, there was no hint of a Geddes axe. It is ironic that a conflict over welfare expenditure led to the resignation of Aneurin Bevan from the Attlee government in April 1951. In the end, a gap of only £13 million was all that divided Bevan from the politically less experienced and unnecessarily rigid Gaitskell in the Cabinet debates on the 1951 budget. Cripps, with his long and close personal relationship with Bevan since the 1930s, had avoided a clash over the 1950 budget by imposing a general ceiling on public health expenditure rather than impose charges; Gaitskell was less adroit. Despite this episode, it is clear that the pledges of both wartime and the polls were generally honoured after 1945, and that Wales, like other regions, experienced a buoyancy unknown for thirty years as a result. The contrast is most clearly demonstrated by the records of the two major social reformers within the two post-war governments. Addison became an outcast in 1921, driven out of Lloyd George's government in disgust at the emasculation of his housing schemes. His reputation as a minister suffered (quite unfairly) as a result. Bevan, in contrast, gained immensely in public stature through the creation of the welfare state, and of the NHS in particular; his eventual resignation did not affect the achievement. The careers of Addison and Bevan, Cabinet colleagues between 1945 and 1951, point the distinction in Wales and other areas in social provision after two world wars.

The greatest difference of all in the two post-war experiences in Wales is to be found in industrial relations, an area which Dr Pelling has made so very much his own. The starting-point in each case is not so very different. Both the Lloyd George coalition in 1918 and the Attlee Labour administration in 1945 aimed at first to maintain the easy access to the trade union leadership that had obtained during the war. Both established 'emergency powers' provisions to deal with industrial disturbances. Both used them several times, Lloyd George in putting down what were, in fact, official strikes of the railwaymen in September 1919 and the miners in April 1921, and Attlee in countering local strikes by London dockers and power workers between 1947 and 1950.

The Lloyd George government made some show of maintaining the wartime consensus with both sides of industry: the National Industrial Conference called in April 1919 embodied the industrial harmony of the war years. But it soon emerged that this façade of conciliaton was superficial. The National Industrial Conference yielded nothing, and broke down amidst much recrimination.[23] Above all, public dialogue with the miners was the most disastrous of failures, one which coloured the relations of the trade unions generally with central government until 1926 and beyond. The failure of the Sankey Commission to get the government to accept nationalization of the mines in August

1919; the chain of events leading to 'decontrol' of the mines that began in the autumn of 1920; and above all the calamitous breakdown of negotiations that produced the miners' lockout between April and July 1921, all testified to the disastrous record of the government, and of Lloyd George in particular. The pretence that he enjoyed a special relationship with the trade unions, nurtured since Board of Trade days in 1905–08, lay in ruins. Horne, a conciliatory Minister of Labour in 1919, was now a most intransigent Chancellor. Points can be put on the other side, of course. The miners, pressing for a 30 per cent wage advance in 1919, were aggressive and hopelessly optimistic in the aftermath of the wartime boom. The handling of the miners' case by Smillie, Smith and the Miners' Federation of Great Britain (MFGB) executive before the Sankey inquiry was the reverse of adroit; they were not politicians, whatever their skill as industrial negotiators. The extent to which the miners were interested in nationalization, as opposed to some kind of wage advance and a pooled system for wages, is very doubtful. For all that, the government manifestly mishandled the course of negotiations throughout the Sankey hearings, while its abject surrender in 1920–21 to the private coal-owners, hated as they were, inevitably caused massive resentment throughout the mining communities.

South Wales reacted the most vehemently of all the mining districts. Indeed, the promise that the post-war period would inaugurate a new era in labour relations here had always been distinctly hollow. Throughout the war years, the Welsh coalfield had been identified as a unique problem area. The Commission on Industrial Unrest in 1917 had reported in ominous terms on the explosive nature of relations between miners and coal-owners. Since at least the Cambrian miners' strike and the turbulence at Tonypandy in 1910, South Wales had been officially regarded as a haven for every variant of extreme socialist ideology. Scotland Yard cooperated with the government in 1919 in dispatching secret reports to the Ministry of Labour on the alleged subversive activities of Bolsheviks and others in the Welsh valleys. It was entirely predictable that South Wales should react the most vehemently of all the British mining districts after the breakdown of negotiations following the Sankey inquiry. The Welsh miners balloted strongly for strike action in September 1920 (141,721 to 40,047). When a national strike was actually called by the Miners' Federation a few weeks later, they voted against a return to work (98,052 to 51,647);[24] moreover, they were foremost in the struggle in April to July 1921 when the mines were returned to the hands of the capitalists and the government subsidy came to an end. Even a man like Vernon Hartshorn, who was always a moderate, was driven into desperate defiance when he succeeded to the presidency of the South Wales Miners' Federation (SWMF), on the death of James Winstone, in 1922. In a famous phrase, Hartshorn had declared that the miners were 'deceived, betrayed, duped' over Sankey.[25] In the local press, he had vividly described how the Welsh miners were becoming 'serfs, demoralised and half-starved'[26] as severe wage cuts were imposed by the coal-owners when international recession took its toll in 1921. In any event, the Welsh mining community was moving rapidly to the left, in confrontation not merely with the government but possibly with the executive of the Miners' union itself. There was a revival of the 'unofficial' movements of pre-war days among rank-and-file miners. Soon they were to issue forth, under Communist leadership, in the Minority Movement within the SWMF.[27] Left-wing figures such as S. O. Davies and Noah Ablett were powerful upon the South Wales Miners' executive. Arthur Cook, backed up faithfully by Arthur Horner in the Rhondda No. 1 District, was becoming the dominant figure in the Welsh miners' union. In 1924, he was to succeed another product of the Welsh mining valleys, Frank Hodges, as secretary of the Miners' Federation of Great Britain.

From this time onwards, the Welsh mining community was in embittered revolt, evolving its own alternative radical culture and its own rival structure of leadership. During the General Strike and miners' lock-out in 1926, the whole community was mobilized; school-teachers, shopkeepers and noncon-formist ministers all lined up in support. The return to pre-war ascendancy by coal-owners and managers such as the Hann family of Powell Duffryn had a disastrous impact upon labour relations in South Wales. The resultant amal-gamation of colliery concerns led to vast profits for the few and mass redun-dancies for the many. The failure of the government to provide any protection against the scourge of mass unemployment drove all the miners' leaders from Hartshorn to Cook into furious antagonism. Worse still, there was a calculated campaign by many coal-owners to break the power of the 'Fed', the Miners' union. Non-unionism, on the pattern of American company unionism, was encouraged in Bedwas and many other collieries. By the end of 1922, a variety of pressures had resulted in SWMF membership falling sharply from a peak of 197,000 in 1920 to 87,000 by the end of 1922. Membership continued to fall, especially after the trauma of the General Strike in 1926. Not until 1935, after a revival of the union leadership under newer, moderate leaders such as James Griffiths and a successful campaign against non-unionism (culminating in the dramatic 'stay-down' stoppages at Nine-Mile-Point colliery), did the tide begin to turn.[28] Only in the mid-1930s did MFGB membership revive and its funds significantly increase. Until that time, the unions and the miners were in implacable opposition to what they regarded as the Tory front that Lloyd George, their one-time hero, had first imposed on them.

After 1945, how different was the mood! The Attlee government had, of course, a most intimate relationship with the Trades Union Congress (TUC), as the presence of Bevin and ex-miners such as Bevan, Griffiths, Shinwell, Hall and Lawson within the administration symbolized. At all levels of the party – the party conference, the national executive, grass-roots constituency bodies – the association between the Labour party and the trade union movement was exceptionally close, probably closer than at any period in the history of the Labour movement. The career of Morgan Phillips, an ex-miner from Aberdare, as Labour's general secretary from 1944, reflected this happy symbiosis. The policies of the Attlee government followed the 1945 manifesto, and this in turn was closely geared to the demands of the unions. The repeal of the 1927 Trades Disputes Act, nationalization of the mines and other industries and services, the maintenance of full employment, the operation of a vigorous regional policy by the Board of Trade, the building up of trading estates and the use of the powers of the Distribution of Industry Act, 1945, were all dear to the heart of the Welsh working community. So, too, was the implementation of the National Union of Mineworkers' (NUM) Miners' Charter, as agreed by Shinwell at the Ministry of Fuel and Power, with the extension of the 'day wage' system, the five-day week and other much needed reforms. The responsiveness of the government to pressure from Wales for economic assistance was notable throughout. In July 1946, when unemployment again seemed to be reaching alarming levels in the mining valleys, Attlee, Cripps and Isaacs were solicitous in the face of protests from the Welsh Labour MPs.[29]

In return, there was a degree of cooperation from the unions in Wales quite unknown after 1918. In the interests of boosting the production record of the Labour government, items agreed in the Miners' Charter, including the five-day week, were relaxed. Whatever the difficulties of labour relations in the new nationalized industries, the industrial atmosphere was immensely more cordial than it had ever been in the 1920s. Major strikes in the South Wales pits virtually disappeared. There was nothing comparable to the prolonged dispute at Grimethorpe and other collieries in southern Yorkshire in August to September 1947. Government decisions such as the implementation of the wage freeze in 1948 or the devaluation of sterling in 1949, which added somewhat to the miners' cost of living, were loyally accepted. Even Arthur Horner, a critic of a 'wage-freeze' policy, accepted it in the cause of labour solidarity. No such concession could have been made over Churchill's return to gold in 1925. The mood in the mining communities by 1950 was remarkably changed. Maerdy, an embittered, besieged community in the 1920s, was by 1950 the beneficiary of a new £5 million investment 'horizon' mining project to connect the upper Rhondda with the Bwllfa colliery in the Aberdare valley. The links that bound the Labour ministers to their own native communities were exemplified by men such as Bevan, Griffiths and Ness Edwards. The new mood continued after 1951 despite a rash of minor stoppages and 'go-slows' that cost 276,000 tons in output in that year.[30] In the thirteen subsequent years of Conservative government, which saw the beginning of a rigorous policy of colliery closures, the unions were never so isolated again. Will Paynter, another Welsh Communist who became secretary of the NUM after Horner, enjoyed amiable relations with ministers. There was nothing resembling the period of victimization which followed the miners' strikes of 1921 and 1926. The Bourbon restoration after 1920 found no similar echo; the communal life of the valleys and other regions of Wales was the healthier for it.

It has been seen therefore, that whatever the elements of continuity in Wales in two post-war phases, there was a marked change of mood in the crucial areas of political conflict, social policy and labour relations. There is, however, one final point that the Welsh historian must consider, namely, what, if anything, the post-war periods added to or subtracted from the sense of Welshness. Was the awareness of national identity, with the institutions and social groups that sustained it, significantly altered by the aftermath of war?

As far as the First World War is concerned, it has already been suggested that the old kind of semi-nationalism, with which the Prime Minister, Lloyd George, was so intimately associated, largely passed away. The reaction against it in 1922 was almost as pronounced in Cardiganshire, Caernarfonshire and Flintshire as in the mining valleys of the south. Old cries such as land reform, temperance and governmental devolution aroused little interest. Disestablishment, the national objective for two generations past and the old prize striven for by Samuel Roberts, Henry Richard, Thomas Gee and other radicals in former years, was achieved in 1920 amidst monumental indifference. Indeed, the nonconformist chapels were henceforth far more apprehensive of the future, once their ambition had been attained, than was a newly-liberated and invigorated Church, whose communicant members in Wales rose steadily in number. Plaid Cymru, formed in 1925, embodied a nationalism of a very different style from that of men like O. M. Edwards before 1914. Some of its key personalities were sympathetic to Roman Catholicism. The party was far more detached in outlook from the English and Imperial governmental and social system than the pre-war nationalists had ever been. Plaid Cymru, in short, was almost entirely the vehicle for the Welsh-speaking minority. That minority itself was becoming increasingly desperate as linguistic censuses in 1921 and 1931 showed incontestable evidence of the decline of the language. The 'Anglo-Welsh' school of writing, heralded by the sardonic short stories of Caradoc Evans, illustrated one kind of reaction. Conversely, the unemployment and economic recession of the interwar period reinforced a sense of class solidarity in the valleys at the expense of either the appeal of community or Welshness. The involvement of some young Welshmen, miners and others, in the International Brigade in Spain in 1936–39 added a new kind of outward-looking dimension to this mood.[31] The post-war years after 1918, therefore, marked the effective end of one lengthy phase of Welsh national achievement, even though such symbols as the University of Wales survived to shape major aspects of the outlook of succeeding generations.

The impact of the Second World War was not so clear-cut. After 1945, there was a general mood in favour of centralization and planning initiated at the centre of economic decision-making. The hopes expressed in the Welsh Reconstruction Advisory Council in 1943 that Wales might become a distinct economic planning unit, a view advanced with especial fervour by James Griffiths, led nowhere.[32] Pressure by Welsh MPs both during and after the war for a Welsh Secretary of State was strongly resisted by the government. Herbert Morrison argued that a Welsh Secretary of State would lead to both bad government and a negation of efficient central planning in the principality. In any case, there would not be enough competent Welsh civil servants available to staff a new Welsh Office.[33] He rebutted James Griffiths' protests when the nationalized electricity services for Wales were divided into two in 1946, so that north and mid-Wales became linked with Merseyside.[34] In the Cabinet, Aneurin Bevan, a stern enemy of both particularism and anything that resembled Welsh devolution, had a more powerful voice in the Cabinet Home Services Committee. So the Attlee government made only the most perfunctory gestures towards Welsh national sentiment, a response strongly endorsed by Morgan Phillips in Transport House. Morrison very reluctantly set up the Council for Wales in 1949. His aim was, in part, to combat the Ministry for Welsh Affairs that the Conservatives proposed to create when they returned to power. But for the next seventeen years of a somewhat ghostly existence, the Council, as a purely advisory and non-elective body, was largely the ineffective talking-shop that Morrison himself had prophesied.[35]

Even so, something did survive the centralization and hostility to nationalism of the Attlee years. Within the Labour party machinery itself, the Welsh Council of Labour was formed in early 1947. The South Wales Regional Council, directed by Cliff Prothero, was merged with eight scattered bodies existing in north Wales and loosely linked with the trade unions there. The central party gave the sum of £100 to facilitate the merger. It was a belated reluctant recognition by the Transport House *apparatchiki* that Wales was a nation rather than a mere region. A battle waged since Arthur Henderson's administrative reforms within the party in 1917–18 was finally won.[36]

The pressure for a Secretary of State went on, despite the government's overall hostility. D. R. Grenfell and W. H. Mainwaring attempted to pressurize Attlee over a Welsh secretaryship, but, predictably, got nowhere.[37] When Labour finally did commit itself to setting up a Welsh Secretary of State in its 1959 party manifesto, even Aneurin Bevan himself endorsed it, although admittedly with great reluctance. However weak the Welsh Office was when it was launched in 1964, its tenure by the veteran James Griffiths inaugurated a new chapter in Labour's attitude towards the Welsh national identity. From

1966 onwards, spurred on by the revival of Plaid Cymru, the Welsh Labour party was even committed to some form of Welsh devolution, although the eventual outcome, the humiliating defeat of the scheme in Wales in March 1979, suggests that backing for it amongst Labour party supporters was skin-deep only. At least, though, it can be argued that some viable notion of Welsh-ness was handed on during the post-war phase after 1945. Unlike the exclusive, sectarian nationalism of the kind favoured by the embryo Plaid Cymru in the 1920s, it was a kind of vision that could appeal to the English-speaking major-ity in Wales as well. As the formation of the Welsh TUC in 1973 suggests, it was relevant to a modern, industrial, technologically-advanced society, and not merely to rural uplands nostalgic for the sentimental idylls of *Cymru Fydd* and an arcadian past. It was, too, an idea of Welshness that could be related to a contemporary secular world instead of the chapel-bred, 'eisteddfodic' intro-verted nationalism that flourished before the First World War.[38] Such a senti-ment could generate a kind of nationhood that could provide a more unified society rather than one embittered, ingrown and riven by linguistic and sec-tarian divisions.

Here again, therefore, in the supreme area of national consciousness, the experience of the two post-war phases is in contrast. More generally, as has been seen, the differences are transcendent in political, social and industrial life. Aneurin Bevan was a prophet, a propagandist but not a philosopher. His diagnosis is inflammatory, rhetorical and often exaggerated. The cautious ac-ademic would hedge his verdicts with all manner of qualifications. Neverthe-less, in broad outline the views expounded in *Why not Trust the Tories?* are unquestionably correct. As far as Bevan's own nation is concerned, the Wales of post-1945 is part of a living, usable past; the Wales that emerged after 1918 is a world well lost.[39]

6

Imperialism and the Labour government of 1945–51

PARTHA SARATHI GUPTA

The first Labour government to enjoy a working majority, and a massive one, was also a government whose senior ministers had served in the wartime coalition, and had thus become familiar with traditional views about Britain's overseas relations. As Ernest Bevin put it: 'You will have to form a government which is at the centre of a great Empire and Commonwealth of Nations, which touches all parts of the world. . . . Revolutions do not change geography, and revolutions do not change geographical need.'[1] In this paper an attempt is made, in the light of recently released archival material, to identify the priorities of the Labour government in its Imperial policy and to see to which pressures it was willing to yield and which it resisted.

Previous interpretations have ranged from contemporary hostile verdicts from the extreme left (like those of R. Palme Dutt or George Padmore) to later judgements which were more sympathetic but which lacked the basis of archival sources (like those of David Goldsworthy and the present author). Dutt in 1949 described British Imperial policy as being subservient to the needs of the USA and explained away the concession of independence to South-Asian countries as a new means of safeguarding British interests.[2] George Padmore, pan-Africanist, ex-Communist and a future adviser to the independent government of Ghana, conceded the reality of South-Asian independence but argued that the Labour party wanted to find new sources of profit in Africa.[3] The Labour party's self-image of its achievements in the election manifesto of 1950 was complacent. South-Asian independence and the adhesion of republican India to the Commonwealth were described as 'a bridge of friendship between the people of East and West'. It was claimed that Britain had subsidized colonial development and welfare and laid the economic and social foundations for democratic self-government.[4] Goldsworthy and the present author, in their different ways, praised Labour Colonial Secretaries for their conscientiousness, but also drew attention to lack of achievement in the sphere of relations between white settlers and Africans and to periodic gaps in communication between nationalists and the government.[5] The

99

present author sought to relate these failures to Britain's desire to play the role of a great power and defend sterling as an international currency.[6] A recent study by a historian who served in the Colonial Office during this period argues, on the basis of Colonial Office records and the papers of a senior civil servant with Fabian sympathies, that just at the time when a case could have been made on economic grounds for exploiting Africa further, the trend in the Colonial Office was for the reverse. Under Creech Jones and Andrew Cohen, traditional assumptions were revolutionized by planning for self-government in Africa within twenty-five years.[7] However, there is as yet no overview of what weight the colonial reformers' ideas carried within the government's overall assessment of priorities.

I

Before examining Labour's policies concerning particular areas of Asia and Africa, it may be helpful to offer some preliminary remarks on the strategic outlook of the Labour government and on how that outlook was affected by domestic considerations. Labour ministers spent a great deal of time justifying Britain's Imperial policy. Such justification was necessary regardless of whether Labour policy was to be the traditional one of maintaining Britain as an imperial power or whether it would be shaped by the electoral pledge of Indian independence and 'the planned progress of our Colonial Dependencies'.[8] On the one hand, criticisms by Labour backbenchers in parliament would have to be met. On the other hand, American misgivings would have to be relieved or deflected. Both the Labour government and the Conservative opposition accepted the need for a close understanding with the United States (US) on questions of defence and diplomacy. Considerable uneasiness remained, however, within the Labour government concerning the US attitude to imperial preference and sterling area. Quite early on in the government's life, Bevin, in a Cabinet paper, defended British policy as having emanated from 'the last bastion of social democracy', the only real alternative to 'the red tooth and claw of American capitalism and the Communist dictatorship of Soviet Russia'.[9] Similar claims were made in 1948 when the Cold War had intensified and Britain was thinking of a Western Union (with associated colonial territories) as a viable bloc between the US and the USSR.[10]

The question of the state of the British economy had an important and complex bearing on both the formulation of Imperial policy and strategic thinking throughout the period under review. In the course of two meetings of the Cabinet defence committee early in 1946, Attlee persuaded his colleagues that only by reducing global military commitments would manpower for domestic reconstruction be released, the balance of payments safeguarded and economic recovery made possible.[11] Imperial status symbols like a large Pacific fleet were to be scaled down, and British troops in India were visualized as a short-term liability only, pending the transfer of power.[12] Bevin believed that a British military presence in the Mediterranean and the Middle East was needed both as a barrier against Soviet penetration and as a line of communication to Middle-East oil supplies.[13] But when he realized that the presence of British troops was blocking treaty negotiations with Egypt, he supported Attlee's proposal for an alternative line of defence based on the development of British equatorial Africa.[14] What attracted him about this plan was 'that the whole heart and centre of command [would] be on British territory', whereas Egypt was a foreign country and the future of the Palestine mandate was uncertain.[15] East Africa would command the Indian Ocean, and a road across Africa would help 'with the uranium deposits in the Congo'. Furthermore, the defence expenditure would be within the sterling area. These arguments convinced Bevin that a new African strategy 'will modernize the whole character of our defence as well as our trade and bring into the British orbit economically and commercially a great area which is by no means fully developed yet'.[16] But the Chiefs of Staff quashed the plan of quitting the Mediterranean by suggesting that the Soviet Union would fill the vacuum created by Britain's withdrawal. The question of the defence and economic potential of British tropical Africa was referred to an interdepartmental committee.[17] The committee approved the idea of reinforcing the economic and strategic value of central and east Africa by railway-building, but postponed any action on the grounds of cost for the time being.[18]

During the next year, as the cost of defence was periodically criticized by Hugh Dalton, Chancellor of the Exchequer, the basic priorities of containing Soviet influence in Europe and keeping a British presence in the Middle East were constants in the government's policy, and were to influence crucial political decisions in Asia as well as their timing. In South and South-east Asia the government sought to come to terms with nationalism in order to prevent Communist movements from spearheading the post-war colonial discontent. It is a mistake to see this merely as a technique for pursuing traditional Imperial purposes by having a client state ruled by a pliant indigenous élite. Such considerations did eventually play some part in Malayan politics,[19] but in India and Burma (and to a lesser extent in Ceylon) the aim was to win the goodwill of representative mass parties, make no preconditions about economic safeguards and ensure assistance in Imperial defence.[20]

Military reports indicate that the average British soldier stationed in India in 1945 welcomed the Labour victory in the elections, but expected to be demobilized at the earliest opportunity.[21] The war had transformed the Indian armed forces from a handpicked loyal team of soldiers of the Crown into a large, more politically-conscious assembly.[22] By April 1946, senior officials could not guarantee that the forces would stay loyal and united if the Indian Nationalist Congress party launched a civil disobedience movement.[23]

The Indian Constitution of 1945 (created by a statute of 1935) did not provide for responsible central parliamentary government and erected special safeguards by which the Viceroy could protect British business interests. However, Indian political leaders and propertied classes had had an opportunity to infiltrate the administrative and political machinery at the provincial level in the years 1937–39.[24] The Labour government ordered fresh elections to the provincial and central assemblies in 1945; this gave the two dominant Indian parties (the nationalist Congress and the separatist Muslim League) control of different provincial governments. The Labour leadership did not like the strident anti-British nationalist tone of the Congress party during the election campaign, nor were they happy, for military reasons, about the Muslim League's demand for a total division of the country. But Attlee and Morrison learnt, to their chagrin, that the British authorities in India had no means of convincing the Indian electorate that under the Labour government the Raj was 'the poor man's protector and friend'. A senior provincial governor, who was the Viceroy's personal emissary in November 1945, was reported to have said that there was no adequate channel of communication between the government and the people.[25] Doubtless it was this that made Attlee decide to send a high-powered Cabinet mission early in 1946 to have direct talks with Indian political leaders.

During these talks the Cabinet mission did not wish to risk the experiment of electing a constituent assembly based on universal adult suffrage, even though as late as 1942–43 Cripps and Bevin had thought of appealing to the Indian workers and peasants over the heads of politicians from the propertied classes.[26] Both Communist and anti-Communist labour leaders in India protested at the inequity of electing a constituent assembly from among legislators who had been themselves elected on a narrow franchise, but the Cabinet mission ignored their constructive suggestions about how to prepare fresh electoral rolls for universal adult suffrage.[27] Behind this concern for a speedy settlement with existing political parties lay a recognition that any new experiment might cause delay and a drift towards extremist political agitation, either by the Congress socialists or by the Muslim League. British business representatives told Cripps that they feared violent agitation was more likely by the Muslim League.[28]

The need for support from the Indian business groups during the war had forced the wartime British administration in India, much against the wishes of Churchill, to agree to debit to Britain military expenditure originating in India. This transformed the subcontinent within six years from a debtor to a creditor country vis-à-vis Britain.[29] A recognition of the economic strength of Indian business interests led the Labour government, despite initial misgivings, to tell expatriate firms in India that it would not press for special safeguards for them in the constitutional talks.[30] The future of British commercial and industrial concerns in India therefore depended on political goodwill.

The federal structure proposed by the Cabinet mission on 16 May 1946, with a central government controlling only external affairs, defence and communication, gave the British Chiefs of Staff what they wanted: a large group of provinces in the north-west which would be logistically defensible in a war with the Soviet Union, could be a base for attack on Siberia if necessary and yet would be linked with the industrial and economic heartland of the rest of India.[31] The truncated West Pakistan that eventually emerged after the rejection of the Cabinet mission plan by the Muslim League and the Congress party had always seemed to the Defence authorities to be very much a second best and to be useless for Imperial defence purposes unless there was some joint defence agreement within the subcontinent.[32]

In the last twelve months of British rule the options before the government rapidly diminished. On 5 June 1946, the Cabinet had refused to set a target date for independence but had also recognized that repression of mass nationalist movements would be unpopular in Britain and would necessitate moving troops from other vital areas.[33] Six months later, the Cabinet overruled the objections of Bevin and the Chiefs of Staff and named a date for the evacuation of British troops and officials.[34] The senior Indian administrative personnel were far more numerous than the British, and their loyalty to the Rāj could not be absolutely relied upon.[35] At home, resources were scarce. The ministers preparing the British economic survey for 1947 reported in December 1946, '. . . we feel bound to question whether the country can afford to devote so big a proportion of its manpower to defence at the present time'.[36] In January, A. V. Alexander, Minister of Defence and a member of the Cabinet mission to India, reluctantly agreed to a 5 per cent cut in defence expenditure.[37] Two months later, when backbench Labour MPs' uneasiness about the length of National Service on economic and moral grounds led to its being reduced from eighteen months to one year, Field Marshal Montgomery put it on record that this was done on the assumption that troops would be withdrawn from India, and that the Palestine problem would be solved satisfactorily.[38]

Against this background of reduced defence capability there were devious efforts to secure some insurance for Imperial defence from the two successor states. Plans to detach the Indian Ocean islands of Andaman and Nicobar and put them under the Colonial Office foundered on opposition from the Indians which was so implacable as to alarm Viceroy Mountbatten.[39] By bringing forward the date of partition, he succeeded, however, in persuading the Congress party, despite its republican orientation, to accept transfer of power on the basis of Dominion Status and at the cost of partition.[40] But British hopes of general supervision of the defence plans of the two dominions were dashed, first by Mountbatten's failure to secure the Governor-Generalship of both dominions, and secondly by the Indo-Pakistani conflict over Kashmir, which started almost immediately after independence.[41]

In Ceylon, defence considerations were paramount. The Soulbury Commission of 1943 on the Ceylon constitution had offered full internal self-government with defence and external affairs under British control. Ceylon was an essential strategic base in the Indian Ocean, and a vital link for the air, cable and wireless communications in the Far East.[42] In the autumn of 1945 the Labour government rejected Ceylonese pressure for Dominion Status.[43] The Ceylonese leaders finally accepted the Soulbury constitution as an interim measure, but by May 1947, even before elections were held under the new constitution, the pressure of events in India and Burma strengthened their demand for immediate independence within the Commonwealth. Even then, though both the Governor of Ceylon and Creech Jones recommended meeting this demand, the Cabinet hesitated lest such a concession would trigger off demands for similar concessions in Malaya and elsewhere.[44] Nevertheless, within a month, after the Ceylonese leader, D. Senanayeke, gave a private assurance that British defence and foreign-policy interests would be safeguarded, the Cabinet agreed to hold constitutional talks immediately after the Ceylonese elections.[45] A military agreement preceded the granting of Dominion Status early in 1948. In the words of a junior Labour minister who visited the country for the Independence celebrations, power had been transferred to an indigenous élite whose style of politics was reminiscent of the Whig landed gentry of eighteenth-century Britain and who were 'terrified by the Left opposition'. The minister also noted that Ceylonese ministers were vulnerable to attacks from the opposition because a military agreement had been made a precondition of Dominion Status. He recommended (though it was not acted on) greater reliance on the Ceylonese leaders' goodwill than on the military agreement.[46]

The planners of Imperial defence had lost the initiative in the Indian subcontinent but retained it in Ceylon. The financial crisis of August 1947 made them readjust their priorities after a great deal of heart-searching.[47] After October 1947 the army outside Britain remained strongest in Europe and the Middle East, followed by Malaya and the Far East. Naval dispositions were weakened in the Pacific and the Caribbean.[48] In February 1948, 40 per cent of the total overseas military expenditure covered Palestine and Egypt and another 30 per cent covered Malaya, Gibraltar and Malta.[49] The inference was obvious. When funds were tight three things mattered most: a firm stand in Europe as long as the West and the Soviet Union remained deadlocked over the German and Austrian settlement, the protection of Imperial communication points and the protection of areas producing oil, tin and rubber.

II

Labour's colonial and Imperial policies after 1945 reflected some of the major political and economic contrasts between the pre-war and post-war periods. Some traditional types of working-class imperialism, noticed before the war, did not recur in the immediate post-war years. Because of shortage of labour in the Lancashire textile industry, one heard little about textile workers being made redundant by the 'sweated' labour of Indian workers.[50] There was no natural demographic pressure for overseas emigration. Ministers were anxious to save manpower, but for reasons of global power politics some ministers approved the principle of encouraging British emigration to Australia and Kenya.[51] Attlee and Bevin hoped that the relatively sparsely populated parts of East and Central Africa would absorb more immigrants from among European displaced persons and provide a home for the Assyrian minority in Iraq.[52] However, there was a reverse flow of migration from the non-white colonial empire to Britain in the post-war period. This aroused misgivings within the party and caused embarrassment to those who believed that the Empire-Commonwealth was, or should be, evolving in a multiracial direction.[53]

The cost of the Second World War made the orthodox Leninist explanation about the imperialism of finance-capital and the export of capital irrelevant. During the war, prospects of a post-war balance of payments deficit made Treasury officials doubt the likelihood of capital exports from Britain.[54] When Britain approached the US for a loan in 1945 and made promises about scaling down sterling balances (which she failed to do in most cases), she became simultaneously a debtor to the richest and some of the poorest countries in the world. Instead of capital, export of goods was necessary to pay off the debt. There was, however, a strong temptation for a weakened Britain to use her powers over the dependent Empire both to get essential supplies and to bridge the dollar gap.

At first these temptations did not surface. It was hoped that economic recovery, return to multilateral trade and the convertibility of sterling would come about as expected. As Bevin put it about the proposed International Trades Organization (ITO), the aim of the 'maximum possible expansion of world trade based upon high and sustained level of employment in every country' was 'in the best interests of the United Kingdom as the world's principal trading nation', and this would promote political stability in all parts of the world.[55] The terms of the American loan of 1945 provoked Aneurin Bevan to talk of the American 'nineteenth century attitude towards international trade', and to suggest (along with Emanuel Shinwell) building up the sterling area bloc as an alternative to the loan. Alexander adopted what was nearly the Beaverbrook approach to the value of Empire trade. Bevin sympathized, but along with the majority of the Cabinet agreed with Cripps and Dalton that to refuse to cooperate with the 'first tentative moves towards an international trade agreement' was against the 'declared policy of the Labour Party', and that the sterling area members themselves wished to move away from tight wartime controls.[56] While there were a few 'early day motions' in the House of Commons from backbench Conservative MPs in favour of Empire trade as an alternative to an open-door world trade policy, very few Labour MPs proposed or signed such motions.[57]

Four years later, in the context of the devaluation crisis of September 1949, Harold Wilson, in a memorandum on Anglo-American economic relations, wrote that the necessary approximate balance in world production and trade which could make multilateralism work had 'never really existed since 1914'.[58] Even with the American loan, Marshall Aid, and other international financial institutions, recovery had been slow, because the 'pump needed far more priming than [was] thought'.[59] At the mid-point of these four years, in the summer of 1947, the hopes of early success through multilateralism had been shattered with the suspension of convertibility of sterling in August 1947. The expectation of general European recovery through the Marshall Plan was, in August 1947, just beginning to be sketched out by western European experts.[60] Meanwhile, the Labour government began to have greater (and partly unrealistic) objectives concerning Britain's Commonwealth relationship, the sterling area and the Colonial Empire. Their purpose was to complement and not to displace trade with a recovered western Europe. The aim was to become as independent as possible of assistance from the US after Marshall Aid came to an end.

As early as January 1947, Bevin had suggested western European economic cooperation (without prejudicing Commonwealth links) as a possible alternative in case the ITO negotiations failed. The rest of the Cabinet preferred to await the outcome of the ITO negotiations.[61] As the months rolled by after the fuel crisis of the winter, problems proliferated. The American loan was rapidly exhausted. Domestic production and the export drive did not match up to expectations.[62] The Ministry of Food received repeated warnings from the Treasury about the level of food imports from the dollar area. It is not surprising to observe, in this atmosphere, a perceptible emphasis on the development of Colonial food and raw material supplies.[63] It is clear that the argument that Colonial development was a solution to Britain's problems was not merely an afterthought.[64]

There had been no reference to it when the *Economic Survey* for 1947 was being drafted. However, only a month after its publication, Attlee approved a proposal from Creech Jones to set up a Colonial Development Corporation (CDC), on an economic and self-supporting basis, to produce foodstuffs, raw material and manufactures 'where supply to the U.K. or sale overseas will assist our balance of payments'.[65] The Cabinet paper on this stressed that an interdepartmental committee would frame guidelines, so that British supply requirements and the balance of payments of the sterling area as a whole were kept in view.[66] After consulting Bevin, Creech Jones got his Under-Secretary, Ivor Thomas, to put a memorandum to the Cabinet arguing that Britain 'should try to re-establish and indeed improve upon the prewar position in which exports of primary produce from the colonies to America were among our principal earners of dollars, the colonies in general having a large favourable balance with dollar countries which they spent mainly in the sterling area'.[67]

Cutting across the spectrum of right and left, spanning the gap between Bevin and Bevan, there was, from mid-1947 onwards, a quest for salvation by means of the sterling-area Commonwealth and Empire, without, of course, turning one's back on Europe. Bevan's intervention in Cabinet early in August showed a hankering after a closed sterling-area bloc.[68] Bevin, in a speech to the Southport Trades Union Congress on 3 September, did some personal kite-flying about a customs union of the Commonwealth and Empire and persuaded the Cabinet to set up a study group on its feasibility.[69] The constant US pressure to eliminate Imperial preferences appeared particularly distasteful when William Clayton, the US trade negotiator at Geneva, repeated them in the crisis month of August with an arm-twisting suggestion that otherwise Britain might not get Marshall Aid.[70] British resentment at this was shown in refusing to yield on any Colonial preferences.[71] Only when the US agreed to relax the legislation requiring the compulsory use of synthetic rubber in American industry and permit a greater use of natural rubber, did the British government, happier at the prospect of more dollars from Malayan rubber, agree to the reduction of Colonial preferences.[72]

Political developments in Malaya and Central Africa were also adversely affected by this preoccupation with the production of dollar-earning commodities like rubber, tin, copper and chromium, but as the position in these areas was complicated from the beginning by suspicion and hostility among ethnic groups, the government's options and decisions in these territories are discussed separately below.

The general idea of a Colonial–Commonwealth endeavour for sterling-area development for mutual benefit, and in cooperation with western Europe too, was announced with a fanfare of bipartisan enthusiasm supported by the back-benchers of both parties.[73] It was given a sharp edge by the simultaneous hardening of the Cold War, with the foundation of the Cominform in October 1947, and the Communist seizure of power in Czechoslovakia in March 1948. Labour ministers were as opposed to western Europe becoming 'permanent pensioners on the United States' as they were of allowing Soviet communism to spread any further.[74] There was general approval in the Labour Cabinet of

Bevin's strong ideological condemnation of the Soviet Union from a social-democratic standpoint. Most western European countries, Bevin wrote, had been 'nurtured on civil liberties and on the fundamental human rights'. He added:

> Provided we can organize a Western European system . . . it should be possible to develop our own power and influence equal to that of the United States of America and the USSR. We have the material resources in the Colonial Empire, if we develop them, and by giving a spiritual lead now we should be able to carry out our task in a way which will show clearly that we are not subservient to the United States of America or to the Soviet Union.[75]

Colonial development was planned with this aim in mind. Official Labour party policy had earlier justified postponement of self-government for the 'primitive' colonies of Africa on the grounds of their social and economic backwardness, and had recommended a policy of balanced growth.[76] The policy then followed was geared to British requirements. The Economic Policy Committee of the Cabinet approved the report of the Plowden Committee which stressed that, for the present, attention should be focused not on the long-range problem of Colonial development but on the short-term problem of solving the dollar gap of the sterling area. This could 'require a particular bias to be given to colonial economic development'. Since without sacrificing British standards of consumption, Britain would not be able to provide finance for Colonial development, grants would be given only for projects yielding a rapid return.[77] A private letter of Lord Addison on the dollar problem shows his great expectations of getting food and raw material out of 'many hitherto far too neglected parts of the colonial territories'.[78] Lord Listowel, the Minister of State for Colonies, noted that the House of Lords was not interested in Colonial political affairs but in Colonial economic development.[79] A year later, Herbert Morrison, worried about Britain's dollar deficit and embarrassed at the idea of asking the US for more direct aid, suggested to Attlee that one way of getting 'the Americans to go on financing the world with dollars as Marshall Aid taper[ed] off' would be to respond urgently to unofficial American feelers on private American dollar investment in the British colonies.[80]

There was awareness at the highest level, periodically prompted by Colonial Office civil servants, that charges of exploitation must be avoided. While approving of the Colonial Development Corporation (CDC), Bevin asked Creech Jones to see that it did not become like the old chartered companies, and Shinwell wished to ensure fair working conditions for its employees. Creech Jones assured them that the Corporation would have to follow local labour and welfare legislation (much of which had been reformed by the Labour government).[81] On these grounds, he rejected the request of the chairman of the CDC for a completely free hand.[82] Even as the Cabinet approved the joint Cripps–Bevin paper for western European economic cooperation with the Colonial territories, it put on record that in opening talks with other European Colonial powers 'any suggestions that colonial territories were to be exploited for the benefit of Europe should be avoided'.[83]

At the same time, riots and disturbances broke out in Accra, the capital of the 'model' African colony of the Gold Coast, which shook the British government. Only four months before, the acting governor had warned that 'a fairly vigorous reaction' and a decline of confidence in constitutional progress was likely to happen if, despite higher export prices for cocoa, the purchasing power of the average man stagnated or declined.[84] The Colonial Office had sent a copy of the governor's despatch to certain Treasury officials hoping that it would be 'good for [their] education'.[85] After the disturbances the commission of inquiry under Aiken Watson recommended further constitutional and political progress to remove the frustration of the politically conscious intelligentsia. These recommendations were modified, but generally approved, by an all-African committee of local experts (the Coussey Committee) whose report was ready by the autumn of 1949. In the meanwhile the Cold War made Labour ministers even more sensitive to charges of exploitation.

In the series of memoranda concerning propaganda against Soviet Communism early in 1948, Bevin had stressed the need to reply to Soviet attacks on British Colonial policy.[86] He took particular interest (even in administrative details) in the education and accommodation of Colonial students in Britain to keep them immune from Communist influence.[87] In the context of the Cold War and the events in the Gold Coast, the credibility of British social democracy in the Colonial territories could only be sustained if the political process started in February 1947 by Creech Jones's despatch on local self-government in the African colonies was not only implemented but accelerated.[88]

Attlee noted with concern that there was 'considerable talk in the colonies of "exploitation" of the Colonial peoples in order to help Britain out of her difficulties' and that the Soviet Union was making use of this.[89] Shortly afterwards, in October 1948, Creech Jones told the Cabinet the views of the unofficial members of the various African delegations who had met for the Africa Conference in London. While they were prepared to reject the exploitation charges, they were afraid that 'when the immediate demand for increased production of certain dollar-earning and dollar-saving commodities became less acute, the local industries would be left to their fate without protection and without adequate markets'. Creech Jones could offer some security through bulk purchase and long-term contracts, but as regards the demand for more capital and consumer goods imports (against their sterling balances) he could help only if he had the cooperation of those departments of the British government which controlled the supplies.[90]

The basic contradiction between the interests of these other ministries and the political preoccupations of the Colonial Office was again evident at a meeting of the Economic Policy Committee of the Cabinet in November 1948. Many members wanted greater central direction from the Colonial Office over local governments on matters such as the greater mobilization of local resources through taxation. Opposition to centralism was voiced on the grounds that it violated 'the fundamental principle of Colonial policy to attempt at this stage to treat the Colonial governments as subordinate departments of His Majesty's Government'.[91] Similar political arguments made a study group under Harold Wilson, President of the Board of Trade, reject the idea of a customs union of Britain and the colonies. 'Politically it would be suspected in the more advanced Colonies and it would be excessively awkward to leave them out and to have only a partial union.'[92]

The opposition of the Colonial Office to the use of all colonies for the benefit of Britain extended to resistance to American pressure for letting in private capital. Creech Jones's official guidelines, drafted in reply to Morrison's suggestions on this, argued that private investors would be welcome as long as they fitted in with Colonial development plans, followed local regulations on labour and welfare and observed a moratorium on the repatriation of capital for ten years.[93] In an undated draft of a speech (written probably around 1949), Creech Jones mentioned that the Americans ought to understand and appreciate that Britain had her own form of the doctrine of 'states rights' in the colonies.[94]

The main injustice perpetrated on some of the colonies in the name of economic development before self-government stemmed from the structure of the sterling area, and the sterling area dollar pool. The sterling area included the Colonial Empire, all Commonwealth countries except Canada and a few other countries. Multilateral transactions were permitted within it, and the dollar earnings of the entire area were pooled together. In the period between 1945 and 1950 some countries were persistently in deficit in their balance of payments on current account with the dollar area, whereas others like Malaya, the Rhodesias and Ceylon tended to run a surplus. The slowness of post-war recovery in Europe prevented Britain from meeting the pent-up demand for manufactured goods in the primary producing parts of the sterling area. Even after Marshall Aid, the efforts to narrow the dollar gap between Britain and the US by an export drive, and at the same time to supply South Asia and the colonies with the goods they demanded, caused considerable strain.[95]

In 1946, Hugh Dalton would have been quite happy to scale down the accumulated sterling balances of India and the colonies. Strong arguments from Sir Sidney Caine at the Colonial Office, and equally strong pressure from the Indian side prevented that from happening.[96] From mid-1947 onwards, however, the differential advantage that political independence brought with it was seen in the way that India and Malaya were treated. India was treated more gently (even when she exceeded her agreed dollar quota). Malaya had only a very limited access to dollar imports, despite the fact that she was always earning a dollar surplus.[97] Other colonies like the Gold Coast were in a similar situation. This gentler treatment of the South-Asian countries was dictated by economic and political considerations. Attlee considered retention of India within the Commonwealth to be vital for political, economic and strategic reasons at a time when China was going Communist and a Communist insurgency movement had broken out in Malaya.[98] Any rough treatment of India's sterling balances might lead to the expropriation of British investments in India.[99] Agreeing to India's requests for extra food imports from the dollar area in 1947 and 1948 was expected to soothe the atmosphere while the question of India's membership of the Commonwealth was still uncertain.[100] Though republican India's adhesion to the Commonwealth was unaccompanied by any commitment to Commonwealth defence, the Labour government considered it a psychological and diplomatic victory.

At the Commonwealth Finance Ministers' Conference in July 1949 (hastily summoned to discuss the dollar shortage of the sterling area and a precursor of the devaluation of sterling the following September) no member state offered to cut their dollar imports by more than the others.[101] Yet before the conference, the Colonies had already been instructed by a directive from London to make cuts in their dollar-import programme which amounted to an overall cut of 10 per cent in their import programme, throwing their development plans out of gear.[102] Pakistan had brought up the question of help to the less developed Dominions, but Creech Jones reminded the Conference that the Colonies had the same problems as India and Pakistan.[103]

Until the devaluation crisis the ministers had periodically noted that some independent members of the Commonwealth were more spendthrift than others, while the Colonies as a whole were in surplus.[104] Not until the Ministerial Conference of July 1949 was a general appeal for economy made, and no institutional means of keeping the sovereign nations of the sterling area under control could be developed. The fact that only some Commonwealth countries had prior knowledge of the decision to devalue did not help in that direction.

Harold Wilson wrote of the sterling area dollar pool in September 1949: 'Pooling of dollars by the sterling area may offend United States prejudices, but it represents a rough and ready way of allocating dollars among several major countries according to their needs.'[105] It was certainly rough and ready. Rough on the dollar-surplus colonies because the others were only too ready to spend the surplus.

III

Even when allowance is made for the distortions caused in the Labour party's programme for 'planned progress in the colonies' by its wish to maintain the sterling area Commonwealth, and even when we recognize the political sagacity shown in the Gold Coast, there remain a number of important areas (Malaya, Central Africa, Kenya and Bechuanaland) where the British government succumbed to the pressure of vested interests whose objectives coincided with its own economic or military aims. All these territories (except Bechuanaland) were ethnically mixed, with the racial groups at different levels of social and political development.

In Malaya and Singapore the pre-war British policy of indirect rule through a decentralized administration ensured the survival of the Malayan Sultans in most areas.[106] The British community dominated both the bureaucracy and business, though prominent businessmen were also to be found among locally-born or immigrant Chinese. By 1945 the indigenous Malay community comprised about 42 per cent of the population. The Malays were relatively indifferent to the rapid collapse of British power under Japanese attack, but the Chinese had resisted the Japanese, and the predominantly Chinese Malayan Communist party (MCP) had played a part in this.

The wartime Coalition Cabinet planned to create a unitary state which would include Singapore, with common citizenship for all races and a political structure in which the Sultans' powers were to be curtailed and the franchise democratized.[107] This was in line with Labour party policy on Malaya.[108] The Malayan Union Constitution, promulgated early in 1946, was, however, in the process of being abandoned by August. Fear of being swamped in their own homeland by a majority of Chinese and Indians led to the rapid emergence of a Malay nationalist party (UMNO) with which a new constitutional settlement was negotiated. Its broad outlines were ready by February 1947. Its citizenship laws had a marked pro-Malay bias, and although it was ultimately to be based on an elected legislature, at that time the legislative assembly had a majority of nominated members. Within two months of the inauguration of this constitution in January 1948, the MCP had started an insurrection which did not end in the lifetime of the Labour government, nor in that of its successor.[109]

Critical judgements have emphasized Britain's need for Malaya's dollar earnings. They have ranged from a description of the first proposals of early 1946 as annexationist imperialism to an interpretation of the *volte-face* and the pro-Malay bias of the second constitution as a design to curb the increasing powers of the Communist-influenced Malayan trade union movement. (The working class was predominantly Chinese and Indian in origin with the Malays comprising only 17.5 per cent of the labour force.)[110] Since the new citizenship laws gave very little scope to the Chinese and were not liberalized until 1952, and since it is accepted that UMNO, though a mass party, was led by western-educated members of the traditional Malay élite,[111] it can be argued that for the sake of dollars from rubber and tin the Labour government divided and ruled, with nominated representatives of the old British business community and the UMNO leadership as its main collaborators. The official version of the Malayan political troubles of the spring of 1948, in contrast, was that a Soviet-inspired insurrection had brought the Cold War to a turbulent area where the government was trying to proceed with its reforms.

On some points there is now little dispute. The demonetization of the wartime Japanese currency (designed to hurt Japanese collaborators and also weaken the MCP) actually led to a transfer of real resources to the returning British, and the burden of inflation was borne by the Malayan labouring and low-paid salaried classes. It has also been convincingly shown that Malayan reconstruction after the war was hampered because Malaya did not have free access to her dollar earnings.[112] The hitherto unused evidence from the Colonial Office, however, shows that a Machiavellian design to divide and rule for the sake of dollars was not a decisive influence during the period of constitution-making prior to early 1947.

Concern for efficiency, democracy and modernization (and not dollar-earning) was behind the decision to create a Malayan Union with a centralized administration.[113] As the ministers discussed the campaign against the Union by the Sultans, old pro-Sultan retired officials and UMNO, what they most disliked were the traditionalist pro-Sultan appeals, and what they anxiously noted were reports that UMNO had become an umbrella organization of Malayan nationalism which was as widespread as it was unexpected. They were reluctant to let it become anti-British in the way that the Indonesians had become anti-Dutch at that time.[114] When the revised proposals were presented to the Cabinet, it was stressed that with regards to nominations to the assembly there should be no mention of interest groups lest it encourage too sectional an approach; while special provisions for Malayans in the citizenship rules were justified as they had nowhere else to go, there should be further consultations about these rules with other communities before finalization. In any case, children of citizens would automatically become citizens. 'This will encourage the growth in [sic] course of time of an increasing body of men and women irrespective of race or creed, who will regard citizenship as a birthright, and an effective bond of common loyalty will then be created.'[115]

Governor Sir Edward Gent had achieved an understanding with UMNO after much tough bargaining and was reluctant to jeopardize it by further talks with non-Malay elements unless UMNO consented.[116] Two loose-knit associations representing Chinese and Indian communities, some radical Malay groups and pro-Communist labour organizations put forward alternative proposals, with an emphasis on citizenship for all residents and constitutional guarantees about a minimum wage.[117] Malcolm MacDonald, the Governor-General of South-east Asia, Creech Jones and Attlee all advised Gent against giving them an open rebuff lest a Communist movement as equally unexpected as UMNO might emerge.[118] However, Gent would not give any respectability to organizations with Communist associations.[119] The parliamentary Under-Secretary of State for Colonies, Ivor Thomas, became concerned, after a visit to Malaya in February 1947, to ensure the unimpeded production of rubber, 'a dollar earning commodity'. He also shared the anti-Chinese and pro-Malay bias of Gent, blamed the estate workers for strikes and frequent wage demands and recommended flogging and banishment as punishments for breaches of law and order.[120]

Creech Jones continued to try for a common citizenship formula throughout 1947 and was anxious that elections should be held as early as possible.[121] Unofficial warning by the economist T. N. Silcock that the local authorities were thinking too much in racial stereotypes impressed him, but his advisers thought that the men on the spot knew best.[122] The result was predictable. When the predominantly Chinese MCP started its insurgency, all classes of the Chinese community were relatively uncooperative towards the counter-insurgency efforts for nearly two years afterwards.[123] In March 1949, while commenting on the strain felt by the European settlers, 'on whom the whole rubber and tin economy depended', Creech Jones despaired of getting help from the Chinese community and wondered whether Britain would not be 'faced with a long war of attrition'.[124] Elections could not be held during this period. Despite efforts to create non-Communist trade unions with the help of visits by British trade-unionists, the gap between workers' earnings and employers' profits was wide. In 1950, rubber workers had benefited somewhat by an arbitration award made by Silcock, but the British tin companies were distributing dividends which, according to the governor, were 'on a dangerously high scale' (between 50 and 65 per cent). He added: 'It must be obvious that success against Communism in Malaya and the continuation of such exploitation on behalf of United Kingdom interests are mutually exclusive.'[125]

After a visit to Malaya in 1950, the new Secretary of State for Colonies, James Griffiths, recognized the need for new political alternatives. He resisted European demands for a public declaration that British rule in Malaya would be maintained for another twenty-five years. He reported: 'Too many of the European population were inclined to hope for a return to the conditions which existed in Malaya before the war. The government would have to make it clear that they had different aims.' These aims included acceleration of the process towards self-government, breaking down the resistance of employers to trade-unionism and convincing 'the workers in Malaya that a non-Communist regime offered them greater opportunities for economic and social betterment than any Communist regime'.[126] To have to state these at the end of a five-year period of Labour rule was an implicit admission of failure.

IV

In southern and eastern Africa, apart from the problem of immigrant European and Asian communities (especially in Kenya and the two Rhodesias), there were other obstacles to a progressive policy. The major difficulties were the racial policies of the Union of South Africa and its claim to the High Commission territories of Bechuanaland, Basutoland and Swaziland, the self-governing status enjoyed by settler-dominated Southern Rhodesia and the fact that the external trade of Northern Rhodesia could only be carried on through the south. In the post-war period these problems were aggravated by additional factors. Wartime assistance given by the Union of South Africa to Britain made her unwilling to offend the former on any international issue. It kept a low profile in the India–South Africa dispute at the United Nations (UN) and supported the South African demand for incorporating South-west Africa into the Union, a demand rejected overwhelmingly at the UN.[127] Despite misgivings at the victory of Dr Malan's Nationalist party in 1948, a lingering hope remained that the pendulum would swing back, and so Britain tried to avoid offending South Africans whenever possible. In June 1950, sometime after having debarred Seretse Khama from the chieftainship of the Bamangwato tribe in Bechuanaland because of his marriage to an Englishwoman, the Secretary of State for Commonwealth Relations noted the universal dislike of mixed marriages among Europeans in South Africa, and added: 'We must also do our utmost to keep the Union solidly in the Commonwealth for strategic, economic, and other reasons.'[128]

As we have seen, the attraction of East and Central Africa providing a British power zone had been suggested by Attlee and Bevin in 1946, and the officials had considered it as a practical possibility when the economy was developed to defray the cost.[129] The Colonial Office handled the defence of East Africa, Northern Rhodesia and Nyasaland together.[130] In October 1947 the War Office suggested bringing Southern Rhodesia into the defence scheme; Andrew Cohen, head of the Africa section of the Colonial Office, considered it worthwhile, though he had some doubts about the native policy of Southern Rhodesia.[131]

Since 1945, the European settlers in Northern Rhodesia had had an unofficial majority in the local legislature. The wartime need for copper production had strengthened the bargaining power of the European Mineworkers' Union, slowed down the prospect of African advancement in the copperbelt, and occasioned the entry of white trade union leaders like Roy Welensky and

Brian Goodwin into the political arena.[132] Andrew Cohen believed that the recent ex-service immigrants in Southern Rhodesia were less racially prejudiced than the apparently increasing stream of Afrikaner immigrants from the Union of South Africa.[133] On this assumption, and on the information that Sir G. Huggins, the Prime Minister of Southern Rhodesia, was supported by such British immigrants, Cohen convinced himself that a Southern Rhodesia under Huggins, augmented by more British immigration, would be a useful partner with Northern Rhodesia and Nyasaland in a regional bloc as a counterweight to the Union of South Africa.[134]

This belief in the superior virtues of the post-war British immigrants appears to have been just a personal impression and is belied by the paper on racial prejudice in Britain prepared by the Colonial Office in May 1946. That referred to the difficulties in recruiting coloured men in the armed forces and of the 'unfortunate series of racial incidents' in the Royal Air Force since December 1945.[135] When the problem of coloured recruitment in the forces was raised by Creech Jones in the Cabinet a year later, the ministers representing the services, with the exception of Philip Noel-Baker (Secretary of State for Air at that time), were reluctant to hasten the pace of recruitment because of rank-and-file prejudice. Anxious to avoid any stigma of colour prejudice the Cabinet asserted the non-racial principle in such a way as to give the authorities discretion in such cases.[136]

Despite occasional proddings from ministers, the desire to reconcile local settler opinion was characteristic of civil servants in Whitehall, even including Andrew Cohen. When the formation of trade unions among African railwaymen in Northern Rhodesia was proposed in late 1945, Cohen 'made the reference a guarded one' because it would raise 'political objections . . . particularly in relation to the copperbelt'.[137] Nevertheless, British trade union organizers were sent out and by March 1949 more than 50 per cent of the African labour force was unionized.[138] Yet the industrial colour bar could not be breached. Detailed suggestions by the British trade-unionist Andrew Dagleish after two visits to the territory were promptly denounced by Roy Welensky.[139] In 1948, Creech Jones, prodded by the Fabian Colonial Bureau, tried without success to find a generally acceptable formula for the implementation of the Dagleish report.[140] Pressure from the Ministry of Supply in Britain for an uninterrupted flow of copper production and the intransigence of the European mineworkers effectively stopped progress.[141] In October 1950 a civil servant in the Colonial Office admitted that progress had been negligible, but displayed characteristic caution in opposing the outspoken parliamentary Under-Secretary of State, J. Dugdale, who had written that effective action on the report would be sufficient to stop Afrikaner immigration into skilled jobs.[142] James Griffiths despaired of governmental action and tried to use international trade union pressure on the European Mineworkers' Union to end the colour bar.[143] Nothing came of this.

In sharp contrast to the accelerated plans for Africanization of the civil services in West Africa after the constitutional changes in the Gold Coast and Nigeria, plans for African education and political advancement in Central Africa were modest, probably because immigrant communities were already in power.[144] The local governments aimed 'first to educate Africans to fill the more responsible clerical posts' and assumed that 'many years' would pass before Africans could hold senior government appointments.[145] African political activity was limited to African local councils, and only two nominated Africans and two Europeans representing African interests were in the European-dominated legislative council. The proposal to grant Northern Rhodesian Africans British nationality under the British Nationality Act of 1948 alarmed the settlers lest some Africans would qualify to vote in the European constituency. Civil servants, including Andrew Cohen, were prepared to meet them half way, and Cohen opposed the common roll, fearing a European backlash. Creech Jones had to step in and write: 'If the seats of Europeans in their small constituencies depend on winning the goodwill of the few Africans admitted to the franchise, their work in the Legislative Council would be tempered with some regard to African development.'[146] His insistence on the argument that 'the franchise [was] symbolic of dignity and equality and racial non-discrimination' prevented official wavering, and by his personal diplomacy during a visit to Northern Rhodesia he persuaded the local authorities to ignore the settlers' protests on this issue.[147]

In July 1948, at a meeting at the Colonial Office, the African representative objected when the Northern Rhodesian politicians raised the question of a Central African Federation.[148] In October 1948, against the background of the Africa conference and efforts at colonial development, Creech Jones wanted some form of regional cooperation which would safeguard native policy but derive the benefits of a large unit. 'Our strategic needs in Africa, the importance of more thoroughgoing development, the desirability of certain common services and regional approach – suggest the need of a closer association of these territories.'[149] He added, 'I am certain we must not advance an inch if it involves us in any surrender of African rights'.[150] Cohen agreed and, against the background of Dr Malan's victory in South Africa, pinned his faith on Huggins of Southern Rhodesia turning to the North to form part of a British bloc.[151] This idea of a British bloc was an argument pressed by the officials in 1950 when maximum pressure was exerted by the settlers for a decision on federation.

In East Africa, the European settlers had managed to increase their representation on the inter-territorial council, which provided the mechanism for regional cooperation. In defending this change in the House of Commons on the ground of efficiency Creech Jones reassured the party experts on Colonial affairs by affirming that Britain would have full powers in all matters affecting African interests.[152] In fact the emphasis laid on economic development by the Governor of Kenya, Sir Philip Mitchell, who was also the chairman of the inter-territorial council, led to a proliferation of technical and developmental officers from overseas without much attempt being made to enlist African participation in the many changes that were taking place.[153] Mitchell's stern paternalism led him to scoff at the sympathy shown by the Watson Commission on the Gold Coast for the frustration of the African intelligentsia. He thought that the Labour government, by speaking about African self-government, had encouraged subversive elements.[154] While Jomo Kenyatta had been allowed to come back to Kenya, Mitchell did not give him much encouragement.[155]

In 1950 all over eastern and southern Africa, critical choices on race relations could no longer be shirked. Three issues called for decision. First, in Bechuanaland there was the question of Seretse Khama's succession to the chieftainship. Second, Southern Rhodesia tried to force the pace for a favourable decision on federation by giving notice to withdraw from the Central African Council, and also by displaying a lack of cooperation in inter-territorial projects.[156] Third, in East Africa an extreme statement by some European settlers temporarily united Asians and Africans. The result was the passage of a resolution in April 1950 of no confidence in the Europeans.[157]

Cabinet discussions on the case of Seretse Khama show that right from the beginning the adverse reaction in South Africa was an important factor. Only at Creech Jones's insistence was an immediate decision to persuade Seretse to give up his title postponed in favour of a judicial inquiry, and it was explicitly recorded that the issue was not to be the merits or demerits of mixed marriages.[158] To the acute embarrassment of the government, the inquiry committee, while accepting the legality and suitability of Seretse, recommended withholding the title precisely on the political grounds that it would offend South Africa and Southern Rhodesia.[159] The government rejected these arguments but did not want to admit that fact lest it spoil its relations with these countries.[160] When a White Paper giving reasons for keeping the chieftainship in suspension for five years was in draft form, some ministers suggested that since suppression of the report of the judicial inquiry committee would cause adverse comment (which it did), it would be better to publish it and indicate the government's points of difference. This was rejected lest it should bring these points into prominence.[161]

Later on in the year, apropos of how Britain should vote at the UN over the question of South-west Africa, James Griffiths and Aneurin Bevan argued that the economic and strategic advantages of British support for South Africa were outweighed by the adverse effects on the British Colonial territories.

Bevan added that the views of many supporters of the Labour party had to be taken into account. The majority of the Cabinet disagreed because South Africa was of great strategic value in 'any struggle against Communism' and because of 'the great value of the military support she seemed likely to promise in the Middle East'.[162] Sir Evelyn Baring, the British High Commissioner in South Africa had noted only a few months earlier: 'So long as the Cold War continues, any U.K. policy which can be represented as directed against Communism will be certain of the maximum possible collaboration from the South African government . . .'[163] The majority of the Labour Cabinet had drifted into a position where fighting the Cold War was an end in itself regardless of the issues for which it was fought.

The paradox was that at the same time as support of South Africa was deemed essential, officials were justifying the Central African Federation proposed by the Rhodesian settlers in the fond hope that it would create a counterweight to the Union of South Africa. The brief prepared by Cohen and Lambert in the Colonial Office for the ministers' meeting with Huggins and Welensky in April and May 1950 started by arguing in favour of a 'solid British bloc of territories in Central Africa . . . to resist economic and political pressure from the Union of South Africa'. Recent transport bottlenecks could be eased by a healthy cooperation between the two territories. The memorandum added that if the British government was itself convinced of the wisdom of the federal idea, then it was 'under no obligation to accept African views'.[164] With this élitist, technocratic, imperial brief before them, Griffiths and Gordon-Walker met Huggins in April and Welensky in May. The Rhodesians asserted that the resources of the territories could only be developed by European capital and entrepreneurship and therefore the Europeans must have firm reassurances of support, especially in view of the progress made towards self-government in West Africa. The British ministers would not budge from their position that African interests would have to be protected and that further political advance for the Europeans in Northern Rhodesia was contingent on corresponding advance for the Africans.[165] But it is possible that these ministers did not disagree about the importance of European entrepreneurship in Central Africa. Even Creech Jones had written, only some nine months before, 'progress depends very largely on the sound relationship of Europeans with Africans, and the realization of a partnership which will give permanent place to European conceptions of development and enterprise in industry and agriculture'.[166]

A final decision was postponed pending an official fact-finding inquiry about the federation. The civil servants wished to handle the settlers gently.[167] Griffiths would have preferred to emphasize British responsibility to the African in the strongest terms, but in announcing the fact-finding committee to the colonies, his language was moderated so as not to offend the Northern Rhodesian settlers.[168]

The embittered relations between Europeans, Asians and Africans in East Africa made Griffiths hold a series of meetings, from May 1950, with the officials and governors concerned. He decided that a public statement of principles was required and got it cleared by the Cabinet. The statement, made on 13 December 1950, stressed that everyone, of whatever race, who had made East Africa his home had a stake in the country and that African social and economic advance should take place in such a way as to enable all communities to live in harmony. The likelihood of the Africans reaching the stage of self-government in the near future was ruled out and paternalist control from London was reaffirmed. It was not a statement likely to appeal to Kenyatta and his followers and its main aim was to prevent a South African orientation on the part of the settlers.[169]

V

Preaching racial harmony in the colonies was easier than practising it at home. The Colonial Office and its ministers were anxious for racial harmony in Britain in order to project a more favourable image in the colonies. Yet the natural constituents of the Labour party, the British working class, did not always express full support for a multiracial Britain.

At the ideological level Attlee recognized the importance of multiracialism. In the wartime Coalition he had criticized the Indian Viceroy Linlithgow for racialist attitudes.[170] He was very pleased at the adhesion of Asian countries to the Commonwealth.[171] During his ideological counter-offensive against Soviet propaganda among colonial peoples, Bevin noted a Nigerian official report which said that 'If it should ever become necessary for us to take a line which would be openly unfriendly to the Soviet Union, we should have the greatest difficulty in putting it across'. This would be due to Britain's inability to meet the Soviet claim to sponsor racial equality.[172]

In November 1945, C. W. Greenidge, a member of the Fabian Colonial Bureau and secretary of the Anti-slavery and Aborigine Protection Society, asked for legislation against racial discrimination in Britain.[173] Three years later, after having examined the evidence, one senior official (Sir Charles Jefferies) and one minister (Lord Listowel) favoured legislation, especially laws against discriminatory clauses in leases or other tenancy agreements, for their 'good effect on public opinion at home and in the colonies'.[174] Creech Jones doubted its practicality and Listowel was unsure about getting parliamentary time that session.[175]

The complexity of racial problems in Britain was further highlighted in 1948. There was panic among eleven Labour MPs when the ship the *Empire Windrush* brought a number of Jamaican job-seekers to Britain. The MPs (of which half were trade-unionists from working-class districts) wanted a ban on immigration so that Britain could continue to enjoy the absence of interracial conflict, and suggested that Colonial Development and Welfare grants ought to provide for the Jamaicans in their homeland.[176] The reaction of the Economic Policy Committee of the Cabinet was also one of panic. Some members suggested that instead of letting them settle in Britain they should be sent to Tanganyika to grow groundnuts![177] As Attlee referred the letter of the MPs to Creech Jones, he wondered whether there was any organization behind the immigration.[178] Creech Jones disabused him of that and took personal care to vet Attlee's reply to the MPs. Attlee finally wrote:

> It is traditional that British subjects, whether of Dominion or Colonial origin (and of whatever race or colour) should be freely admissible to the United Kingdom. That tradition is not, in my view, to be lightly discarded, particularly at a time when we are importing foreign labour in large numbers. It would be fiercely resented in the colonies themselves, and it would be a great mistake to take any measure which would weaken the goodwill and loyalty of the colonies towards Great Britain.

He added that only if 'a great influx of undesirables' occurred the policy might, 'however reluctantly', be modified, but this would not happen 'except on really compelling evidence' which did not exist then. Furthermore, all the Jamaicans who had come were skilled and easily absorbed into various occupations.[179] After this, Attlee circulated Creech Jones's memorandum to the Cabinet for information and avoided further discussion.[180] The Prime Minister's decision to play down this episode must be seen in the context of contemporary developments. In June 1948 the riots in the Gold Coast were only three months old, the Malayan insurgency had started and British plans for African development were under attack as exploitation. Attlee was also keen to retain India in the Commonwealth.

News about labour shortage in Britain attracted many potential immigrants. One stowaway who had landed said, when questioned, that 'he had come in answer to Sir Stafford Cripps' appeal for textile workers'.[181] Some Colonial governors made inquiries about openings in Britain for their surplus labour.[182] This resulted in an interdepartmental working party on this problem.[183] The whole question of continuing the policy of free access or repatriating colonials was also discussed by another committee in February 1949, at the request of some police commissioners to the Home Office.[184] These investigations and discussions brought out two significant trends.

In the first place, there was strong opposition from trade unions to coloured workers. Informal soundings by the National Union of Mineworkers and that of Agricultural Workers revealed this, as did reports from the regional controllers of the Ministry of Labour.[185] The final report of the committee on the employment of colonial workers wrote:

The leaders of the Trade Union movement generally take the line that while they themselves have no objection in principle to the introduction of coloured workers from British territories, the decision whether or not to go on with a recruiting scheme must in every case be left to the local branch in the area of prospective employment. The local trade union officials usually say that they would help if they could but that the workers in their particular area are not prepared to accept coloured workers into their place of employment.[186]

In the second place, the Colonial Office representatives investigating the rules on stowaways and the repatriation of immigrants successfully upheld the principles of the British Nationality Act of 1948. They rejected the repatriation of the generation born of immigrant parents in Britain, and of able-bodied persons who were not a persistent charge on public funds.[187]

The entire controversy over immigration had overshadowed the original request for legislation against racial discrimination. The Fabian Colonial Bureau revived the issue in February 1949, when Lord Faringdon proposed a private member's bill in the House of Lords. Lord Listowel was willing to seek parliamentary time, but the Lord Chancellor objected on two counts: it was not practicable, and it went against the grain of lawyers to pass legislation merely as a gesture, when there was no public demand for it.[188] In resisting the pressure of backbench MPs over the influx of Jamaicans in 1948, the government had upheld the special role that it had assigned to Britain within the Commonwealth. The failure both to press the trade unions to take coloured colleagues and to take steps towards anti-discriminatory legislation (especially in housing) showed, however, that for most members positive steps towards promoting the multiracial ideal took a low priority.

In discussions of immigration during two meetings of the Cabinet, held after the general election of 1950, worries were voiced by a substantial number of ministers. It is not possible to say whether it figured as an election issue at all. That it had introduced a disturbing element for Labour ministers, however, was plain enough. The first Cabinet (on 20 March 1950) was told of West Indian complaints about obtaining jobs. Its reaction was to note the 'serious difficulties' that would arise if coloured immigration were to continue.[189] For the next meeting Griffiths produced a memorandum describing his policy of dispersing immigrants from overcrowded areas and helping them to assimilate. He did not question the open-door policy. The memorandum was simply noted, not accepted. The discussion in the Cabinet 'turned mainly on the means of preventing any further increase in the coloured population of Britain'. Attlee was asked to review the situation.[190] At the same time, however, the growth of racial prejudice in some Commonwealth countries (especially the Union of South Africa) led to a remarkable demonstration by ninety-seven Labour MPs (including thirty-one trade union MPs), who signed an 'early day motion' on 26 February 1951 in favour of racial equality in the

Commonwealth.[191] It is quite likely that this partly neutralized the pressure of those who wished to restrict immigration and made Attlee decide that the situation had not changed materially since 1948. At a time when, in the international and Commonwealth arena, Britain was trying to live down the Seretse Khama episode and was preaching racial harmony in East and Central Africa, it was impolitic to suggest that Britain could not cope with a multiracial society.

VI

It has been argued that the 'Labour ministry decided that what the British Empire needed, even in epilogue or afterthought, was logic'.[192] Logic and consistency are precisely what the Labour government's record does not show. The reason for this is not the absence of thinking or planning by Labour ministers, especially those in charge of the dependent Empire, but the multiple contradictions in Britain's post-war imperial predicament. She aspired to a global role, but she was a debtor country. She thought herself to be the centre of the Commonwealth, but the reality was that the Commonwealth was a house with many independent mansions. She had made blueprints for planned progress in the colonies, but found her resources severely limited.

Whichever government had come to power, these would have been the contradictions in running an Empire. For a party with a working-class base, and some degree of commitment to Fabian gradualist ideology of reform, the burden of reforming the Empire proved too much. Where the Empire was relinquished gracefully, no problem arose. Where there was a wish to form power blocs and at the same time modernize the 'backward' people, scarcity of resources on the one hand, and the divergent expectations of the party's natural constituents and the élites who ruled the independent commonwealth countries, or who were aspirants after power in the dependent colonies, on the other hand, created potentially explosive situations. Wherever the policy-makers of a reformed Empire came in contact with the hard realities of valuable raw materials or exciting prospects of a great power role as the bastion of social democracy against communism, the reforming zeal petered out under pressure from vested interests. It was doubly unfortunate for the reformers that these strategically- or economically-valuable territories would also bristle with political tensions associated with multi-ethnic plural societies. The imperial role of the Labour government, then, is neither as unselfish as the official manifesto would lead us to believe, nor as single-mindedly Machiavellian as some of its critics have claimed, both then and now.

records up to the end of December 1950 were available for inspection at the time of research. The research on this paper was done while the author was Smuts Visiting Fellow in Commonwealth Studies in Cambridge, 1980–81, and he wishes to thank Cambridge University for the opportunity.

II

The working class in British society

7

Work and hobbies in Britain, 1880–1950

ROSS McKIBBIN

In 1856, R. W. Emerson concluded that while an Englishman might eat and drink 'not much more than another man' he laboured three times as much: everything in England 'is at a quick pace. They have reinforced their own productivity, by the creation of that marvellous machinery which differences this age from every other age.'[1] Fifty years later such a view was not the predominant one. If anything, conventional opinion held the reverse to be true: Englishmen laboured less hard than others; they were ill-adapted to even more marvellous machinery; their work irritated them; ingenious Americans and docile Germans passed them on all sides. The argument that industrial life and division of labour had become intolerably monotonous to many workers was, of course, a commonplace of the nineteenth century. When Marx wrote that 'the worker feels himself at home outside his work and feels absent from himself in his work' there were few who would not have conceded that he was at least partly right. By the end of the nineteenth century, when the British economy appeared to flag, it came to be argued not only that boredom demoralized the worker but that it also damaged the economy by undermining his efficiency. Thereafter it was implied in the reports of royal commissions, departmental committees of enquiry and delegations of concerned persons. It was, of course, argued explicitly as well, both by employers and by workers themselves. The London engineering employer A. Bergtheil told the Tariff Commission that not only was 'the foreign workman – I speak more particularly of the German and the Belgian – a more intelligent and better class of labourer . . . but he takes more actual interest in his work'.[2] At the same time, W. J. Davis of the Brassworkers' Union could write that Berlin brassworkers 'appear to enjoy their work more, and to be able to work more easily, and with more satisfaction, and also to have a better time than our brassworkers in Birmingham'.[3] Boredom had allegedly gruesome consequences: a decline in craft skills and inattention to detail and design,[4] irregular attendance at work and dogged resistance to technological changes that would further accelerate and decompose labour.

The doctrine that boredom makes men inefficient is a pretty simple one. It had, however, a more subtle variation whose proponents shifted the emphasis from work to leisure. In brief, they argued that the mental energies necessary for effective industrial work were being diverted to, and absorbed by, substitute work: by sport and by hobbies. This variant was a considerable advance on the argument from which it was derived. It accepted that the British working class was in fact more disciplined, more sober, more regular at attending work than it had been. Non-vocational interests rescued workers from the inanition of factory labour and from its usual antidote: the bottle. 'It would be pretty hard', C. B. Hawkins wrote, 'to show that the increasing sobriety of Norwich . . . does not owe something, at any rate, to this new habit of watching football matches.'[5] Proponents of this view even accepted that men were not always bored by formal work; they just did not care one way or the other. The Englishman, Margaret Loane thus wrote, liked work, as long as it was someone else's work he was doing.[6] In the Edwardian period it was Shadwell who argued the case most strongly, and although he was catholic enough to attack all classes, the weight of his assault fell heavily on the working class. Britain was, he argued, 'a nation at play'; Englishmen were still interested in beating records, but only sporting records; their competitive drives and ambitions now centred not on the workplace and its product but on cricket and football and their product, betting.[7] The case was even more violently urged at the end of our period. Writing with the admittedly grim post-war years still clearly in mind, and anxious to assert that the desire to work is culturally and not biologically determined, the industrial psychologist J. Cohen wrote that in Britain there was 'a universal spivery, with its major industry in gambling, horse-racing, dog-tracks, football pools etc. If half the working population spends a goodly proportion of leisure completing coupons for football pools, this can only mean that large numbers of workers are moved by the desire not to have to work.'[8] Even at first sight both Shadwell and Cohen over-argued their case,[9] but since it appeared to fit in with much other evidence it is a hypothesis worth examining. In this essay I would like to test it by trying to answer three questions. What is the evidence that hobbies began to occupy more and more of the British working man's waking time? Is there any evidence that interest in hobbies led to a deterioration in formal work? What satisfactions did hobbies provide in their relation to formal work?

At the outset we need to be clear as to what can legitimately be called a hobby. Until recently no distinction was commonly drawn between 'craft' hobbies and sporting interests: it was assumed that both demanded the same kind of energy and skill, or at least were the same kind of activity. How eclectic these activities were can be seen from the contents of the inaugural number of

Hobbies magazine (October 1895): fretwork and inlaying in wood (its celebratory project was a fretwork model of St Paul's Cathedral), photography for amateurs, stamps and stamp collecting, magic lanterns, bazaars and how to decorate them, cycling, football, athletics, bent iron work and so on.[10] C. E. B. Russell wrote of working-class 'pals' that 'they invariably spend the evening together and usually share the same hobby'[11] and in context it is clear that he meant the same interest. C. B. Hawkins put the cinema and music-hall on one side as 'amusements', and football, angling and hobbies (including in Norwich, of course, canary breeding) on the other as 'interests'.[12] As late as 1922, Margaret Phillips could make a similar distinction: between 'personal' interests, of which the basic was sex, but which also included the cinema (or both, presumably, at the same time) and 'objective' interests which in the case of young men 'may be an interest in sport, or in engineering and mechanical inventions connected with their work: in the case of girls an interest in housecraft or clothes'.[13] J. G. Leigh thought that most working men's hobby was sport and he conceded that it had all the satisfactions normally associated with a hobby.[14] What, then, were the satisfactions normally associated with a hobby? First, it was an activity freely chosen, though not exclusively practised in free time; it might, for example, be talked about at work. Second, it was neither random nor disorganized, but required regularity and physical and/or intellectual discipline. Third, it demanded knowledge and sustained interest. Finally, it was usually accompanied by the creation and discharge of some kind of mental or physical tension. All the activities I will discuss in this paper have these qualities, and if we argue that the following of a sport and the practising of a 'craft' hobby should both be classified in the same way, as hobbies, we are accepting a tradition that only the most up-to-date sociology has broken.[15]

It would be difficult to say exactly when hobbies as a significant activity outside formal work became widespread; contemporaries usually only notice these things after they have become frequently adopted; commercial institutions as often reflect as create a market: the publication of *Hobbies* magazine in 1895, for example, though indeed indicative, clearly post-dates the growth of organized hobbies. The New English Dictionary gives 1816 as the first year for which there is literary evidence of the word being used in its modern sense (Scott, *The Antiquary:* 'I quarrel with no man's hobby'). But there is a certain 'Englishness' about hobbies which suggests pre-nineteenth-century antecedents. In every European language the phrase for 'killing time' is the same – *tuer le temps, die zeit totschlagen*, etc. – but only English has the word 'hobby', which all others have eventually borrowed, even when, as in French, there were already antique words of some charm. Domestic gardening was always popular in the industrial towns wherever it was physically possible, and that popularity came from a long tradition of a competitive and refined artisanal horticulture.[16] Emerson noted in the early 1850s how passionately the

English of all classes decorated their homes and how fond they were of improving them.[17] The habit of 'pottering around the house', for which Dumazedier suggests there is no real European equivalent,[18] is clearly one of immense age. All forms of animal husbandry were ebullient English activities long before dog and pigeon breeding became working-class pastimes. Games and sports, of course, were endemic to English life. We must assume that the nineteenth century probably drew upon pre-industrial traditions which were only re-shaped, not made, in the last quarter of that century. What characterizes hobbies thereafter is their intellectual systematization, physical organization and commercial exploitation. To an extent they also became vicarious. With some the emphasis was increasingly upon individual effort and skill, for example with carpentry, gardening and dog-running. In others, most obviously sport, it was upon information and knowledge, and the individual was not so much a participant as an informed observer. The reshaping of these traditions seems to have taken place in the 1870s and 1880s. By 1885, T. H. S. Escott could write that there was no better way of measuring the advance in 'popular amusement' than by comparing the newspapers of 'to-day' with those of less than fifty years before.

> One would look in vain now for the announcements of pugilistic encounters between bruisers of established and growing reputation, cock-fights, dog-fights, and performances of terrier dogs . . . One would have looked in vain then for the accounts of cricket-matches . . . which now occupy entire pages of sporting journals; for the notices to excursionists that are a regular feature in every newspaper during the summer season; for the miscellaneous pro-grammes of picture exhibitions, lectures, theatres, music-halls . . . Within the last five-and-twenty years cricket and football clubs have been formed in all the towns and most of the villages of England.[19]

He pointed to the proliferation of reading rooms, clubs, lecture-halls in the north and the popularity of athletic sports of all kinds. In the potteries and around Manchester, 'rabbit-coursing, with a peculiar breed of little grey-hound, is much in vogue'.[20] By the 1890s it was assumed that a man would as like as not spend his leisure time on a hobby. To the members of the Royal Commission on Labour it went without saying that a man would dig in his lot, and they were surprised when this sometimes turned out not to be true.

> Then in your experience the workpeople have not ill-used the greater leisure they have had? – No, I do not think they have. There is no greater leisure now except the two hours . . . The men, then, in your experience have no more time to attend to their plots of land now than they had when you commenced operations? – There are not many plots in our district.[21]

Hobbies magazine was always insinuating that no fully-equipped human being could be without a hobby. 'The chief object of these articles on Pigeons', it wrote in January 1896, 'is to induce those readers who have no favourite hobby to try their hands at Pigeons . . .'[22]

There can be little doubt that from the 1880s onwards, substantial, and almost certainly increasing amounts of time were given to hobbies. In those industries where legislation or trade union pressure had significantly reduced working hours, make-work activities were often simply forced upon workmen. As Ernst Dückershoff noted of the Northumberland miners: 'Their spare time impels them to contrive things to smarten their homes.'[23] For children of skilled artisans (particularly) adoption of craft-hobbies was partly a result of parental training and partly the result of possession of a back garden. R. A. Bray wrote of artisanal gardens:

> This useful appendage to the dwelling even though shared by more than one family, opens out a rich field for the development of new interests. Rabbits are often kept in a hutch . . .; pigeons are hung in a cage just outside the back door; fowls are encouraged and even ducks may flourish with an occasional swim in a tub of water. A few flowers are grown in the garden, which in addition affords room for a mild game of cricket or football. All this may seem very trivial to the general reader, but as a matter of fact this small outgrowth of the dwellings possesses a significance not easily overestimated. The boys are indeed crushed out of the house, but can overflow into the yard, where various hobbies occupy their attention and invest the dwellings with a new colouring and a new importance.[24]

But for most working men and boys an overflow into the yard was not a possibility. As late as 1944, with the exception of Wales, in not one British industrial region was there a majority of households with a back garden.[25] This put allotments even more at a premium. From 1892, when Collings' Small Holdings Bill was finally enacted, there was a large and unsatisfied demand for urban allotments.[26] As with back yards, so with allotments: their ubiquity was exaggerated and their provision inequitable. The 1892 Act and the subsequent legislation of 1907–08 were not fully implemented until the First World War and local authorities were often less willing than private companies to provide plots: the railwaymen, and to a lesser extent the miners, became famous gardeners because their employers were fairly ready to rent out company land cheaply.[27] But employers had no doubt that allotments were popular and that men spent much time in them. C. J. Wilson, president of the South of Scotland Chamber of Commerce, argued the case for cooperative housing before the Royal Commission on Labour precisely because the houses had garden plots. 'Do they use their time in these plots? – Yes, greatly.'[28] The First and Second World Wars occasioned an increase in the number of allotments and there is no evidence that time occupied in their cultivation was in any way reduced. The post-war Departmental Committee of Inquiry into Allotments found that lot-holders spent around an hour-and-a-half per day on allotments in summer and almost as much in spring:

Hours spent on allotment by the average allotment holder (England and Wales)[29]

Season	Total time spent on allotments (hours per week)
Spring	10
Summer	12½
Autumn	8
Winter	3

What other spare-time activity, the Committee chirpily asked, 'receives so much attention from its adherents?'[30] In their study of the mining town, 'Ashton', Dennis and his colleagues found (in 1953) that some allotment-holders, though a minority, 'spend so much time there as to separate themselves from their families for considerable periods'[31] which is presumably one reason why they did it, and one reason why so many working-class wives were suspicious of their husbands' hobbies.[32]

How much time was spent on 'home-hobbies', repairing, making, decorating, tinkering, is, at least for the period before the 1950s, not known, except that it was extensive.[33] 'Private' hobbies were most resistant to amateur survey, particularly the most private of them all, betting.[34] This, however, is not true of animal raising: dog breeding, canary breeding and the prime 'fancy' itself, pigeon breeding, were necessarily active consumers of time, particularly if individuals were breeding for profit. Canary breeding, always satisfying and sometimes profitable, but also very difficult and chancy, could easily upset the domestic economy and force men to dodge formal work.[35] We have similar evidence about sporting hobbies. This was so partly because the late nineteenth-century absorption in sport was obvious to anyone with eyes to see, and partly because casual or 'boy' labour, the *locus classicus* for organized sport, was deemed to be an Edwardian social 'problem' and thus fit for study. To a foreigner like Dückershoff there was almost nothing to be said: 'all is sport in England. It is sucked in with the mother's milk.'[36] C. E. B. Russell noted that to most Manchester 'lads' outdoor games meant only one thing, football. 'Football is as popular in summer as in winter, and were it not for the fact that the rules governing the game prohibit the playing of games during the summer months, doubtless it would be played from one year's end to the other.'[37] Freeman wrote (in 1914) that 'football is the greatest single interest in the life of the ordinary working boy' and his printed diaries of working life emphatically support that judgement.[38] Paterson argued that the London working adolescents had three real interests: smoking, clothing and conversation. But in a boy's 'click' conversation, in effect, meant sport talk.

> For the greater part of the year football holds the stage. Cricket is never quite such an engrossing topic, though the fortunes of the Surrey county team are followed with that breathless and extravagant interest which demands a copy of every edition of the 'Star'. A most amazing knowledge is betrayed of the personal appearance, character, and moral weakness of each individual player . . . None of the Heads [his 'click'] are [sic] without a cricket or football guide in the inside pocket of his coat . . .
>
> This genius for hero-worship is not confined to the cricket or football fields. Boxers or wrestlers, runners and cyclists, weight-putters, and dog-fanciers . . . are in the sweetstuff shop assumed to be national celebrities, their times, weights and records stored away in minds that seem capable of containing little else.[39]

Freeman, like Paterson, noted that attention was not confined to sports that could actually be played. For industrial workers before 1914, cricket, for example, was not a game that most knew. Many young workers could hardly tell one end of a bat from the other; yet, Freeman wrote,

> it is strange that in the face of this, and the comparatively small extent to which boys play the game, they nearly all take a great interest in County Cricket. The evening papers are eagerly read each night, and scores of boys who never play themselves are able to name at any time the runs made by prominent cricketers . . . and in seasons like the present, discuss readily and ably the claims of the individual members of the Australian cricket team to be considered really worthy exponents of the game.[40]

Alfred Williams was not the first, but was probably the best placed, to assert that sport drives out politics. 'Politics, religion, the fates of empires and governments, the interest of life and death itself must all yield to the supreme fascination and excitement of football.'[41] There is no reason to believe that any of this changed before 1950; even by then Ferdynand Zweig could write that 'sport has an indescribable fascination for the British worker . . . It may sound absurd, but one could say that sport has bewitched [him].'[42]

It seems indisputable, therefore, that the British worker spent a considerable part of his non-working life either on craft-hobbies or on sporting interests that had the same characteristics and provided the same satisfactions as craft-hobbies. But is there any evidence that such hobbies encroached upon formal work by diminishing the interest and energy that men might otherwise have devoted to it? It would be wrong to pretend that the question can easily be answered; we know little enough of people's attitudes to work at the best of times and have almost no accurate knowledge for the period before the 1930s. As for how people see the relation between work and leisure, or, in this case, between one form of work and another, we can only proceed by the most delicate inference. The real obstacle is the absence of a corpus of autobiographical or biographical information. Of that which survives, little suggests that hobbies significantly changed attitudes to paid work, though it strongly suggests that for many, hobbies alone made work bearable, and for some, absorption in hobbies precluded interest in work altogether.

The sample of adolescent labourers whose diaries Freeman published certainly points to the dreariness of work and the attraction of hobbies, but not much more:

> I do hinge making and grinding on Emery wheel.
> It requires no intelligence it can be picked up in a few minutes.
> Not so hard but very monot.

For this boy waking life had value only when he played his banjo to which he was addicted.[43] Both Durant in the 1930s and Zweig in the 1940s found it common for men to be so absorbed in their hobbies that working life became almost intolerable. Durant, the pioneer of the Gallup Polls in England, carried out a survey of young East London working men one of whose published diaries demonstrates the tension between the hatefulness of work and the compulsion of hobbies in its most extreme and poignant form.

> On the Sabath day, I am unlike most animals, I do not lay in bed from noon till night, semiquaver! I take my parents a cup of tea, and take my fellow animal, the dog, for a stroll and a swim in the balmy waters of Wanstead Flats pond. I then have breakfast and traverse to church. After dinner, I sleep till tea-time, then I practise on my viola with piano-forte accompaniment.
>
> On Monday I get up at seven o'clock and tone up my muscles for work with aid of chest-expanders, springs. I then breakfast and go to hell – in other words – to work. I work in that hatred, a wretched debt [i.e. department] – the Grocery. Monday night's I go to night school.
>
> On Tuesday night's I go to Band Practise, because I am in the (YMCA) intermediate string orchestra. On Wednesday night's I go to Gymnasium to learn gymnastics and acrobatics. Thursdays I go swimming with the swimming club.
>
> Friday night I do my night-school homework, which takes me about three hours instead of 1 hr, because as far as *arithmetic* is concerned my name is, (*dense*).
>
> Saturday night I go to music lessons, unless I have a (date) with my viola or violin.
>
> My favourite hobbies are music, which I spent all my money on, and put my heart and sole to.
>
> Also gymnasium, swimming and reading English Litterature. Altogether my full repertwar of hobbies is: – football . . . Also Boxing and Acrobatics arts and crafts and reading, music and gymnastics, are my hobbies.
>
> Semibreve –
> full stop.[44]

Ferdynand Zweig, who wrote more extensively than anyone on working-class attitudes to both work and hobbies, was convinced that 'for a man who takes a passionate interest in dog-racing or football or making models, the job becomes of secondary interest. Sometimes the hobby can be so absorbing that it takes his mind off his work and lowers his efficiency.' Whereas most men were never entirely certain whether they worked simply in order to live or because it also gave some creative satisfaction, 'men with absorbing hobbies had no doubt at all'.[45]

There is, therefore, some evidence that the Shadwell–Cohen 'thesis' has weight; nevertheless, few, of whom Zweig is the most plausible, were prepared to argue it explicitly. Its major premise is both inarticulate and unproven. It presupposes that pre-industrial work was in some way expressive and purposive; that before labour became divided, *en miettes* in Georges Friedmann's phrase, work and leisure were integrated, part of a unified mental and material world and mutually enriching. Although this assumption is fundamental to many critiques of industrial capitalism, not least that of Marx,[46] there seems very little to suggest that it is true; more likely, as Anderson has observed, it is simply 'romantic and wishful thinking'.[47] To argue successfully that hobbies emerged as therapy for the pathological symptoms of extreme division of labour (as Friedmann does to the point of bone-headedness[48]), for a labour force in some sense 'denatured', it would be necessary to demonstrate that industrial work was unquestionably more monotonous and less autonomous than the kind of work which preceded it. This has not been done and I would be surprised if it could be. It would also be necessary to show that *within* the workplace itself there were no means by which boredom could be tempered. In fact, it can be argued that in some trades workmen actually paid more 'attention to work' as the factory system developed, and in other trades the patterns of industrial life were so disjointed as to significantly lessen the tedium of factory work.

Employers who gave evidence before the Royal Commission on Labour were nearly unanimous in believing that increasing leisure made their men 'steadier' at work and happier in their lives, even if they also believed, rightly in my view, that in an important sense those same men remained wilful and ill-disciplined.[49] W. A. Valon, president of the Incorporated Gas Institute (which represented engineers, managers and secretaries of the gas companies) was questioned by the Commissioners as to the changed character of the gas workers.

> What do you say as to the general character and conduct of the gas workers in your experience? Have the men improved in this respect and become more temperate? – Yes. More orderly? – Yes. Thirty years ago it was sometimes painful to go into our retort-houses. At that time we had to employ . . . a special class of men for lifting the very heavy scoops. Every chance they got

they drank a large quantity of beer, and the result was that we had a great deal of trouble with them from time to time. Since then the managers and engineers of companies have laid themselves out to have reading-rooms on the works, to supply the men with tea and coffee etc.[50]

The Commissioners, not unnaturally, were anxious to establish this point and pushed and coaxed employers hard.

And is it according to your experience that increased wages and greater leisure tend to produce more attention to the work and greater constancy to the work? – It depends entirely upon the use that is made of the leisure. I think our population has been improving. It has been improving during the time they have had more leisure. Therefore I should say that on the whole they have been spending their leisure wisely. A wise and better educated man would probably give better attention to his work than an unwise man; so that I think I may answer your question by saying, yes. You find in your experience the greater wage and reduced hours have been the means of causing your workman to pay more attention to work than otherwise would be the case? – That is true with limitations – distinct limitations. The factory system in Scotland is not an old one, and the factory system has been growing up by degrees, and it simply means this, that where improved machinery costing a large sum of money, is employed, that machinery must be carefully and effectively worked; and that, of course, tends to the improvement of the workman as well as to the improvement of the work. I think that is the answer.
But has increased wages and more leisure interfered with them in any way, or has [sic] it increased the tendency to fire attention among the working men? – I cannot speak very decidedly on that point . . . Since reaping these advantages have the workmen become more attentive to their work or less so? – I think rather more so.[51]

One might argue that this was evidence painfully extracted and ambiguous in its implications; since, however, the whole point of employers' evidence before the Commission was to show how badly done by they were, any admission that the work force was more placid and docile than it had once been has to be treated with respect.

More characteristic than apathy was simple ambivalence: workers were often bored, but sometimes (or even often) interested. Pre-industrial craft pride carried over into factory life; men prided themselves on their strength; work routines were easily disrupted by non-attendance or strikes; the workplace became an important social institution. Craft skill, and satisfaction in it, did much to mitigate the effects of increasing simplification of industrial routines. Alfred Williams noted the élan and craft-sense of the carriage finishers at a Swindon works. Of their meticulousness and style, he wrote:

The carriage finishers and upholsterers are a class in themselves, differing by the very nature of their craft, from all others in the factory. As great care and cleanliness are required for their work, they are expected to be spruce and clean in their dress and appearance. This, together with the fact that the finisher may have served an apprenticeship in a high-class establishment and one far more genteel than a railway department can hope to be, tends to create in him a sense of refinement higher than is usually found in those who follow rougher and more laborious occupations.[52]

Even in trades where there was little craft-skill or where it no longer existed, men could endow their work with intense craft-pride.

> The bricklayers are nevertheless very jealous of their craft, such as it is . . . Occasionally it happens that a bricklayer's labourer, who has been for many years in attendance on his mate, shows an aptitude for the work, so that the foreman, in a busy period, is induced to equip him with the trowel. In that case he at once becomes the subject of sneering criticism: whatever work he does is condemned, and he is hated and shunned by his old mates and companions.[53]

These techniques, though infuriating for management (and perhaps bad for efficiency), helped to give work a value it might not otherwise have possessed. This was also true of pride in strength, a pride particularly important in heavy labouring where it was probably the only 'skill' the job possessed. Dennis *et al.*, whose book is partly a chronicle of work-shirking, nevertheless stress that 'pride of work' was a 'very important' part of the miner's life.

> Old men delight in stories of their strength and skill in youth. A publican or a bookmaker will often joke about the number of tons 'filled off' each day in his establishment by the old men. Older men in the pit who go on to light work will confide that they can still go as well as the young 'uns' but they think they deserve a rest.[54]

Occasionally such pride took on menacing proportions. Williams tells the sad tale of 'Herbert' who achieved prodigies of physical labour, but whose appetite, alas, grew in the eating. 'In reality, such a man as Herbert is a danger and an enemy of his kind, though he is quite unconscious of his conduct and does it all with the best intentions, he must be forgiven', Williams comments unforgivingly.[55]

We can see the same ambivalence in attitudes to machinery. There was, in fact, very little Luddism in British factory work: machinery as such was rarely at issue, though levels of manning often were,[56] and there is little evidence that workmen were able to resist the introduction of new machinery where management was determined on it. But this was so partly because workmen themselves were often keenly interested in machinery and took pleasure in examining and discussing it. Gerhard von Schulze-Gävernitz, who believed (like his compatriot Dückershoff),[57] contrary to received wisdom, that the British worker was better educated and technically more acute than the German, noted that 'technical problems awaken [the] most lively interest' in the British factory worker. Salutary for the continental observer, he wrote, was 'a visit to some machinery exhibitions in the industrial districts. The operatives here crowd around the exhibited objects and discuss their advantages and failings'.[58] Even Shadwell conceded that the British workman, though perhaps less quick and inventive than the American, was much sharper than the German.[59] Machine-tool operators delighted in comparing American and British machines (American light, speedy but rackety; British heavier, slower, but more reliable) and their views usually corresponded with those of their employers. Fifty years later Zweig still thought many British workers took pleasure in machines and in the handling of them.[60] In any case, we might doubt whether all workers found repetitive work boring; some, as Viteles argues, clearly got 'satisfaction not observed by the spectator: at the successful working of complex machinery' for example.[61]

Men could even develop covetous attitudes to new machinery. Williams (again) tells an extraordinary story of a frameshed foreman, 'an inventor himself', who could not keep his hands off other people's machinery.

> More than once he was known actually to purloin a machine from the neighbour foreman's shop in the night and transfer it to his own premises. Once a very large drilling machine, new from the maker, and labelled to another department at the works, came into the yard by mistake, but it never reached its proper destination. Calling a gang of men, he removed the drill from the truck, caused a foundation to be made for it, fixed it up in a corner half out of sight, and had it working the next day.

Successful in this, he failed in his greatest coup, the attempted theft of three large drop hammers.[62] As for men, like carpenters, in journeymen trades where machinery was slow to intrude, it is doubtful if the factory system made much difference at all. 'Not for us the years and years in the same factory, the same office, the regular routine . . .' Max Cohen wrote.[63]

Even if attitudes to machinery were simply hostile or work generally just got too much, there were ways in which routines could be made bearable. One was plain non-attendance. 'St Monday' was common in most industries, not just mining. In mining itself 'Mabon's Day', the first Monday of each month (an agreed holiday) was capable of almost indefinite extension, and managers were fatalistic about it. The exchange between George Caldwell, the former president of the South Lancashire and Cheshire Coal Association, and James Mawdsley is not atypical, even if Caldwell laid it on pretty thick. Caldwell doubted if an eight-hour day would make much difference:

> . . . my experience of colliers is that they like a day or two a week under any circumstances . . .
> What do they do on that day that they lose . . .? – Dog running, pigeon-shooting, and things of that kind, any kind of enjoyment . . . What do the employers do with these men? – Nothing, they let them go their own way; we cannot control them; we have no power to control them.

Have you taken into consideration the advisability of insisting upon more regular attention to work? – We have thought about it many times, but it is no use; we cannot help ourselves; we are entirely in the hands of the Miners' Union; we have no control whatever.[64]

This is admittedly lachrymose evidence; but sixty years later Dennis *et al.* came to the same conclusion. It was, they argued, 'generally assumed that a man who has won the weekly draw in "Ashton" or a dividend on the pools will not turn up for work on Monday'.[65] Foreigners were startled at the irregularity of work in England. De Rousiers, observing Birmingham smithies, thought that few worked their nominal week. 'One, for instance never arrives before nine o'clock; others occasionally extend the Sunday holiday until Tuesday or Wednesday, if last week's pay is not exhausted. [The employer] complains greatly of these irregularities but bears them in silence in order to keep his men.'[66] Dückershoff, refugee from a country where they did things differently, was less surprised at the casual attendance than at the fact that so little was done about it.[67] Before 1914, only in the textile industry were serious attempts made to enforce strict attendance, but with limited success even there. In casual trades like building or the docks 'come-day, go-day' was elevated to an art-form.

In the 'newer' industries, particularly those based upon high-speed production lines, this kind of slap-happiness was harder to accomplish. Yet even here it would be difficult to argue that tedium was entirely unmitigated. For those workers who did not take pleasure in machinery there were a number of routine-breaking techniques. Where permitted, the most basic was conversation; and the most basic conversation was about how slow, or how fast, time was passing. Mass Observation recorded the following dialogue between two girls in a wartime machine-tool factory.

It [time] went quick this morning, didn't it?
Yes, it went lovely and quick between eleven and twelve, but it dragged after that I thought.
Yes, just after the twelve o'clock buzzer. It started to drag then.
Funny, wasn't it? It usually goes so quick after the twelve o'clock buzzer.
I hope it will go as quick this afternoon.
Hope so. You can always tell, can't you? If it goes quick up to half-past two, then its going to go quick all the afternoon.
It's funny that.[68]

Girls seemed to derive considerable pleasure from this sort of nattering and, as Mass Observation suggested, it substituted interest in time for non-interest in work.

The opportunities for men to vary routines were probably greater than for girls. Horseplay and practical jokes were common and popular,[69] just as they were for the machine-tool workers of Saxony studied by the evangelical pastor, Paul Göhre.[70] Furthermore, for men, more than for women, the workplace was an important social institution. Men did not just *work* there, it was in the factory more than anywhere else that they had their social being. Brown, Brannen, Cousins and Samphier, in their study of the 'occupational culture' of shipyard workers, argue that 'this sociability is an important intrinsic work satisfaction', and partly explains the otherwise inexplicably large number of men who had their lunch in the yards.[71] Williams reported that smithies were often 'in love' with their forges and he was incredulous that 'men cling to the shed as long as they possibly can; they have an unnatural fondness for the stench and smoke!'[72] Thus it was the loss of the social relationships implied by work as much as the loss of the work itself that made long-term unemployment so catastrophic for so many men in the interwar years.[73] One final activity almost certainly ameliorated monotony: the creation of tension via strikes, unofficial stoppages and workshop disputes. While it might be the case that the majority of strikes in this country are economic in origin, though I think the case by no means unarguable, their rituals are not necessarily so: they are one way of raising interest in the workplace, if not in work, and the number of unofficial stoppages in highly automated industries is presumably not accidental. Men when bored will create tension. De Grazia even claims that there is a Mediterranean game, *passatella*, which was so successful in creating tension it had to be suppressed by law,[74] and it would have required instruments of coercion available to neither the state nor management to prevent its creation in British industry.

In the late 1940s, Zweig concluded that, at most, only about one-third of the British working class were affected by 'dull, repetitive and uninteresting jobs', but he doubted whether even this one-third were actually bored with their work.[75] Zweig underrated, I would guess, the degree of technical change in British industry. He was over-familiar with the mining and textile industries and underfamiliar with the rest, but it would be hard to quarrel with his conclusion. It is, furthermore, easy to underestimate British labour productivity before 1940. Writing in the 1880s, when clouds no bigger than men's hands were being detected on every horizon, the Scottish industrialist Alexander Wylie was urging workers to go easy: the 'tide of over-labour' had inundated the country 'with desolating effects' on the hard-wrought workman.[76] Although the casual attitude of British working men worried him, de Rousiers was astonished at their capacity for work:

> . . . Everybody works very quickly here . . . There is no effort wasted and no talking. French workmen, so energetic by starts, would find it difficult to equal the rate of production . . . [A] merchant of precious stones told me he had often tried to introduce French workmen . . . The experiment had never succeeded: the masters found that the work was not turned out fast enough.[77]

The 'pace' of British industry did not slow down before 1914 (except perhaps in mining); the evidence suggests the contrary and Britain's was the only European economy where 'Taylorism' had been adopted on any significant scale.[78] Although the relative rate of its growth was probably decelerating, labour productivity was considerably higher than in (say) Germany and although that gap continued to narrow in the 1920s it widened again in the 1930s. The apparent débâcle of British productivity since the Second World War, while almost certainly a continuation of longer-term trends, is much more remarkable than those trends actually imply.

Nor is there any evidence that the British factory proletariat was more alienated from its work than the continental work force: it can be argued, indeed, that the reverse is true.[79] Similarly, it is hard to see that the 'work-experience' of continental workmen differed much from that of the British. To read Paul Göhre's famous *Three Months in a Workshop* after reading Alfred Williams' *Life in a Railway Factory* is like seeing the replay of a silent film with German instead of English sub-titles. What is clear, however, is that British management permitted, or was compelled to permit, techniques for ameliorating boredom and stress that were not permitted by European or American management, or only in a much-attenuated form. The conclusion from that is plain: those sectors of British industrial life in which monotony or work was most tormenting were in the minor clerical, distributive and packing trades where such ameliorating techniques were hardly possible. Not only was the work itself intrinsically hopeless but the 'occupational culture' was equally impoverished. Evidence to the Royal Commission on Labour on the condition of shop assistants, warehousemen and packers is among the most dispiriting of all. A. J. Mundella asked W. Johnson, the secretary of the National Union of Shop Assistants, why it was so difficult to organize shopworkers. 'We must look at this', Johnson replied, and added:

> The average warehouse clerk and assistant goes into the business at an early age. Indeed, from the time he goes in as a rule he is shut from all communication with the world and he does not know really the changes that are taking place around him. He does not read the daily papers . . . and knows nothing of the outside world . . . [Mundella] But how is it that intelligent men cannot combine as well as working-men who have less education and less intelligence? – Because working-men have the opportunity for social intercourse with each other and for discussing these matters, which shop assistants have not.[80]

This is the world of Durant's hobby-obsessed London grocery assistant[81] or the petty clerks of the 1960s who found their work almost unrelievedly repellent.[82] It is, to some extent, also the world of casual and boy labourers, amongst whom work was not discussed, and whose 'restlessness' and 'excitability' convinced the Edwardians that the 'nerviness' of the town was characteristic of industrial life generally. But these men, since they did not work directly in production, should probably be excluded from the original Shadwell–Cohen 'thesis', though it might be true they more neatly fit it than most. There is even evidence that individual workers were as often interested in their work as bored by it, and little evidence that their work suffered even if they were bored. If we can argue both that industrial division of labour did not necessarily lead to monotony and that, anyway, it is unlikely to have been much more monotonous than the work which preceded it, then the simple antithesis between work and leisure (or work and not-work) proposed by the Friedmann–Dumazedier school hardly stands. By this proposition, industrial work, synonymous with highly divided labour, is almost always deleterious and its consequences sometimes pathological. Leisure is 'time liberated' during which men can recover from one day's tedium in order to arm themselves against the next day's.[83] This is close to Shadwell's argument and not far from that of Zweig, who argued that men always chose hobbies unrelated to their work: clerks preferred manual work and railwaymen gardening, but labourers would avoid heavy work.[84] But there is, so to speak, no such unilinear relation. For one thing, too many hobbies were simple extensions of work itself. The hobby of many carpenters or painters was carpentry or painting. Most artisans liked 'pottering' and pottering could mean building all the furniture in a house or even rebuilding the house itself. 'In the evening he prosecutes his craft at home and manufactures furniture and decorations for himself and family . . . Very often the whole contents of his parlour and kitchen – with the exception of iron and other ware – were made by his hands.'[85] Not only did carpenters prefer carpentry, but manual labourers were energetic gardeners. Lady Bell, in her survey of the reading habits of Middlesbrough iron workers, noted how often men borrowed books on subjects 'connected with their work'.[86] After 1918 many men in automobile factories found their hobby in the product of their work – in making racing or rally cars, repairing, tinkering, reading auto magazines. Here again work routines defined the hobby.[87] Indeed, the most notorious case of men refusing to entwine work with leisure was not that of industrial workers but that of agricultural labourers whose allotments were, and still are, much less cherished than town lots.[88] Even if men selected hobbies unrelated to their work the hobbies had all the characteristics of work: indeed that is their fundamental quality.[89]

In any case, the relation between work and hobbies is as likely to be 'organic' as 'dialectic'. We have already seen that for skilled craftsmen the hobby was often simply an extension of ordinary work routines with the crucial modification that routine was replaced by autonomy and choice. Furthermore, before 1914, when tools of the trade were normally the personal possession of the craftsman (and expensive) it is improbable that many unskilled men would buy tools in order to practise a craft hobby. Despite Zweig's assertion that men choose hobbies unrelated to their work, the direction of the evidence, so far as the historian is able to tell, points the other way. Men with the most complicated or 'leisure-enriching' hobbies appear more likely to be those whose work is itself 'enriched'. Caradog Jones and his colleagues found that hobbies 'are less common . . . among male manual workers than in other social classes'.[90] Young and Willmott comment, with obvious surprise, that they 'did not find in the working classes as many men who were enthusiasts for a sport or hobby, in compensation for the relatively greater dreariness of their work, as we did amongst other classes who (one would think) needed the compensation less'.[91] It seems fair to suggest (as a rule of thumb) that craft 'make-work' as a hobby was confined chiefly to the skilled working class while the principal hobby of the unskilled labourer was certainly sport. But this must be a rough rule: it is by no means clear whether (say) pigeon-fancying is a sport or a craft, nor is it clear that the miners who were its most enthusiastic adepts can be classified as skilled or unskilled workers. A more reasonable statement, therefore, of the Dumazedier–Friedmann–Zweig position is a simple functional one. In other words, hobbies helped to make work acceptable ('without a hobby you might as well be dead' Zweig was told[92]) rather than that hobbies made men inefficient workers. Yet even that is not established. It is equally arguable that for many men there is *no* relation between work and leisure, work time and free time, and that preferences between the two are as much temperamental as occupational; or, indeed, that the *only* relation is a negative one: a dreary job means a dreary hobby.

This can, however, only be a partial conclusion. Hobbies had two other characteristics which were almost certainly connected with working habits. The first is that they gave an autonomy to working-class working life, even skilled working life, that was denied by the industrial division of labour and no doubt by pre-industrial labour as well. This was true even of activities such as football which eventually became mere simulacra of commercial capitalism. The free nature of hobbies is obvious. They were as complicated and as prolonged as the individual decided: only self-satisfaction determined whether the model was finished, the garden dug or whether the canary was a good singer or not. Though there were some constraints, seasonal for example, individual control of time was perhaps the main difference between formal work and hobby work. This freedom could also be collective. The cooperative organization of hobbies provided rare opportunities for working-class collective activity without managerial and middle-class intervention. Pigeon, dog and canary breeders met frequently and eventually developed national organizations for the control and growth of the hobby. The tendency for publicans to provide premises and act as officials of such organizations perhaps gave them a new function when the old one of simply pouring alcohol down thirsty throats was declining.[93] Spontaneous organization was also true for football. C. E. B. Russell was startled at the 'businesslike methods' adopted by working-class youths in establishing football clubs. They were 'in some cases surprisingly well managed and controlled, and it is, in every way, a good thing that young lads should learn to organise and work for their fellows'.[94]

The second of these characteristics is that most hobbies were intensely competitive. Even when men banded together to promote them, the implied object of their cooperation was individual competition. In many hobbies this is self-evident: the whole point of the elaborate breeding of pigeons and dogs was to win races; of canaries to produce new colours and a better song. In these cases a man's success at his hobby was measured by public competition. It is self-evident also of gardening. Flower and vegetable shows were always competitive. When asked in 1892 by the Royal Commissioners on Labour whether there had been 'an increasing tendency' to cultivate allotments, C. J. Wilson replied: 'Oh increased . . . because the advantages of them have been seen, and because interest has been taken in them, and [there is] a certain amount of vieing with one another as to whether they shall have better vegetables, fruits, and gardens than their neighbours, and that is how it has come about.'[95] It was a competitive spirit cunningly and profitably encouraged by the government in both world wars. Competition even came to dominate the brass bands and their 'idealist' origins were almost entirely lost. 'Contesting', Brian Jackson commented, 'has altered the whole movement, quite as radically as the introduction of beer has altered the working men's clubs.'[96] Sport was, of course, intrinsically competitive. Moreover, when hobbies were not directly competitive their individualism could imply competition. Most hobbies, however private, usually involved some public display and this was unquestionably exploited by the commercial salesmen of hobby perquisites.

The individualism of hobbies was, and is, in clear contrast to the work experience of most of their practitioners. The gradual elimination of competitive stress from working life by technological change and (to some extent) by the work force itself helped to make that life more tolerable for those who led it; but it conceivably diminished it as well. Stress and tension are disagreeable yet necessary. It was one of the functions of hobbies, therefore, to provide an acceptable competitiveness to lives otherwise circumscribed both by the requirements of increasingly mechanized work routines and (indeed less certainly) by the demands of group loyalties. That is why for so many men some kinds of betting (though not, for example, betting on dogs) were ideal hobbies. They created and released physical tension and intellectual energy while, in effect, being as competitive as other organized hobbies where the competition, the winner and the prize were more obvious. It is a mistake, and a palpable one, to assume that all manifestations of working-class life were, or should be, collective; or to conclude that leisure activities 'set within definite limits, the most fundamental of which was the acceptance of the individualistic value of hegemonic ideology' were typically those of the middle and lower middle classes because of the absence of those 'sustainable alternatives' found in working-class culture.[97] Working-class hobbies certainly had their collective organizations but it is hard to see how they differed from the associative bodies that absolutely underpin middle-class leisure. In any case their competitive nature was quite as typical, and this, arguably, was part of their attraction. When other sides of life, working and domestic, were all too collective, the pleasure of an activity that emphasized privacy and solitude seems explicable on grounds other than those of borrowed ideologies.

Hobbies had one more function: they permitted a socially-acceptable level of intellectual activity. The degree to which the British working class rejected what we might call an official culture must not be exaggerated, but it is true that attempts to impose such a culture on it very largely failed. There was, however, no difference in the kind of intellectual activity that each class devoted to its own pursuits. The mastery of a craft-hobby or a sport demanded accuracy, knowledge, discipline and skill: all the qualities that the elementary educational system attempted to promote with such little obvious success. Hobbies, however, were socially-permissible outlets for these qualities. It was for this reason that Paterson, having spent several years teaching in a Southwark board school, concluded that twenty years of compulsory education (he was writing at the turn of the century) had done little in a formal sense, but that 'in the organization of games as a definite and regular part of the school-work lies the hope of the future'.[98]

We can accept, therefore, that hobbies met a number of individual and collective needs; that they stood in a complicated, but very ambiguous, relation to work. Nevertheless, the 'thesis' that hobbies were undermining the British workman's interest in vocational work must fail. The evidence that there was a kind of 'work fund', a given sum of intellectual and emotional energy being drained by hobbies, though it exists, is not convincing. Yet if that is so, why should the thesis ever have been proposed? The most obvious reason is that hobbies (or, at least, one of their manifestations, mass sport) were by the turn of the century very conspicuous. Employers had learnt to live with large-scale absenteeism during 'big' mid-week football fixtures, however much they disliked it. But that worried them less than what appeared to be happening in the workplace. One does not need to look far for evidence that management felt it was losing control, that in some sense the rate of production was being determined by others, that its continental and American competitors were unfairly favoured. Much of this was, of course, pure fantasy. Managers always fear they are losing control; German and American employers almost certainly felt the same thing. Furthermore, there is little evidence that the labour force was working less hard, was effectively opposed to technological change when management was determined on it or was much more irritated by labour than one would expect given the nature of the work. Yet it appeared to management that workers, if just by deadweight, were devising only half-resistable techniques to defeat measures that would individuate the work force and make it internally competitive. The extent to which these techniques were successfully used is debatable; that they were used and had some success is not.

What explains even this partial success? One answer may be found in the social traditions of British life; the emphasis upon group loyalties and corporate affiliations which both worked against individualist practices. The physical representation of this was the trade union which the employers could not wish away and against which they were feebly armed. A second, and most likely explanation, is to be found in the 'collective' nature of so much British factory work, usually undertaken either by gangs or by an artisan with one or more assistants, and the whole edifice propped up by the continuing vigour, or at least the continuation, of the apprenticeship system.[99] Both traditions reinforced each other, and the attitudes they produced ('dead-levelism' the mid-Victorians called them[100]) were something that management disliked but knew it could not overcome. It was for this reason that attempts to introduce bonus payments were so often resisted in England and it was this that Zweig meant when he described the British work force as 'defeatist' and 'without ambition'.[101]

In these circumstances it is not hard to see why so many should claim that work *itself* was the problem. Both sides had an interest in perpetuating this view. Management, apparently incapable of managing as it thought it wished it could and conscious of competitive weakness, was happy enough to blame anything that would excuse itself. The political left was attracted by an argument which suggested that divided labour was intrinsically pointless and that organized leisure alone liberated a man under capitalism. As a slogan, 'the right to useful labour' had a doubly pleasing resonance: work could provide both utility *and* self-satisfaction. In fact, neither work nor hobbies was the 'problem'. The 'problem', insofar as there was one, was in social codes. As we have seen, the casualness of British discipline always surprised foreigners; whether or not they approved of it depended on the political point they wished to make. The real difference between England and its competitors was not in attitudes to work but in factory discipline and the ability of management to enforce the order of production. The British ideology, for in effect that is what it was, ensured a high degree of social cohesion but not social integration. Associations, groups and classes lived and let live; they knew there were certain boundaries that could not be crossed and rights that could not be infringed. This had its inevitable effects in the factory: within certain broadly accepted limitations the British workman went his own way.

8

Credit and thrift and the British working class, 1870–1939

PAUL JOHNSON

'A knowledge of proletarian conditions,' wrote Engels in 1845, 'is absolutely necessary to be able to provide solid ground for socialist theories, on the one hand, and for judgements about their right to exist, on the other; and to put an end to all sentimental dreams and fancies pro and con.'[1] The burgeoning of social and labour history in Britain in the past twenty years has been directed primarily towards increasing our knowledge of these conditions. There have been studies of paupers and poverty, housing, leisure, conditions of work and apprenticeship, diet, drink, welfare, crime and punishment, education, and so on, not to mention the countless publications on specific industries and industrial areas, on the rise of labour and on the political organization of labouring men.

These histories have been written from a wide variety of ideological standpoints, but they are all, more or less, materialist; they accept that the material conditions of life are key determinants of personal and social behaviour. The strength of this underlying consensus makes the apparent neglect of the foundations of these material conditions – personal income and expenditure – a surprising one. There are, of course, a number of indices of prices and wages, and these have been very thoroughly reworked and analysed at a national level by Charles Feinstein, but little attention has been paid to the way in which individual families eked out a living by balancing their income with their expenditure.[2] Yet in a wage economy where most of the population has a negligible holding of capital, it is the success or failure of this balancing act which determines the extent of hardship or ease, of hunger or plenty.

This essay will consider some of the more important ways in which working-class households attempted to balance their budgets, in the belief that such a study can tell us much about both the economic conditions under which the majority of people lived, and the aspirations, both individual and collective, that they had. The essay is divided into three parts. The first outlines the typical economic behaviour of a household in conditions of uncertain income and expenditure, and puts forward a tentative and elastic definition of 'the work-

147

ing-class population'. The second part examines credit and thrift institutions in some detail to see whether and when they were used in an 'economically rational' way. The conclusion suggests how a study of patterns of saving and borrowing may give broader insights into the development of some working-class institutions by considering the motivation behind mass membership rather than the more frequently studied actions and attitudes of a small number of leaders. Many organizational histories, because they are written from the crucial but narrow perspective of institutional records, display elements, if not of hagiography, then at least of those 'sentimental dreams and fancies' which it is the purpose of social history to dispel.[3]

I

In conditions of uncertain or erratic income and expenditure, most people attempt to balance their budget by some form of borrowing or saving. We might expect to see a great deal of this behaviour among the working population of Britain during the period covered by this study, 1870–1939, since there is little doubt that income and expenditure were erratic.

Unemployment fluctuated between the extremes of 0.4 per cent in 1916 and 15.6 per cent in 1932,[4] and the chronic casualization and short-time working in many trades made a constant income unknown to a large number of workers. In the poorest households where the housewife took regular paid employment, the fall in income and increase in expenditure associated with childbirth could bring acute financial hardship; in the relatively prosperous homes of skilled crafts-men, technical change, foreign competition or a fall in aggregate demand could all rapidly reduce an apparently assured earning potential.[5] Expenditure patterns varied too, particularly before the introduction of state welfare services, if there was illness or death in the family. A further budgeting problem arose because, very often, the years of peak family expenditure did not coincide with those of peak family income.[6] And for many, even the savings that could be made during the best years were insufficient to provide for them in old age.[7]

The saving and borrowing of government, industry and commerce were far larger than the gross sums involved in working-class budget management, but the small scale of this behaviour did not mean that it was unimportant for the individuals concerned, or that it was unobservable. Wage labour and weekly wage payments were almost universal for the working class in these years, and earnings in kind were insignificant even for agricultural labourers,[8] so we should be able to observe the response of working-class families to erratic income and expenditure flows by looking at the financial dealings of households.

However, before examining these dealings, some attempt should be made to define the 'working-class population'. Two approaches can be followed which may be of use to the historian. One procedure is to define some indicator, perhaps income, employment or ownership of the means of production of a population to be called 'the working class', and then to see to what extent members of the group so defined adopted the sort of behaviour or made use of the institutions and facilities that are the subject of the historical inquiry. But for present purposes this approach has severe drawbacks. The income figures for individuals are far from complete, those of ownership of productive assets even less so, and in aggregate form they tell us very little about the budget management of individual households. We cannot conduct questionnaire surveys on dead populations, and so for the more detailed information required we have to rely on the self-selected information presented in the form of autobiographies and letters, Charity Organisation Society (COS) case papers,[9] and the several social surveys carried out from the 1880s onwards.

The autobiographies and COS case papers of necessity deal with exceptional cases, and so whilst they may be useful in testing and highlighting views gained from a wider sample, they cannot be an adequate substitute for that sample itself. The social surveys are broader in coverage,[10] but they involve a working-class population that may be much more inclusive or exclusive than we would wish. Furthermore, the particular interests of the surveyors (for example Booth's concern with religion and Rowntree's with drink) may colour both the survey method and the interpretation of the results finally published.

The alternative method is to define the working-class population by means of the opinions held or institutions used, on the testable hypothesis that only people with specific income patterns and social linkages that may be termed working class behaved in these ways. As with all such attempts at definition, this is to some extent arbitrary and circular, but it does seem to be in line with then-current feelings on the subject, which saw working-class credit and provident institutions as a distinct group. In two published works on working-class thrift institutions, E. W. Brabrook, the Chief Registrar of Friendly Societies, divided these institutions into two sorts, those that dealt with thrift by means of saving, and those that catered for it by means of insurance.[11] In the former group he included the Post Office and Trustee Savings Banks, building societies and cooperative societies, and in the latter group he put industrial assurance companies and friendly collecting societies, affiliated and local friendly societies, and trade unions. We may wish to quibble slightly over some of the categories. Building societies, for instance, seem to have received some working-class savings, but made loans principally to building speculators or 'the middle classes'.[12] Yet the essential distinction between these institutions and others, such as ordinary life assurance companies, joint stock banks and the Stock Exchange, remains. It is a distinction of both scale and time period, for the working-class institutions accepted small savings at short intervals, epitomized by the 1d a week insurance with the Prudential. They were designed to (and did) serve people with small incomes paid frequently. Similarly, with credit or lending institutions, we would exclude those such as merchant banks, plate dealers and large-scale money lenders on the grounds of too large a scale or periodicity of loan. But we would include as working-class lending institutions those which were prepared to lend, week by week, sums often much less than the average weekly wage – pawnbrokers, small-scale money lenders and local shopkeepers willing to advance shop credit.

Even so, this class distinction is rather vague, and we need some more certain categorization in order to make some estimate of the size of the population we are concerned with. Routh's occupational distinctions may prove to be of use here. For 1911, the last five categories of his occupational grouping – clerks and foremen, and skilled, semi-skilled and unskilled manual labourers – accounted respectively for 4.8 per cent, 1.3 per cent, 30.6 per cent, 39.5 per cent and 9.6 per cent of the total occupied population of Britain.[13] In other words, the manual work force accounted for fractionally less than 80 per cent of the total labour force. In terms of income, the median earnings for male manual workers in 1906 stood at 26s 7d, with the lower and upper quartiles standing at 20s 9d and 34s 3d respectively.[14]

It is very difficult to confirm these earnings figures or occupational classes by reference to the institutional records surviving, for few thrift or credit institutions took any note of the average earnings or occupation of the members. The institutions that were interested were insurance or friendly societies, since to some extent they could use occupation to estimate risk of unemployment, sickness or death. One large set of records holding details of employment, namely the policy proposal forms of the Royal London Mutual Insurance Society, dates from the early years of this century, but the many million individual forms would make acquisition of even a representative sample a Herculean task. Two other, more manageable, sets of insurance documents also give details of occupations. These are the membership lists drawn up at the time of incorporation of the Blackburn Philanthropic Friendly Collecting Society in September 1913, and the policy registers of the Royal Standard Benefit Society. The former was a burial club run on a door-to-door weekly collection basis and the latter was a mutual sickness and life assurance society which worked by means of monthly meetings at which members paid their dues. More than 10 per cent of the members of the Royal Standard Benefit Society gave their occupation as 'clerk', and virtually all the rest were skilled artisans. There was, however, a sprinkling of schoolmasters, accountants and even a professional golfer.[15] In the Blackburn Philanthropic Friendly Collecting Society lists, only 0.15 per cent of members whose occupations are recorded were clerks, and membership was heavily concentrated in Routh's unskilled or semi-skilled groups.[16] These distinctions are important for what will later be said about income variations between members of different types of club; the crucial point to note here is that even within the Royal Standard Benefit

Society, a small-scale, élitist and expensive society,[17] the bulk of the membership came from the manual labour group, albeit from the upper echelons.

Admittedly, not all the people who used these credit and thrift institutions were working class, and not all the working class made use of the institutions, but, as the evidence in the next section of the essay will show, the range of coverage within the working class was very wide. An indication of this coverage can be gleaned from the COS case papers previously mentioned. The financial status of each household making an application to the society for charitable assistance was recorded in the case paper. As would be expected of households which, by definition, found themselves in financial need, the majority of them had debts outstanding. Of ninety-seven case papers surveyed, forty-six of them mentioned rent arrears, forty-seven the possession of pawn tickets and forty-two referred to other forms of debt. Only twenty-one of the cases appeared to be debt-free. But, perhaps more surprisingly, eighty-three of the case papers listed some form of thrift, the most common being payments to a life assurance company or burial club. Sixty-six of the ninety-seven cases displayed both savings and debts.[18]

This conjunction of debt and saving in the same household is itself highly suggestive, but these results are of use here in supporting the view that most working-class people used at least the thrift institutions listed by Brabrook, for if those who were forced to seek charitable assistance could pursue these forms of accumulation, it seems reasonable to assume that those with a greater discretionary income did so to a greater degree.

Although this view of class and the use made by the working class of the institutions named is underpinned by relative income levels, it is not just an income definition dressed up in new clothing. Routh shows that in 1913–14, the average annual earnings of clerks and skilled manual workers stood at exactly the same level, £99,[19] but it has been pointed out that, despite similar wages, clerks behaved in a much more independent manner when saving and insuring than did the skilled manual workers.[20] They very often preferred self-help to mutual aid, and among the mutual aid societies preferred the impersonal centralized ones like the Hearts of Oak and the National Deposit to the conviviality of the Oddfellows' lodge or the Foresters' court.

To sum up, the definition of the working class taken in this paper is one not only fashioned by a consideration of income and occupation, but also crucially determined by the degree of mutuality displayed in borrowing and saving behaviour.

II

Credit institutions

Probably the most important form of working-class credit, that given by shops and tradesmen, is completely unquantifiable, largely because it was not institutionalized. There was no credit traders' society,[21] no government regulation, no trade paper. Credit trading was generally local, small-scale and unpublicized, but, judging from such evidence as can be found, it appears to have been widespread and much used.

Credit trading was of two different types, which we might call spontaneous and premeditated. Spontaneous credit was that allowed by shops to regular customers for normal supplies when they were in particular distress, on the understanding that the debt would be paid off when personal circumstances permitted. This was generally described as a 'booking trade', the customers having their purchases entered up in a 'tick book'.[22] Generally the tick book ran from pay-day to pay-day, and was only extended to longer periods at times of particular distress, although the pattern could be one of a longer regular cycle. Booth pointed out that London workers tended to live on credit from local shops in the lean winter months and pay off their debts in the summer.[23] Frank Bullen, a small shopkeeper who was eventually driven into the bankruptcy court by his bad debtors, wrote of this system:

> Many hundreds of families would come to the workhouse long before they do, especially in hard winters, but for these small tradesmen giving them credit for the bare necessities of life, and thus tiding them over the pinching time. This system of first aid can hardly be called philanthropy, since those who extend it do it for a living, and yet in the multitudinous life of poor London it is a huge and most important factor.[24]

The bad winter of 1879 followed by a trade depression meant that many casual labourers in London could not earn enough to pay off the debts of the previous winter, and this apparently forced many small tradesmen into bankruptcy.[25]

Premeditated credit was that deliberately entered into in order to obtain goods that were usually fairly expensive by means of payment by instalments. A survey by the Women's Co-operative Guild in 1902 reported that 'Drapery and hardware clubs at drapers' and other shops abound; in fact we found that practically every poor person we spoke to bought boots, drapery and furniture through these clubs.'[26] Lady Bell found exactly the same pattern among the women of Middlesbrough,[27] and in Birmingham in 1914 'the bulk of the credit trade with working men [was] done in wearing apparel and household requisites'.[28] This behaviour had, as a complement, another form of premeditated credit, that negotiated with the tallyman or 'scotch draper', an itinerant salesman. Again, no certain view of the extent of the tallyman's trade can be arrived at, but the critical attention he received from the pens of social commentators suggests that his trade was a large one.[29]

We thus find the extent of credit trading impossible to quantify, but apparently prevalent among 'working men' and large sections of 'the poor'. However, these two terms are not synonymous; many skilled industrial workers and artisans with incomes of 30s or more a week were not poor, and lived their lives untouched by both 'primary' and 'secondary' poverty. Some of the social divisions within the working class can be emphasized by looking at the different behaviour of this higher income group.

In the Salford of Robert Roberts, 'all goods one saved for, of course, and bought on the nail, or at worst through weekly clubs run by local shops – a method much frowned on . . . Clothing clubs existed, but respectable folk eschewed them altogether.'[30] Likewise, Harry Gosling's father, a licensed Thames lighterman, would 'never buy anything unless he could pay ready money for it'.[31] But this pattern was not true everywhere. Mrs Bosanquet tells us that among 'better class' families, 'very frequently there will be some piece of furniture – a mangle, a sewing machine or even a piano – which is being bought on the hire system'.[32] A family buying a piano was clearly one with an income well above the poverty line, and a strong desire for social betterment and respectability. That this respectability could be achieved despite a hire-purchase arrangement suggests that the mechanisms of social influence and respect were far from uniform. A reconciliation between the views of Roberts and Gosling and that of Bosanquet can probably be made by reference to the cost of purchase. The goods Bosanquet mentions are all expensive, costing well over a week's pay to purchase, those that Roberts hints at – the normal trade of the weekly clubs such as boots, clothes and blankets – cost a good deal less. The distinction is not properly between those who used credit and those who did not, but between those who used it deliberately to purchase luxury goods, and those who could not do without it if they were to fill their bellies and cover their nakedness.

This is not the whole story, for we find that the relation between respectability and absence of small-scale credit does not hold fully in one key area, the Co-operative movement, which was the stronghold of well-paid skilled craftsmen and industrial workers. The movement was not the cash trader of Co-operative folklore, but in fact extended credit to its customers on a scale that increased markedly from 1886 at least.[33] However, this credit does appear to have been used to overcome short-run emergencies rather than long-term income deficiencies. The few very sharp regional or local variations in the amount of credit advanced are closely linked to acute industrial distress. For instance, during the coal dispute of 1921, the credit allowed by the Dowlais Co-operative Society rose from £3,017 to £30,518, and in the Western Division of the Co-operative Union, which encompassed primarily cooperative societies in South Wales, the average amount of credit extended per member rose from 16s 5d at the end of 1920 to £3 15s 5d at the end of 1921.[34] The credit advanced by cooperative societies was often limited to some fraction of the paid-up share capital of the member, and so can be seen more as a drawing upon savings than as a borrowing. In this sense status was not damaged, for membership of a cooperative society involved a certain respectability that was not easily undermined by a short-term drawing upon savings resting in the society itself.

If the extent of shop credit and its social implications are difficult to estimate, the cost of it to the consumer is even more so, since interest was often charged indirectly by selling inferior goods at inflated prices to customers tied by their tick book to a particular shop. It is therefore impossible to say whether widespread working-class use of trade credit was an optimal purchasing strategy, given budget (and time) constraints. Nevertheless, the subject is one that deserves further study, and which has importance for work in other areas. The new-product consumerism of the interwar years had much closer ties with hire purchase sales techniques than did pre-war consumption. It has been suggested that this was due to a fundamental change in the way that living on credit affected personal respectability within the community,[35] a change that Roberts sees as being brought about by the social upheaval caused by the First World War.[36] Alternative explanations might stress changes in the real cost of credit, or an increase in the gap between the purchase price of the new consumer goods and average weekly wage or net household savings. A further possibility is that habits did not change at all, but that, as hire purchase became more organized and subject to legislative control, it became more noticeable to outside observers than was the club draper or furnisher.[37]

The other great credit institution of the period was the pawnshop. The number of licensed pawnbrokers in England and Wales stood at 3,049 in 1870 and had risen to 4,611 by 1914.[38] This represented about one pawnbroker to every 7,500 people, but in large towns this ratio was lower at about 1:3,500. Even so, there were strong local variations, particularly in ports which tended to have a ratio of 1:1,800.[39] This is not surprising. If recourse to the pawnbroker is made in time of erratic income or expenditure, we would expect there to be a greater demand for pawnbroking facilities in towns where industrial depression strikes hardest, and in ports which are subject to the seasonal whims of the weather as well as the cyclical ones of trade. The Select Committee on Pawnbrokers estimated, in 1870, that the annual average number of pledges received by a pawnshop was 45,000 for the provinces and 60,000 for London. Such figures led Cuthbert Keeson to calculate that in 1902 there were, in London, more than six pledges to each head of population, or one pledge per family every two to three weeks.[40]

Aside from this statistical evidence, there exists a wealth of impressionistic accounts of the primacy of the pawnbroker in working-class economic life. Mrs Bosanquet pointed out that 'to many thousands the pawnshop is their one financial recourse, their one escape from charity or the Poor Law . . . to raise money on the home is not among the lower classes the last expedient of despairing misfortune, but the ordinary resource of the average man'.[41] This view is exactly echoed by Arthur Newton in his description of childhood in a well-to-do working-class home in Hackney before the First World War: 'At that time there were very few people indeed who could truthfully say that at no time in their lives they had not pawned something to get ready cash. I have even known my parents do this. Not more than two, perhaps three times, but they did it nevertheless.'[42] Many other accounts, particularly in the Select Committee minutes of evidence, tell the same story. Indeed, so entrenched was the practice of pawning in working-class life that it established a place for itself in children's street games.[43]

These sources also tell us a great deal about different pawning habits. Some people would regularly pawn goods week by week: most often the Sunday clothes. Sometimes this was a matter of physical convenience, there being nowhere to store these clothes in cramped living quarters,[44] but usually the money received for clothes pledged on a Monday morning was used for immediate payments for food, rent or the tallyman. In many cases, it seems, goods bought on credit from the tallyman would end up in pledge before they were fully paid up.[45] In 1876, a London credit draper, M'Rooster, thought that 'in nine cases out of ten those who get their best clothes on tally carry them to the pawnshop'.[46] In other cases, the sort Newton describes, the pawnbroker was the poor man's banker in times of exceptional need and sudden emergencies such as illness or death.[47] And sometimes the pawnshop was used seasonally in much the same way as shop credit; goods were pawned in the winter and redeemed during more prosperous summer months.[48]

This different pawning behaviour was dependent upon two interrelated factors: household income and social status. Among households with very low or erratic incomes, pawning was the norm: a visit to 'Uncle' was as common as a visit to the butcher (the very use of the term 'Uncle' to describe a pawnbroker indicates the way in which he was often viewed as a familiar and friendly standby in times of need). Yet even with this group of habitual pawners, there was, it seems, a degree of shame associated with the act of pawning. Entrances to pawnshops (at least, to the pledging side of them) were often discreetly placed away from the main shop window, and the pledging counter was commonly divided by high partitions into cubicles so that one customer could not see what another was pawning.[49] And we know that, in 1870 at least, many customers gave false names and addresses. As a pawnbroker's assistant said to the Select Committee on Pawnbrokers, 'the person who visits the pawnbroker has a great degree of shame, and does not want to be seen'.[50]

It may at first sight seem peculiar that people went to such lengths to disguise such a common practice as the pawning of household goods, but they were apparently shamed by their behaviour, and tried to retain an image of financial sufficiency. It is suggested that this image was important because it was through the appearance of financial security that respectable status was achieved within each small working-class community. The best way to display a financial reserve, and so gain status, was to convert it into some possession, an overmantle, or a new suit, perhaps, which could be made open to view. Hence the importance of the 'Sunday best' clothes. Alfred Hardaker, secretary to the Liverpool Pawnbrokers' Association, described the typical behaviour of the weekly pledger: 'The wages [paid on Friday] are generally disbursed in clothing necessary for Sunday wear . . . The pledge is brought back again on the Monday, and then the money is laid out again for the requirements of the week: to pay rent, and buy the necessary flour and bread for the week.'[51] This process resulted in an effective annual rate of interest of over 100 per cent; it was obviously inefficient. It was carried on week after week in order to maintain appearance and status within the community.

Of course, status and economic well-being were intimately linked. In close-knit working-class communities with a pawnbroker to every few hundred families, the pledging of goods acted as an economic signal: 'News of domestic distress soon got around. Inability to redeem basic goods was a sure sign of a family's approaching destitution, and credit dried up fast in local tick shops.'[52] In some cases, perhaps, interest of 100 per cent per annum seemed a small price to pay for the maintenance of both status and a good credit rating in the local community.

If the sense of shame and loss of community status was apparent among the regular pawners, it must have been acute for the occasional pawner who, because of sickness or unemployment, had to raise some money for food or rent by pledging clothes or household articles. But if a whole community had to turn to the pawnbroker because of widespread distress, individual stigma was no longer attached to pawning which became a community-wide response to a general problem. Pawning, rent arrears and shop debts became not an indicator of personal financial failure and decline, but a social ill borne by the whole community. A case in point is that of the skilled artisans affected by the engineering dispute of 1897–98. In 1898, the *Pawnbrokers' Gazette* published a revealing clipping from a Newcastle paper about the effects of the strike on household finance:

> At the West-End of Newcastle the landlords of houses, the occupants of which were as sure as the bank with their rents, have had to let the rent days pass over, hoping against hope that the tenant would be back to work again and recover his lost ground. A pawnbroker at Benwell has had to take the tenancy of two empty houses in which to store the goods and chattels pledged with him, and three pawnbrokers at the West-End have for a long time closed their books against further pledges, the offers in that way being altogether beyond the limits of their business. These facts will give but a slight notion of

the hardships that have been suffered by families; and there must yet be many a day of steady employment before formerly comfortable homes recover their old appearance.[53]

It seems that with pawnbroking, as with credit trading, the manner in which people used the facility reflected on their social standing. The mechanism is neither simple nor easy to discern. Membership of a particular social stratum might demand or preclude use of some specific borrowing or saving institution, but on the other hand, use of a specific borrowing or saving institution could help to determine social status. The links between security, independence and respectability will be returned to later.

One very important but not immediately obvious result of the widespread and competitive market for the advance of loans upon the security of items of personal and household property, was that it in effect provided a substitute savings bank for low-income households. The expenditure of money upon, say, a new chair, was not a commitment to consume a certain sort of seating until the chair was worn out: in times of distress money could quickly and easily be raised on the security of the chair to buy food or medical services. As Robert Roberts wrote of Edwardian England: 'For many in the lowest group the spectre of destitution stood close; any new possession helped to stifle fear.'[54] Gareth Stedman Jones found this pattern of consumption prevalent among the casual labourers of London. 'The most usual method of anticipating the winter, was what came to be called thrift in reverse. Workers regularly bought luxury items like furniture, clothing, domestic utensils and ornaments in the summer, which they pawned off one by one in the winter to help tide over bad times.'[55] Of course, such behaviour was quite incomprehensible to the patronizing middle-class ladies of the COS like Mrs Barnett. 'I have counted', she wrote, 'as many as seventeen ornaments on one mantelpiece – three or perhaps five are ample. She who aims to be thrifty will fight against yielding to the artificially developed instinct to possess.'[56]

The role of goods in the budget management of households was a crucial one, particularly before the First World War, but has been generally neglected by observers both at the time and since.[57] Goods were so important because, given the extent of the pawnbroking market, they had the status of near-money that perhaps only demand deposits have today. Goods were certainly more liquid than money held in the Co-op, the Post Office Savings Bank or a building society, from which cash withdrawal required a week's notice. We do not need to delve into obscure anthropological studies of acquisitive societies[58] to explain the flight of china ducks to the walls of so many working-class homes during this period. They were decorative, and a status symbol of sorts, certainly, because of their cost. But they were also a readily realizable store of value.

The wide use made of this mortgage market in second-hand goods, and the large number of pawnbrokers serving it, suggests that it was both efficient and competitive. The competition came not by manipulation of the interest rate, which was fixed by Act of Parliament in 1872 at 25 per cent per annum,[59] but in the assessment of the value of the good to be pledged. If pawnbrokers did not 'lend quite up to the hilt, and even above it',[60] the goods would be taken to a competitor to see if a larger advance could be negotiated. Any more accurate measure of the degree of efficiency of the market is lacking. Pawnbrokers giving evidence to the Select Committee in 1870 stressed that fierce competition and regulated interest rates pared their profit margins to a very great degree, but they were hardly an unbiased source of information. Certainly profits were not guaranteed. Of the six pawnbrokers' shops that closed in London in 1897, two did so because their owners went bankrupt,[61] but failures could have been due as much to incompetence as to competition.

The picture is even less clear when we attempt to assess the relative costs of credit from different institutions. The pawnbroker's annual rate was 25 per cent, charged by the month, but the real rate paid by the customer varied with his or her pawning habits. An article pledged and redeemed each week bore an annual rate of interest of over 100 per cent. In contrast, the local chandler's shop or tallyman seldom charged interest on sums outstanding, but instead sold goods at an inflated price in order to cover potential bad debts and outstanding credit. One pawnbroker stated explicitly that 'shopkeepers charge more for such credit than the pawnbroker does for the loan of his money', and in illustration of this he pointed out that many working-class people preferred to pawn with him and buy from the adjacent baker in cash rather than rely on trade credit.[62] But there is simply not enough information available about the real cost of trade credit to test the generality of this statement.

The overall view of credit institutions is that their geographical spread was wide, their market coverage extensive among the 80 per cent or so of the population categorized as the manual working class and their cost to the customer high, even though the effective interest rates charged may have done little more than cover the high risk of default.[63] The fact that many people were prepared to pay a very high rate of interest despite having little or no spare cash and many unfulfilled wants, suggests that the subjective benefits derived from such credit were similarly large.

Probably the only way to interpret sensibly the very high charges certain families were prepared to pay for what were fairly standard community-wide goods such as bread or Sunday clothes, is to consider the existence of discontinuities in each family's utility schedule. We can imagine that the possession or non-possession of certain goods might affect the utility or well-being of a family to a degree quite disproportionate to their total value. For instance, for a family on the verge of starvation, a shilling's credit from the baker might be just sufficient for it to survive independently, without having to turn to the parish for relief. Pauperdom was the ultimate disgrace. It represented a complete loss of independence, respectability and community status and esteem, and it was worth avoiding almost regardless of cost.[64] Old debts could be paid off more quickly than the stigma of pauperdom would fade in the memory. Likewise with the 'Sunday best'. It was not the intrinsic value of the cloth that determined its worth to the wearer, but the value of community identification and esteem that wearing the clothes ensured. The non-appearance of the Sunday clothes was the most public of signs that a family was on hard times. Only when we consider both the low discretionary income of the average working-class family and the thresholds of community respectability that certain possessions or behaviour described, can we begin to understand the reason for the complex and often costly manner in which working-class people used the credit facilities available to them.

Thrift institutions

For those working-class households that had an excess of income over expenditure, and which did not use the whole of this excess to buy pledgeable goods, there was available a large choice of savings institutions which were of two basic types: for saving by personal accumulation and for saving by insurance. Much middle-class frustration at the apparent thriftlessness of the working class stemmed from a failure to understand the economic role of these different institutions. Very often to a middle-class observer, saving meant the acquisition of a stock of liquid assets in a savings bank or similar institution and possibly the purchase of house property. To the working class, saving most often meant purchase of a contingent property right with a friendly society, trade union or industrial assurance company. This difference in emphasis was due to differences in both income and social environment.

Low and erratic income receipts made it difficult for working-class households to accumulate a stock of savings. A strike, unemployment, illness or death could quickly drain the net savings of a household and leave it quite incapable of sustaining similar occurrences in the future.[65] And for just the same reasons it was difficult to build up a sufficient sum of money to finance jamborees like Christmas or even major household expenditures such as those on furniture. This is how one advocate of mutual thrift described the problems of individual accumulation:

> The everyday demands upon the average workman's wife to spend the weekly earnings as she gets them are too strong to resist; the nest-egg of a few weeks, collected by great sacrifice and often after bitter reflection as to the wisdom of undergoing present suffering on the chance of reaping future comfort, she sees again and again dissipated by some unlooked-for calamity, until the efforts to provide for the future – heroic efforts in many instances – become fewer and less sustained, and the hand-to-mouth existence becomes established.[66]

The most popular means of circumventing these difficulties was by way of regular contribution to some club or society. This was done partly for the straightforward reason of simplifying household budgeting, since a number of small regular deductions from income cause less interference with regular consumption patterns than do several large ones. Hence the profusion of Christmas goose clubs, holiday clubs, didly clubs and the like.[67] (The corollary to this process of club saving is that of making small regular payments after the receipt of the good, that is, of credit purchasing.) Payment of small regular sums, whether as advance saving or as debt repayment, imposed an external discipline without which any saving or acquisition of durable goods out of a near-subsistence income may well have been impossible.[68]

But regular payments into friendly societies and slate clubs did more than just impose the discipline of saving or even out expenditure flows. They also provided insurance against the financial deprivation caused by the most usual shocks to working-class income and expenditure patterns, thereby effectively giving the insured a large stock of savings at, and only at, the time when it was especially needed. This was to be used in lieu of personal savings which either did not exist in liquid asset form, or, if they did exist, could be preserved for other uses.

Insurance against a number of different contingencies, unemployment, sickness, old-age and death, was available to the working population but the cost of the insurances varied, and they were adopted on widely differing scales. Looking at the insurance market between 1870 and 1939, it is clear that both the cheapest and the most popular form of insurance used by the working class was death or burial insurance provided by the Friendly Collecting Societies registered under Section 30 of the 1875 Friendly Societies Act, and the industrial life assurance companies. The biggest institutions were, from the former group, the Royal Liver and the Liverpool Victoria, and from the latter, the Prudential. In giving evidence on this type of insurance in 1888, J. M. Ludlow, the Chief Registrar of Friendly Societies, said:

> the large collecting societies address themselves to the very poorest part of the population. It may seem strange, but the poorest class think more of providing for their burial than of providing for themselves in sickness . . . it is the lowest form of providence, that of providing for your burial; and it becomes thereby convenient to receive, in very small sums, the insurance money for the purpose. These being very poor people it is convenient for them to pay only a penny or a halfpenny a week, instead of paying, as they would do in an ordinary friendly society, one shilling a month or something of that kind.[69]

The total number of people who bought this form of insurance is difficult to estimate accurately, because most of the statistics refer to the number of policies, not the number of insured people. When an insured person wanted to increase the amount of his insurance, he simply took out another policy for another 1d or 2d a week. So over time, as income increased, and in inflationary periods, when monetary values were debased, many policies would be issued to people already holding at least one policy. A change in the way that the Liverpool Victoria Friendly Society made its annual returns to the Registry of Friendly Societies shows that in the three years 1917–19 it had four policies in force for every three members.[70] There is no way of checking the representativeness of this ratio since the other large societies and assurance companies kept records according to policy number rather than by name, and so did not know how many individual members they insured.[71] Furthermore, some people insured with more than one institution, and there can be no way of cross-checking this.[72] But an idea of the enormous extent of this sort of life insurance is given by the unadjusted figures of the number of Friendly Collecting Society and Industrial Assurance Company policies in force in certain years. They are for 1880: 7.8 million, for 1915: 45.5 million and for 1935: 84.4 million.[73]

More impressionistic surveys also point in the direction of very widespread coverage, particularly among the poorer sections of society. Clara Grant observed that 'the Poor Law Guardians must grant burial where really necessary, but insurance is practically and rightly universal'[74], and this was for an area of Poplar coloured black (lowest class) and blue (very poor) by Booth. Rowntree, in his second survey of York in 1936, gained information on the insurance premiums paid by 267 poor families living below the poverty line. Of these, forty-five paid no insurance money, ninety-nine paid less than 5 per cent of their income in insurance, ninety-three paid between 5 per cent and 10 per cent of income, and thirty paid between 10 per cent and 20.9 per cent.[75] But most of these observers joined in the barrage of middle-class criticism of burial insurance as a means of thrift, for reasons echoed by John Hilton in 1944 when he wrote 'let us rail at the system under which more than half the pitiful sums [the poor] pay goes in expenses and lapsed policies. Not six pennyworth of value do they get for any shilling so hardly spared.'[76]

Undoubtedly the lapsing and expenses rates were high. Even in the Prudential, generally the most efficient of the societies or companies, expenses took 40 per cent or more of income until the early 1920s when the introduction of a more efficient collection system reduced the expenses ratio by 14 percentage points in only four years. The rate of lapsing in the Royal Liver during the period 1877–88 varied between 7.87 per cent and 18.7 per cent, and for the period 1909–23 between 4.95 per cent and 24.8 per cent, with a general tendency to be high in years of trade depression and low when trade recovered.[77]

What seemed peculiar was the willingness of millions of working people to pay regularly a substantial part of their low incomes for a form of insurance that was sold in an inefficient way with a very high service charge, and their habit of using any policy payments not for judicious investment, but for ostentatious funerals. To many observers, burial insurance of this kind seemed quite the opposite of thrift. In Liverpool, the home of two of the largest societies, one newspaper that regularly urged workers to be more thrifty printed the following piece on burial societies.

> Some men argue that the fact of such large sums of money being collected from the working classes, for the purpose of providing assistance in the hour of need, goes far to prove what a hold provident habits has taken upon them. This is an error. There is nothing that shows so much indifference, inconsideration, utter want of thought, reckless mode of wasting means, as the *mode* in which these contributions are *generally paid*.[78]

And a Charity Organisation spokesman criticized this sort of insurance not for the high cost of contribution, but because of the way any receipts were spent. 'Insurance against necessary burial expenses is a perfectly proper provision' he conceded, 'but there is no need to spend on the funeral what would keep the survivors of the family for a month.'[79] But such criticism brought no striking changes. In 1914, Mrs Bosanquet was regarding burial insurance as 'a misdirection of expenditure so general that it seems hopeless to try to remedy it'.[80]

Views of this kind came from people who assessed the worth of burial insurance in purely financial terms, but to make sense of the enormous demand for this insurance, we have to consider more than just money. The main purpose of burial insurance was to prevent pauperism. A writer on burial societies in 1869 stated:

> Amongst the humbler classes there is nothing of more importance than a proper provision for decent interment. The notion of having recourse to the parish for assistance is very torture to a poor man and his family, and therefore there is nothing met with greater punctuality than the weekly call of the collector for the burial-club money.[81]

Rowntree's survey of York sixty-seven years later showed exactly the same behaviour: 'many a poor family is prepared to suffer hardship for long years, spending on insurance premiums money sorely needed for food, in order that they may make sure that they, and the members of their family, may be "decently put away"'.[82]

Among a sample of long-term unemployed people surveyed in Liverpool in November 1936, there were:

> Several instances . . . of what a decent death meant. In one Liverpool case £24 was received in death benefit, and £18 spent on the funeral. There is something peculiarly macabre in the sight of the plumed horses, the rows of black carriages or expensive cars, the family in deep mourning, and the flowers piled high on the coffins, as a funeral *cortège* moves from the door of a Liverpool hovel, where maybe there are two or three families living in five or six rooms. It is a triumphant but misguided assertion of the rights of man. If a man cannot

live an independent life, at least his death shall be a charge on no one but his own family.[83]

The survey goes on to suggest that 'this abhorrence of a "pauper's grave" seems to be at bottom an assertion of independence . . . This particular manifestation of the sense of respectability is apparently almost universal among the poorer classes'.[84]

The reason why families were prepared to pay so much of their income for burial insurance was that the subjectively assessed cost of non-insurance could be so high. Of course, financial inadequacy was commonplace for many working-class families, and assistance could be summoned in many different ways. The most subtle ones of shop credit and small-scale pawning could often be concealed. But the openness, indeed, the public display, of financial need that went with a pauper funeral had the most damaging effect. In a society in which independence and respectability were the goals, an expensive funeral was an outward exhibition of such independence; a pauper burial in a common grave the clearest sign of economic decline and moral neglect. It reflected on the social morality of a family, for only the most shameless would be untouched by an interment that was not 'decent'.

Higher-income sectors of the working population, further away from the threshold of pauperdom and with more money to devote to savings of some sort, tended to insure not only against death, but also against other contingencies, especially sickness. The institutions that provided the facility for this were the local and affiliated friendly societies and sometimes the craft unions, though usually not the New Unions. In 1880 ordinary friendly societies in England and Wales had about 1.6 million members, and affiliated societies (that is those with branches like the Oddfellows and Foresters) numbered just over 600,000. By 1915 the figures were (for the United Kingdom) 3.8 million and 2.8 million respectively, and for 1935 they were 5.3 million and 2.9 million.[85] Whilst collecting societies insured primarily women and children, ordinary and affiliated societies were very largely composed of adult male workers, and so therefore covered a large section of the working population.

The evidence amassed by several government investigations of Friendly Societies suggests that, in general, the lowest sectors of the population (lowest in terms of income and status) did not join this sort of friendly society. In 1871, the provincial corresponding secretary of the Oddfellows told the Friendly Society Commissioners that his membership was 'Generally the more respectable class of tradesmen and clerks; it embraces also some in a lower class, but they oftentimes retire from it by non-payment' and he reckoned no Oddfellow earned less than 20 s a week.[86] Bentley Gilbert, in his study of national insurance in Britain, points out that this sort of friendly society 'made no appeal whatever to the grey, faceless, lower third of the working class. Friendly society membership was the badge of the skilled worker.'[87]

For those who did join, the societies provided some or all of the following: death benefit for the member, his wife and children under a certain age, sickness benefit, lying-in benefit, support for the member whilst migrating in search of work, unemployment pay and fellowship. This last was a distinguishing feature of the higher type of friendly society. Instead of cash being collected from the house each week, it would have to be taken once a month or fortnight to the society or branch meeting. Very often these meetings would be at a public house, and they would involve some organized entertainment – a lecture, debate or music. The Oddfellows and Foresters in particular had regalia and ritual modelled on freemasonry and designed to increase by mutual knowledge the bond of brotherhood between the members.

Compared with burial societies, this sort of friendly society gave a much better return on money invested. Expenses were kept to around 10–15 per cent of income, as against 40 per cent or more for collecting societies, and the lapsing rate in the Oddfellows was about 3 per cent compared with 13 per cent per annum in the Royal Liver.[88] Even so, they were not considered by their members to be simply efficient insurance organizations. Membership implied not only increased financial security and independence, but also increased status within the community, as noted by Crossick in his detailed study of Kentish London.[89]

Membership of these more expensive and comprehensive friendly societies was important for individual status not so much in the negative sense of a burial society, by preventing a fall into publicly displayed destitution, but in a positive way, by displaying economic security and well-being. This, perhaps, explains why fellowship, feasting and ritual were such important parts of friendly society organization despite the hectoring of outside observers who wished to divorce entertainment from insurance. Financial security and independence can bring respectability and social status only if they are to some extent displayed. The possibility of weathering the financial deprivation of unemployment or sickness on a friendly society dole, although the most important part of mutual insurance, was a very unobtrusive benefit. For community esteem to be placed on friendly society members, membership had to be advertised, hence the lodge meetings, feasts and parades with their paraphernalia of banners and other regalia. Friendly society membership was, quite literally, 'the badge of the skilled worker'. And although some of this ritualized behaviour seemed to be no more than the aping of various middle-class actions and attitudes, it was much more directed towards the working-class peer-group.

For even higher contributions, an annuity or old-age pension could be bought from some friendly societies, as it could also from the National Debt Office via a

Trustee Savings Bank, or through the Post Office. Even in peak years no more than 3,000 contracts were concluded for the government-sponsored schemes, and although private annuity schemes were more popular, they never reached a very wide audience. This was due to the high cost over and above that payment required for sickness and death insurance balanced against the relatively low probability of reaching old age. J. M. Ludlow, in giving evidence to the Select Committee on National Provident Insurance, said:

> I do not myself believe . . . that deferred annuities will ever be largely assured for by the working class; for the simple reason that, whilst death is a certainty and sickness is virtually a certainty, the reaching of a given age is a mere contingency . . . I think that a young man from 18 to 21, who wants to do the best he can for himself and for others in life, has much better uses to put his money to than by providing for himself on the contingency of his reaching 60 or 70 years of age. I think that later on, when he marries, and when he has got children about him, he still has much better purposes to which he can apply his money.[90]

The difficulty for the working man of making adequate provision for himself and his wife in old age was recognized by the several Royal Commissions and Select Committees which were appointed to study the working of the Poor Law and to investigate schemes for a system of national insurance. And, of course, it was for this reason that the first old-age pensions scheme was of a non-contributory nature. As Lloyd George said when moving the second reading of the Old-Age Pensions Bill:

> if it were within the compass of the means of the working classes to make provision for old age, the fact that they had provided for sickness, that a good many have provided against unemployment and accidents of that kind, would in itself be a proof that they would have provided superannuation for old age if they could have done it.[91]

As far as the pre-1909 period is concerned, Mrs Bosanquet was quite right when she wrote: 'The most important institution, then, for the maintenance of old age is the natural and legal provision made through the family.'[92]

Of direct-saving institutions, by far the most important were the savings banks. The Trustee Savings Banks together had 1.38 million depositors in 1870, 1.9 million in 1914 and 2.48 million by 1939. The Post Office Savings Bank, for the same dates, had 1.1 million, 9.2 million and 11.6 million accounts open. The average amount in each account was slightly higher in the Trustee Savings Banks than in the Post Office until 1927, when in both it stood at something over £28.[93]

But with savings banks it is likely that the institutional delineation of the working class begins to break down. It has been argued that one of the great concerns of working-class household budget management was the creation or maintenance of as high a social status as possible within the working-class community. The importance of certain goods and patterns of behaviour as delineators of status can explain why they were not always acquired or adopted in the most financially efficient manner. No such similar justification can be made for the use of a savings bank. Their use did not secure status except by the purely financial means of establishing a liquid reserve fund to be used in emergencies, because savings bank deposits were in general entirely secret and could not be used for any sort of social display unless converted into some other form.

The implication of this is that savings banks were used either by people who placed a relatively low utility ranking on the status-giving attributes of the other working-class financial institutions, or by those who could afford to purchase goods and insurance to secure and display their financial strength, and who used savings banks as the most efficient way of accumulating excess liquid funds. The first group comprises people displaying lower middle-class aversion to any form of financial and social mutuality, the second comprises those of the working class who were particularly well and regularly paid. Occupational breakdowns of savings bank membership are few and far between, but one such account of the Aberdeen Savings Bank for 1880 is suggestive:[94]

	Per cent
Mechanics, artisans, etc.	28½
Black-coated and professional	9
Servants	14½
Women workers	4
Labourers	4½
Seamen	4
Agricultural	5
Shopkeepers, etc.	5½
Women not otherwise classified	10
Children	15
Total	100

As Horne puts it: 'The savings bank was still mainly the bank of the skilled worker, the domestic servant, widows and children, and the small middle-class man and woman. The unskilled, so far as they saved at all, patronized the friendly or benefit society or trade union, which helped them to tide over short periods of sickness or unemployment by means of small weekly contributions while in work.'

The Post Office believed its savings bank reached a poorer class of depositors than did the trustee banks, and the lower average level of deposit until

1927 to some extent justifies this view. But the difference was exaggerated before 1909 by accounting procedures; in that year the removal of dormant accounts from the Post Office calculations raised the average deposit from £14 11s 7d to £20 16s 0d.[95] A better estimate of the type of Post Office deposit comes from a survey of the occupations of all people making deposits during a three-month period in 1896.[96]

	Per cent
Professional	1.55
Official	2.81
Educational	1.01
Commercial	3.88
Agricultural and fishing	1.83
Industrial	18.43
Railway, shipping and transport	2.96
Tradesmen and their assistants	8.14
Domestic service	8.61
Miscellaneous	0.37
Married women, Spinsters, Widows, and Children	50.41
Total	100.00

The different classifications used make comparison of the two surveys difficult, but it is by no means clear that the Post Office attracted more working-class custom. The obviously non-working-class depositors in the first four categories of the Post Office list account for almost 10 per cent of the total, or 20 per cent of those in paid employment. The most striking feature of both sets of figures is the number of women and children. It was estimated that women and children counted under specific occupations in the Post Office survey would raise the total of the last category to 60.59 per cent. If we assume that most of the servant depositors in the Aberdeen bank were female, this gives us an estimate for women and children of about 43 per cent. It is clear from the fact that these women and children had money available to deposit that they did not come from the poorest ranks of the working class, but there is no indication as to whether they were from manual or white-collar families.

One contemporary estimate was that 75 per cent of depositors belonged to the 'industrial classes',[97] which would suggest that in 1914 some eight million savings bank depositors were working class. But with well over half of all depositors being women and children, this probably represents less than four million working-class households: considerably fewer than the six million or so ordinary and affiliated friendly society members, the great majority of whom were heads of households. This tentative estimate at least does not contradict the hypothesis that only those working-class families with an income more than sufficient to buy contingency insurance are likely to direct their surplus funds to the savings banks.

At the top of the hierarchy of savings institutions were the building societies: at the top because of their cost and their role as status-givers. Ownership of property was perhaps the best possible indicator of financial security, and a sure way to preserve a respectable standing. But it was expensive. The strict rules for regular payments by both lenders and borrowers that were general for at least the earlier years of this study meant that only people with a very secure income could become members. As pointed out above, most of the borrowers seemed to belong to the middle class; many of the depositors no doubt did as well. In numerical terms, the impact of the societies was initially not very great. By 1913, they had only 617,423 members, borrowers and depositors combined.[98] Between the wars, the societies became increasingly important as financial institutions. Their assets and liabilities expanded more than ten-fold between 1913 and 1938,[99] but this was particularly due to fundamental changes in the housing market and the special income-tax arrangements made by the societies with the Inland Revenue.[100] These factors made building societies even more the preserve of the substantial investor, as is demonstrated by the figures of the Abbey Road Building Society in which in real terms the average size of deposit rose by 64 per cent between 1913 and 1932.[101]

III

In this essay it has been argued that for the low income–low asset group of manual workers under consideration, self-interest was intimately linked with social state. So, although some saving was undoubtedly determined by economic factors such as income levels and rates of return, much of it took place in response to social pressures. Some distinction can be made between causation and scale. The scale of income had strong bearing on the type and amount of saving or insurance indulged in, but the cause of saving, the individual desire for security and respectability, was independent of income.

The social influence on personal economic behaviour has long been recognized, although seldom fully considered, by economists. Duesenberry, in his seminal work published in 1949, wrote:

> When the attainment of any end becomes a generally recognised social goal, the importance of attainment of this goal is instilled in every individual's mind by the socialization process. In psychoanalytic terms the goal is incorporated into the ego-ideal. When this occurs the achievement of a certain degree of success in reaching the goal becomes essential to the maintenance of self-esteem. The maintenance of self-esteem is a basic drive in every individual.[102]

This essay has suggested that a crucial working-class goal was financial security, or independence from the adverse effects of income and expenditure fluctuations, and that this independence was closely related to an idea of respectability. For instance, even for financially pressed working-class households, 'it was of supreme importance to keep intact the "front room", hardly ever used, but conferring somehow through its shiny furniture a feeling of independence and status to them'.[103] The most respectable members of the working class were those who did not have to turn to the pawnbroker, local charity or the Poor Law Guardians in times of low transitory income or high transitory consumption. For if they could weather the storm in times of hardship, they could do much more in times of plenty. They had the financial capacity to obtain more leisure and recreation, more knowledge, and greater independence at the workplace, all 'marking services'[104] that could extend their personal influence among their own class group. This behaviour has usually been seen as an aping of middle-class actions and pursuits, but it had strong status-creating effects within the working class, and it was more towards this group that such behaviour was directed. Financial security was demonstrated by the behaviour that established respectability. Respectable things – goods like suits, pianos, tea-sets and newspapers, services like medical aid, education and apprenticeship, displays such as holidays and 'proper' burials – were all impressive, but expensive.

The crucial social importance of respectability is demonstrated by the openness of almost all saving behaviour. Here it is necessary to break with Duesenberry, who argued that 'most people do not know how much their neighbours save or what their assets are. Consequently they cannot be directly affected by other people's saving decisions.'[105] This may be true of post-war America; it certainly was not the case in working-class communities in Britain in the years covered by this study. There was a positive desire to display the extent of savings and wealth because these were so important in determining the ranking of individuals in the working-class hierarchy. So ornaments were collected and arranged in the parlour for display to visitors, and 'Sunday best' was worn even by the irreligious. So also did friendly societies and trade unions organize various parades and rituals, and almost everyone attempted to fund some ostentation at weddings and funerals.

The very wide coverage provided by working-class credit and thrift institutions, and their general growth throughout the period certainly belie the view, widely held by middle-class social improvers at the time, and since adopted by some historians, that 'working class men and women spent little time speculating about the future . . . they refused to torment themselves by trying to plan ahead for something different'.[106] It suggests that although working-class household budgeting was in part an attempt to plan ahead, to establish long-run financial security in times of income or expenditure variance, it was also directed towards the more immediate establishment of social status. These twin aims were reached by the same economic action, and they tended to induce a predominantly conservative outlook. In the long-term, the individual worker was concerned with his personal economic position and the maintenance of his earning power and such job-security as he might have, and so was unlikely to support any collective movement for speculative change. In the short-term, he was motivated by a desire for display within an established social environment in order to demonstrate his claim to a particular position within the hierarchy of respectability, so he had a vested interest in maintaining the established environment within which display could be made on known terms.

Much historical writing on the years 1870 to 1939 has been directed towards explaining the lack of any collective expression of working-class consciousness. The growth of self-governing working-class institutions like trade unions and Friendly and Cooperative societies has been pointed to as an indicator of the latent class organization that never found any coherent political outlet. In this essay the growth of these institutions is seen as part of a much broader and essentially non-radical attempt to balance the household budget, to establish some personal financial security and to achieve and maintain as high a position as possible within the working-class hierarchy of status. This is not to deny the existence of a certain exclusive working-class cohesiveness that rejected many bourgeois ideals and values, nor that this cohesiveness existed in working-class mutuality institutions, but rather to point out that the institutions were, in class terms, introverted. They were used by the individual for bettering or maintaining a position within the working-class hierarchy, rather than by 'the workers' for striking the first blow of class warfare.

9

Intelligent artisans and aristocrats of labour: the essays of Thomas Wright

ALASTAIR REID

In recent years, there has been a significant revival of the debate over the usefulness of the notion of a 'labour aristocracy' for the analysis of mid- and late nineteenth-century Britain. The idea was first introduced into serious historical discussion by Eric Hobsbawm in 1954, when he argued that it was possible to identify an upper stratum of about 10 per cent of the working class which had high and stable earnings and which corresponded, more or less, to those workers organized into trade unions in the period.[1] Although not attempting simply to revive Lenin's crude attack on the reformism of the Second International, Hobsbawm was clearly influenced by it and certainly intended the security and prosperity of the 'labour aristocracy' to be a central part of his explanation of the political peculiarities of the British working class in the period, particularly of the absence of an independent party of its own.[2]

While this masterly article soon established its position as the basic account of the social history of the period, it was another twenty years before the advance of research on the second half of the nineteenth century produced further elaborations in Robert Gray's analysis of Edinburgh and Geoffrey Crossick's case study of south-east London.[3] These attempted, rather unsuccessfully in my opinion, to develop Hobsbawm's suggestions about social mobility and the relationship between piece-masters and subcontracted labour into a coherent account of the social formation of an 'upper stratum' of skilled workers. Gray was rather more successful in his development of the analysis of the impact of casual labour and unemployment on different occupations and in re-emphasizing that, as a result, not all skilled workers were 'labour aristocrats'. But the main contribution of both authors was their analysis of the ideology and values of the 'artisan élite'. They succeeded in reconstructing the practices of 'self-improvement' in some detail, but emphasized, against the predominant current,[4] that 'labour aristocrats' had not just passively echoed the values and beliefs of their employers. On the contrary, Gray and Crossick argued that within the limits of the dominant culture, skilled workers had played an active role in the formation of their own world view by giving their own meanings to such key words as 'respectability'.[5]

However, the more general advance of research into the social history of the second half of the nineteenth century has recently given rise to widespread criticisms of the notion of a 'labour aristocracy'. I find most of these convincing, and would summarize them by saying that skilled workers were less economically privileged and secure and less socially and politically incorporated than the proponents of the 'labour aristocracy' have argued. In effect, this is a restatement of Henry Pelling's much earlier criticisms in his perceptive response to Hobsbawm,[6] although it could also be said that it pushes some of the most important insights of Gray and Crossick a little further than they were prepared to do.

Thus I would argue that unemployment affected almost all skilled workers, exposing them to cyclical and seasonal insecurities and reducing in the long term their standards of living.[7] Simultaneously, the incomes of the less-skilled were frequently higher than the 'labour aristocracy' model has assumed, suggesting that there was probably a broad band of the moderately well-off rather than a narrow 'upper stratum' of the very prosperous.[8] The same points could be made about skill, for even the most highly-skilled workers were rarely immune from employer pressure, nor were they a group totally distinct from the 'unskilled'.[9] Rather they merely formed the top grades in a complex hierarchy of knowledge and aptitude which was being continually redefined both by employers' attempts to raise productivity and by trade unions' attempts to defend occupational 'custom and practice'.

Just as those men with the highest skills and largest incomes were probably not as economically distinct from the rest of the working class as proponents of the 'labour aristocracy' theory have claimed, so their values and political beliefs were even further from those of their employers than Gray and Crossick have argued, and closer to those of their work-mates and neighbours. It is now widely agreed that adherence to the norms of 'respectability' was not confined to a superior minority, and Gareth Stedman Jones has argued that working-class notions of 'respectability' were almost completely self-contained. Indeed, in so far as they involved rather reckless expenditure on 'keeping up appearances' in front of other workers they were often in conflict with middle-class notions of 'thrift'.[10] As for political behaviour, Patrick Joyce's stimulating account of Lancashire indicates that party divisions were often between workplaces and localities rather than between grades of the work force, while Keith McClelland's work on radical politics in the Tyneside region suggests that the Reform movements were not supported exclusively by skilled workers.[11]

While there are signs that the force of these criticisms is causing fundamental rethinking among some of the major proponents of the 'labour aristocracy',[12] the theory continues to have some purchase among historians of the period. I think this is partly because, in the absence of a fully developed alternative, many are reluctant to abandon the established method of matching up forms of employment, levels of wages, cultural pursuits and political views to create coherent 'social strata' whose rise and fall can be used to explain political changes. But it is also partly due to the existence in nineteenth-century sources of many references to 'labour aristocrats', 'well-to-do artisans' and 'respectable working men'. If such a stratum did not exist, it can be asked, why did Victorians keep talking about it? The problem with this line of argument is that it is tautologous, for it is only if we begin by assuming the existence of a 'labour aristocracy' that we shall take all such contemporary comments to be references to it. In this respect one of the most interesting features of the recent debate has been the increasing sensitivity on all sides to the complexities of Victorian social classification, to the variations in meaning attached to the same words and to the effects of specific political contexts on the formulation of statements which seem at first sight to be simply descriptive.

In order to contribute to this line of inquiry, I have devoted the rest of this essay to a detailed consideration of three books written by Thomas Wright, 'The Journeyman Engineer', in the late 1860s and early 1870s.[13] Wright was a skilled metal worker still employed in his trade when he wrote the essays collected in these volumes. This makes him an almost unique voice in the records of the period. Not surprisingly, he has been extensively quoted and referred to, not only in almost every account of the 'labour aristocracy' but also in discussions of workplace customs and leisure activities, to such an extent that he has indeed become a 'hero of a thousand footnotes' even though the course of his own life remains obscure.[14]

I

The 1860s and 1870s were a period of significant increases in working-class industrial and political pressure, as a result of which substantial legislative concessions were granted. The key incidents, especially the 'Sheffield Outrages' and the agitation over the Second Reform Bill, are, of course, well known, and at the time provoked an enormous outpouring of middle-class opinions about the working class. Broadly speaking, there was a confrontation between supporters and opponents of Reform, and the latter found their most celebrated images in Robert Lowe's denunciations of violent and criminal trade-unionists, drunken labourers and a general absence of decency and morality among manual workers.[15] In response, the supporters of Reform attempted to give more substance to Gladstone's image of responsible working men who could be trusted with the vote by compiling literary and statistical evidence to present a picture of acceptable forms of collective organization: of moderate trade-unionism, friendly societies, building societies and retailing cooperative societies.[16] Combined with arguments about increases in working-class literacy and general education, this was taken to show that, despite Lowe's condemnations, workers possessed the qualities required of responsible citizens. However, as there was no intention of enacting universal adult male suffrage, largely because of the electoral expenses that would have been involved, it was either implied or explicitly argued that these qualities were concentrated in the upper layers of the working class.

While this debate over the franchise was by no means the origin of attempts to categorize workers, it may have been one of the crucial influences on the development of the notion of social 'strata' according to which ways of life and sets of views corresponded to positions in an economic hierarchy, in this case defined by the levels of rent paid. Certainly the advocates of the 'labour aristocracy' theory have drawn heavily, and rather uncritically, on the pro-Reform literature of the late 1860s.[17] The usual procedure has been to take the required information on wages, savings, education and so on from the middle-class sources and then to call in Thomas Wright as a witness from within the working class to the same process of stratification that was observed from outside it.[18]

> Between the artisan and the unskilled labourer a gulf is fixed. While the former resents the spirit in which he believes the followers of 'genteel occupations' look down upon him, he in his turn looks down upon the labourer. The artisan creed with regard to labourers is, that the latter are an inferior class, and that they should be made to know and kept in their place.

Exactly what significance Wright himself attached to this statement will be explored in a moment, but first it ought to be stressed that he would not have been very pleased to find his own words quoted in confirmation of material drawn from the other contributions to the then-current debate over the working class. After all, one of his major intentions in publishing his essays was to combat the images presented by *all* of the external commentators on the working class, even those who set themselves up as its friends. Each of the books he published in these years began with a reference to the flood of writing on the subject, which he condemned for its ignorance, its oversimplification and its misrepresentation of the ways of life and points of view of the 'great unwashed'.[19]

> The best of these portraits are idealised from observations necessarily superficial and generally made with a view to their suiting some preconceived theory, while others are 'adapted' to the interests of parties, or boldly evolved from an inner consciousness or a rich imagination, by persons who wish to *father* their own interested designs upon the working man.

Obviously there was an element of self-promotion in these criticisms, but Wright genuinely did have a distinct, and more nuanced, view of the class to which he belonged.

Admittedly his first attempt to give an account of the composition of the working class, in his essay 'Working Men', was heavily marked by the prevailing images, written as it was at the height of the debate over Reform. Obliged to accept the truth of many of Lowe's accusations of 'drunkenness, ignorance, violence and venality', he attempted to defend the working class as a whole by arguing that such characteristics were to be found mainly among its 'poorer sections'. Not that these were composed of worse individuals who therefore ended up in poverty, but rather that poverty and ignorance reduced working men to the level of the 'rough': living in dirty and overcrowded houses, loafing about on street corners and outside public houses, prone to drunkenness, bad language and wife beating, and willing to barter their votes for drink.

These moral and political failings did not apply to the rest of the working class who broadly fitted the then-current category of the 'intelligent artisan' as being 'earnest and honest in his political beliefs, upright in his dealings with his fellow-men, and sober, industrious, prudent, and independent in his mode of life'.[20] This polarization between 'artisans' and the 'poor and rough' might seem at first to fit neatly into the 'labour aristocracy' model; however, Wright clearly intended his use of the category 'intelligent artisans' to include the bulk of the working class, while it was the 'rough' who were in the minority.[21] Furthermore, while accepting some parts of the pro-Reform case, Wright was also concerned to expose its exaggerations. Although certainly equipped with native shrewdness and intelligence, the average 'artisan', or worker, was far from educated; on the contrary, he was 'bigoted, narrow-minded, and unjust' and over-influenced by anachronistic popular traditions. Wright claimed that the average worker was ignorant of the principles of political economy and the constitution of society, and while unwilling to sell his vote cynically, was rather too prone to be influenced by professional agitators. On the whole these would lead this prototypical worker to believe that labour was the sole source of wealth and that the working class was therefore very badly treated by its current rulers among whom the worst offenders were the landed aristocracy. As a consequence he was inclined to place too much confidence in the possible benefits of future legislation, and of having the vote, and inclined to undervalue the importance of 'self-improvement', particularly through education.[22]

If the majority of the working class had the minimum requirements for political citizenship, those with the virtues touted by the pro-Reform writers were, in Wright's view, a very small minority indeed, largely because of the inadequacies of the then-current educational system. As a result of its emphasis on the rote-learning of more or less useless information, even the best-educated workers left school with very low levels of literacy and numeracy, and a real taste for reading was kindled only in a few and only by chance.[23] The 'educated working man', the third type, which Wright juxtaposed between the 'artisan' and the 'rough' was therefore a rare and entirely 'accidental being'[24] and the degree to which his more moderate and sophisticated views on current issues had an impact on his work-mates was ambiguous.[25] On the one hand, they relied on him as a fund of information and a writer of trade petitions to the employers: 'But while trusting to him and allowing him to exercise a considerable amount of influence on some matters, his mates are "down on him" in regard to others. They are inclined to think that he is a bit of a prig, or, as they put it, that he tries to "come the grand" over them.'[26] This was partly a result of his own attitudes, for the 'educated working man' was often openly frustrated by the tone of life in his workshop and locality and frequently tried to use his literacy to 'improve himself *out* of the working classes'.[27] As a result, he tended to hold himself aloof from much of the social life of his work-mates, only attending union and friendly society meetings when there was real business to be conducted and usually then taking an idiosyncratic and unpopular line. Again, there are some features of this type which might seem to confirm the existence of a 'labour aristocracy', especially the higher level of literacy, political moderation, ambiguous relationship with other workers and aspirations for upward mobility. But for Wright these workers did not comprise a coherent stratum. There might have been only one or two, or perhaps no, men of this type in a given workshop, and their characteristics were not connected to any particular occupation or level of income but rather to preferences arising from their individual psychological make-up. He wrote that

> . . . they must be regarded as exceptional beings: the exceptions that prove the rule, that the working classes, as a body, are not as well educated as they might and ought to be, or as, from the manner in which they have been belauded by admirers more ardent than judicious and well informed, large numbers of those belonging to other sectors of society believe them to be. They must be regarded as so exceptional as to make the somewhat prevalent idea, that intelligent artisans are a large and well-defined section of the working-classes, an utterly erroneous and misleading one.[28]

II

Most of the terms of this tripartite division were retained in Wright's later essay 'The Composition of the Working Classes', but their place in the structure of the argument was slightly different. While in the earlier essay the infinite variety of working men had been acknowledged in passing, in the second version of his position this occupied a more central part of the argument and subsumed the main divisions indicated in 'Working Men'. Thus he began his discussion by emphasizing the diversity of types of worker, once again in opposition to the bulk of then-current writing on the subject, and proposed six main pairs of opposites. As before, there was a contrast between the educated and the ignorant, and one between 'a sober, steady, saving section, and a drunken, unsteady, thriftless section',[29] but to these were added the further contrasts between the political and the non-political, the trade-unionist and the non-trade-unionist, the regularly employed and the irregularly employed and, of course, the artisan and the labourer.

Whereas in his earlier writings the word 'artisan' had been used very loosely to apply to the majority of manual workers, in this new polarization it had a more specific occupational reference: to skilled workers in sectors in which training was based on apprenticeship and a large number of adult workers were permanently restricted to the role of assistants to the fully skilled men. Indeed the gulf which was fixed between the 'artisan' and the 'labourer' was not so much a general social differentiation as a reference to the quite specific tensions which arose in the workplace between tradesmen and their helpers.

> In the eyes alike of unionist and non-unionist mechanics, any clever or ambitious labourer who shows a desire to get out of his place, by attempting to pick up or creep into 'the trade' to which he is attached as an unskilled assistant, is guilty of a deadly sin, and deserving of the abhorrence of all right-thinking members of the craft.[30]

The 'artisan' creed that 'labourers' were 'an inferior class, and that they should be made to know and kept in their place' was not, therefore, the quasi-irrational piece of social pretension which traditional interpretations portray, but rather a practical strategy to defend occupational territory. Moreover, it derived not so much from an arrogant sense of privilege as from a feeling of insecurity: the 'artisan' was hostile from fear of being 'dragged down'[31] by the erosion of his ability to restrict entry into his craft. This hostility was mutual; the 'labourers' not only resented their subjection to the authority of 'artisans' but also enforced their own restrictive practices.[32]

> A mechanic when out of employment can scarcely take work as a labourer, even if it is offered to him. If he were to do so, labourers would strongly object to his being brought amongst them. 'Here', they would say, 'is a fellow with a trade in his fingers, and yet he is coming to take the bread out of the mouths of us poor labourers.'

This polarity between the 'artisan' and the 'labourer' might still be easily assimilable to the 'labour aristocracy' model, particularly if it was assumed that Wright's other pairs of opposites matched up with it to produce, on the one hand, 'artisans' who were regularly employed, sober, educated, members of unions and non-political and on the other hand, 'labourers' who were irregularly employed, drunken, ignorant, non-trade-unionists and political. However, Wright himself did not intend to give such a picture and in his own analysis any one of these key characteristics might be associated with any of the others. Thus, as will already be obvious from the quotation above, there were 'unionist and non-unionist mechanics'. Equally, while 'artisans' were likely to have had more *schooling*, it was not that which determined whether a workman picked up a real taste for self-education, 'for a labourer to be a better educated man than the skilled workman whose assistant he is, is a common phase of workshop life'.[33]

Furthermore, each of the polarizations had its own specific dynamics. For example, the educated had a tendency to treat the uneducated with contempt and were in turn resented. Meanwhile, whatever his individual beliefs, the political working man would be prone to express them in a 'rather hectoring fashion' and was in turn accused by non-political workmen of pursuing his own personal ends under the guise of programmes and parties.[34] Similarly, trade-unionists regarded those eligible to join their societies but remaining outside them as either threatening or stupidly selfish, to which non-unionists responded by forming their own closed shops in order to resist the 'offensively dictatorial' influence of the unions.[35] Thus while there were important distinctions and tensions between 'artisans' and 'labourers' in Wright's account of the composition of the working class, this division did not play any special role in creating an overall pattern. This must, at least in part, have been a result of his own first-hand experience of the economic insecurities in the life of the skilled worker, a theme which recurs persistently throughout his books.

It was obviously an advantage to be outside the casual labour market, and a further protection to be a member of a union, but even this '*élite* of the trade'[36] was not immune from unemployment as, he pointed out, a glance at the uses of their societies' benefit funds or an acquaintance with their customs of 'tramping' would reveal.[37] Even if a given occupation did not suffer from an absolute surplus of labour, most were subject to relative surpluses for all but six months of the seven year trade cycle; for four years out of seven the demand for labour would average from 10 per cent to 20 per cent below full employment and for six months would bottom out at 90 per cent unemployed.[38] Thus Wright estimated that only 10 per cent of the work force in large-scale industry (or 5 per cent of the whole working class) would have belonged to that '. . . set of hands who are virtually regarded as a staff, and who, so long as the works are kept open, will be retained in employment'. But unfortunately there was no known way in which an individual workman could guarantee to end up with this relative security whatever occupation he chose and however hard he worked, for 'chance, as well as character and qualifications, has a part in deciding who shall be the fortunates of the working classes'.[39]

In Wright's view, another crucial area in which chance would affect the long-term prospects of the 'artisan' was in his choice of a wife, for in the absence of domestic servants, the degree of comfort in his home life would depend on how good she was at 'managing'.[40] On the whole, Wright thought that the level of housekeeping among the working class was lower than desirable, partly as a result of the spread of the 'pernicious idea so prevalent in other grades of society, that the performance of housework is degrading'.[41] A second cause was the lack of training in domestic techniques offered by the jobs most frequently done by young working girls: even domestic servants were liable to be either too specialized in one particular area or over-worked and incompetent. However, there were some exceptions, and if a working man was lucky enough to meet one, and prudent enough not to marry too soon,[42] he could enjoy a better standard of living than his mates. 'Whatever sanatory [*sic*] or architectural improvements may be made in artisans' dwellings, it will still be found, while wives remain as they are, that of homes supported on like incomes, one will be a veritable 'little palace' in point of comfort, while another will be a domestic slough of despond.'[43]

A common reaction of men who found themselves in a 'slough of despond' was to take refuge in drinking and male society at the local public house, but skilled men did not have to be driven to it to become heavy drinkers. The custom of paying sums of money, or 'footings', into a common workshop fund for occasional bouts of drinking may have been in decline but it was still prevalent in the 1870s, while the main function of the meetings of friendly societies was, in Wright's opinion, to provide an excuse for practically enforced unrestricted drinking. These were occasions on which the line between the 'steadier men' and the 'lushingtons' of the same trade or locality became blurred as the two groups mixed freely, and even if they did not lead to a permanent dissolution of the distinction, they could make severe inroads into the family budgets of even the more prudent.[44]

In Wright's view, then, there was no simple correspondence between particular occupations, or even wage rates, and particular standards of living. Nor was it a matter of having the material necessities and then deciding whether or not to join a 'respectable élite'. In the first place chance played an important role in determining whether a man ended up 'on the staff' or facing recurrent spells of unemployment, whether he lived with a 'managing wife' or a 'trollop' and whether he ended up as a chronic heavy drinker. And, in the second place, the values of 'respectability' were not, in Wright's eyes, restricted to a privileged minority. Even in his first essays, written at the height of the controversy over working-class morals, he had argued that the majority of workers were intelligent, sober and industrious, while the vices of 'roughness' were largely restricted to those who lived their lives out in poverty. After the passing of the Reform Act in 1867, much of the heat went out of the controversy and, as the requirements of defensive strategy were loosened, it became possible to soften the contrast. Some elements of 'rough' behaviour were acknowledged to exist among ordinary working men, especially heavy drinking, while a large number of those in even the most poverty-stricken environments were shown to adhere to the norms of 'respectability'.

The basic distinction that Wright made was between those who were still wage labourers, or at least looking for employment, and those who had become 'idle' and were willing to keep their families alive by manipulating charity in a shameless and skilful way. Indeed, while the 'idle' poor had lost all sense of self-respect, and no longer felt 'the proverbial coldness of the hand of charity'[45] or the 'degradation' involved in entering the poor-house, they were generally better off. Those who suffered most from poverty were those who retained a sense of self-esteem and maintained a front of 'respectability': even when they were willing to look for assistance they would rarely have been successful because they did not *appear* to be poor. Thus the 'respectable poor' were little mentioned in writings on the subject because they were largely invisible.

> In many instances they have within the working class range seen better days, and carry the habits of those days with them into the lower grades of poverty. Though they may be without a chair to sit upon, and their bedding may consist of a pile of rags, they will have a curtain for their window, they will keep their ragged children out of sight as much as possible, and they will endure the direst hardship rather than seek aid from the hand of charity . . . Except in so far as their sense of independence may be a compensation to them, they are a degree worse off than the more reckless, more shameless, more pauper-spirited poor . . .[46]

Again and again in his essays Wright made this connection between 'respectability' and 'independence' which, while a 'glorious privilege', belonged to every man who could support himself and his family by his own efforts. 'Independence' was at one and the same time the freedom from dependence on economic patronage or charity and a guarantee of political integrity and incorruptibility, and as such was potentially the property of all wage labourers.[47] For Wright, 'respectability' was therefore an intrinsically working-class virtue, adhered to even by the most politically radical, while he referred to those who aped the values and ways of life of higher social groups as the 'genteel'.[48] Every working man took pride in having smart clothes to wear in the evenings and a proper Sunday suit, but only those with aspirations to 'gentility' wore gloves to hide the effects of manual labour on their hands.[49] The demarcation between who was and was not 'respectable' was not in Wright's account a means of identifying an 'upper stratum', but on the contrary only came into operation at the *other* end of the working-class spectrum among those who were at risk of becoming dependent on economic assistance and consequently becoming politically unreliable. Among the majority who came above this line there were other cultural distinctions, the most important of which were between the educated and the uneducated, the political and the non-political, the sober and the drunken.

In those pieces of his writing which describe working-class leisure activities, other differences emerge which are very suggestive of the texture of working-class life in these years. One obvious distinction which had wide-ranging implications for life-styles was that between the married man and the bachelor. The latter, generally a younger man, was usually more mobile and consequently a bit better-off, and was more active in workshop bands, the Volunteers, rowing clubs and trade-union affairs.[50] The married man was more likely to spend his free time at home and when he went for an outing it was usually for a 'comfortable and economic' family picnic.[51] Younger married men with social pretensions might have gone out 'quite genteel', though, and would then have preferred to eat in restaurants where they would have tried to convince the waiters 'that they and their young ladies are members of the aristocracy, who are merely indulging in a working-class holiday by way of a novelty'.[52] On their days out, the single young men tended to form groups of two main types: 'the jolly and dashing' on the one hand and the 'sporting' on the other. Groups of the first variety hired smart traps and drove about in search of pretty girls and dancing, while 'sporting' young men were found at boxing matches, race courses and local athletics contests.[53] When we consider that there were also important geographical distinctions, between the metropolis and the rest of the country, between regions and between cities and small towns[54] we will be inclined to agree with Wright that

> In no other section of society are there so many and so widely-differing castes as among the working classes. There are working men and working men in such infinite variety, that any one man embodying the distinguishing characteristics of the various types that go to make up the aggregation would be simply a monster of inconsistency. There is no typical working man.[55]

However, having made sure that his readers had grasped the diversity and complexity of the social life of the working class, Wright suggested another version of the division into three 'schools' as a 'proximate generalisation' to facilitate the understanding of popular politics. This time the guiding principle was, as Henry Pelling has already observed, the difference between the experiences of *generations*.[56] The 'old school', about a third of the male working class in 1870, was comprised mainly of those who had been born before 1820 and had been influenced by the Napoleonic Wars and a particularly harsh political and economic climate. This was a generation deeply marked by a combination of crude national chauvinism and crude class hatred, and still carrying with it the atmosphere of the popular Toryism of the previous century. Men of this school thought of themselves as 'rough and tough', were contemptuous of 'mere book learning' and were the core audience of the popular weeklies like *Reynolds'* and *Lloyds'*. They were firmly self-reliant, would normally have had some savings and often have owned their own houses, but had absolutely no pretensions to 'gentility' and no time for other classes of society.[57]

The 'school of the day' was in Wright's eyes, and as its name suggests, the predominant generation and probably made up almost half of the male working class. Most of its members would have been born in the 1820s and 1830s, affected by, but also growing away from, the 'old school' as a result of the 'explosion of old ideas ere they had ingrained themselves in comparatively young minds, and the influence of new institutions, experiences, and knowledge'.[58] The 'school of the day' was still marked by a tendency to believe that manual workers were the sole producers of wealth and yet treated as outcasts by the rest of society, and it too was strongly influenced by the popular weekly press. At the same time, however, its members were less narrowly chauvinistic and more ready to believe that other nations were serious economic competitors. Consequently, they preferred arbitration and compromise as the means of settling industrial disputes, and were more careful in their use of strike action. Though not much better educated than the previous generation, the middle-aged generation regretted it and struggled to give its children the opportunities which it had lacked.[59]

The main distinguishing characteristic of the 'coming school', largely born after 1840 and amounting to about a quarter of the male working class, was therefore its greater degree of education. The general environment in which it had grown up had been less harsh than that of the previous generations, in large part because of earlier successes in building a network of working-class institutions and gaining legislative reforms. The rising generation was much less crudely prejudiced against other social classes, more critical of the remaining shortcomings of working men, and inclined to read *The Times*, the *Saturday Review* and the *Beehive* as well as the more popular working-class press.[60] This was Wright's own generation and, as he pinned his hopes on its future predominance, he was inclined to attribute to his immediate contemporaries more of his own ideas than they probably held. In Wright's eyes, the man of the 'coming school'

> Believes that education, abundant and easily accessible literature, and the resources of modern science have already placed means within the reach of the working classes which, rightly appreciated and used by them, would diffuse a far higher and more general happiness among them than is to be found at present. Believes that a time may – probably will – come, when self-organised, self-supporting 'Working Men's Clubs' will supersede the public-house, intelligent intercourse the 'booz-ing' and horse-play of the tap-room; a time when a choicely-filled little bookcase will be an ordinary article of furniture in working-class homes . . .[61]

III

Although the distinction between the educated and the uneducated took different forms in Wright's first and second accounts of the composition of the working class, it remained for him the central distinction as far as further improvement in the well-being of his fellows was concerned. In the mid-1860s it seems to have been part of a political commitment to mainstream Liberalism, but severe disappointments with several aspects of Gladstone's first Ministry led Wright to support the formation of a working-class party with the aim of bringing about a substantial redistribution of the nation's wealth. The leading role of the educated minority remained, and its main enemy was still the popular weekly press which cultivated a mindless class antagonism among its readers. Wright did not deny that such feelings were usually based on real grievances, but argued that the men who expressed them failed to specify realistic ends and practical means, drove away potential allies in other social classes, and failed to identify their real enemies as a result of their obsession with the landed aristocracy.[62] In a remarkable passage which was the closest he came to using the phrase 'aristocracy of labour', Wright used the adjective 'aristocratic' to describe not an incorporated minority but a tendency towards mindless class antagonism among the majority.[63]

> While he constantly rails against the aristocracy, thus speaking of them as the natural and avowed enemies of the working classes, he is himself generally the most aristocratic – in his own offensive sense of the word – of working men. . . If a foreman, he scorns the idea of associating in any but a business way with the men under his command; if a mechanic, he would indignantly repudiate any proposition to associate him with a labourer; and even when a labourer he will usually find some set of persons with whom he will refuse to associate – upon some such plea as maintaining the dignity or the rights of labour, or of upholding the respectability of the order to which he belongs.

Wright's development away from Gladstonian Liberalism and towards a more oppositional radicalism seems to have exposed him to the notions of a moderate élite of privileged workers common among revolutionary writers of the period, though not necessarily referred to as a 'labour aristocracy'. Thus the phrase itself does not appear, but a similar idea is obvious in several passages in *Our New Masters* in which he pointed to the possibility that the most prosperous members of the working class would be inclined to be politically apathetic under normal circumstances and, if put under pressure in a major social upheaval, might support the *status quo*.[64] This would be a result of a mixture of economic influences: having security of employment and lacking experience of economic deprivation, having savings and therefore a stake in private property or being piece-masters or participants in cooperative production and therefore involved in making profits out of the labour of other workers. However, he concluded that the possibility that 'the natural vanguard of the army of labour would be discovered forming a rank and file under the great captains of capital' was not likely to be realized.[65]

For Wright, the main obstacle remained the prevalence of unthoughtful class antagonism and, on the other side of the same coin, sectional antagonism between groups of workers. Although in the abstract belonging to one class dependent for its income on manual wage labour,[66] in practice working men were divided by occupations and life-styles into separate and antagonistic groups, and as a result, 'though notoriously the most clubbable section of society, having vital interests in common, and being supreme in numbers where numbers should be supreme, they are still politically powerless'.[67] Apart from any general suspicion that a working man involved in politics was self-seeking, there were powerful obstacles of trade exclusiveness standing in the way of a working man's success in elections even at a local level. Wright spoke from experience here, having canvassed for a local School Board candidate whose views were approved of by the working-class voters who, however, refused to vote for him because he was a baker. 'No, they said, they were not going to vote for a fellow who carried home twopenny dinners.'[68] As Wright concluded:

> The working classes really are, as we hope we have shown, divided and sub-divided; and not only that, but divided into antagonising sections. They are as a house divided against itself. To use the point of the old fable, they are a *number*, but not a *bundle*, of sticks. Their strength is wasted and made ineffective by want of coherence. Though all schools and sections of them have broad interests in common, they are so divided in feeling as to be incapable of united action even for a common object.[69]

IV

Thomas Wright's essays, then, if read carefully, by no means give unambiguous support to the notion of a 'labour aristocracy'. There are some passages where he comes very close to adopting such an analysis, but interestingly enough these parts of his essays have not yet been quoted in accounts of the 'upper stratum' of the working class. The reason, I think, is that they do not contain the word 'artisan', and in looking to Wright for validating the notion of a 'labour aristocracy' it is passages containing *this* word which have been selected. However, as I have argued in this essay, Wright's own use of the word varies from article to article and even from passage to passage, so it is not safe to assume that each time it appears the word 'artisan' is intended to refer to the same group of workers. It is true that on some occasions Wright does use it to refer to skilled workers who have served a craft apprenticeship, but on other occasions it seems almost interchangeable with the phrase 'manual worker'. Some of the most interesting passages are those in which workers are referred to as 'artisans' precisely because of their moral qualities or even because of their involvement in the politics of Reform. I suspect that this usage was quite common in the mid-Victorian period and that workers of whatever levels of skill and income were frequently referred to as 'artisans' if they participated in what were considered to be 'artisan activities'.

In order to avoid making false correlations between political opinions, social attitudes and workers' occupations, historians therefore need to pay closer attention to the language of their 'sources', and need to be sensitive to the possibility of variations in meaning of the same word or phrase in different contexts. I have tried to show the importance of this in the case of one writer of the mid-Victorian period, but clearly there is still an immense amount of work to be done before we shall have a clear map of contemporary usage of the terms 'respectable', 'independent', 'artisan' and 'aristocracy of labour'. This should not be a formal exercise in the analysis of texts yielding a consistent set of meanings for a given period. Rather it should be a way of exploring the process by which individuals assigned themselves to different social groups and constructed images of the other groups around them.

In the case of Thomas Wright we have a skilled manual worker, an active trade-unionist and a man who, through self-education, was able to leave the world of manual labour behind and become a school inspector: in many ways an archetypal example of the historians' 'labour aristocrat'. However, this was not his own view of himself, or indeed of any of his fellow workers. Even the most highly skilled were still, in Wright's view, subject to variation in the demand for their labour caused by severe economic fluctuations. They were therefore ultimately no more secure than their fellow workers, but this did not give them any straightforward sense of being 'working class'. For while such a class could be considered to exist at a high level of abstraction, in everyday reality workers were divided into rival groups largely by their own responses to the structured and chance events of their lives. In Wright's view, some of the most important of these influences varied from generation to generation, for not only were they affected by different political and military events, but in addition the rising generations grew up in a context significantly affected by the successes and failures of their elders.

In the final analysis, then, I think that Wright saw himself and his fellow workers as having made career and cultural choices within the broad contours of a particular generation. We are now less likely than he was to assume that the succession of generations has a benign evolutionary character, but otherwise this perspective remains an extremely valuable one. For example, using this approach in the analysis of trade unions would help to provide an alternative explanation of their internal conflicts to that which emphasizes the inevitably corrupting effect of bureaucratic organization. Conflicts between officials and members could be explored in terms of the differences in attitude between the younger men and their elders who controlled policy and had been influenced by different experiences of the economic climate. The study of generations might also provide an element of an alternative approach to attempts to correlate shifts in working-class political attitudes with the underlying changes in the occupational composition of the work force. Rather we might emphasize the succession of different generations each with a distinct experience of institutions and of international war. The development of analysis in this direction would have the further advantage of displacing relatively static structural models and restoring us to the realm of specifically historical ways of thinking.

10

Anglo-Marxism and working-class education

CHUSHICHI TSUZUKI

Any history of Marxism in Britain has to deal with the complex personality and ideas of H. M. Hyndman. He was the first protagonist of Marxism, albeit of his own peculiar brand, in this country.[1] His idiosyncratic presence, though, can distort the record of Anglo-Marxism by making it fit the oddly-shaped mould which he and others fashioned at the end of the nineteenth century and after. It is the intention of this essay to re-interpret aspects of the history of Anglo-Marxism not in terms of his personal beliefs, but rather in terms of the development of an institution which attempted to work out the legacy of his Marxism and that of the Social Democratic Federation (SDF) in the years after his death. The organization in question is the National Council of Labour Colleges (NCLC), which started out as a vehicle for the dissemination of Anglo-Marxism and within two decades ended up as part of the Trades Union Congress (TUC), dedicated to forwarding the ideas of the Labourist consensus. In this transformation it is possible to see some of the peculiarities and contradictions which have beset Marxism, English-style, in this century.

I

The origins of independent working-class education can be traced back to the foundation of the London Mechanics Institute in the 1820s and further back to the activities of the London Corresponding Society at the time of the French Revolution. For our purposes, however, we can begin with the history of Ruskin College, more especially with the strike in 1909 of its students, who were determined to resist an attempt to make their college into something of a preparatory school by means of which the working-class élite could enter the University of Oxford. Noah Ablett, a Ruskin student from the Rhondda Valley, advocated workers' control of the college in *'Plebs' Magazine*, the organ of the students.[2] According to the official history of Ruskin College, the main issue to be decided was 'whether Ruskin should be a "Marxist" college or should continue to be untied to any officially adopted body of doctrine, political or religious'.[3] What was the role of Marxists in this conflict?

George Sims, a carpenter by trade and SDF member in Bermondsey, who was the leading spirit among the students, had studied Marx sufficiently to 'enable him to do a great deal to compensate for the almost complete ignorance of Marx's works shown by the Ruskin lecturer on political economy'.[4] W. W. Craik, a member of the Amalgamated Society of Railway Servants, who acted as Sims' aide-de-camp, later recalled that in the 'self-service classes' at Ruskin each participant was 'given one of the more difficult sections of the first volume of *Capital* . . . to explain to the class what he understood it to mean'.[5] It appears that the Ruskin students' desire to study Marx and Marxism was the bone of contention in their clash with the college authorities.

The strike lasted three weeks, and some of those who did not return to Ruskin when it ended, took the lead in founding the Central Labour College (CLC), an event which they regarded as 'the declaration of Working Class Independence in Education': the workers would 'think for themselves . . . free from the spell of a servile tradition and a slave philosophy'.[6] The Plebs League that had been set up by the Ruskin students prior to the strike now issued a record of the dispute under the title *The Burning Question of Education*, the tone of which, according to J. P. M. Millar, the author of the recent book *The Labour College Movement* (1979), was 'messianic'. Millar, who for many years acted as general secretary of the NCLC, called attention to the fact that the Plebs' account of the strike 'contained not one reference to Marx or Marxism'.[7] Was this omission deliberate? Or did it happen because what really mattered was to find '*their* theory'? The Plebs' pamphlet declared that their 'great ideal' was three-fold: 'the workers in their march towards emancipation shall have three great armies: – the industrial, to look after the interests of the mine and workshop; the political, to look after the interests in Parliament; the educational, to give both of these a constant supply of vitality and ideas'. The CLC 'is a triumphant testimony to what can be done when men travel along the road to which the facts of evolution point. . . . Its course is determined by the supreme struggle of economic classes; its function is to create a conscious recognition of that struggle by the class whose triumph will make society both classless and strifeless.'[8]

Dennis Hird, formerly the Principal of Ruskin College, who had been very popular among the students, was invited by the CLC to become its first Principal. An Anglican minister, he had joined the SDF and had to renounce Orders for his lecture 'Jesus the Socialist' and other similar sermons and writings. He popularized Darwin's theory of evolution and explained the march of man from the state of a brute to that of a brother in terms of the guidance of reason, itself 'one of the gifts of Evolution'. This freed man from false ideas about his origins and would bring him to 'a true order of life', that is, to some form of socialism. By socialism Hird meant Sidney Webb's collectivism or socialization of various functions of society. 'We are struggling to extend this Socialisation. It has been of slow growth, but all Evolution *is*.'[9] He taught sociology at Ruskin and also at the CLC, using as his text-books the works of Professor Lester F. Ward, an eminent American sociologist. Professor Ward visited Europe in the summer of 1909 and stayed at Oxford for the opening of the CLC. At its inaugural meeting he spoke on 'Education and Progress' before an audience of 200 including representatives of seventy labour organizations. He argued that natural inequalities in the capacity of mankind would mean 'intellectual individuality' and as such would broaden the functions and activities of mankind, whereas artificial inequalities in intelligence and capacity produced artificial social classes. Hence he advocated universal education which would bring down artificial classes and declared:

> The first and second estates were supplanted by the third and now the fourth estate is coming on and will ere long supplant the third estate. What do we hear all over the world? Nothing but the subterranean roar of that great mass of mankind, infinitely larger numerically than all the other classes put together; that class is rumbling and seething and working, and coming to consciousness; and when they do come to consciousness they will take the reins of power in their hands, and then will have been abolished the last of all the social classes.[10]

These were words both befitting the birth of the CLC and appropriate for combining the two main facets, as it appears, of CLC Marxism: the Darwinian theory of evolution and the Marxist doctrine of class struggle. 'Those who were present at the evening meeting in "Taphouse Room" on that August Bank Holiday', recalled Dennis Hird, 'will never forget the burning oratory of that frail, tired, old man, or the blazing enthusiasm of those who heard it.'[11]

In 1911, the CLC was driven from Oxford to London, where it plunged into the militant trade union movement of the day. '"The Labour Unrest" must be given greater voice', wrote Sims in the pages of *Justice*.[12] Hyndman and his party's preoccupation with politics, however, drove the CLC into the hands of trade unions in the heyday of Syndicalism and Industrial Unionism. *The Miners' Next Step*, the famous revolutionary programme for reorganization of the South Wales Miners' Federation, was prepared by its 'Unofficial Reform Committee'. Noah Ablett and W. H. Mainwaring, who was soon to become a CLC student, were among its chief spokesmen, and their scheme, as Henry Pelling has pointed out, 'marked the high water of syndicalist influence in British trade unionism',[13] and illustrated some of the peculiarities of CLC Marxism. The policy of reconciliation, they declared, had led to 'an antagonism of interests' between union leaders and the rank-and -file. 'They, the leaders, become "gentlemen", they become MPs, and have considerable social prestige because of this power. . . . Can we wonder that they try and prevent progress?' Ablett and his friends called for 'a united industrial organisation, which recognising the war of interest between workers and employers, is constructed on fighting lines, allowing for a rapid and simultaneous stoppage of wheels throughout the mining industry', and advocated 'a programme of a wide and evolutionary working class character, admitting and encouraging sympathetic action with other sections of the workers'. In short, theirs was a fighting manifesto for the workers' control of all industries. They were opposed to nationalization of mines which they regarded as a kind of state capitalism. 'Our only concern is to see to it, that those who created the value receive it. And if by the force of a more perfect organisation and more militant policy, we reduce profits, we shall at the same time tend to eliminate the shareholders who own the coalfield.' They would support political action in order to 'wrestle whatever advantage' they could obtain 'for the working class'. Their main concern, however, was industrial action, the basic philosophy of which was derived from the same theory of the worker's right to the whole produce of his labour as that which Thomas Hodgskin had taught when, a century before, he upheld the cause of organized labour. The Welsh miners, just like Hodgskin in 1825, urged trade unions to fight to reduce profits and thus to eliminate the capitalists.[14]

It was no mere coincidence that the CLC gained the official support of the two unions most prominent in Industrial Unionism, the South Wales Miners' Federation (SWMF) and the National Union of Railwaymen (NUR). During the First World War, the College was closed for a while; local classes, however, were allowed to continue. The Scottish Labour College, the founding of which had been inspired by John Maclean, had classes in which a total of 1,500 workers participated in 1918.[15] Other local labour colleges, especially those in Manchester and Sheffield, began to advocate closer coordination between colleges and classes.

Furthermore, the Workers' Educational Association (WEA), their serious rival in the field, was making a great effort to solicit trade union support by founding the Workers' Educational Trade Union Committee. The WEA itself was an outgrowth of the university extension movement, and was then in a period of educational enthusiasm in which barriers of party, class and creed were said to have been broken down. R. H. Tawney, 'the most respected spokesman of the WEA' as he was called, argued that 'the idea of solidarity which is the contribution of the working-classes to the social conscience of our age has its educational as well as its economic applications'. His plea, however, appeared to the advocates of independent working-class education to favour class-collaboration.[16] Militants then stressed the need for a national organization of their own if only to counteract the influence of the WEA. The Plebs League took the lead, and at a conference held in the old Clarion Club at Yardley, Birmingham, in October 1921, the NCLC was founded. The CLC (now the Labour College, London), the only residential college, was unwilling to abandon an expansion scheme of its own, and only reluctantly threw in its lot with the national movement.

Prominent among the leaders of the NCLC were J. F. Horrabin, the editor of *Plebs*, which became its organ, and J. P. M. Millar, the district organizer of the Scottish Labour College (Edinburgh) who acted jointly with George Sims as honorary secretary of the new organization. Sims, however, remained as secretary of the CLC and was advised by his old friends to cease his efforts to secure the support of national trade unions for the NCLC which they feared would become competitive. Before jealous counsels and divided loyalty overwhelmed him, Sims had managed to negotiate the affiliation of the two national unions: the Amalgamated Union of Building Trades Workers (AUBTW) and the National Union of Distributive and Allied Workers (NUDAW).[17] George Hicks, general secretary of the AUBTW, became a firm supporter of the NCLC; he was also a member of the Hyndman Club that was founded at about this time to commemorate the founder of the old SDF. Ellen Wilkinson, the national organizer of the NUDAW, backed the affiliation of her union. Once described as a 'sharp-tongued little fury just out of college',[18] she was a member of the Plebs League and the Independent Labour party (ILP). Her militancy was unquestioned, though her membership of the Communist party was only of short duration. Other unions followed: by 1924, the Amalgamated Engineering Union, the Electricians' Union, the Sheet Metal Workers' Union and the Tailors' and Garment Workers' Union adopted the NCLC education schemes. By 1925, the number of affiliated unions rose to twenty-eight, and the number of postal course students increased from thirty-nine in 1923 when the course was introduced, to 2,373 in 1926. The NCLC received grants from the Labour party, the Co-operative Union and the TUC. Although there were frictions, especially with the WEA, over TUC education schemes, the NCLC had by then firmly established itself as the one viable organization dedicated to independent working-class education.[19]

Nevertheless, as Craik said, 'ominous rifts' soon developed in the relations between the NCLC and the CLC, and competition between them for trade union support dealt a fatal blow to the CLC and later, as Craik saw it, led to 'the disappearance of the NCLC itself as an independent entity'.[20] Craik may well be suggesting that the demise of the CLC deprived the NCLC of much of its integrity as a Marxist body. The CLC was perhaps more overtly Marxist than the NCLC, but was its Marxism really different in kind?

II

The CLC retained the tradition of Industrial Unionism and Syndicalism, and it came very close to the Communist party when that tradition was woven into the texture of Communist unity. Already in August 1918, Maxim Litvinov, the Soviet representative in Britain, attended the annual meeting of the Plebs League and duly impressed many militants who were there, including leaders of the South Wales miners.[21] Two years later, the Communist party of Great Britain (CP) came into existence through a series of meetings and two unity conventions. Unlike the major Communist parties on the continent, which sought to win the bulk of the main working-class movement in each country, the British party was to be formed by 'assembling together a number of tiny left-wing groups'.[22] The British Socialist party (BSP) (the internationalist majority of the old SDF), the Socialist Labour party (SLP) (an unofficial group), the Workers' Socialist Federation ('the party of the poor' according to its leader, Sylvia Pankhurst,[23] or alternatively the party which had 'no real body of membership outside of a few active women in London' as the BSP saw it[24]), the South Wales Socialist Society (SWSS), the National Guild League and some others took part in the negotiations. The SWSS, though it became defunct by the summer of 1920, was represented in a unity conference by Ness Edwards, who held a SWMF scholarship at the CLC at the time, and two former CLC students from the Rhondda, George and Frank Phippen.[25] Indeed, the CLC was so favourably inclined to the CP that 'about one third of the students joined [it] almost as soon as it was formed', wrote Craik: 'Some of their successors were already members of the CP even before they arrived at the College.'[26] Even the Plebs League contributed some of its executive members – Horrabin, Raymond Postgate and Maurice Dobb – to the party.[27]

Plebs, an independent Marxist journal, had served as a vehicle for debate on the nature of the dictatorship of the proletariat and the Soviet system since the Russian Revolution. Eden Paul, a retired medical practitioner, who jointly with his wife Cedar translated a good many European works on socialism, including Marx's *Capital*, into English, suggested that Russia, through the Soviet idea, might attain the short cut to socialism. He emulated Alexander Herzen who believed that the Russians had the advantage of being free from the restrictive traditions of Europe: its religion and its bourgeoisie.[28] Maurice B. Reckitt, a Christian Socialist and member of the executive committee of the National Guild League, remarked that the Soviet system involved 'a hopeless confusion of civic with industrial functions', and would 'lead to a progressive domination . . . of minorities' and 'inevitably (quite apart from Bolshevik "atrocities") to a dictatorship *over very large sections of any proletariat'*.[29] The Pauls admitted the force of Reckitt's argument and proposed a neologism, 'ergatocracy' meaning 'workers' rule' as a better expression than 'dictatorship of the proletariat'.[30] They also contended that the British counterpart of the Russian Soviet was the Shop Stewards and Workers' Committee Movement.[31] J. T. Walton Newbold, a convert from the ILP, now calling himself 'a Bolshevik', declared that he would regard parliament as 'an institution for which there will be no place under Socialism'; 'I would use St. Stephen's to house Madame Tussaud's.'[32] Nevertheless, he became the first Communist MP, as he believed he could use parliamentary elections for Bolshevik propaganda. T. A. Jackson of the SLP and of the North-Eastern Labour College, who along with Walton Newbold was remembered as the best-known winter tutor of the NCLC, argued that 'direct action or parliamentary' was a false issue and the bloodiness or otherwise of a revolution would depend upon the counter-revolutionaries and also upon the efficiency of the workers' class organization which could be ensured only by education.[33] A similar discussion was going on in the pages of the *Call*, the organ of the BSP, where Theodore Rothstein, the most persistent opponent of Hyndman in that party, under the pseudonym of 'John Bryan', defended the institution of the Soviet against both parliament, which 'embodied the rule of the capitalist class', and trade unions, which in Russia proved 'conspicuously unimportant as revolutionary factors'.[34] He was in favour of 'the "direct action" of the masses themselves'.[35] His son Andrew explained the Soviet idea to *Plebs* readers as 'the direct representation of the massed labour'.[36] In fact, the *Plebs* remained friendly towards the emerging Communist party as long as the Soviet was interpreted as 'a Russian version of Industrial Unionism'.[37]

J. T. Murphy, the leader of the Shop Stewards Movement in Sheffield, attended the second world congress of the Comintern held in the summer of 1920 and was shocked to learn that his movement could not affiliate because it was considered to be a mass organization similar to trade unions.[38] Murphy, however, overcame what Communists saw as Industrial Unionist prejudices on his own through reading Lenin's *Left-wing Communism, an Infantile Disorder* and also after having spoken to Lenin himself. William Gallacher, who attended the same congress of the Comintern as the representative of the Clyde Shop Stewards, was similarly converted.[39] Indeed, Lenin was the architect of Communist unity in Britain. In his book referred to above he had criticized anti-parliamentary elements in the movement, stressing the need for 'proletarian "class politicians"'. The British Communist party, as it emerged, underwent the painful process of 'Bolshevization' in which syndicalist influences and decentralizing tendencies were wiped out, while 'democratic centralism' and iron discipline were gradually introduced. It could not long remain 'the sort of party which had previously existed on the extreme Left in British politics, with its strong nonconformist traditions'.[40]

It was almost inevitable that at the beginning of its 'Bolshevization' the party came into conflict with the Labour College movement. Murphy, now a good Bolshevik, wrote an article for *Plebs* entitled 'Wanted: the Marxism of Marx' in which he criticized the Plebs League and the Labour Colleges for being 'the custodians of the Marxism of the epoch of imperialist expansions'. The Plebs' advocacy of workers' control of education and their assertion that 'the fact of the Class Struggle' was the foundation of independent working-class education, belonged, Murphy argued, to 'the pedantic formalism of the so-called Marxian theorists of the epoch of the Second International'. 'Shall we spend months unravelling the Theory of Value, and never mention the elementary fact that the workers must have a revolutionary workers' party – lest we be accused of party politics?' In short, Murphy wanted the Plebs League to be committed to the Marxist–Leninist principle of the conquest of political power and allied more closely to the Communist party.[41] Several prominent Plebs tackled Murphy's criticisms, and the most forceful argument came from Craik of the CLC. Their education, he wrote, was concerned not so much with the conquest of power as with

> the *road to power*, which is not a ready-made road that one might find indicated in the Directory of the Russian Revolution (made in England) with the injunction, 'This is the way; walk ye in it', but a road which the workers themselves must make, conscious of their power to make it and of the materials which evolution has furnished for their historical task.[42]

Murphy rightly sensed that 'the syndicalist elements within the Labour Colleges and Plebs League dominate them, and it is these who resent the new competitor'. 'Instead of the Plebs and Labour Colleges having been a preparatory school for a Marxist party', he deplored, 'we are finding that some of the stiffest opposition to the development of the Party comes from them in the name of Marxism.'[43]

In the NCLC that was formed shortly after the creation of the unified Communist party, Millar and Jack Hamilton, secretary of the Liverpool Labour College and president of the NCLC, and a stonemason by trade, were strongly opposed to Communist attempts to win over their movement for fear that 'the prospects for gaining substantial union support would be reduced'.[44] The CP, however, soon decided not to rely on the Labour College movement for political education but to build up its own system. 'Fortunately', wrote Millar, 'the [Communist] orientation was short-lived since all but one of the Plebs executive committee members who had joined the Communist Party soon left it.'[45] The one who did not was probably Maurice Dobb who advised the Plebs League not to become 'anti-party' though it could remain 'non-party'.[46] J. F. Horrabin resigned from the Communist party 'quite deliberately, because the British Party chose, equally deliberately, to act in a manner calculated to injure a movement they were professing to support – the movement for Independent Working-Class Education'. He could not work, he added, with 'little Machiavellians'.[47] The Plebs Summer School held in July 1925 at Cober Hill near Scarborough, both attested to their Marxism *and* revealed its latent liberalism. The main speakers included Murphy and Gallacher for the Communist party, C. L. Malone and George Lansbury for the Labour party, and Mark Starr and J. F. Horrabin for the Plebs League. Such ample room was provided for discussion of the 'various "group" points of view' among the left wing that the participants sometimes found it difficult to control their emotions. The Communist 'attempt to "discipline" people's thinking' was denounced as 'absurd', and it was pointed out that the work of the Labour colleges and the Plebs League, 'vitally important' as they were for all revolutionists, could not be carried out under any party name.[48]

III

There was no difference of views on the Communist party and its 'iron discipline' between the NCLC, with the *Plebs* as its organ, and the CLC, of which Craik remained as a chief spokesman, although the CLC students often came under the Communist influence. The collapse of the CLC in 1929 had certainly more to do with financial rivalry than any ideological differences between the two bodies. The animosity between them had been accentuated when the Countess of Warwick offered Easton Lodge for conversion (with the financial support of the TUC) into a great residential Labour college which would absorb the CLC and Ruskin College. The NCLC was sceptical of the project, for its own classes would have suffered if the plan had been adopted as it would have caused a diversion of trade union funds from its own educational schemes. The Bournemouth Congress of the TUC in 1926 voted against the Easton Lodge plan to the delight of the NCLC and equally to the discomfiture of the CLC and also of the WEA. Millar even went so far as to suggest that Sims in 1923 and Craik in 1925 had been dismissed from the CLC for misusing some of the College funds.[49] The details and circumstances of this allegation are not clear, but Craik was apparently bitter against the NCLC and almost believed that this body and the Plebs were virtually responsible for the failure of the Easton Lodge scheme. The end of that plan 'was also to be the end of the Labour College', he wrote.[50] Yet it was surely the General Strike of 1926, which had depleted trade union funds, that was really responsible for the failure of the scheme.

Millar gives the following account of how the CLC came to an end. Towards the end of 1926 a section of the executive of the NUR, one of the two controlling unions, proposed to terminate its financial support of the CLC. They felt that their union derived little benefit from the CLC: fourteen out of the twenty-nine former NUR students were no longer working on the railways. The NCLC intervened and sought to persuade the NUR to continue to share the costs of running the college jointly with the SWMF and possibly with the NCLC itself, and the annual meeting of the NUR defeated the executive's move to close the CLC. Financial worries were aggravated by ideological discord. It was disclosed at about this time that some ten CLC students, of whom eight were Communists, were actively engaged in organizing Communist cells in some trade unions. Other students objected and the trouble was eventually reported to the NUR representative on the CLC board who had not been favourably disposed to the College and was now determined to wash his hands of it. Some of the students were expelled, and the NCLC was blamed, perhaps wrongly, for the expulsions.[51] The NCLC made 'last-ditch efforts' to save the CLC, but its offers were turned down by the college board headed by W. H. Mainwaring of the SWMF, the other controlling union, which unlike the NUR had been given great service by its former college students. A piece of vanity or jealousy perhaps played its part in this case. The fate of the CLC was thus sealed. 'The governors did not offer the NCLC any part of the College equipment, which was sold out at public auction', wrote Millar.[52] As Ness Edwards, a former SWMF student and later a Labour MP recalled, however, the CLC was 'to all intents and purposes a victim of the General Strike'.[53] In a sense the CLC was an educational form of Industrial Unionism which had just about burnt itself out in 1926. Its demise, therefore, was inevitable.

The NCLC survived, though the slump in the early 1930s weighed heavily on its finances with payments from the affiliated unions being sometimes reduced or even terminated. The recovery came with the affiliation of the NUR whose contribution turned out to be greater than that of any other union. The SWMF followed suit when economic recovery became more apparent. By the end of 1938, the number of trade unions with standard education schemes had increased to twenty-seven, while the total number of those fully affiliated or otherwise associated was forty-eight. At the last annual conference before the outbreak of the Second World War, the NCLC found itself 'in a stronger position . . . than ever before'.[54]

An ideological battle between some NCLC members and the Communist party went on intermittently in this period. After the General Strike of 1926, Maurice Dobb blamed the 'great betrayal' of the right-wing leaders for its failure, while Ellen Wilkinson refrained from what she described as 'futile denunciations of "treachery" and "cowardice"' and called for a thorough study of the historic event.[55] When the NCLC published such a study entitled *A Workers' History of the General Strike*, William Paul in the Communist *Sunday Worker* suggested that the Plebs were 'moving to the right'.[56] John S. Clarke, formerly an SLP and subsequently a CP member, who along with Gallacher had represented the Clyde Shop Stewards at the second world congress of the Comintern, later left the CP and joined the ILP. When the NCLC issued his book, *Marxism and History*, which was originally written for ILP readers, T. A. Jackson attacked it with an article in the *Sunday Worker* entitled 'Where is the NCLC? Is it Deserting to Marx's Enemies?' He criticized Clarke for his 'banal metaphysical trick of talking about the "economic factor", the "moral factor", the "psychic factor", the "geographical factor"'. Jackson himself felt that these were merely differing aspects of one and the same human society.[57] Jackson stuck to his guns. His dialectical materialism began to assume the characteristic of a metaphysical orthodoxy, despite the volley of Plebsian protests including one from J. F. Horrabin who wrote: 'when the *Sunday Worker*, and certain other critics, say that we're not Marxist, what they really mean is that we're not *Communist*'.[58]

A similarly heterodox position was stated by Arthur Woodburn, for many years secretary of the Scottish Labour College (Edinburgh), and subsequently president of the NCLC. He had written an NCLC text-book, *Outline of Finance*, and gave evidence on economic questions on behalf of the NCLC to the Macmillan Committee on Finance and Industry, which reported in 1931. He recounted his arguments for *Plebs*. The gold standard should be maintained as it was in line with 'the law of currency as established by Marx'. The cause of economic crises and unemployment was 'overproduction' which he paraphrased as 'unorganised production.' 'The remedy for this is control of production, not "monkeying" with the currency'. Yet he was in favour of a managed currency: 'the development of socially desirable trade should determine how much cash is required' and 'the only limit to the creation of credit is the amount and quality of unemployed labour'.[59] At the Cober Hill Summer School of that year, however, the quality of his Marxism was questioned by his critics who asserted that his terminology was not Marx's, his method was not 'dialectical', and his biological view of society was not Marxist.[60]

Ideological differences appear to have been a convenient screen to hide disciplinary matters. James Younie, a former NUR student at the CLC and then an NCLC organizer, who was dismissed for some irregularities, attacked Millar, the man who dismissed him, and published a pamphlet in which he declared that in the NCLC he could no longer detect revolutionary Marxism but only 'a feeble policy of gradualism'.[61] Even the tone of the special Karl Marx number of *Plebs* commemorating in 1933 the fiftieth anniversary of his death was not harmonious. T. A. Jackson, as ever, pleaded for the dictatorship of the proletariat, while A. L. Rowse, Fellow of All Souls College, Oxford, and Labour candidate for Penryn and Falmouth, argued that Marx was 'very much less sectarian than his interpreters are apt to be, less rigid and one-sided in his interpretation'.[62]

Less than two months before this, Hitler had come to power. The threat from Nazi Germany that soon loomed large and the resulting changes in Comintern tactics towards popular fronts, however, did not improve the relationship between the NCLC Marxists and their CP critics. 'It must be rather difficult to be a Communist just now', wrote Ellen Wilkinson in 1935:

> I don't mean one of those decent fellows who has heard that there is a class-war on, and weighs in to help, but those theoreticians whom the Germans expressively called 'ink coolies', who have to watch carefully which side the Soviet cat washes its whiskers each morning, in order to keep up with the swift changes of policy in Moscow. And if they don't watch out, they make awkward mistakes.[63]

It was not easy to watch out. It was even harder to foresee. Between communists and socialists, awkwardness and bad temper remained.

Already in the general election of 1929, the NCLC claimed a fair share in Labour's victory and was proud of eight Plebs' MPs: Ellen Wilkinson, Willie Brooke (a former CLC student), Charles Brown (an NCLC organizer), J. F. Horrabin, Will Lawther, John S. Clarke, George Daggar (an old SWMF student at the CLC) and Philips Price (author and for many years a member of the Plebs executive committee). In 1945, Millar jubilantly reported to his executive committee:

> Among those elected are three who signed the Round Robin which was the declaration of the strike at Ruskin College in 1909. They are Arthur Jenkins, Hubert Beaumont and Meredith Titterington. Among NCLC MPs four are members of the Cabinet – Ellen Wilkinson (Minister of Education), Aneurin Bevan (Minister of Health), Jim Griffiths (Minister of National Insurance), E. J. Williams (Minister of Information). The following are parliamentary secretaries: Arthur Jenkins, Ness Edwards, William Leonard [first secretary of the Scottish Labour College], Arthur Woodburn and Ellis Smith. . . Four members of the NCLC executive have been elected, viz. A. Lyne, W. Coldrick, Arthur Woodburn and T. Williamson. W. N. Warbey, ex-NCLC organiser, has also been elected as have a number of ex-NCLC executive members as well as tutors and four postal course examiners. . . The result of the General Election is likely to stimulate a considerable interest in the NCLC's work.[64]

There were many other prominent members of the NCLC outside parliament. As noted above, Morgan Phillips, secretary of the Labour party, was an old CLC student, as was Will Lawther, now president of the National Union of Mineworkers; Ebby Edwards, general secretary of the same union, was a Ruskin student at the time of the 1909 strike and remained an active Pleb.[65]

By 1929, the NCLC fully identified itself with the Labour party and the trade unions. It had provided the Labour movement with facilities for education for class war. This, the NCLC felt, would ensure the development of the independent political and industrial forces of labour. With the advent of the Labour government in 1945, a change of emphasis took place in the NCLC

Marxism. Apparently there was the need for constructive rather than critical socialism. As time went on, wrote Millar, 'the proportion of classes and postal courses explicitly dealing with Marxist theories decreased because the needs of the Labour Movement demanded new classes and courses designed to equip workers for practical problems and responsibilities arising from their industrial and political struggles and to help them in their efforts to improve their condition'.[66] The absorption of the NCLC by the TUC, which finally came in 1964, was an inevitable outcome of this practical approach to what they had advocated for so many years: independent working-class education.

IV

The NCLC Marxists, like Hyndman before them, searched for a British way to socialism and found it in the Labour party and the trade unions. When they found it, they tried to be as practical and helpful as they could, and by doing so parted with whatever remained of that critical and revolutionary socialism that had been closely linked with the movement of Industrial Unionism and Syndicalism. The doctrine of 'labour unrest', as we have seen, had been inspired by the Hodgskinian claims of the worker's right to the whole produce of his labour. It was Hodgskinian with a difference, however, for what they demanded was not the individualistic right to the fruits of one's own labour but the right of the workers as a class to control industry. Just as the critical doctrine of the right of nature, the theoretical weapon of a bourgeois revolution, had given way to the more constructive theory of utilitarianism, the philosophy of the triumphant bourgeoisie, so did the NCLC Marxism evolve from Syndicalism into utilitarian Labourism when Labour appeared victorious.

Many years before 1945, it was already apparent that NCLC Marxism, like Hyndman's, was the Marxism of the Second International in the sense that it was revisionist at heart. It was neither Hegelian nor Leninist. Dialectical materialism was too metaphysical, and political dictation too Machiavellian for its taste. It adapted itself to the mundane British world of utilitarianism and evolutionism. Prominent Plebs thus turned into Labour politicians, trade union leaders and functionaries. But if Labour's political success in 1945 was the direct cause of the natural death of the old NCLC, disillusionment with the outcome of that victory could easily bring forth out of the remains of the old creed a new form of 'Anglo-Marxism' dedicated to the ideal of 'true' working-class education.

11

Did British workers want the welfare state? G. D. H. Cole's Survey of 1942

JOSÉ HARRIS

Many commentators on British politics in the early twentieth century assumed that extension of state social welfare would be one of the inevitable consequences of opening up the franchise to members of the working class. As Sidney Webb put it in 1894, collectivist social policies were the 'economic obverse of democracy': a view that has been widely quoted ever since by historians of the welfare state.[1] However, a few years ago the assumption that workers automatically equated state welfare with the promotion of their own interests was criticized by Dr Henry Pelling. He argued that such evidence as was available suggested that British workers were much less interested in state welfare schemes than in the more tangible benefits of secure employment and cheap food.[2] Other recent studies of early twentieth-century social history have stressed the ambiguities in workers' attitudes to welfare. Popular support for more extensive social provision was often mingled with such factors as fear of bureaucratic power, dislike of form-filling and regimentation, defence of the traditional voluntary ethic and (in the case of skilled workers) resentment against the state's efforts to extend minority privileges to majority groups.[3] Dr Pat Thane, in one of the few direct comments on Dr Pelling's thesis, plausibly suggested that early twentieth-century workers' organizations welcomed some forms of state welfare and resisted others; they disliked those which subjected workers to remote and impersonal forms of official regulation or which took the form of disguised regressive taxation; they welcomed those which allowed for a high degree of participatory democracy and encouraged working-class traditions of self-help.[4]

A full historical analysis of workers' perceptions of state welfare would clearly raise numerous problems of definition and methodology, and would require a great deal of detailed and varied research covering different historical periods. In this paper discussion will be confined to a limited period and to a single source. Working-class attitudes to welfare will be considered in the context of one of the major turning-points in British social policy: the Beveridge plan of 1942. Evidence will be gleaned from the special survey of popular attitudes to welfare carried out for Beveridge by G. D. H. Cole and the Nuffield College Reconstruction Survey. Just how far this survey was an authentic expression of grass-roots opinion may be questioned, and was indeed questioned at the time. The aim of this paper is not to present Cole's findings as a mirror image of working-class attitudes, but, bearing in mind the limitations of this source, to see what information may be extracted from it in default of evidence of a more exact and comprehensive kind.

The investigation of popular attitudes to welfare was undertaken for the Beveridge Committee by Cole and the Nuffield College Reconstruction Survey (hereafter Survey) late in 1941 and completed in the summer of 1942. The Survey had been set up in 1940 to monitor the impact of war on industrial structure and on the working of the social services, and to formulate proposals about 'general problems of social and economic reorganisation' after the war. The work of the Survey was coordinated by a group of Oxford economists and statisticians working under Cole's directorship; but the actual field-work was done by a nation-wide team of local investigators who had been collected together by Cole to do research for Beveridge's manpower survey of 1940. The local investigators included a doctor, a solicitor and a barrister, but the majority were university teachers and lecturers to the Workers' Educational Association (WEA). Initially, the Survey was funded by a Treasury grant and was to receive full cooperation from Whitehall departments. But by mid-1941 there were signs of suspicion and hostility in official quarters, particularly in the Ministry of Labour. The Survey was accused of 'socialism', of 'snooping' and of sheltering refugee economists with unreliable views. The confidence of Whitehall was further eroded by Cole's handling of the research for the Beveridge Committee; and the Survey's government grant and semi-official status were eventually withdrawn in 1943.[5]

Cole's remit from Beveridge was to produce a report on the working of the social services 'from the consumer's end'. He was to 'find out what the recipients thought of the present form and substance of these services, where the shoe pinched, and what changes in them were most urgently needed or desired'. No specific mention was made of 'working-class' opinion, but since the bulk of the social services were either means-tested or subject to an income limit, it was clear that the vast majority of the 'consumers' investigated would, in fact, be working-class. No attempt was to be made to look at the social services from the angle of workers as industrial producers, an omission that is perhaps surprising in view of Cole's guild socialist past, but one that seems consistent with the development of his political thought in the 1940s. Initially, it was hoped to carry out the research with the aid of a house-to-house survey, but this was specifically forbidden by the government partly on wartime security grounds and partly for fear that it might raise false hopes of future welfare schemes in the minds of the populace. It was therefore decided to circulate questionnaires only to the Survey's local investigators. They were to fill in the questionnaires after informal contact with trade-unionists, social workers, Citizens' Advice Bureaux, local newspapers, solicitors, WEA members and panel doctors. The inquiries of the local investigators were to be classified under three broad headings – (i) popular opinion about the working and deficiencies of the social services, (ii) 'consumers' wants and needs not fully met by existing schemes' and (iii) 'problems and difficulties of Social Insurance and Assistance as seen by social workers'.[7]

The field-work of the investigation was carried out in the early months of 1942. On 7 February a conference of local investigators was held at Nuffield College; Beveridge strongly emphasized his interest in sounding out grass-roots opinion and outlined the kind of issue that he wanted to see aired. He was particularly interested in gathering information about attitudes to the 'contributory' insurance principle, about the need for 'coordination' between the different social services, about the treatment of long-term unemployment and about whether old-age pensions should be made conditional on retirement. His talk was followed by prolonged discussion among the investigators concerning methods of collecting information and how the concept of 'consumer' should be defined. Some doubt was expressed as to the procedure of the Survey by one delegate who 'said that, as a psychiatric social worker, she was not much in contact with economic problems'; but in general the investigators were confident that an accurate picture of popular opinion could be easily obtained.[8] Over the next two months a wide variety of different survey methods was put into practice by investigators in twenty-seven different areas of England, Scotland and Wales. Some got information through personal interviews with individual clients of the social services; others relied mainly on information from professional bodies such as organizations of social workers and housing managers; while the more ambitious called together group meetings of 'trade unionists, WEA students, industrial workers and other persons interested'.[9] One consequence of this difference in technique was that the social background of the informants varied widely from area to area. In South Wales, Edinburgh and Southampton opinions were gleaned almost exclusively from working-class sources. In Leeds and York informants appeared to be mainly middle-class interpreters of working-class opinion such as social workers, factory welfare officers, the staff of Citizens' Advice Bureaux and Public Assistance officials. In Bristol the only working-class sources mentioned were women: mothers at infant welfare centres and women's cooperative guilds. More typically, investigators called upon a fairly wide range of sources; informants in Aberdeen, for example, included health visitors, almoners, trade union and friendly society secretaries, a retired soldier, a funeral undertaker, an office cleaner, a carpenter, an engineer, a tram-driver, a journeyman cooper, several working-class women and an unspecified group of 'working-class friends'. Wide variations were also recorded in the degree of local enthusiasm generated by discussions of social reform. In South Wales the response was 'so vigorous and positive in almost every case that it has been very easy to evaluate the strength of feeling'. But investigators in Manchester reported 'widespread ignorance and apathy', and in Oxford working men found it 'mildly comical' that they should be asked to contribute to such a debate.[10] In addition to these local surveys, information was gathered from bodies like the Association of Family Case Workers and the Society of Women Housing Managers, together with a rather rough-and-ready sample of general practitioners in London, Leeds, Basingstoke and Carlisle.

The results of the Survey, which Cole claimed consisted solely of a summary of local information without any kind of editing by himself, were submitted to the Beveridge Committee in June 1942.[11] Conclusions were presented in an entirely impressionistic form with no attempt to quantify the different opinions recorded. The report was divided into five main parts – on national health insurance, old-age pensions, the Unemployment Assistance Board, the Public Assistance system, and workmen's compensation.[12] Of these, the section on national health insurance was by far the most detailed and thorough, and suggested that, from the point of view of the working-class consumer, it was health that was the first priority of future social reform. With few exceptions,[13] the report recorded an almost universal dissatisfaction with the 'panel doctors' available under the existing national health insurance, a dissatisfaction based partly on the enormous size of many panel practices, and partly on the conviction that panel patients were given markedly inferior treatment to that given those who paid.[14] It was complained that panel doctors would not visit patients at home, that their surgeries were dirty and ill-equipped, that they frequently prescribed 'coloured water' or cut-price drugs and that their manners were 'curt, brisk and hurried'. There were many 'pin-pricking differentiations' between panel and private patients, reported a local investigator in Cumberland, 'which are of no real importance, but leave a sense of inferiority which is not unimportant'. In some areas it was reported that the concept of the 'family doctor' was in decline, though this was to a certain extent belied by the fact that in many households the 'panel doctor' who treated the insured breadwinner was also employed privately to treat his uninsured wife and children. However, lack of confidence in the panel system was indicated by an increasing tendency for well-paid workers to employ a private physician, and by a revival of the nineteenth-century practice of taking ailments straight to hospital out-patients' departments, thus bypassing the general practitioner. Reports varied on the cherished medical principle of free choice of doctor. Some investigators reported that it was of no practical significance and that many working-class people did not bother to enrol with a doctor until they fell ill. Choice was based on purely random factors, and 'academic qualifications are of no importance'.

Others reported that free choice of doctor *was* important, particularly to women and Roman Catholics; and in the East End of London it was found that many people 'definitely prefer a coloured doctor for superstitious reasons – a type of inverted black magic'. Virtually no use was made of the statutory right to change one's doctor, partly through dislike of form-filling and partly through embarrassment at the thought of giving offence. The latter feeling was particularly strong in rural areas, where 'the doctor is regarded as gentry'. The report concluded, however, that the right 'was appreciated in theory, and there might be objections to its elimination'.

Similar dissatisfaction was expressed with the 'approved society' system, which had been set up under Part One of the National Insurance Act of 1911. The existence of a large number of approved societies, each offering 'additional' benefits which supplemented statutory health insurance, was designed to achieve two goals. It was supposed to enable the consumer to exercise rational preferences and to shop around for whichever package of benefits suited him best; and it was also supposed to preserve the local democratic fraternal ethic of the nineteenth-century friendly society movement. Even in theory it might be objected that these two goals were incompatible; and certainly in practice neither was being very successfully achieved in 1942. Among a minority of skilled workers serious attempts were made to assess the relative performance of the different approved societies; but reliable information was almost impossible to obtain without prolonged research in public libraries, and 'the whole thing is wrapped in mystery so far as the ordinary workman or woman is concerned'. A majority of workers were either apathetic about the whole system, or based their choice of a society on accidental or personal factors such as family tradition, surrender to high-pressure salesmanship or following the example of their mates.' 'Children are more or less born little Oddfellows, Ancient Shepherds, Rechabites or Free Gardiners', it was reported from Edinburgh. Patterns of membership revealed a widely varying and anarchic local pluralism. For example, detailed analysis of a small factory in Devon showed that 328 workers were distributed between no less than thirty-one approved societies, ranging from the Prudential with fifty-nine members and the Rational Assurance with forty-six through to the Catholic Thrift with two members and the Orange and Protestant with one. Where a large number of workers in the same industry did decide to join a society specific to the industry, it could have disastrous actuarial consequences totally unforeseen by the unwary consumer, as in the large number of miners' union approved societies which were on the verge of financial ruin. Some resentment was expressed about the pressure put upon workers by union officials to stay in such schemes even when they were obviously breaking down.[15] There was widespread criticism of the virtual exclusion from approved societies of people with long-term ailments; epileptics and disabled people, for example, often could not gain entry to an approved society even when they were employed in regular, full-time work.[16] Resentment was strongest, however, against approved societies which were run by the large industrial assurance companies and which had played an increasingly large part in the administration of health insurance since its inception in 1911. In Birmingham and South Wales it was reported that working people made little distinction between trade union and 'friendly' approved societies on the one hand and the big insurance companies on the other; but in all other parts of the country the reverse was the case. The insurance companies, with their large army of professional door-to-door weekly collectors, were accused of depersonalizing and delocalizing social insurance and destroying the rituals of dinners, fraternal meetings and distinctive regalia which had been a central part of mid-nineteenth-century friendly society culture. Moreover, it was believed that 'the Trade Unions and Friendly Societies want to help their members get what they are entitled to, whereas the industrial companies try to dodge payment if they can'. Particularly resented was the Prudential Assurance Company which was accused of being 'thoroughly rotten', of making 'every effort to avoid payment' and of taking longer to pay benefit than any other approved society in the country.[17] Such observations may have been true or false, but they cannot be ascribed simply to the anti-commercial bias of Cole's investigators, since it was repeatedly emphasized that approved societies set up by large private companies for the benefit of their employees were extremely popular; Harrods' and Debenhams' Approved Societies, for example, were among those noted as being both 'very personal and friendly' and ultra-efficient. In respect of both large and small approved societies, numerous complaints were made about lack of machinery for redress of grievances. Insured workers were almost universally ignorant of their statutory right to complain to the local Insurance Committees which had been established under the 1911 National Insurance Act, and indeed the very existence of such committees was widely unknown. Moreover, in both large and small societies the self-governing procedures prescribed by the Act were virtually a dead letter; schemes were run by small cliques of officials, and most approved societies were 'as remote as a Nazi election from any reality of democratic control'.

The third main item of grievance about national health insurance was the low level of weekly benefit paid: only 10s 6d for disablement and 18s for short-term sickness with no allowance for dependants (compared with the 20s a week plus allowances for wives and children paid to the insured unemployed). Sickness benefit had deliberately been fixed low in 1911 so as not to undercut the voluntary insurance movement; but, although voluntary working-class saving had continued to grow in the intervening years, it was disproportionately concentrated on 'assurance' rather than 'insurance', that is to say, on provision against the ultimate certainty of death rather than against the unpredictable risk of occasional sickness. The consequence was that few workers had adequate voluntary insurance with which to eke out their basic statutory sickness benefit,and common sources of supplementation were partial payment of wages, Works Benevolent funds, help from friends and relations, Post Office savings, pawnshops, getting into debt, rent arrears, charity and Public Assistance committees. In London, never famous for its thrift, 75 per cent of beneficiaries of national health insurance were simultaneously receiving public assistance, but even in small provincial towns with a much stronger tradition of saving, the figure was as high as 40 per cent. Enforced resort to what was still regarded as indistinguishable from the old Poor Law caused widespread resentment, and was one reason why unemployment benefit was apparently regarded as considerably less stigmatic than sickness benefit. It was widely recorded that fear of being thrown upon the Poor Law drove many sick workers to return to work prematurely, 'with consequent disastrous results to their health'. Fear of the Poor Law also opened up self-conscious lines of demarcation between different sections of the working class. In a few areas such as Poplar it was observed that there was no longer any 'social aversion' to public assistance, but in many places old attitudes died hard. 'However much the [Public Assistance] committees may be humanised, the ignominy of respectable working-class families being compelled to seek assistance through the same channels as the unemployables, the destitute, the infirm and the flotsam of the population is felt keenly.' Even in the case of contributory insurance benefit there was some evidence of refusal to claim benefit 'out of pride', but this feeling had virtually 'died out among the present generation'. Failure to claim benefit was ascribed by local investigators mainly to ignorance, dislike of filling in forms, over-optimism and, in a few cases, to sheer fecklessness.

Considerable criticism was levied not only at the low level but also at the narrow scope of health benefits. Throughout the country there were complaints about the exclusion of wives and children, though this issue was debated in less detail than might have been expected. Similarly, there was an almost 'unanimous feeling' that dental treatment, ophthalmic treatment and surgical appliances, in that order of priority, should be included among the statutory benefits. People were at a loss to understand why some approved societies could pay such benefits whilst others could not; and there was a widespread demand for standardization of benefits for all insured contributors. There was an almost equally strong feeling in favour of a statutory funeral benefit, 'in order to remove the present abuses of commercial insurance against death'. A more controversial issue was the demand that maternity benefit should be payable over an extended period and that it should be available to all mothers regardless of whether or not they were insurance contributors.[18] One objection recorded was that increased maternity benefit would merely raise midwives' fees, another that it would 'all go on drinks for the husband' and a third that childbirth should be a charge on national taxation rather than on social insurance. A related grievance concerned the widely varying quality of local maternity services, and the fact that in geographically contiguous areas the proportion of pregnancies admitted to hospital could vary from 0 per cent to 90 per cent.

After health insurance, the second major section of the report dealt with the three different types of old-age pensioner – non-contributory, contributory and supplementary. The Survey reported that among the three types of pensioners less than 5 per cent were still in the labour market, a figure that seems extraordinarily low, given the wartime shortage of labour. If anything like true, the finding certainly challenged the then-current trade-unionist belief that working pensioners contributed substantially to problems of employment among younger workers. Some evidence was found to suggest that pensioners were being dumped by their relatives in old people's homes, but there was far more evidence of the contrary kind, that 'children do not encourage parents to enter homes and make great efforts to look after them'. Among old people themselves there was an overwhelming demand for 'almshouse type accommodation' which was strongly preferred to old people's homes, and in many cases seen as preferable to living with one's family.

Most discussion of old age centred, however, on the financial issue of pensions. As with sickness benefit local investigators reported a unanimous feeling that the level of contributory, insurance-based pensions was 'hopelessly inadequate'. There was, nevertheless, no evidence of hostility to the contributory principle, in fact quite the reverse. Beneficiaries of non-contributory 'Lloyd George' pensions (mainly people who had been self-employed or who had left the labour market before 1926) were strongly in favour of being transferred to the contributory system. At the same time there was widespread reluctance to apply for the supplementary pensions introduced in 1940, and general support for 'the abolition of the principle of supplementation and the introduction of a higher flat-rate'. Reasons for preferring the contributory principle were not fully spelt out, but were almost certainly linked with dislike of means tests and administrative discretion, and with the feeling that non-contributory payments were 'unfair to the thrifty'. There were few complaints against the Assistance Board's administration of supplementary pensions, but some criticism of the personnel of the local pensions committees who administered the non-contributory system. Such committees were supposed to consist of 'sympathetic persons' with a 'working knowledge of the working-class'; but particularly in rural areas membership was almost solidly middle class 'and the working knowledge is, therefore, obtained across the fence of middle class prejudice'.

The administration of unemployment insurance was deliberately excluded from the Survey because of abnormal wartime conditions in the labour market.

The investigation did, however, look closely at the working of the Assistance Board, whose peacetime duties were mainly concerned with the long-term unemployed. Here the investigation found less national unanimity than on the issues of health and pensions; in fact, popular attitudes to the Assistance Board varied enormously from area to area. Reports from North Wales, Edinburgh and Aberdeen were extremely hostile, while those from Dundee, Huddersfield, Cambridge, Hull and south and west London were highly favourable. Between these two extremes the work of the Board appeared to have earned a mixture of suspicion and grudging respect. The most important variable in determining local attitudes was almost certainly the personal outlook and behaviour of the Assistance Board staff. 'The bullying type of investigating clerk' was deemed to have 'practically disappeared', but, nevertheless, it was complained in some areas that staff were untrained, demoralized and particularly hostile to claimants with large families. In South Devon the Board's chief investigating clerk was a retired policeman 'whose conception of his office was that of a detective whose duty it was to spy upon suspected malefactors'. Old people claiming supplementary pensions 'resented being questioned about their incomes and the way they spent them by young girls who might be their grandchildren'.[20] Particularly unpopular were offices without waiting-rooms where clients were forced to queue on the stairs or in the street, and offices where walls were plastered 'with posters proclaiming pains and penalties for breaches of the regulations'. On the whole, however, claimants' criticisms against the Assistance Board were noticeably less hostile than those of the professional social workers who gave evidence to the Survey. 'They have good intentions', complained the Brighton Social Service Centre about Assistance Board clerks, 'but no knowledge of social legislation or psychology. They miss countless opportunities of doing highly valuable social casework, because they have no idea how to set about it'. But attempts by the Assistance Board to introduce a 'social work element' into the handling of claims had not found favour with clients, many of whom viewed it as an interference with personal liberty or as an oblique way of tightening up the means test. Predictably, all forms of means test were universally resented and there were many complaints that the Personal Needs Test introduced in 1940 was merely the old, discredited Household Means Test in disguise. By its operation, so it was objected, thrift was still penalized, relatives were still pursued for contributions, children were still driven from home.[21] Attached to each local office of the Assistance Board there were local advisory committees, composed of representative employers and workers. There was, however, much variation in opinion about how effective these were in protecting claimants' interests. It was widely believed that meetings were dominated by, and often solely attended by, employers – non-attendance of working-class representatives being ascribed in some places to the fact that committees only met in the evening and elsewhere to the fact that they only met during the day. Appeals against the Board's decisions were rare, partly because clients were ignorant of their rights, partly because the nature of an appeal tribunal was widely misunderstood. One investigator recorded that 'people are said to be afraid of the very word "tribunal" which suggests punishment'. In Wales it was complained that tribunals were useless to many among the local population because proceedings were held only in English. Chairmen of tribunals were 'too remote from the working-folk, too legalistic and insufficiently human. This is particularly true of the mining valleys, where the professional classes constitute the aristocracy in an otherwise classless territory.'[22] In Bristol on the other hand, workers' representatives on appeals tribunals were said to be usually 'harder on the applicant' than were their middle-class counterparts. In only four of the twenty-seven regions surveyed – Devon, south Wales, west Wales and Aberdeen – was the tribunal system perceived as inherently hostile to the interests of the working class.

Attitudes to the Public Assistance bureaucracy also appeared to vary widely. Investigators from some areas reported that in both principles and personnel it was indistinguishable from Poor Law Boards of Guardians which it was supposed to have replaced, others that the traditional stigma attached to public relief had almost disappeared. Reasons given for the local variation in attitudes were more complex than in the case of the Assistance Board. Public Assistance committees were less unpopular in urban than in rural areas, less resented by the young than by the old. There was some difference of opinion about whether people preferred the old-style, Poor-Law-trained relieving officers, or the new-style relieving officer recruited by examination and trained in office management. The old guard were often 'mean and lacked imagination', but were more personal and human than their successors, they would occasionally 'unbend' and 'go out with their clients for a drink'. As with the staff of the Assistance Board, relieving officers of both kinds were subject to wide-ranging attacks from professional social workers for their 'lack of sociological and psychological knowledge'. 'If applicants were treated . . . with the case-work approach', reported one Welfare Officer, 'I think that the reluctance of people of good standards to apply to them would disappear'. One important factor in determining attitudes to assistance was undoubtedly the wide variation in local scales of relief. Weekly benefits for a married couple varied from eighteen shillings in North Staffordshire to thirty-five shillings in Glasgow. Rent allowances varied from nothing in most agricultural areas to more than twelve shillings a week in most industrial towns. Such variations were partly dependent on local politics: Glasgow Public Assistance committee, for instance, was dominated by socialists, and working-class representatives controlled a majority of Public Assistance committees in Wales. But another important factor in producing these variations was recent social history; it was recorded that areas which had experienced hunger marches, for example, had noticeably higher scales than elsewhere, regardless of the political complexion of the local Public Assistance committee. Nearly all areas operated a wage-stop to keep relief below the level of local wages; but, although this was mentioned as a grievance in certain areas, it was believed to have declined in importance because of the rise in wages during the war. The Public Assistance means test was less resented than that operated by the Assistance Board, presumably, although this was not clearly spelt out, because the Assistance Board was concerned with payment of benefits that people believed that they should have been getting as a contractual entitlement. One area in which the Public Assistance system emerged in a surprisingly favourable light was provision of medical care. Evidence from most areas suggested that 'medical provision under Public Assistance is at least as good as, and in many respects better than, panel service'.

The final section of the investigation dealt with workmen's compensation, though local investigators had gathered less information on this than on other welfare issues. Once again a 'unanimous view' was recorded that benefit levels were inadequate. 'Men simply do not understand why they should not get full wages when injured at work', reported the investigator in South Wales. Other repeated complaints centred on the long delays involved in meeting claims, and the reluctance of firms to keep on partially-disabled workers in light employment. Much criticism was expressed of the 'pernicious effect of lump sum payments', which were 'often invested in a business which fails', though in Wales cases were recorded of injured miners who had used their lump-sum settlements to pay their way through university. Workers were baffled by workmen's compensation law, and there were many demands for a separate system of workmen's compensation courts, staffed by laymen and not bound by normal legal rules. This view was not shared by trade-unionists in South Wales, however, where formal courts were seen as less hostile than lay tribunals: 'at the present time most County Court judges interpret existing legislation in the workmen's favour . . . the atmosphere of the County Court is said to be a strain but the judges are not viewed unfavourably'.[23] From some areas came support for the idea of unifying workmen's compensation with national insurance, a demand which was totally at odds with the current official policy of the Trades Union Congress (TUC).[24]

Throughout the different sections of the Survey, fragments of evidence appeared about working-class involvement in voluntary and informal systems of welfare outside the state and approved society systems. Voluntary activity of the 'friendly' ritualistic kind seemed to be mainly confined to the older generation: older men 'were proud of being Rechabites or Oddfellows . . . especially where the Society has regalia, there is quite an "old school tie" feeling about its members'. Membership of voluntary schemes of a more informal kind still appeared, however, to be widespread in all age groups, and in particular, schemes for private medical provision were universally popular. A 'typical' transport worker whose pattern of saving was analysed in detail was found to subscribe, in addition to his approved society contribution, to a Co-operative Society sick scheme, three slate clubs, a hospital contributory scheme, a district nursing scheme and the Transport and General Workers' Union convalescent home. Most popular of all were the various hospital contributory schemes such as the Saturday and Sunday funds, which received 'little but praise' and only one mildly adverse comment in any part of the country. Throughout the regions surveyed there were still innumerable public house benefit schemes, tontines and 'Sick and Divide clubs', which performed the dual function of paying benefits to the sick and sharing out the residue as a bonus at Christmas. 'Doctors' Clubs', run by local medical-aid societies or by doctors themselves, were still important in the north, but had virtually died out in London and the south-east. In a growing number of local-authority areas such as Birmingham, Northampton, Oxford and Mansfield, the panel system was supplemented by a local-authority-organized 'Public Medical Service', which provided medicine for non-insured working-class people in return for voluntary contributions of 1/4d per family per week. Very poor areas, such as Bethnal Green and parts of North Staffordshire, were reported to be 'riddled with back-door insurance touts', who 'seem to prey on the poverty and ignorance of the people'.

The results of the Survey were presented to the Beveridge Committee in June 1942, and on 23 June Cole himself gave oral evidence, together with four of his local investigators. Under cross-examination many of the methodological and conceptual weaknesses of the Survey were ruthlessly exposed by the Beveridge Committee's civil servant members.[25] Particularly scathing was the chairman of the Assistance Board, Sir George Reid, who trapped Cole into admitting some embarrassing errors of fact. Complaints about Assistance Board offices without waiting-rooms were found to boil down to one isolated incident that had occurred in the middle of an air raid. The failure of tribunals in Wales to conduct proceedings in Welsh was found to apply only to the Swansea area, where virtually everyone spoke English. The number of complaints recorded against the Prudential had to be set against the fact that it was by far the largest approved society with over four million insured contributors. In general, the official members of the Beveridge Committee complained that the Survey report was 'a document of almost unrelieved gloom', which concentrated disproportionately on people's grievances and ignored the possibility of widespread silent satisfaction. It was objected that little attempt had been made to get information from official sources, and that the findings of the Survey were unduly influenced by the views of social workers 'who are by the very nature of their calling apt to be more concerned with the abnormal and "interesting" case'.[26] Cole denied all these charges under cross-examination. He claimed that, in his efforts to present a balanced picture, he had if anything exaggerated such evidence as was favourable to the existing system. Officials had not been used as a source of information, partly because they would have every opportunity to present their own evidence to Beveridge and partly because the whole object of the inquiry was to get behind the conventional cloak of welfare officialdom. Opinions had been sought from such people as social workers not because they were an ideal source, but because the government had specifically forbidden a more direct house-to-house inquiry. Beveridge himself defended Cole's work, pointing out that what he had specifically asked for was not a scientifically-impeccable academic survey, but a rapid, impressionistic, descriptive view of national consumer opinion at the grassroots.

Many of the official criticisms must be admitted by the historian concerned with assessing the authenticity of Cole's evidence. The Survey report certainly contained errors of fact (perhaps not surprisingly in view of the amazingly short period in which it was carried out). More seriously, it was by no means always clear in Cole's summary whose views were being reported: those of the Oxford academics who directed the Survey, those of the local investigators who collected the information or those of the social welfare beneficiaries whose opinions were under review. Moreover, as mentioned above, the variety of research methods used meant that to a certain extent different layers of consumer opinion were being transmitted from different local areas. Many of the people employed on the Survey had strong preconceived opinions about the need for reform and these preconceptions undoubtedly coloured the kind of questions that were asked and the interpretation of the answers: it was scarcely surprising, for example, that when claimants were asked if benefit levels were adequate their answer was a univocal No. In no sense, therefore, can the Survey be regarded as a scientific assessment of consumer or working-class opinion in the period. Against this, however, must be set the fact that Cole's investigators did make great efforts to record variations in opinion, and that much of his report consisted of verbatim quotations from the consumer's mouth. A great deal of the evidence collected was undeniably subjective, but subjectivity is not without its significance in the recreation of historical experience, particularly when such an intangible factor as 'consumer opinion' is being sought. Cole and his assistants were perfectly well aware of the limitations of the material presented to the Beveridge Committee: material which they viewed simply as an 'interim report', to be followed up at a later stage by a much more thorough final report after all the data submitted by local investigators had been carefully sifted.[27] This process of more thorough analysis began in the summer of 1942, but it was forcibly abandoned and no final report ever appeared, because of a ruling by the Ministry of Reconstruction that

papers once submitted to a Cabinet committee automatically became secret
'classified' material.[28] As a consequence, the mass of data collected by local
investigators was never properly analysed; and it is in this local data, rather
than in the highly condensed summary presented by Cole to the Beveridge
Committee, that the most valuable aspects of the Survey may be found.

What, if anything, does the evidence collected by Cole's local investigators
tell us about consumer attitudes to welfare in the early 1940s? At the time of
writing this paper I have analysed in detail only six of the twenty-seven local
reports, together with the preliminary digest of evidence from the twenty-
seven localities compiled by Cole in June 1942. Any general conclusions must,
therefore, be tentative. Nevertheless several quite striking features appear to
emerge. One very obvious fact was that Lloyd George's compromise of 1911,
whereby approved societies were employed to administer public funds, had
singularly failed in most areas to harness the 'friendly society' ethic to the state
system. Enthusiasm for voluntarism was powerful and widespread, but found
expression largely outside the sphere of statutory social insurance. Linked
with this was the fact that certain areas of welfare were seen as much more appropriate to voluntary action than others. Schemes for the voluntary provision of
medical and hospital treatment, for example, commanded widespread support
and passionate local loyalty; schemes for cash benefits, on the other hand,
were supported grudgingly 'as a matter of necessity', and were seen as a service
that could more efficiently be provided by the state. A second striking factor
was the widely-expressed hostility of workers who were themselves contributors to commerical schemes towards the intrusion of commercialism into
welfare. Commercialism and voluntarism were seen, not as the complements,
but as the antipodes of each other, a distinction often lost sight of in more
recent discussions on the role of the private sector. Commercially-based insurance was seen as exploitative and destructive of the voluntary self-help ethic,
and although a few witnesses appeared to welcome the insurance agent's visits,
the vast majority saw such visits as a 'nuisance', an intrusion on privacy and at
times as a very crude form of behavioural control. In contrast, 'the state' was
viewed as generally benign, an attitude that is perhaps surprising in view of the
hostile comments passed on some of the state's front-line welfare officials.
'The State is looked to more and more as the best guardian', reported the local
investigator from north Wales, which, paradoxically, was one of the areas in
which existing welfare administration was least popular. What seems clear,
however, from the reports which I have examined so far, is that when witnesses
favoured increased state intervention they had in mind increased provision
from Whitehall rather than an extension of existing local services. The possibility that central government welfare might in certain circumstances be just as
destructive of localism and voluntarism as advanced commercial enterprise
was not seriously considered. There was strong general support for the con-

tributory principle within the state system. Witnesses in several areas suggested that the worker's share in the costs of contributory insurance might be diminished, but only an isolated witness in west Cumberland remarked that there was 'no real reason' why the whole social security system should not be paid for out of direct taxation. One final point that should be made is that the degree of fundamental discontent with prevailing welfare arrangements was essentially limited. Witnesses gave expression to what were obviously in many cases deeply-felt specific grievances against the existing system; but, in spite of hopeful prodding from the prophets of reconstruction, there was little coherent conception of what should take its place. On occasion, Cole's investigators could scarcely conceal their impatience at the degree of 'ignorance and apathy' that the Survey revealed. 'People remain dissatisfied but inactive', observed the interim report. 'Few concrete proposals of reform submitted, most rather vague and uninteresting', commented the investigator for Oxford. In east London people took a 'perverse pride' in 'refusing to bother their heads' about social welfare arrangements. 'Some seemed to be quite satisfied in an inarticulate sort of way', complained the investigator from Manchester, '. . . the majority just *did not know*'. In general, the tenor of the evidence was more modest and less ambitious than that of the reforms proposed later in 1942 in the Beveridge Plan. Criticisms of health provision and social insurance fitted in very closely with those made by Beveridge, but there was little foreshadowing of Beveridge's demands for a reconstruction of the labour market and abolition of family poverty. 'More of the same' rather than radical change was the wish of most respondents. There was no evidence to suggest that grass-roots opinion was harbouring any wider vision of more far-reaching social revolution.

12

Images of the working class since 1930

ARTHUR MARWICK

My title is ambiguous. In this essay I shall be touching on all three of the possible questions implied in it: how do the workers see themselves? how do they see the rest of society? how does the rest of society see the workers? But these clear statements may not immediately erase all danger of confusion. Alas, the study of class has long been monopolized by a few narrow theological fraternities who not only insist that the word 'class' shall be used as they decree, and in no other way, quoting from the texts as they go, but now also assume that any usage of the phrase 'images of class' must conform to precedents established by certain leading sociological writers. After bowing to Marx, Weber and Durkheim, one is then expected to stumble along in the footsteps of Willener, Ossowski, Bott, Lockwood, Goldthorpe and Bulmer.[1]

Such has been the influence of the work of these and other scholars that to talk of 'images of class' is to suggest that by definition one is going to be concerned with questions of ideological perspective, of 'power' models and 'pecuniary' models. Moreover, there is the implication that, as the authors of the classic study of the 'affluent worker' put it, one is concerned with 'the *destiny* of the working class' [my italics].[2] It is perfectly possible to share the view of Westergaard that 'class imagery involves . . . a series of perhaps contradictory, conflicting, rather confused and ambivalent pictures of what society is like and where the individual fits into it' without reaching his conclusion that in all images of class 'there are inevitable political elements, whether they are explicit or not'.[3] To argue in this way is to empty the word 'political' of any precise meaning. Similarly there is force in the argument that 'working classness' extends 'outside the immediate locality, outside the particular conditions of an occupational community'. But it is a central assumption of this essay that concepts of class can retain their analytical force even (or perhaps only when) they do *not* require that workers, to constitute a class, must have 'at least a tentative vision of an "alternative society"'.[4]

Indeed it is well worth going back to a fundamental question: 'How do we know that class exists?' The approach of some social scientists has always been that *something* exists (manifest inequality in the distribution of power, wealth, etc.), and that that 'something' can appropriately be described as 'class'.

Having thus created the term, social scientists feel that it is perfectly reasonable that they should administer the rules by which it is employed. The trouble is that we know that ordinary individuals and groups in society, quite without the benefit of social science, also speak, write and act as if they believe in the existence of class as something real and tangible. Thus my answer to the question just posed is 'because people write, speak and act as if class did indeed exist'.

The problem remains, though, that the class that individuals and groups clearly have in mind frequently does not coincide with the class of some sociological research. The response from one sociological corner is unequivocal: we should not allow ourselves to be confused by the usage of 'ordinary language'.[5] I take an exactly opposite view: only through studying the 'ordinary language' can we come near not only to demonstrating that class does indeed exist but also to understanding what it really is. The task at hand is to probe what lies behind the everyday usage of the language of class. If we can also find out *why* people talk about class, then we may be well on the way to understanding the complex meaning of the term 'social class'.

If one rejects the presuppositions of some sociological studies of the problem, then what is left? For historians, the answer is an elemental one: the sources. I write then of 'images of class' not because of any *a priori* concern with the sort of issues identified by contemporary sociologists but because essentially what letters, diaries, acts of parliament, novels, films, political speeches and, indeed, the treatises of social scientists yield are images. Inevitably these images are confused and they do not really bear out the hypothesis, advanced by Elizabeth Bott and accepted by Lockwood and others, 'that when an individual talks about class he is trying to say something, in a symbolic form, about his experiences of power and prestige in his actual membership groups and social relationships both past and present'.[6] People use the language of class because it is *customary* to do so:[7] class offers a handy and accepted means for dividing society up into broad categories that are recognized throughout society. The employment of these categories quite clearly implies social and cultural differences. Such categories *may* also imply inequalities of various sorts. (Inequality is also attributed to factors other than class: luck, for instance, or having a 'good' job or a 'bad' job. I cannot myself accept the quick jump so often made by which occupation suddenly becomes equated with class.)[8] Once we have derived from the sources the actual categories in use in a particular society, we can integrate these categories with the objective evidence on the gross inequality in the distribution of power, income and wealth in contemporary societies. (I am highly dubious as to whether 'prestige' has any great significance outside the questionnaires of social scientists; just as, indeed, I am dubious about the use of the word 'deferential' to describe manual workers who recognize that they *are* manual workers and are proud of it.)

This essay, then, is concerned with the working class not as an historical agency, but as an important constituent of British society. It rejects the assumption that having fixed our sights on the working class we can assume that the rest of society consists of one homogeneous group which can be referred to as 'the middle class'. It is concerned with the relationship of the working class to other social classes and, above all, with how these relationships have changed, under the pressure of major historical events, since the 1930s.

I

The paradox of the 1930s is that while there was everywhere a straightforward acceptance that a coherent, well-defined, easily recognizable working class existed, outside the professional fields of social investigation and social legislation great discretion was exercised in actually talking about the working class, or, for that matter, about any other classes. *The New Survey of London Life and Labour* comprised both a street survey of the entire population in which, in order to maintain continuity with Charles Booth's original categories, the distinctions employed were those of income,[9] and a house sample which quite explicitly was concerned only with 'the working class'.[10] The approach (a very simple one) was essentially that described in A. L. Bowley's *Livelihood and Poverty* (1915). Right away houses which were 'obviously middle-class' were excluded; after that there was a refined list by which further exclusions could be made[11] thus leaving, as a distinctive residue, the working class.

> Middle-class households are distinguished primarily by the occupation of the head. But some measure of discretion must be employed.

> ### SPECIAL CASES

> 1. Professional and clerical occupations to be ranked middle-class. This includes commercial travellers, insurance agents, etc.
> 2. All publicans to be ranked middle-class.
> 3. Shopkeepers to be ranked middle-class unless the shop is subsidiary to the work of the principal wage-earner, *or* the income from the *shop* is definitely below £250.
> 4. Self-employers, small employers, master-men, etc., not to be ranked as middle-class unless their incomes are definitely over £250 a year.
> 5. Hawkers, street-traders, etc., to be ranked working-class.
> 6. Shop assistants to be ranked working-class unless their work is managerial or supervisory (e.g. departmental head or shopwalker) *or* unless their wages suggest middle-class rank.
> 7. Police Sergeants to be ranked W.C., Inspectors M.C.[12]

It was recognized in the post-war survey that there was probably a greater discrepancy than there had been at the time of Bowley's original survey between holding middle-class social status and earning a middle-class income, but nonetheless the category 'middle class' was distinct enough. The discrepancy could be taken as 'a significant though rough indication of the effects of "mechanisation" and other economic developments in transforming clerical and distributive occupations, and leading to the growth of a "black-coated" group, whose earnings are comparable with, and sometimes even lower than those of skilled manual workers, though they are still regarded by themselves and by their fellows as belonging socially to the so-called "lower middle class" '.[13]

The Social Survey of Merseyside,[14] though it used a number of different classifications for different specific purposes, was also fundamentally concerned only with 'the working class', and again it used the rules laid down by Bowley.

> These rules were faithfully followed in working through the directory, but a certain amount of discretion had to be left to the investigators, because the occupation was quite frequently not recorded in the directory or, when recorded, it was a marginal case which could only be decided by a visit. For instance, a man who describes himself as a shop-assistant without further qualification may or may not belong to the class defined above, and even after enquiry the matter cannot always be settled beyond the shadow of a doubt. The result is that some cases have been included in the survey which by a strict reading of the above definition should have been omitted, but they would all be somewhere near the borderline and we do not think there has been any conscious bias or serious error arising from this cause.[15]

Why should there be, when give or take a few marginal instances, it was evidently so easy to recognize members of the working class? In undertaking the research for his *The Unemployed Man: A Social Study* (1933), the young American academic E. Wight Bakke had no difficulty in finding a working-class family with which to take lodgings in Greenwich, and Sir Hubert Llewellyn Smith in his preface to the study wrote confidently of the 'working-class' area in which Bakke lived and of his 'working-class' friends.[16]

That there was a statutory working class becomes clear from a study of the social legislation of the time: quite simply, welfare provision was intended solely for what the relevant acts termed 'the working classes', the plural usage being in the nineteenth-century tradition which recognized the range and variety of occupations and skills within what was nonetheless obviously perceived as one single social class. A background paper to the Addison Housing Act of 1919, noting that the houses to be built must be 'for the occupation of the working classes' proposed to define this term by an upper income limit of £200 per year, a figure computed by taking the £160 per annum which was then the upper income limit for those covered by workmen's compensation and national health insurance and adding a further element to take account of inflation.[17] Ministers, however, preferred to proceed on the same assumption as Llewellyn Smith, Caradog Jones and others, that you did not need to know a man's income to tell that he was working-class. Questioned in the House of Commons in April 1930, Arthur Greenwood maintained that 'The term "working classes" is generally well understood, and I am not aware of any practical difficulty in its interpretation.' 'The local authorities', he added after a further question, 'have never found any practical difficulties in defining it for themselves.'[18] However, when it came to slum clearance, where property rights and guarantees of rehousing were at stake, it was necessary to go beyond definition by instinct. The 1902 Select Committee of both Houses of Parliament on the Housing of the Working Classes had offered a definition of what it called the 'labouring class' and this was used as the basis for the fifth schedule of the Housing Act of 1925, 'an act to consolidate the enactments relating to the Housing of the Working Classes in England and Wales'. The definition was repeated in the 1936 Housing Act; legally, it must be stressed, it had force only in matters of slum clearance. The expression 'working class', the Act decreed

> includes mechanics, artisans, labourers and others working for wages, hawkers, costermongers, persons not working for wages, but working at some trade or handicraft without employing others except members of their own family, and persons other than domestic servants, whose income does not exceed an average of £3 a week, and the families of such persons who may be residing with them.[19]

One of the most illuminating statements on the distinction, taken for granted by the great and the good, between the wage-earning working class, the proper object of state-sponsored social welfare, and the salary-earning middle class which was expected to survive through its own providence and higher earning power, was the 1936 Report of the Unemployment Insurance Statutory Committee on Remuneration Limits for Insurance of Non-Manual Workers. The Chairman of the Committee was Sir William Beveridge. Noting that the communication from the Ministry of Labour which had placed the matter before them had spoken of raising the 'salary' limit for those covered by unemployment insurance, the Committee pointed out that 'the term used in the Unemployment Insurance Act is neither "salary" nor "income" but "remuneration"', the essence of the matter being that the remuneration limit applied to 'persons who would normally describe their remuneration as wages, rather than salary, and are practically indistinguishable from other wage-earners'.[20] The Committee did in the end recommend raising the remuneration limit from £250 to £400. But the essence of the matter comes through in the minority report, signed by two out of the seven members of the Committee, which favoured a figure of £300: their argument in support of this was that the main Unemployment Insurance Act of 1920 had clearly intended the inclusion of only 'That body of non-manual workers which corresponded in the matter of income to the general body of manual workers'.[21]

The same sense of the existence of a separate and definable working class governed national health insurance legislation. Free medical attention was a definite indicator of working-class status. The Orphans and Old-Age Contributory Pension scheme introduced at the end of the 1920s contained fewer exemptions than any of the other social security programmes of the 1920s. It provides the most complete guide to the composition of the statutory working class of the time. A similar attitude to class was revealed when the Amulree Committee took up the question of holidays with pay. This committee saw itself as being concerned with 'working people coming within the employment field, including the unemployed, who are either manual workers, or non-manual workers in receipt of not more than £250 a year'.[22] And it brought out the explicit distinction between 'salaried employees' who for eighty years or more had had an entitlement to holidays with pay, and 'wage-earning employees' who generally had no such entitlement.[23]

II

Did members of the working class perceive themselves so clearly? The sources are fragmentary but the phrase occurs often enough, and in a sufficiently clear way, to suggest an affirmative answer. In his perhaps rather self-conscious memoir published at the end of the war, Max Cohen remarked that he 'had been brought up in what is known as the proud, independent working-class spirit'.[24] The night-watchman, Charles Fiske, writing in the late 1920s, described his landlady's family as 'rough-and-ready people, clean working-class people that wouldn't see you without'.[25] Among the *Memoirs of the Unemployed* collected by Beales and Lambert in 1933, a house painter referred to himself as 'a working-class parent' dealing with the 'usual small grocery store of a poor working-class district';[26] a skilled wood-carver remarked on how he could no longer afford butter, dripping and lard, 'the elementary ingredients of a working class diet' and explained how he had lost faith in the power of organization to bring 'the working classes the freedom they claimed';[27] and a skilled engineer declared that he had met with sympathy and friendliness 'amongst the working class'.[28] A Cumbrian carpenter's son employed as a stable boy – 'I was still working-class' – was quickly able to detect the working-class character of his boss, a former railway porter who had risen slightly in the world.[29]

It is appropriate to speak of a high level of 'class awareness' (that is, the definite sense of belonging, culturally, to a distinctive class, without necessarily believing in any form of political activism on behalf of that class[30]), but far less so to speak of 'class consciousness'. Bakke, who can scarcely be accused of prejudice on this score since his American studies were concerned to bring out the growth of class consciousness among American workers, noted that 'dogmatic and relentless class loyalty among the workers with whom I lived is a myth'.[31] Moreover, while the leading articles in, for example, *Railway Review* were strongly Marxist in tone, there was open recognition on other pages of an absence of class consciousness among ordinary railwaymen.[32] Describing himself as 'a keen socialist', an unemployed fitter lamented that the main thoughts of his fellow unemployed 'seemed to be only on sport'.[33] A view cited by Bakke might well be taken as representing the very extreme of 'deference': 'these agitators, they say, "Away with the bosses," but what will they put in their place? We need bosses, don't we? Otherwise we are like sheep without a sheep dog.'[34] Yet the label 'deferential' does not sit well with the manifest pride in a good, 'respectable', job well done which comes out so often in the sources.[35] Rather the distinctive feature is a determination to leave management to the managers. 'I do not for one moment desire to interfere with the Management of your Company in any shape or form', wrote the secretary of the Wallpaper Workers' Union in response to an announcement of short-time working:

> I know the position is very awkward and it is not every Company that will carry increased stocks to the extent you have done, still I repeat, it takes a lot of explaining to those who have to exist on £2.4.0 – £2.8.0 and £3.0.0 per week as the case might be.
>
> Please do not take this letter as a moan or even criticism, but rather let it be an appeal that if circumstances compel short time, let the week be broken into as little as possible.[36]

If Professor Margaret Stacey was correct in her conclusion that the widest range of 'knowledge and social recognition' between status groups (that is to say, groups *within* classes) was 'two groups distant from your own' then it is perhaps not surprising if there are no very clear working-class images of the overall structure of society.[37] A miner, Conservative in politics, identified, without actually using the label, a lower middle class of 'local jumped-up people, with a small car and an equally small mind', people who made their money out of the miner 'by selling him bacon, pit boots, and insurance policies'.[38] Another miner spoke in general of 'the employing class',[39] while a carpenter, after praising his own employer, declared that something that did make him 'see red' was 'the pictures and descriptions of such things as society weddings, court functions, and so on'.[40] In the BBC radio programme of 1938, *What do We Mean by Class?*, trade union leader George Isaacs put forward the view which lay at the heart of what ideology of class there was among working-class members of the Labour party: the working class included 'the oft quoted "middle class", together with artisans, labourers, shop-keepers, housewives and all the professions'; on the other side of the only significant class divide stood 'the so-called leisure class'.[41] Such as it is, the evidence from the 1930s scarcely supports the notion of the working class perceiving the social structure in terms of power relationships.

There can be no doubt, as the *New Survey of London Life and Labour* indicated, as to the existence of a lower middle class with a very clear sense of an identity distinct from that of the working class. In 1933, for example, the Guild of Insurance Officials and the Bank Officers' Guild organized 'a Conference of Middle-Class Workers'. At a branch meeting of the former it was noted that 'employees, whether working-class or middle-class, have been forced to form themselves into trade unions and associations to protect and further their interests'.[42] The clear sense of distinction does not seem to have been accompanied by any strong sense of hostility or conflict; perhaps that is what is implied in describing the middle-class model of society as 'hierarchical'. But, apart from the rest of the middle classes – *the* 'middle class' (*tout court*) and the 'upper middle class' – there was at least one further group at the top of society which may, perfectly properly I believe, be called the 'upper class'. Members of this class were not always very good at distinguishing between the working class and the lower middle class: any manifest outsider in their milieu was likely to be described as 'working class', as was Goronwy Rees, the son of a Welsh Presbyterian minister, when he arrived at Oxford in 1928.[43] Upper-class status did not necessarily, of course, prevent a man from being a socialist or a member (almost invariably a leading one) of the Labour party. Being a leader of the Labour party did not necessarily mean having empathy with the working class. Commenting on Chamberlain's encounter with Hitler at Berchtesgaden, Hugh Dalton confided to his diary that 'if Hitler had been a British nobleman and Chamberlain a British working man with an inferiority complex, the thing could not have been done better'.[44] The custom was to see in the working class certain psychological states or cultural habits; certainly not to see the working class as a political threat. When J. H. Thomas had to resign from the government in 1936 for leaking budget secrets, Stanley Baldwin privately opined that Thomas had 'fallen a victim to the two weaknesses of his class': he had been 'a terrific gambler'; and 'most likely' he had 'let his tongue wag when he was in his cups'.[45]

III

As is well known, there was quite a fashion for novels of working-class life in the 1930s, though the label itself, while used (by critics, for example) to describe these novels, did not often appear in the novels themselves, and there was usually little sense of a relationship, whether about 'power', 'hierarchy' or 'deference', with other social classes. What one is presented with is the working class as a cultural enclave, as a fit object for study, as in the social surveys. A similar impression is conveyed by the somewhat patronizing films of the documentary movement of the time. Feature films, however, scarcely ever included scenes from working-class life, save when they formed a kind of stock background to the performances of Gracie Fields or George Formby; Jeffrey Richards has accurately referred to the sense of a 'hermetically sealed' working class which these films present.[46] In the novels 'written from the inside' by authors themselves brought up within a working-class environment, the sharpest divide is between the employed and the unemployed. Walter Brierley's *Means Test Man* (1935) is about the psychological and physical pains of an unemployed miner in a Derbyshire chapel-going community:

> . . . he passed a gang of County Council workers, re-laying a stretch of road. Obviously the foreman was not there, for the men stood leaning on their tools, picks and shovels, talking and smoking. They were workers, honest workers, who drew their money each pay-day and knew that they had a right to it. They could put it down for shop things, beer, tobacco – anything, and say, 'I'm swapping my sweat and toil for your goods.' He couldn't say that.[47]

The sense of cultural distinctiveness is strong, yet so also is the sense of values shared across society. In *Love on the Dole* Walter Greenwood introduces the working-class district of Hanky Park by stressing the custom of scouring steps and window-sills: certainly a peculiarity of the Northern working class but not, in its objectives, very alien to what is often thought of as middle-class ideology.[48]

The most curious feature of the format of Greenwood's novel is the use, at the beginning, of a series of quotations which emphasize struggle and class conflict.[49] The first, from *Those United States* by Arnold Bennett, refers to the 'sinister toxin' of not having enough of anything and of 'too much continual strain on the nerves'. From Siegfried Sassoon's *Memoirs of an Infantry Officer* comes the phrase '. . . and in 1917 I was only beginning to learn that life for the majority of the population, is an unlovely struggle against unfair odds, culminating in a cheap funeral'; from the letters of D. H. Lawrence the phrase 'I get more revolutionary every minute'; and from Rosa Luxemburg 'We are witnessing . . . a whole world sinking'. Finally an Austrian middle-class woman is quoted as saying that the middle class had been reduced to a proletariat and forced to thrust culture aside to join the fight of man against man. Yet in the novel itself there is no overt feeling of the struggle of class against class. Perhaps the prefatory quotations expressed what Greenwood felt he *ought* to say (as sociologists feel bound to address themselves to certain questions), while the novel itself expresses what he really saw.

But then also, as noted, public discussion of class was deeply inhibited. It was only after years of agonizing that the BBC eventually put on a series of talks on class in which George Isaacs had his innocuous say. The 'official' view was that presented by Carr-Saunders and Caradog Jones (who seemed to find it easy to lock away in a professional compartment the results of their investigations into the Merseyside working class): 'Is it not a mis-reading of the social structure of this country to dwell on class divisions, when in respect of dress, speech, and use of leisure, all members of the community are obviously coming to resemble one another?'[50] Discretion and reticence about class became the hallmarks of the two most public of all the media, films and radio. One need not have any conspiratorial theory of British cinema in the 1930s to see that in such images of the working class as it did project, it was above all governed by the convention that class was not something to be talked about or stressed. However, the newsreels of the time, bland and reassuring though their commentaries were, could not fail to bring out that in 'dress, speech, and use of leisure' (and many other characteristics as well) industrial workers were very different from other members of the community.

Through all the confusion and pretence, though, one fundamental and agreed characteristic of the working class does emerge: that is the feeling of what Gareth Stedman Jones has termed the working-class 'life sentence'; that sad hallmark of working-class life enduring, despite social change, till this day, whereby for all but a small minority life will continue, for sons as well as fathers, mothers as well as daughters, to be lived out in a particular, arduous, working-class ambience.[51] If there are hints of social aspiration in this passage from *Means Test Man*, the crushing weight of the last sentence really lies in the fact that the miner's wife had got no further than being a servant:

> Mrs. Cook insisted that her husband should not use the dialect when speaking to their son; she quite realised that in the streets and at school it must inevitably beat into his nature, but at home, at least, he must know that there was another language. Later she would tell him that unless he could use this other language, there would be small chance of his escaping from the poverty and dullness which even now he was beginning to see limited him. His mother, in her youth, had had lessons in elocution, and it was her speech and manner which had made her such a success as maid to the local doctor.[52]

Old Harry Hardcastle, musing at the end of *Love on the Dole* echoed the phrases of Siegfried Sassoon that his creator had quoted on the frontispiece of the novel: 'One long succession of dreary, monotonous years, toiling moiling, with a pauper or near-pauper funeral and [*sic*] the end of it.'[53] This sense of a common lot tends to swamp what hints there still are of that contrast between 'respectables' and 'roughs' emphasized in Robert Roberts' classic autobiography *The Classic Slum*; if classes are to be considered as seen from the outside as well as from the inside, too much weight need not be given to such recollections of the time as this: 'A gentle, amiable woman with numerous children, she was not quite up to the standards of respectability of the rest of the road. She was, it was felt, more the type who should be living in the "poorer" road parallel with ours on the other side of the Quaggy.'[54]

IV

A significant feature of both the war and post-war years was the talk, starting on the very day that war broke out,[55] of drastic change in the class structure and improvement in the position of the working class. Despite all the welter of talk about 'the abolition of class distinctions', 'the flattening of the social pyramid' and 'the levelling of classes', it is very clear that these phrases were used within the context of an acceptance of the continuance of the basic features of the British class structure. The point can be simply conveyed by quoting some sentences from the longest, and one of the most celebrated, letters published in the letter columns of *The Times* during the war years. The issue was that of the future role of the public schools and the letter took the form of a report by a Labour MP and former textile worker, George Muff, of a visit which he and a number of colleagues had paid to some leading public schools.

> We were miners or textile workers – all with ripe experience of public admin- istration in Liverpool, the L.C.C., Hindley, Manchester, the West Riding, Lanark, Durham, Hull, Bradford, and South Wales. We were of the opinion that the 'two nations', vividly portrayed by Disraeli, were nurtured on pre- judice and foolish class distinctions. Some of us believed that class separation of the people commenced in our middle school years. There was a gulf be- tween the public school and the elementary school – a caste system; when all the while we knew the child of the worker was neither 'untouchable' nor belonged to a depressed class. The free places in our great grammar schools have proved, by the output to our universities, that given an equal chance the son of a bricklayer can take his place as a mental equal with the son of a barrister. . . .
>
> We want more boys to share the heritage of our public schools. We want the boy from an industrial home to be as proud of the school tie as his dad is of the trade union badge. . . .
>
> I ask – nay challenge – all headmasters and governors to see how far part of their endowments can be used to educate boys from working-class homes.[56]

The Parliamentary Secretary to the Board of Education was James Chuter Ede, a figure who needed no novelist to invent him: ex-elementary schoolboy, ex-pupil teacher, ex-elementary schoolteacher, graduate of Cambridge, ex-regimental sergeant-major, Labour MP for South Shields, Ede had no vision of education as a means for changing the class structure of the country. Among the many illuminating thoughts which he confided to his diary were the following:

> Some public schools in my view wd. remain outside public subsidised schemes. Families traditionally associated with them wd. make enormous sacrifices to

send their sons to them. The *nouveau riche* wd. also patronise them. I thought some rich men, if they did not exclude others, sd. be allowed to go to Oxford & Cambridge. State scholars needed more careful selection.[57]

Both the manual workers & the small trading classes believed that in the clerical posts gained from Secondary Schools there were greater security of tenure & better prospects of a reasonable superannuation.[58]

. . . we did not want to educate people to go out of their classes, but to live the life most appropriate to their individual aptitudes. We had to rescue them from the extraordinarily prevalent fallacy that the most skilled craftsman was the inferior socially of the most inefficient clerk.[59]

Compare with this the remarks made during discussions of the Butler Education Bill by Harold Laski:

I do not believe that our educational system could even pretend to be democratic so long as the 'public' schools are kept in being. And that is true even if they are persuaded to take some scholarship boys and girls from the elementary schools. All that this concession will really mean is that a small percentage of the nation's children will escape the drudgery and toil of working-class life in order to act as hostages for the privileges of the children of the well-to-do.

There is no answer to the demand for the common school: and the common school will never become what it might be until the children of well-to-do parents are educated there.[60]

In his diary, Ede correctly noted, 'the Labour Party programme does not include either of the two items'.[61]

The war certainly brought considerable social upheaval and, without doubt, a general levelling of living standards.[62] Yet the fact that British class attitudes were firmly fixed is sharply brought out if one glances for a moment at the American war-boom community of Willow Run.

Trailer occupants at Willow Run were all kinds of people from all over the United States. Middle-class professional and business people from Michigan and Minnesota parked cheek by jowl with rural hill-billies from Tennessee and urban foreign-born mechanics from Weehawken and St. Louis. They came from everywhere, and they had all kinds of backgrounds: college degrees and middle-class comfort; fourth-grade semi-literacy and working-class insecurity.[63]

It is impossible to imagine anything quite like that happening in wartime Britain.

There was, then, still a recognizable, coherent, working class in the post-war years. But there was no longer a statutory working class. Social legislation was, at first, in principle universalist; in practice it steadily became selective, but its selectivity was directed at the unfortunate, the underprivileged and the victims of family circumstance, rather than at the working class as a class. Much welfare legislation, as is well known, was of special benefit to the lower middle class. Social surveys ceased to be directed at the working class as such, but rather at entire communities, or at single industries or at the middle class.[64] The epoch-making volume edited by D. V. Glass, *Social Mobility in Britain* (1954), represented the first main results of a programme carried out by the Department of Sociological and Demographic Research of the London School of Economics. The starting-point was 'the formation and structure of the "middle classes" '.[65]

Basic structures had not changed and many traditional assumptions persisted; the change, rather, was in attitudes and relationships, in how individuals in different classes saw each other and saw themselves. For the working class, as W. G. Runciman has put it, 'both work and maintenance became not aspirations but fixed expectations';[66] not, of course, expectations likely to alter the broad outlines of the class structure. While high levels of economic demand had pulled up working-class living standards, they had also accelerated the compression of the range of working-class incomes. Though, no doubt, those human sensibilities which give rise to the notion of there being a distinction between 'the respectable' and 'the roughs' continued, the distinction had further diminished in real terms. A University of Liverpool inquiry into social relationships on a Liverpool housing estate reported that

> . . . many inhabitants of the estate distinguish between a 'better' and a 'lower' end in spite of the marked homogeneity of its population . . . at the 'lower' end of the estate fewer people work in the factory, while after the war, when some bungalows became vacant, a number of people moved in from bombed areas of the city and settled there as squatters. Amongst these there is a slightly higher proportion of people whose standards of life are regarded by the other residents as socially inferior, and, in consequence, the problem of establishing satisfactory relationships is generally regarded as being more difficult here than elsewhere on the estate . . .

> . . . but the differences between different parts of the estate can be over-emphasised and the problem of achieving 'privacy' or establishing and maintaining satisfactory neighbourly relationships must be regarded as a general one. Such differences as exist are in degree rather than in kind.[67]

If we compare the results of opinion polls conducted in Britain with results obtained in France and the United States we see very clearly the strong sense that a large number of British people still had of belonging to a working class. See the table overleaf for the responses given within a period of two years to open questions about which class people allocated themselves to.[68] The total of 47 per cent in the British middle class taken as a whole is actually surprisingly high and perhaps suggests a confused response to the ideas of reform, progress and equality then in the air. For those who doubt the reality of class in this period, the really significant comparative statistic is the tiny number of people in Britain (5 per cent) unable to find a class label for themselves. We can also see that among members of the working class there was now a clearer perception of overall class structure as is suggested by the results of F. M. Martin's investigations, which were conducted in Greenwich and Hertford in September and October 1950: 'The great majority of our subjects thought in terms of a three-class system, and most of them described these classes by the same set of names – upper, middle and working.'[69]

Britain (1948)		France (1950)		USA (1950)	
	Per cent		Per cent		Per cent
Upper	2	Bourgeois	7.9	Upper	·5.4
Upper middle	6	Middle	22.5	Middle	45.2
Middle	28	Working	27.1	Working	10.6
Lower middle	13	Peasant	13.7	Farming	0.8
Working	46	Poor	7.5	Lower	4.0
No Reply	5	Other	2.3	Other	6.5
		No Reply	19.0	No Reply	27.5

V

In the post-war period, British feature films were more open in their present-ation of class differences and of a distinctive working class than ever they had been in the 1930s. *The Guinea Pig* (1948) faithfully echoed the ideas about class and the public schools put forward by Muff, Chuter Ede and the Con-servatives, though, in this case, the 'working-class' boy who is steadily ab-sorbed into the ways of an exclusive public school was in fact the son of a Walthamstow tobacconist. (In the boy's 'comic' *Adventure*, it may be noted, 'Smith of the Lower Third' was the son of a grocer; 'school stories', that is to say stories set in public schools, such as 'Cripple Dick Archer' in the *Hotspur,* continued to be featured throughout the period; and whenever schools were shown in films, they were almost invariably public schools, as, for instance, in *The French Mistress* of 1958.) *His Excellency* (1952) was about an ex-docker (Eric Portman) who was sent by the Labour government as Governor-General of a colony modelled closely on Malta and about the working relationship he developed with his upper-class Lieutenant-Governor (Cecil Parker). Other figures mentioned in the film who had similarly risen at least came from the true industrial working class. There is a moment of sharp truth about the precariousness of working-class 'escape' when Eric Portman's daughter (Susan Stephen) tearfully remarks that if he fails, that will be the end of him. The documentary ideal of the 1930s, with most of the patronizing quality filtered out, reached its peak in *The Brave Don't Cry* (1952), the portrayal of a Scottish mining disaster. The closely integrated local community is well presented: the brave neither cried, nor did they protest.

Two films released in 1959 achieved notoriety in left-wing circles for the hostile view they were seen to present of the British working class. *I'm All Right Jack*, as I have suggested elsewhere,[70] was, in fact, a social satire of considerable sensitivity and perception. The plot structure of *The Angry Silence*[71] was undoubtedly clumsy and unconvincing. A slightly mysterious figure, Travers, played by Alfred Burke, who communicates by telephone with his mysterious bosses, deliberately stirs up trouble in an engineering factory which has an important government contract on its books. He operates through the traditionalist shop-steward, Connolly ('my Dad led the Hunger March'), played by Bernard Lee. Travers contrives first a strike, and then the sending to Coventry of Tom Curtis (Richard Attenborough) for refusing to participate in the strike. It is made clear that Tom is a rather obstreperous character: when Connolly repairs his television set for him he is still dissatisfied. Tom also acknowledges the point of view of those who have sent him to Coventry: 'They think they're doing right too'. Eventually, Tom is beaten up by one of the two loutish characters (Eddie and 'Gladys') who are strongly featured in the film, and loses an eye. At last Tom's inarticulate, sensual friend Joe (Michael Craig) who has gone along with the herd, fumblingly speaks out: 'We let it happen'; 'I feel I've done something dirty'. Michael Craig's stumbling cockney drawl is beautifully realized (though the film is set, and was shot on location, in Ipswich); screenwriter Bryan Forbes (John Theobald Clarke), himself the (distanced) product of an East End working-class background, later wrote that 'the extent of my aims and the sum total of my achievement' was that 'in the language I used I perhaps got closer to colloquial working-class speech than some of my contemporaries writing directly for the cinema'.[72] Once the cumbersome plot structure is forgotten, the powerful tension between slightly cranky individualism and herd instinct is well conveyed. The class imagery is striking, and rather more persuasive than the plot. At the start we see the factory workers arriving at the Ipswich engineering shop: they are on foot or on bicycles, they are in their working clothes and they are *en masse*. The same image can be found in *I'm All Right Jack* and it contrasts with that of commuters gathered together on their railway platforms before *separating out* to their different offices which was so often used to bring out an equally important truth about the class above. *The Angry Silence* presents a clear three-class structure. Mr Martindale, boss of Martindales, is defined by accent, attitudes and vulgar bow tie as a self-made middle-class figure. But he has to deal with directors from the controlling company whose ignorance, expense accounts and Bentleys he mocks as he tells them to get back to London. The most sympathetic figure is the works manager, Davis (Geoffrey Keen), who 'worked out there' and who brings in the union to deal with what, it is stressed throughout the film, is wholly unofficial action.

The Angry Silence certainly portrayed an unflattering picture of the working class. But other individuals, groups and classes do not come out well either. The upper-class figures are incompetent; Martindale has no principles at all and does not 'like lone wolves on either side'. Above all, the mischievous role of the press, and, in particular, of television is stressed: this is historically of some interest. Alan Whicker made a personal appearance just as Malcolm Muggeridge did in *I'm All Right Jack*. For my purposes the important point is that this film both presented a generally pessimistic view of human nature and a notion of classes as carefully delineated cultural entities.

In the late 1950s and early 1960s, a new 'working-class novel' emerged with, hot on its heels, a new working-class film. The key elements in *Saturday Night and Sunday Morning*,[73] when compared with the novels of the 1930s, are the 'affluent' living standards, the general alienation which the main character, the young factory worker Arthur Seaton, feels from organized society and his contempt for the older, docile members of the working class. This last point of generational difference was also made in *The Angry Silence*, though in a much nastier way. In *Saturday Night and Sunday Morning* there is no sense of class antagonism, nor is there any sign of an aspiration to break out of class boundaries: there is pride; there is independence; but it is clear that Arthur Seaton will live a working-class life till the end. In introducing the 1968 reissue of the novel in the 'Heritage of Literature' series, Alan Sillitoe, after noting 'the fact was that I came from the so-called "working-class"', declared:

> The greatest inaccuracy was ever to call the book a 'working-class' novel for it is really nothing of the sort. It is simply a novel, and the label given it by most reviewers at the time it came out, even the intelligent ones who should have known better, was simply a way of categorising a piece of work they weren't capable of assessing from their narrow class standpoint.

Certainly it was not a *political* novel, but, as David Craig has stressed, the book did indeed embody 'the mixed feelings and experiences' of the working class.[74]

VI

The challenging notion put forward in 1969 by Goldthorpe, Lockwood and their associates was that the clearly defined, distinctive, working class had given way to a new middle social grouping including both former working-class and former middle-class elements. That image is a very usual one in the United States, where the phrases 'middle class' and 'working class' are often used indiscriminately and, apparently, as synonyms.[75] However, what is most striking about changing class perceptions in America is the way in which in the most recent period this confusion has lessened and the phrase 'working class' is more and more used in what might be regarded as a traditionally British way.[76] My conclusion would be that the economic changes of the 1940s, 1950s and 1960s did indeed inject an 'American' element of confusion into British class imagery, but that this represents a minor modification rather than a major reversal. All the most recent developments in Britain as well as in America indicate a reassertion of the enduring realities of the working-class situation. Much of the evidence is, anyway, contained within the Goldthorpe survey of 1969 itself and in such works as Huw Beynon's *Working for Ford*.[77] Documentation of the traditional sort is thin for the very recent period but, obliquely though it is expressed, the enduring voice of the British working class can be heard in this protest of 1968:

> All my life I have been a very strong trade Unionist and firmly Believe that the Socialist way of life is the Best way of life for the workers. I also believe that every man has a right to defend himself against exploitation.
>
> I consider that I am a good worker who has worked hard all my working life. I see no reason why the Austin Management should refuse me further employment, I have never been disciplined by the management for anything. I have been a good time Keeper and have only lost time through illness.[78]

From the mid-1970s onwards there was far more public discussion of class in Britain than there had been at any time within the period under review in this paper.[79] There was irony in this sharp contrast with the discretion and reticence of the 1930s: undoubtedly the easy assumptions of the 1930s about who was and who was not working class had been overlaid by new complexities; undoubtedly the divide in living standards between working class and middle class was now far less distinct; undoubtedly there was much greater mobility out of the working class.[80] But whatever new abstractions social scientists might coin in the hope of making sense of a changing society – 'traditionalists' and 'non-traditionalists', 'quasi-groups', 'service class'[81] – it was clear that the old imagery of a 'working class' set within a society containing an 'upper class' and various types of 'middle class' still had much life in it[82] as the most appropriate way of describing divisions still felt to be social, economic and cultural rather than political.

13

Unemployment, nutrition and infant mortality in Britain, 1920–50

JAY WINTER

The paths of labour historians and demographic historians have crossed all too rarely in Britain. Part of the cause of separate but equal development is a barrier of mutual suspicion, largely based on misapprehensions, which should have been broken down long ago. Among some labour historians there is a profound distrust of quantification, either as the art of proving laboriously what we already know, or as a cult replete with mysteries into which all but initiates enter at their peril. Among demographic historians, the explicit political commitments of some historians of labour seem to violate canons of scholarly objectivity, as if population questions and policies had no ideological content.

The present plea for collaboration is based on the view that it is both profitable and necessary. Scholars in the fields of labour history and demographic history have distinctive contributions to make on many subjects of mutual interest. Among them is the history of the health of the working population. Demographic historians can learn much from studies of class structure about the changing meaning and complexity of the social and economic variables which they relate to vital statistics by means of sophisticated statistical analysis. Labour historians can learn much from demographic analysis about the costs of social inequality and the degree to which working people have managed to cope successfully with chronic deprivation and economic insecurity.

Scholars of both disciplines can also help in different ways to unravel the difficult problem of what is the appropriate time scale on which to analyse the relation between trends in public health and variations in levels of employment or income. In some quarters, a short-term perspective is adopted *faute de mieux*, and movements in vital statistics are reduced to reflex reactions to changes in economic variables. In these cases a joint effort is necessary in order to bring current historical and epidemiological research to bear on problems of public health in the past. Only then will it be possible both to relate short-term developments to long-term trends and to transform abstract economic and social categories into descriptions of real and at times contradictory social situations.

A case in point is the relation between unemployment and mortality rates.

In the American context, one student of demographic trends has argued recently that unemployment was a killer.[1] The victims were not workers, but rather their infants, whose survival chances, it is claimed, were significantly reduced immediately after surges in unemployment in the United States in this century. Partly by adversely affecting the physical or emotional health of the mother, partly by reducing expenditure on public health care and partly by diminishing the quantity and quality of the food intake of infants, economic slumps quickly took their toll of the lives of the most vulnerable sections of the population.

In the light of recent employment trends in Britain, this subject has more than historical significance.[2] No one denies that deprivation has made the struggle to improve public health much more difficult in this century, but few have succeeded in untangling the complex web of relations between economic fluctuations and infant mortality. In order to do so, we must go beyond the short-term perspective of studies such as that cited above. One of the objectives of this essay is to show why this is necessary, with reference to the experience of Britain in the years 1920–50.

This period is an appropriate one about which to pose the methodological and substantive problems related to the question of the effects of employment levels on infant survival chances, since between 1921 and 1948, statistics which accurately reflect fluctuations in levels of unemployment among workers were collected under the workings of the National Insurance Act. Between 1911 and 1921, only workers in certain 'precarious' trades were covered by the insurance scheme, and for the period before 1911, the historian must deal with statistics drawn from trade union records, the representative nature of which is highly doubtful. After 1948, virtually the whole population, whether in the labour force or not, came under the protection of the Act. Since accurate unemployment statistics are essential to this study, it is necessary to restrict it to the three decades after the end of the First World War.

There are other reasons why this period has been chosen as a test case. The contrast between mass unemployment in the interwar years and 'full employment' in the periods during and after the Second World War is a commonplace of economic and social history.[3] It is well known too, that a major redistribution of income levels took place in the period 1938–48, thereby significantly reducing income inequality in this country.[4] By focusing on the second quarter of this century, it is possible to see in what ways a major break in the pattern of unemployment and income distribution affected infant health.

The conclusion that will be drawn is that unemployment was not the decisive cause of fluctuations in infant mortality rates during this period. It will be shown that while short-term changes are important, we must look both before and after this period to appreciate the full demographic meaning of economic instability. On the one hand, we must seek in much earlier developments the primary source of movements in infant mortality rates in these years. By doing this, it is possible to see how the slow but steady progress of sanitation and nutrition since the 1850s is reflected in the demographic experience of later generations. The shadow effect of the rise in working-class living standards over the past century is at once more subtle, more significant and more stubbornly irreversible than many students of the period have acknowledged. These gains have left (and still leave) a legacy that even foolish economic policies or politically imposed impoverishment cannot obliterate completely. It is in this context that we must place the downward trend of infant mortality in the period 1920–50. On the other hand, we can find evidence of the deleterious effects of the Depression of the interwar years and the beneficial effects of economic conditions in the 1940s in certain aspects of infant mortality trends in the years since 1950. The development of a long-term perspective is, therefore, the key to an understanding of one important part of the history of public health in Britain over the last one hundred years.

What I propose to do in this essay is to describe first the character and components of infant mortality in the period under review. Secondly, I shall examine the statistical evidence to show that in the British case, it is a vast over-simplification of the interaction of economic and demographic behaviour to argue with M. H. Brenner that there is a demonstrable, direct, short-term relation between 'national economic changes and infant mortality under one year in each of the major age categories'.[5] Thirdly, I shall discuss the ways in which the upheavals of the Second World War affected infant mortality rates in England and Wales. Finally, I shall try to relate the arguments about short-term and long-term changes to an interpretation of aspects of the demographic and social history of Britain.

The course of infant mortality decline in Britain, 1921–48

During the period 1921–48, infant mortality rates in England and Wales declined by more than 60 per cent, from 83 to 33 deaths per 1,000 live births. A decline of similar magnitude was registered in Scotland. This constituted a continuation of the trend towards increasing infant survival rates which began at the turn of the century. Similar improvements were made in Europe during this period, as figure 1 illustrates. While experiencing significantly lower infant mortality rates than Scotland and France, England and Wales lagged behind the Netherlands and Switzerland in terms of infant survival chances throughout most of the period.

Three aspects of the trend are clear. First, between 1929 and 1948, there seems to have been a periodicity of two to four years in the appearance of peaks of mortality. Increases in infant mortality punctuated the trend of economic decline in a number of European countries in 1929, 1932, 1935–36, 1940–41, 1944–45 and 1947. Some of the fluctuation in infant mortality in this period may be a function of the virulence or periodicity of viral and bacterial

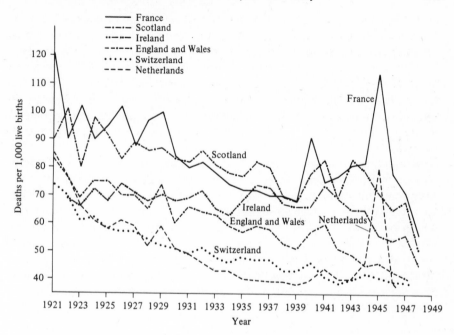

Fig. 1 Infant mortality rates in selected European nations, 1921–48.

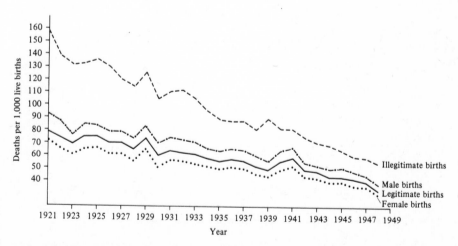

Fig. 2 Infant mortality rates for legitimate, illegitimate, female and male births in England and Wales, 1921–48.
Source: *Registrar-General's Annual Report for England and Wales*, 1921–49.

infections.[6] During the Second World War, peaks of infant mortality such as those in the Netherlands in 1945 and in France in both 1940 and 1945, were obviously attributable to war conditions. The fact that increases were registered in the war years by countries occupied (France and Holland), unoccupied but combatant (Britain) and neutral (Switzerland and Ireland) suggests that part of the upward disturbance in infant mortality rates between 1939 and 1945 probably would have occurred even had war been avoided. There is an epidemiological component of the history of infant mortality which cannot be ignored.

Secondly, as is shown in figure 2, the upward surge in infant mortality in 1940–41 in England and Wales is shown in all categories of births with the exception of illegitimate births. The steady decline in illegitimate infant mortality rates after 1939 suggests in part that the maternity services reached many unmarried mothers and thereby reduced the greater risks that their infants faced in the first year of life. In addition, the proportion of married women among all women who gave birth to illegitimate children rose to about one-third of the total. Herein may be one reason for the wartime continuation of the tendency for a narrowing of the gap between legitimate and illegitimate infant mortality rates.

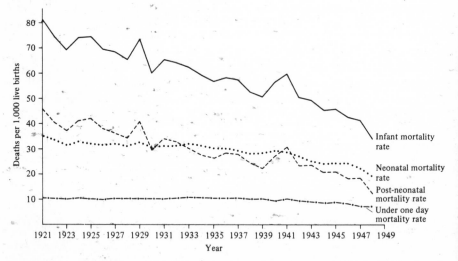

Fig. 3 Infant mortality rates at different periods of the first year of life in England and Wales, 1921–48.
Source: *Registrar-General's Annual Report for England and Wales*, 1921–49.

Thirdly, it is possible to compare the contribution of different periods within the first year of life to the overall trend of decline. A glance at figure 3 will suffice to show that mortality rates under one day and neonatal mortality rates (under one month) for England and Wales were virtually static throughout

Table 1. *Infant mortality rates from certain causes, England and Wales, 1937–46 (deaths per 1,000 live births)*

	1937	1938	1939	1940	1941	1942	1943	1944	1945
All Causes	57.68	52.81	50.57	56.77	60.04	50.62	49.12	45.44	46.00
I Infectious diseases excluding tuberculosis	3.23	2.43	2.28	2.81	4.24	2.09	2.60	1.98	1.81
II Tuberculosis	0.63	0.60	0.51	0.60	0.67	0.54	0.51	0.44	0.42
III Diarrhoea and enteritis	5.30	5.07	4.31	4.44	4.82	5.17	4.94	4.84	5.12
IV Developmental and wasting disease	26.91	24.94	24.76	25.41	25.56	23.79	21.69	20.40	20.33
V Other causes	21.61	19.77	18.70	23.50	24.75	19.03	19.38	17.78	18.32

Source for tables 1 and 2: *Registrar-General's Annual Report for England and Wales, 1921–49.*

most of the period under review. Neonatal mortality rates started a more precipitate decline in the late 1940s, but throughout the period 1921–48, much more significant reductions in infant mortality appear in the post-neonatal period, that is, after the first month of life. Post-neonatal mortality trends governed the movement of infant mortality trends, a point to which we shall return.

The deterioration in infant survival chances in 1941–42 was primarily a function of higher mortality in the post-neonatal period, during which most babies are weaned and, in time, lose the protection of their mothers' antibodies against infectious disease. In contrast, gains in survival rates for infants in the second half of the Second World War were registered at both the early and the later stages of the first year of life. The point is supported by data presented in table 1, which describe wartime declines in both the developmental and wasting diseases, which primarily affect neonatal mortality rates, and infectious diseases, which primarily affect post-neonatal mortality rates. It is equally striking that diarrhoea and enteritis, historically the great scourge of infant life among malnourished populations, did not contribute to either the increase in infant mortality rates in 1940–41 or their decline in the later years of the war.

An overall trend of declining infant mortality rates in Britain was interrupted, therefore, but not reversed, during the Second World War. The same is true for maternal mortality rates, the decline in which began in the mid-1930s. Chemotherapy was not the sole cause of this important development, but the introduction of sulphonamide drugs in the 1930s enabled doctors to control puerperal sepsis, the greatest single cause of maternal deaths.[7]

The war period was a turning-point, though, in the trend of still births. Reliable statistics are available only from the late 1920s, when the still-birth rate for England and Wales stood at 40 per 1,000 total births. Virtually no change occurred in the decade before the outbreak of war, but, as we can see in table 2, a decline of approximately 30 per cent took place throughout England and Wales between 1938 and 1946. The greatest gains were registered in the mining regions of South Wales (Wales I) and in the industrial regions of Lancashire and Cheshire (North IV), with other regions, more rural and agricultural in character (South West), not far behind. Of course, massive internal migration makes regional comparisons between pre-war and post-war populations highly suspect. It is best, therefore, to interpret the decline in still-birth rates in this period as a reflection of a process which affected the population of Britain as a whole.

That process, it will be argued below, was set in motion long before the outbreak of the Second World War. Much smaller gains were made, both relatively and absolutely, in infant survival chances during the war against Hitler, than during the First World War a generation earlier.[8] It was perhaps easier to effect a reduction in the infant mortality rate when it stood at about 100 per

Table 2. *Still-birth rates, England and Wales, 1938–46, by region (deaths per 1,000 total births)*

	1938	1939	1940	1941	1942	1943	1944	1945	1946
England and Wales	38	38	36	35	33	30	28	28	27
South East	32	31	30	30	29	27	25	24	24
Greater London	31	31	29	30	29	26	24	24	24
Rest of South East	34	33	31	29	28	27	25	25	25
North	42	42	40	39	37	33	30	30	30
North I	39	40	40	36	37	32	30	31	31
North II	37	39	36	39	35	30	29	30	29
North III	41	42	39	38	36	32	30	30	29
North IV	46	44	41	40	38	34	31	30	31
Midlands	38	38	36	34	33	30	26	27	26
Midlands I	37	38	36	34	33	30	26	27	26
Midlands II	39	38	36	33	33	31	26	28	25
East	37	36	34	34	32	29	26	28	27
South West	39	37	36	32	32	30	27	26	26
Wales	51	49	47	43	40	36	34	34	33
Wales I	51	49	47	44	39	36	34	35	33
Wales II	48	47	47	39	41	35	33	32	33
County boroughs	40	40	38	36	34	31	29	29	29
Other urban districts	41	40	38	36	34	32	28	29	28
Rural districts	38	37	37	34	32	30	27	28	26

Regions

South East
Bedfordshire
Berkshire
Buckinghamshire
Essex
Hertfordshire
Kent
London
Middlesex
Oxfordshire
Southampton
Surrey
Sussex
Isle of Wight

North I
Durham
Northumberland

North II
Cumberland

Westmorland
Yorkshire–
  East Riding
Yorkshire–
  North Riding

North III
Yorkshire–
  West Riding
Yorkshire–
  County boroughs

North IV
Cheshire
Lancashire

Midlands I
Gloucestershire
Herefordshire
Shropshire
Staffordshire

Warwickshire
Worcestershire

Midlands II
Derbyshire
Lincolnshire, parts of
Northamptonshire
Nottinghamshire
Peterborough,
  Soke of

South West
Cornwall
Devon
Somerset
Wiltshire

East
Cambridgeshire
Ely, Isle of
Huntingdonshire

Lincolnshire, parts of
Norfolk
Rutlandshire
Suffolk

Wales I
Brecknockshire
Carmarthenshire
Glamorganshire
Monmouthshire

Wales II
Anglesey
Caernarvonshire
Cardiganshire
Denbighshire
Flintshire
Merionethshire
Montgomeryshire
Pembrokeshire
Radnorshire

1,000 live births in 1914, than when it was about 50 per 1,000 live births in 1939. But the greater impact of the earlier conflict must be understood in the context of pre-war social conditions which were significantly worse than those of the interwar years. Our interpretation of the stability of mortality trends in the period 1921–48 rests on the assumption that they were determined largely by prior changes in the standard of living of the British working class.

In order to complete the general demographic picture, it is necessary to examine the possibility that movements in the birth-rate influenced the course of the decline in infant mortality. By the 1920s, resort to contraception was, if not universal, extremely widespread in British society. The decline in fertility, dating from the 1870s, enabled working-class parents to provide more food and greater attention to each child in a smaller completed family. In the inter-war years, however, the long-term trend was either interrupted or broken, a distinction which depends upon an interpretation of demographic trends today. There is no argument, though, that the birth-rate moved downward in the first half of our period (1921–34) and upward in the second half (1935–48). Since infant mortality rates declined both during the upswings and the downswings of the birth-rate, and since changes in maternal age and parity in this period were dismissed long ago as decisive factors in the downward mortality trend,[9] we can conclude that purely demographic changes were not directly responsible for the gains made in infant survival chances during the period under review.

Unemployment and infant mortality

Time-series analysis
With this set of descriptive statistics in mind, let us consider the nature of the relation between unemployment and infant mortality during this period. Professor Brenner's case is that standard statistical methods can establish both the existence and nature of a strong correlation between movements in employment levels and movements in infant mortality rates. His approach is fairly simple. In order to make the unemployment rate consistent with other major but positive economic indicators, he used what he called an 'inverted' unemployment rate, namely 100 minus the percentage of the labour force unemployed. This was deemed to be the independent variable, the trend of which he determined. With the trend line equation in hand, he then calculated annual deviations from the trend. When a positive deviation was recorded, it indicated better than average employment conditions. Conversely, a negative deviation from the trend indicated worse than average employment conditions. Using US data for the period 1915–67, the bad years of the 1930s and the good years of the 1940s stand out clearly (figure 4). Against this set of deviations from the trend of employment, some of which were smoothed out by the

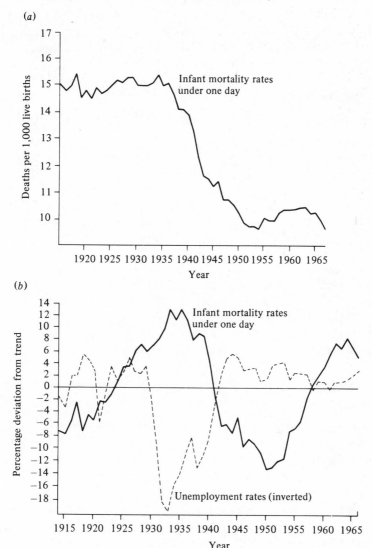

Fig. 4 (*a*) Infant mortality rates under one day in the United States, 1915–67. (*b*) Percentage deviations from the trends of under one day mortality rates and unemployment rates (inverted), 1915–67 (relation shown at one-year lag).

Source: M. H. Brenner, 'Fetal, infant, and maternal mortality during periods of economic instability', *International Journal of Health Services*, III, 2 (1973), p. 5.

Note that (*b*) illustrates deviations from a *linear* trend. A glance at (*a*), where the crude data are shown, would lead the reader to doubt the linearity of the trend.

use of moving averages, Brenner plotted deviations from the trends of under one day, post-neonatal and infant mortality rates. A positive deviation from these trends meant higher than average infant mortality; a negative deviation, lower than average infant mortality. What Brenner was after was a sort of 'double helix', confirming his hypothesis that employment levels and infant mortality rates were related in a statistically significant way. His primary conclusion was that when unemployment rose, mortality in the first day of life rose one year later, and post-neonatal mortality and infant mortality as a whole rose three to five years later.

There are theoretical objections to the method Brenner used to generate his evidence of the supposed inverse relation between employment and infant mortality, and I shall discuss these difficulties below. It seems reasonable, though, to try to test Brenner's hypothesis in an indirect way, by repeating the exercise for data on unemployment and infant mortality at various stages of the first year of life in Britain in the period 1921–49.

Fig. 5 Percentage deviations from the trend of infant mortality rates during the first day of life and from the trend of unemployment rates (inverted) in England and Wales, 1921–48 (unemployment rates moved forward by one year, three-year averages).

The results using British data are strikingly different from those reported by Brenner in his examination of the American case. On the one hand, his hypothesis seems to be confirmed in the case of early infant mortality. Figure 5 displays the 'double helix' predicted by Brenner in the case of day-one mortality in England and Wales. The mirror image of the two curves describing percentage deviations from the trends may be measured in terms of negative correlation coefficients which appear at lags of zero, one, and four years for day-one mortality, and at lags of zero and one year for week-one mortality in England and Wales (appendices 1 and 2). Similar negative correlations appear in the case of early infant mortality in Scotland at lags of one and four years. On the other hand, though, Brenner's findings are not replicated at later periods of the first year of life. Indeed, as in the case of total infant mortality in England and Wales, the numerous positive correlations imply that when unemployment rose, infant mortality actually fell, which is completely at variance with Brenner's argument. The weight of the statistical evidence concerning Britain, therefore, is against the contention that movements in infant mortality 'respond' to movements in unemployment.

I shall argue below that the positive findings in support of Brenner's hypothesis are probably statistical aberrations. It is necessary, though, to consider the possibility that early infant mortality is a special case. Time-series analysis seems to show two contradictory things: (i) when employment rates dipped below the trend line for the period 1921–49, first-week mortality rates either rose to levels well above the trend or failed to fall with it; (ii) no such relation existed at later stages of the first year of life. It is extremely difficult to accept at face value this apparent indication of a correlation between unemployment and early infant mortality, since there is no evidence that unemployment resulted in deprivation which affected new-born babies in the first seven days of life but not thereafter. It could be argued that unemployment interfered indirectly with the access which women had to hospitalization or professional care at home immediately after childbirth, but this argument is unconvincing for several reasons. First, the proportion of all deliveries undertaken in hospitals was rising throughout this period. Secondly, even before the outbreak of war in 1939, major improvements had taken place in provision for antenatal and postnatal care in maternal and child welfare centres. Both developments helped to protect the maternal population against the worst effects of the Depression. The exception was in South Wales, where maternal morbidity and mortality rates rose in the aftermath of increases in unemployment. Fortunately, the state of health of women in childbirth in the mining communities of South Wales was not representative of that of British women as a whole. When the decline in maternal mortality rates for Britain as a whole did come in 1936, it was not as a result of declining unemployment rates or the alleviation of the fear of unemployment. No one would deny that joblessness created stress among working women and the wives of working men, but the evidence that such anxiety affected pregnancy or its outcome is too weak to be conclusive.

Other doubts must be raised about accepting the contention that unemployment affected early but not late infant mortality rates. The most rigorous examination of the effect of unemployment on aspects of the mortality experience of the British population is the analysis of rheumatic heart disease among children in the period 1927–38 by Morris and Titmuss. They demonstrate conclusively that an increase in unemployment led to an increase in juvenile deaths due to rheumatic heart disease. A time lag of three years separated the two trends and represented the latent period of the disease.[10] Its toll was undoubtedly a reflection of malnutrition and squalor, conditions which also affect infant survival chances as a whole, and in particular those during the later months of the first year of life. If corroboration for the findings of Titmuss and Morris are to be sought in application of Brenner's method to British data, then it is to the post-neonatal period that we must direct special attention. And it is precisely at this later stage of infant mortality that Brenner's hypothesis is refuted by the data.

Another line of reasoning about the relation between unemployment and infant mortality is that a decline in protein intake during pregnancy increased early infant mortality due to congenital disease and deformity. There is some confirmation for this argument in the fact that the infant mortality rate due to spina bifida and anencephalus increased in the early 1930s. This rise continued, however, in the later 1930s when unemployment rates dropped, and during the Second World War when unemployment reached negligible levels.[11] It is puzzling, though, that infant mortality after the first week of life does not register evidence of diminished resistance to disease through maternal protein deficiency. A further problem is that it is very difficult to reach firm conclusions about nutritional levels in general or those of the unemployed in particular for this period. Lord Boyd Orr's work suggests that aggregate protein intake was constant over the period 1924–34, but that in the same decade, consumption of animal fat, fruits and vegetables increased significantly. During the Second World War, it was precisely these foodstuffs that were in very short supply.[12] A link between protein intake and early infant mortality is therefore plausible but unsubstantiated for the period under review. The shadow effect of such food deprivation after the Second World War is a point to which we shall return below.

Another look at figure 3 will suffice to show a further, more technical, reason for doubting Brenner's hypothesis. Statistically significant correlations between deviations from the trends of unemployment and infant mortality were found for the case of mortality in the first week of life, that is, in a time series which shows little or no absolute movement over three decades. The method of fitting a trend line to such data may exaggerate tiny changes and make them appear to be of equal significance to much greater movements around different trend lines. Brenner's use of a *linear* trend line in the case of day-one mortality is highly debatable, to say the least,[13] and it is no accident, therefore, that the relation between post-neonatal mortality and unemployment was found to be non-existent, while such a relation seemed to be proved in the case of early infant mortality. The method itself may produce such anomalies. Indeed, some statisticians raise objections to the way in which trend lines are 'fitted' to data, regardless of their character. As a *reductio ad absurdum*, it can be shown, using this approach, that sunspot eruptions cause business cycles. For this reason, alternative techniques of time-series analysis have been devised. Among them is a sophisticated procedure known as the 'Box–Jenkins' method. Through the integration of an autoregressive and moving average model, the Box–Jenkins approach solves problems built into more traditional modes of detrending series. It is also a powerful tool in the analysis of the structure of time series and of any lagged relation between serially correlated variables, which is precisely what we need.[14] Using this method, I was unable to identify any correlation between unemployment rates and infant mortality rates at any lag from one to ten years.[15]

Class differentials in infant mortality rates

In other ways too, we can show that it is necessary to view the relation between unemployment and infant mortality in a manner more complex than that suggested by Professor Brenner. Let us examine evidence related to the infant mortality experience of different social classes, regions, and urban administrative areas.

The shift from high to low unemployment in the 1930s and 1940s seems to have left undiminished class differentials in infant mortality. Evidence on this point has been available since the 1920s, when Registrars-General started regularly to use a five-tiered taxonomy of social classes to measure in a very rough way the demographic disadvantage of being born into a working man's family. Not too much should be made of such comparisons, which rely upon an inadequate definition of social class in terms of male occupation. Still, we can learn something from them. As is shown in table 3, in 1911 the mortality rate of infants born to the families of unskilled workers was double that of infants born to professional men's families. Between 1911 and 1939 the aggregate infant mortality rate for England and Wales dropped from 130 to 51 deaths per 1,000 live births. Yet over the same period, the advantage of Class I over Class V babies was not only maintained, but actually increased. This was only marginally true in the first month of life. At ages between six and twelve months though, when infectious diseases predominate, the advantage in survival chances which infants of well-to-do families had over those of poorer families increased substantially in the period between 1911 and 1931–32.

Assuming for a moment the very unlikely fact of low inter-class mobility, it is possible to compare only very imperfectly trends in demographic inequality in the pre-war decade and in the years between 1939 and 1951. Again we see that shifts in levels of unemployment were not decisive determinants in shifts in relative levels of infant mortality. In the 1930s, the gap between Class V and Class I narrowed both at ages six to twelve months and in terms of infant mortality rates as a whole. By 1951, the elimination of mass unemployment ought to have had some differential effect on the relative position of families of unskilled workers, if the Brenner hypothesis is valid. The evidence, however, points the other way. The excess of Class V infant mortality rates over those of Class I in 1951 and 1939 was virtually the same.

Table 3. *Infant mortality rates of legitimate children, England and Wales, 1911, 1920–22, 1930–32, 1939 and 1951 (deaths per 1,000 live births), with respect to excess mortality in Social Class V compared to Social Class I*

	1911	1921–23	1930–32	1939	1951
Neonatal Mortality					
Class V	42.5	36.9	32.5	30.1	22.8
Class I	30.2	23.4	21.7	18.9	14.0
Excess	12.3	13.5	10.8	11.2	8.8
% Excess	40.7	57.7	49.7	59.3	62.9
Post-neonatal Mortality					
Class V	110.0	60.1	44.5	30.0	18.0
Class I	46.2	15.0	11.0	8.0	4.7
Excess	63.8	45.1	33.5	22.0	13.3
% Excess	138.1	300.1	304.5	275.0	283.0
Mortality at 6–12 months					
Class V	50.0	24.6	19.4	10.4	–
Class I	18.3	5.8	3.6	2.3	–
Excess	31.7	18.8	15.8	8.1	–
% Excess	173.2	324.1	438.9	352.2	–
Infant Mortality					
Class V	152.5	97.0	77.0	60.1	40.8
Class I	76.4	38.4	32.7	26.9	18.7
Excess	76.1	58.6	44.3	33.2	22.1
% Excess	99.6	152.6	135.5	123.4	118.2

Sources: R. Titmuss, *Birth, Poverty and Wealth* (1943), pp. 44–5. *Registrar–General's Decennial Supplement. England and Wales 1931. Part IIB. Occupational Fertility. 1931 and 1939*, Table Q1, p. 86.
Registrar–General's Decennial Supplement. England and Wales 1951. Part II, vol. 2, Table 14A, Occupational Mortality.

Regional differentials in infant mortality rates

It is a commonplace of the history of the interwar years that the slump completely bypassed large parts of the south and east of England. It did not require
Orwell's journey to Wigan pier to make known the fact of wide regional and
industrial variations in economic hardship. Among the worst-hit populations
were those who lived in the 'Special Areas' of England, encompassing the
counties of Durham, Cumberland and Northumberland, and the 'Special
Areas ' of Wales, that is, Glamorgan, Brecknock, Pembroke and Monmouth.
In each of these counties, unemployment rates in the early 1930s reached between 30 per cent and 40 per cent, or double the national average. In parts of
these areas, unemployment rates of 70 per cent to 80 per cent were not
unknown. What does the experience of infant mortality in these regions during
the age of mass unemployment in the 1930s and in the period of 'full employment' in the 1940s contribute to the debate over Brenner's hypothesis?

The first point to be made is that these regions are highly heterogeneous,
and that, therefore, we should expect wide fluctuations in their demographic
behaviour. Still, it is no comfort to supporters of Brenner's case that improvements were registered in Northumberland in the early 1930s, in Glamorgan in
the mid-1930s, and in Durham in the late 1930s, despite the persistence of very
high unemployment rates compared to the nation as a whole throughout the
pre-war decade. It is even more surprising that in the years 1945–49, when the
Attlee government made certain that there would be no immediate return to
the age of mass unemployment, there occurred in Glamorgan and Durham a
slow-down in the rate of decline of infant mortality. Data on county boroughs
in these regions show the same pattern of irregularity in the relation between
unemployment and infant mortality.

Statistics relating to areas outside those worst hit by unemployment also
show a persistent trend for the better during the 'bad' 1930s and the 'better'
1940s. If anything, there are indications that the difference between the
national rate of infant mortality and that of industrial regions in the post-war
period was actually greater than in the pre-war period. For instance, infant
mortality rates in Lancashire and Cheshire in 1937 were 21 per cent above the
national average. Ten years later, the gap had grown to 32 per cent. The
greatest gains in infant survival chances were registered in London and the
South-east, that is to say, in those areas which were not afflicted by mass
unemployment in the 1930s.

Variance in infant mortality rates in urban administrative areas

Finally, let us compare the trend of infant mortality in smaller administrative
areas. Brenner's hypothesis suggests that the pace of infant mortality decline
was greater in areas of low unemployment such as Oxford and Eastbourne
than in high unemployment areas such as Wigan or Sunderland. If this assump-

tion were true, it would mean that the variance among the mortality rates of all county boroughs would increase when unemployment hit some harder than others. The statistical variance among all county boroughs of England and Wales and among all metropolitan boroughs of London in the period 1920–50 is, though, astonishingly uniform. Whatever their experience of unemployment, virtually all urban areas went through the process of infant mortality decline together, as it were.[16] Here again it appears that demographic trends cannot be reduced to reflections of the workings of the labour market.

Infant mortality during the Second World War

The decline in infant mortality in England and Wales was unshaken by the slump. It is hardly surprising that there was a further drop in the later 1930s: partly because of a brightening economic climate and partly because of the introduction of the early sulphonamide drugs. As the late Richard Titmuss showed, these gains were not only maintained but in some respects amplified during the Second World War.[17] In this context the importance of short-term social and economic changes for improvements in public health can be seen in sharp relief.

It was inevitable that an increase in civilian mortality rates would occur in the aftermath of aerial bombardment. To avoid such casualties over one million Londoners and other city dwellers were evacuated as the war began. When the anticipated Blitz did not materialize, there was a drift back to the cities. This trend was reversed, though, when bombing began in earnest in late 1940. On balance, migration took out of the line of fire, and probably saved the lives of, a significant number of mothers and infants. In March 1942, when the worst of the first phase of the Blitz was over, more than 600,000 people were still billeted in government reception areas.[18] Such policies helped to ensure that operations of war did not significantly add to infant mortality rates in the period 1940–42, as is shown in table 4.

The dislocation, anxiety and hardship caused by evacuation and relocation of bombed-out families apparently did not endanger the health of pregnant women or their children in early infancy. Infant mortality rates due to prematurity and to birth injuries declined slightly in 1940–41 compared to those of the immediate pre-war period. A widespread outbreak of German measles in 1940–41 was probably the source of a small, but real, increase in the rate of death due to congenital abnormalities in 1941–42. The slight decline registered in 1940–41 in neonatal mortality rates as a whole, though, further supports the view that the disruption of war did not undermine the progress made in the pre-war period in terms of the survival chances of mothers or their infants in the early period of the first year of life.

It is rather in the context of post-neonatal mortality that we can find evidence of the deleterious consequences of the upheaval of the first three years of the war. Migration and overcrowding in relocation areas helped to spread viral and bacterial infections. Less parental supervision and more exposed gas pipes and electric leads were responsible for an increase in fatal household accidents and in 'overlying' or asphyxiation of infants. At the same time, a sharp fall in food supplies, particularly in meat, fats, sugar and fruits, added to increased stress and overwork among women, reduced resistance to infection among mothers and infants. If we recall that rehousing of bombed-out families often took place in inadequate dwellings and that the winters of 1939–40 and 1940–41 were unusually cold, it should come as no surprise that infant mortality due to bronchitis and pneumonia, as well as to other bacterial and viral diseases, increased sharply at this time.[19]

Table 4. *Infant mortality rates by cause and sex, 1940–45 (deaths per 1,000 live births)*

	1940–42		1943–45	
Cause	Male	Female	Male	Female
Whooping cough	1.05	1.24	0.75	0.89
Tuberculous diseases	0.64	0.54	0.49	0.42
Measles	0.42	0.37	0.28	0.29
Convulsions	1.41	0.94	0.77	0.51
Bronchitis and pneumonia	13.23	10.18	10.35	8.22
Enteritis and diarrhoea	5.60	3.98	5.71	4.16
Congenital malformations	6.97	6.14	6.01	5.31
Premature birth	16.07	12.38	12.93	10.73
Injury at birth	3.13	2.07	2.96	1.91
Asphyxia, atelectasis	2.39	1.88	2.50	1.83
Haemolytic diseases	0.68	0.44	0.80	0.49
Operations of war	0.25	0.28	0.07	0.08
Other violence	1.52	1.28	1.46	1.23
Other and ill-defined causes	9.22	6.63	7.05	5.06
All causes	62.61	48.35	52.13	41.13

Source: *Registrar–General's Statistical Review of England and Wales for the Six Years 1940–45*, vol. 1, Medical, p. 50.

The evidence in table 4 confirms Titmuss's view that it is essential to divide the demographic history of the Second World War into two periods, 1939–42 and 1943–45. The first period is one of marked deterioration in infant survival chances; the second, of striking and substantial gains in infant survival rates. The causes of the transition from phase one to phase two lie in part in the vagaries of enemy action. Of perhaps greater importance, though, is that by 1941, the British population had been insulated from some of the worst features of this country's economic frailty by specific policy decisions.

It was a central tenet of the economic strategy of Churchill's Coalition that the cost of the war should not be placed on the shoulders of those least able to bear it. Consequently, increases in wages were not passed on to consumers but were covered by subsidies. These kept down the cost of the relevant commodities and of other goods, the prices of which were unaffected by rising wage bills. It took time, though, for the mechanism of price controls to operate effectively. Hence only in late 1942 did the index of weekly wage rates finally catch up with and surpass the cost of living index. Because of overtime and piecework, as well as separation allowances for wives of servicemen, family incomes may have reached the price level even earlier. At the same time, a more progressive tax structure helped to redistribute income away from salaries, rents, interest and profits, that is, middle-class incomes, and towards wages.[20] The period of undeniably rising real incomes in 1943–45 coincides, therefore, with the period of steeply declining rates of infant mortality.

Effective food rationing, the provision of free milk under the National Milk Scheme, strict limitations on the production and distribution of alcoholic beverages and rent control helped to stabilize the family economy of the working class more than that of the middle class. This was largely because manual workers' families spent a much greater proportion of their incomes on food, drink and rent than did families of non-manual workers or professional people. A rise in the price of luxury items, or in the costs of motoring, travel and services significantly affected the cost of living of the middle class. Such relatively minor deprivation, annoying though it may have been, in effect paid for the improvement in working-class incomes and indirectly in working-class nutritional levels during the war.

Still, the per capita consumption of food dropped by 18 per cent in the difficult years of 1938–41 and was 10 per cent below the pre-war level three years later. Consumption of milk, poultry, eggs, meat and fish was substantially reduced. The nutritional effect of the inevitable shortage of animal protein and fats in the nation's diet was balanced in part by an increase in consumption of vitamins and minerals due to the greater prominence of vegetables in the diet. Such adjustments meant that there was only a 2 per cent drop in the daily per capita calorific intake over the decade 1934–44. This relatively minor squeeze in food consumption would have been much worse, though, had not home farmers succeeded in raising agricultural output which, together with lend-lease aid, kept food supplies at a safe level throughout the war. Similar developments had occurred in muted form in the 1914–18 war, but a generation later, agricultural and food policy was more effectively planned and carried out.[21]

A similar parallel may be found between the two world wars in terms of a growing commitment by the state to defend the health of mothers and children as casualty lists lengthened. The fact that until D-Day in 1944 more civilians than soldiers died from enemy action no doubt helped to bring civilian needs to the fore. The demands of the war economy also made the extension of provision for mothers and infants into an act of national importance. Factory crêches, nurseries and child and maternal welfare centres were built at an unprecedented rate during the war. In addition, women's attitudes changed. By 1943, and for the first time, a majority of pregnant women attended antenatal-care centres early in their pregnancy. By the end of the war, it had become much easier for doctors, nurses and midwives to identify problem cases, to remedy deficiencies in nutrition during pregnancy and to ensure effective care during and after labour. By 1945, over 70 per cent of the infants born in the previous year were brought to infant welfare centres.[22] Between 1939 and 1945, therefore, the pre-war patchwork of voluntary and local authority-sponsored institutions began to take on the unified form in which the maternity service exists today, and more women began to see it as a right rather than as a privilege.

It is more difficult to locate the impact of wartime medical provision on the deterioration in infant survival chances in 1940–42 or in the pattern of improvement in 1943–45. As in the First World War, civilians had a much diminished chance of seeing a doctor in wartime due to military mobilization.[23] Titmuss estimated that fully one-third of general practitioners were called up and that of the remainder, a substantial number were old-age pensioners. The scarcity of medical attention was particularly marked in rural areas.[24] Some of the gap was filled by the patent medicine industry and the corner chemist, but more seriously ill people were undoubtedly disadvantaged during the war. When tuberculous people were sent home early in the war to make room in sanatoria for the wave of bombing casualties which never came, the disease was bound to spread. The data in table 1 show that, fortunately, infants in Britain did not suffer from this recrudescence of the 'White Plague'.

It is possible, though, that wartime medical developments helped to control the spread of disease. Advances in chemotherapy and in the efficient operation of the blood transfusion service, which were of direct use in dealing with war casualties, may have helped civilians as well. It is likely, however, that the military had first access to the limited supplies of penicillin and other drugs, and that it was only long after 1945 that the civilian population enjoyed the full fruits of the pre-war chemotherapeutic breakthrough. Medical intervention was, therefore, less important than economic and social policy in curbing the hardships of the early part of the war and in ensuring that Britain's military effort did not undermine the health and survival chances of mothers and infants.

Conclusions and implications

This examination of a chapter of the demographic history of modern Britain has tried to establish that the relation between economic change and demographic change is anything but a simple one of short-term cause and effect. It is profoundly misleading to treat unemployment as an independent variable and infant mortality as a dependent variable, in the way Brenner has done. To make sense of the immediate consequences of unemployment, it must be seen as part of a network of economic relations, support systems and social attitudes that are deeply embedded in the class structure. The worst way to approach the problem of unemployment is to reify it. In addition, Brenner's analysis assumes that unemployment is one phenomenon, when, of course, it is many. We need to know much more about the way in which unemployed people and their families cope with the undoubted difficulties of joblessness. To assume that men and women who lose their jobs will by definition be unable to support their families or to keep their children alive is unwarranted and demonstrably untrue.

In the period under review, one reason why infant mortality rates did not follow in the immediate wake of movements in unemployment rates is that unemployment insurance, however miserly and demeaning in its application, and council housing, however drab and dispiriting in its appearance, provided a buffer for the unemployed which helped to separate deprivation from destitution.[25] Perhaps these forms of state support distinguish the British and American cases, and provide the basis for a comparative study of the impact of economic crises on different populations.

On another level, though, the lack of symmetry between economic change and demographic development suggests that it is necessary to use different time perspectives in analysing these discrete phenomena. Even in the twentieth century, demographic history may require a touch of what French historians call the style of '*la longue durée*'. In other words, we shall not be able to appreciate the demographic costs of a depression or a war by concentrating solely on the events themselves.

Some immediate repercussions of either political or economic upheavals can, of course, be seen. It is clear that the combination of aerial bombardment in the first part of the Second World War and delays in the emergence of an efficient war economy contributed to the increase in infant mortality in 1940–41. Abundant evidence exists too about the beneficial effects of rising real wages and extended social provision for the health of mothers and infants in the latter part of the war. It is necessary, however, to take a longer-term view in order to place both the pre-war and war-related events in their appropriate context.

If there is any single change which ought to govern comparisons of the social history of the late nineteenth century with that of the twentieth century, it is the eradication of much of the appalling poverty which was endemic in Victorian cities and in large parts of the Victorian countryside. Alterations in the labour market and the growth of state and local authority provision were in part responsible for these developments. Consequently, communities where unemployment was high in the interwar years did not bear the worst features of nineteenth-century capitalism, and it would be foolish to look for demographic evidence that it did so. Similarly, the deprivation occasioned by Hitler's war did not alter in any lasting way the pre-war pattern of improvement in social conditions and in public health.

The demographic experience of this turbulent century can be understood fully, therefore, only by adopting a long-term view. The case of the Netherlands during the Second World War may help to clarify this point. In 1944–45, there occurred in Holland a man-made famine imposed by the Nazis on Dutch city dwellers in the aftermath of a railway strike intended to spark off an insurrection or at least to interfere with German troop movements after the Normandy landings. Unfortunately for the Dutch, the Allies finally arrived only in the last days of the war, by which time nutritional levels had been reduced below subsistence. The consequence was a severe short-term demographic crisis. Mortality rates soared, and the birth weight of new-born babies conceived in this period diminished significantly.[26] But the crisis struck a population whose nutritional standards had been rising over several generations. Once normal conditions had been restored, the trend of infant mortality continued on its downward path. Twenty years later, indeed, the new-born babies of the 'hunger winter' were found to be virtually indistinguishable in physical and mental characteristics from people born either slightly earlier or slightly later. At least on one level, the physical scars of war healed almost without trace.[27]

Nothing even remotely like the 'hunger winter' of 1944–45 occurred in Britain during the Second World War. It is true, nonetheless, that the capacity of the civilian populations of both Britain and Holland to adjust to the shortages, deprivations and injustices of war was a reflection more of the trend of nutritional and sanitary improvement over the generations preceding the 1939–45 conflict than of any particular aspect of the war itself.

The trend towards better nutrition was initiated by the sustained rise in real wages during the third quarter of the nineteenth century. Working-class children born in the 1850s and 1860s were the first to receive unambiguously some of the fruits of economic growth. As they grew into adolescence and early adulthood, their death rates began to decline. The same generation married in the 1880s and 1890s and were more likely by the turn of the century to give birth to infants with an improved chance of surviving the first year of life. Improvements in parental, and in particular in maternal health, were, therefore, prerequisites of improvements in infant health. After 1900, the secular improvement in standards of living and nutrition continued and was reflected both in increasing life-expectancy for adults and in significant increases in the age-specific height and weight of schoolchildren.[28]

Better nutrition meant increased resistance to viral and bacterial infection. In addition, sanitary and medical intervention helped to reduce exposure to disease. After 1936, advances in chemotherapy enabled doctors to control many previously lethal diseases. Before this period, though, the enhancement of recovery rates from endemic infant diseases such as diarrhoea and measles was a result of improved nutrition, both among pregnant women and among their children. Unfortunately, we do not have relevant morbidity and case-fatality rates to prove this argument beyond question. The overwhelming evidence from studies of the synergistic relation between nutrition and infectious disease[29] leaves little doubt, though, that a sustained decline in infant mortality rates such as Britain experienced before the 1930s was impossible without major improvements in the quantity and quality of the per capita food intake.

The way in which a female child is fed is likely, a generation later, to affect her ability to conceive, to carry a pregnancy to full term and to give birth to a baby healthy enough to survive the first year of life. By examining this cohort effect it is possible to see, finally, that the shadow of chronic deprivation is just as important as the shadow of nutritional improvements. In a series of remarkable studies, Sir Dugald Baird and his colleagues at Aberdeen have shown conclusively that the quality of a mother's environment before and soon after *her* birth influences her reproductive efficiency and the survival chances of her children a generation later, and even those of her children's children two generations later. For instance, there was a rise in the perinatal mortality rate due to low birth weight in Aberdeen in 1968–72. Particularly affected were the 15–19 and 20–24 cohorts who had been born in 1949–57 and 1944–52, when the incidence of low birth weight was also high. *Their* mothers had been born between 1928 and 1932, during the worst years of the depression.[30] Similarly, in Scotland as a whole, there was an increase in the perinatal mortality rates due to central nervous system malformations among three cohorts of babies: those born in the early 1930s, those born in the 1950s and those born in 1971–72.[31] Here is evidence of the human costs of the depression, which Brenner's short-term approach could not detect.

Similarly, Baird has shown that the full effects of wartime food policies can only be seen after one generation. As we have noted, the still-birth rate fell substantially between 1940 and 1947. Among deliveries in Aberdeen, it dropped sharply as well after 1963 for women in the 20–24 age group, after 1967 for women in the 25–29 age group and after 1972 for women in the 30–34 age group. In other words, it is in the 1970s that we can see the beneficial outcome of giving priority in food allocation to pregnant women and children in the 1940s. We can understand, therefore, why girls born in the mid-1940s had greater reproductive efficiency in the period 1974–79, when there occurred a 38 per cent drop in the perinatal mortality rate.[32] A recognition of such cohort effects is thus essential to an interpretation of the relation between economic and demographic change.[33]

There is, in sum, a momentum in Britain's demographic history which is the product of slow but cumulative changes in the adequacy of the diet of the working population. The record is certainly not one of uniform and unbroken improvement. On balance, though, it is only by recognizing the significance of the long-term legacy of better nutrition that we will understand why the process of infant mortality decline survived intact the economic dislocation of both the slump and the Second World War.

Appendix 1. *Estimates of trends in unemployment rates (inverted) and in infant mortality rates at some sub-periods of the first year of life in Britain, 1921–49*

Infant mortality rates	Equations used to detrend rates	R^2
England and Wales 1921–48		
Day 0–1	$y = -0.019\,059\,12x + 0.000\,042\,480\,94x^3$	
	$-0.000\,000\,000\,545\,092\,3x^6 + 10.383\,37$	0.91
Days 1–7	$y = +0.157\,189x - 0.000\,001\,467\,553x^4 + 8.115\,394$	0.91
Days 7–28	$y = -0.248\,112x + 0.000\,000\,002\,723\,914x^5 + 17.145\,70$	0.90
Days 0–28	$y = +0.061\,225\,82x - 0.000\,002\,617\,767x^4 + 32.321\,86$	0.94
Months 1–12	$y = -0.983\,647\,4x + 0.000\,000\,203\,922\,5x^4 + 63.586\,06$	0.89
Year 0–1	$y = -0.919\,807\,9x - 0.000\,002\,421\,507x^4 + 95.842\,95$	0.92
Scotland 1922–49		
Days 0–7	$y = -0.039\,577\,98x + 0.000\,144\,799\,5x^3$	
	$-0.000\,000\,001\,472\,994\,6x^4 + 22.85896$	0.84
Days 0–28	$y = -1.470\,707x + 0.000\,792\,620\,5x^3$	
	$-0.000\,000\,004\,488\,805x^6$	0.90
Months 1–12	$y = -2.120\,373x + 0.000\,624\,291\,3x^3 - 0.000\,000\,003\,472\,773x^6$	
	$+96.37800$	0.86
Year 0–1	$y = -3.605\,271x + 0.001\,438\,913x^3 - 0.000\,000\,008\,067\,815x^6$	
	$+158.4418$	0.89
Unemployment (inverted) in United Kingdom		
	$y = -0.505\,902\,9x + 0.000\,005\,956\,640x^4 + 96.247\,21$	0.63

x = year
y = infant mortality rate or unemployment rate (inverted)

Appendix 2. *Correlation coefficients between percentage deviations from trend of unemployment rates (inverted) and trends of infant mortality rates at sub-periods of the first year of life in Britain, 1921–49*

	No lag		1-year lag		4-year lag	
Rate	No average	3-year average	No average	3-year average	No average	3-year average
England and Wales 1921–48						
Day 0–1	−0.4077[a]	−0.7058[a]	−0.5788[a]	−0.8798[a]	−0.1442[a]	−0.5235[a]
Days 1–7	−0.3257[a]	−0.4467[a]	−0.4413[a]	−0.5170[a]	+0.0437[a]	−0.0220
Days 7–28	+0.2749[a]	+0.2940[a]	+0.2556[a]	+0.3288[a]	+0.1241[a]	+0.3993[a]
Days 0–28	+0.0294	−0.0549	−0.0896[a]	−0.2035[a]	+0.0110	−0.0549
Months 1–12	+0.0401[a]	+0.6296[a]	+0.3940[a]	+0.6201[a]	+0.0883[a]	+0.1634[a]
Year 0–1	+0.3396[a]	+0.5604[a]	+0.3052[a]	+0.4928[a]	+0.0787[a]	+0.1434[a]
Scotland 1922–49						
Days 0–7	−0.0185	−0.0003	−0.2577[a]	−0.2694[a]	−0.1374	−0.3286[a]
Days 0–28	+0.1237[a]	+0.1944[a]	−0.0971[a]	−0.1011[a]	−0.2655[a]	−0.4914[a]
Months 1–12	+0.0941[a]	+0.1190[a]	+0.1242[a]	+0.2052[a]	+0.1424[a]	+0.2331[a]
Year 0–1	+0.0926[a]	+0.1524[a]	+0.0686[a]	+0.1114[a]	+0.0284[a]	−0.0116[a]

[a] Significant at the 5% level.

The Durbin–Watson test showed positive serial correlation only in the case of the trend of unemployment rates. Since none of the time series of infant mortality rates displayed evidence of autocorrelation, it is possible to accept the significance of the correlation coefficients shown above.

The published writings of Henry Pelling

1 Books

Origins of the Labour Party (Macmillan, 1954; 2nd edn, Oxford University Press, 1965; Oxford Paperback, 1966).

The Challenge of Socialism (A & C Black, 1953. British Political Tradition Series. 2nd edn, 1968).

America and the British Left: From Bright to Bevan (A & C Black, 1956).

(With Frank Bealey) *Labour and Politics, 1900–1906: A History of the Labour Representation Committee* (Macmillan, 1958).

The British Communist Party. A Historical Profile (A & C Black, 1958; reprinted with new introduction, 1975).

Modern Britain, 1885–1955 (Thomas Nelson, 1960. Nelson History of England, vol. 8. Cardinal Paperback, 1974).

American Labor (University of Chicago Press, 1960. Chicago History of American Civilisation. Paperback edn, 1960. Special Student edition, New York, 1962).

A Short History of the Labour Party (Macmillan, 1961. Also Papermac edition. 2nd edn, 1965; 3rd edn, 1968; 4th edn, 1972; 5th edn, 1976; 6th edn, 1978).

A History of British Trade Unionism (Pelican Original, 1963. 2nd edn, 1971; 3rd edn, 1976. Also hardback editions by Macmillan, 1963, 1972, 1976).

Social Geography of British Elections, 1885–1910 (Macmillan, 1967).

Popular Politics and Society in Late Victorian Britain (Macmillan, 1968. 2nd edn, 1979).

Britain and the Second World War (Collins Fontana, 1970. Fontana History of War and Society).

Winston Churchill (Macmillan 1974. Pan Books edn, 1977).

2 Essays in books by other authors

'The Rise of American Labor', in H. C. Allen and C. P. Hill, *British Essays in American History* (Arnold, 1957), pp. 263–73.

'Great Britain: The Communist Party and the Trade Unions', in J. J. Kirkpatrick, *The Strategy of Deception: A Study in World-wide Communist Tactics* (Farrar, Straus & Co, New York, 1963), pp. 310–40.

3 Books by other hands edited by Henry Pelling

C. Tsuzuki, *H. M. Hyndman and British Socialism* (Oxford University Press, 1961).

4 Articles

'H. H. Champion: Pioneer of Labour Representation', *Cambridge Journal*, vi (1953), pp. 222–38.

'The American Labour Movement: A British View', *Political Studies*, ii (1954), pp. 227–41.

'The Rise and Decline of Socialism in Milwaukee', *Bulletin of the International Institute of Social History*, (1955), pp. 91–103.

'The American Economy and the Foundation of the British Labour Party', *Economic History Review*, 2nd ser., viii (1955), pp. 1–17.

'The Knights of Labor in Britain, 1880–1901', *Economic History Review*, 2nd ser., ix (1956), pp. 313–31.

'The Early History of the Communist Party of Great Britain, 1920–9', *Transactions of the Royal Historical Society*, 5th ser., viii (1958), pp. 41–57.

'Manuscript Sources of British Labour History in the United States', *Bulletin of the Society for the Study of Labour History*, no. 5 (1962), pp. 39–40.

'La Classe Ouvrière Anglaise et les origines de la Législation Sociale', *Le Mouvement Social*, no. 65 (1968), pp. 39–54.

'Wales and the Boer War', *Welsh History Review*, iv (1969), pp. 363–5.

'Corvo and Labour Politics', *Times Literary Supplement*, 6 Feb. 1969.

'On Writing a New Churchill Biography', *The Times*, 11 July 1974.

'The 1945 General Election Reconsidered', *Historical Journal*, xxiii (1980), pp. 399–414.

Article on 'Trades Union Congress' in *Encyclopedia Britannica*, mid-1960s.

5 Review articles

'Religion and the Nineteenth Century British Working Class', *Past and Present*, no. 27 (1964), pp. 129–33.

'Taylor's England', *Past and Present*, no. 33 (1966), pp. 149–58.

'State Intervention and Social Legislation in Great Britain before 1914', *Historical Journal*, x (1967), pp. 562–6.
'Communists in Britain', *Times Literary Supplement*, 27 March 1969.
'Working-class Conservatives', *Historical Journal*, xiii (1970), pp. 339–43.
'The Impact of Labour', *Cambridge Review*, 7 May 1971.

Notes

All works published in London unless otherwise indicated.

Introduction: labour history and labour historians

1 E. P. Thompson, 'An Open Letter to Leszek Kolakowski', *Socialist Register* (1973), p. 55.
2 *Essays in Labour History*, ed. A. Briggs and J. Saville (1960).
3 Thanks are due to Professor Royden Harrison for enlightenment on this matter.
4 For examples of their work, which extends well beyond the confines of labour history, see: A. Briggs (ed.), *Chartist Studies* (1959); J. F. C. Harrison, *Living and Learning* (1961) and *Robert Owen and the Owenites in Britain and America* (1969); R. Harrison, *Before the Socialists* (1965); E. J. Hobsbawm, *Labouring Men* (1964); S. Pollard, *A History of Labour in Sheffield* (Liverpool, 1959); J. Saville, *Rural Depopulation in England and Wales 1851–1951* (1957); E. P. Thompson, *The Making of the English Working Class* (1963).
5 P. Joyce, *Work, Society and Politics. The Culture of the Factory in Later Victorian England* (Brighton, 1980), p. 93. See also: J. Femia, 'Hegemony and Consciousness in the Thought of A. Gramsci', *Political Studies*, XXIII, 1 (1975), pp. 29–48; A. Gramsci, *The Modern Prince and Other Essays* (Eng. edn, 1963); R. Gray, *The Aristocracy of Labour in Victorian Britain c. 1850–1914* (1981); H. Newby, 'The Deferential Dialectic', *Comparative Studies in Society and History*, XVII, 2 (1975), pp. 139–64; P. Thompson, *The Edwardians* (1975); G. Stedman Jones, 'Working-class Culture and Working-class Politics in London 1870–1900: Notes on the Remaking of a Working Class', *Journal of Social History*, VII (1974), pp. 460–508.
6 S. Meacham, *A Life Apart* (1978); A. Mason, *Association Football and English Society 1863–1915* (Brighton, 1980); R. W. Malcolmson, *Popular Recreations in English Society 1700–1850* (Cambridge, 1973); D. Vincent, 'Love and Death and the Nineteenth Century Working Class', *Social History*, V, 2 (1980), pp. 223–47; and many contributions to *History Workshop Journal*.
7 For example, A. Campbell, *The Lanarkshire Miners. A Social History of their Trade Unions 1775–1874* (Edinburgh, 1979); J. Obelkevich, *Religion and Rural Society* (Oxford, 1975); Joyce, *Work, Society and Politics, passim*; J. Foster, *Class Struggle*

in the Industrial Revolution (1974); J. White, *The Limits of Trade Union Militancy* (1978).

8 For example, J. Cronin, *Industrial Conflict in Modern Britain* (1979); G. Crossick, *An Artisan Elite in Victorian London* (1974); J. R. Hay, 'Employers and Social Policy in Britain: the Evolution of Welfare Legislation', *Social History*, 4 (1977), pp. 435–55; J. Zeitlin, 'Employers' Strategies in the Engineering Industry 1890–1914', in W. Mommsen (ed.), *Trade Unions in Britain and Germany 1880–1914* (1982); L. J. Williams, 'The Coalowners', in D. Smith (ed.), *A People and a Proletariat: Essays in the History of Wales, 1780–1980* (1980).

9 L. Stone, 'The Return of the Narrative', *Past and Present*, no. 84 (1979).

10 *The Challenge of Socialism* (1953), p. 8.

11 See the list of his published writings on pp. 257–9.

12 *Popular Politics and Society in Late Victorian Britain* (1968), p. 165.

13 For an introduction to such work, see: R. Harrison (ed.), *The Independent Collier* (Brighton, 1979); R. Harrison (ed.), *Workmen of Our Class* (Brighton, 1982); J. Hinton, *The First Shop Stewards' Movement* (1973); E. Hunt, *British Labour History 1815–1914* (1980); R. Hyman, *Strikes* (1973); Mommsen (ed.), *Trade Unions in Britain and Germany, passim*; M. J. Daunton, 'Down the Pit: Work in the Great Northern and South Wales Coalfields, 1870–1914', *Economic History Review*, 2nd ser., xxxiv, 4 (1981), pp. 578–97; and, R. Price, *Masters, Unions and Men: Work Control in Building and the Rise of Labour, 1830–1914* (Cambridge, 1980).

1. The social democratic theory of the class struggle

1 See Peter Jenkins' appreciation of Crosland, *Guardian*, 21 Feb. 1977.

2 G. Bernard Shaw (ed.), *Fabian Essays in Socialism* (1889), pp. 187, 147; Bernard Shaw, 'The Impossibilities of Anarchism', in *Socialism and Individualism*, Fabian Socialist Series, no. 3 (1908 edn), pp. 47, 28.

3 Winston S. Churchill, *Liberalism and the Social Problem* (1909), p. 75; London Municipal Society, *The Case Against Socialism* (1908), p. 4.

4 J. Saville, 'The Ideology of Labourism', in R. Benewick, R. N. Berki and B. Parekh (eds.), *Knowledge and Belief in Politics* (1973), p. 215; G. D. H. Cole, *The World of Labour* (1913; reprinted, ed. John Lovell, Brighton, 1973), pp. 31–2.

5 As it happens, Crosland disliked the label 'mixed economy', but this is the thrust of his approach. See *The Future of Socialism* (1956; paperback edn, 1964), p. 34. There is an adumbration of this argument in L. T. Hobhouse, *The Labour Movement*, 3rd edn (1912), p. 88: 'The type of society to which we are working, largely under the impulsion of the Labour Movement, is neither Individualist nor, in the narrower sense, Socialist.'

6 Hobhouse, 'The Moral of Failure', *Nation*, 25 May 1907, p. 478; *Liberalism* (1911), p. 214; *Social Evolution and Political Theory* (New York, 1911), p. 183.

7 *Government by the People*, People's Suffrage Federation pamphlet (1910), p. 24; *Democracy and Reaction* (1904; reprinted, ed. P. F. Clarke, Brighton, 1972), p. 221.

8 Open letter by David Owen, William Rodgers and Shirley Williams, *Guardian*, 1 Aug. 1980; Crosland, *The Future of Socialism*, p. 134; E. Durbin, *The Politics of Democratic Socialism* (1940; new impression, 1957), p. 187, italicizing the sentence quoted; J. A. Hobson, *The Science of Wealth* (1911), pp. 54–5, and *Work and Wealth* (1914), p. 276.

9 R. H. Tawney, *The Acquisitive Society* (1921), p. 113; review of *The Town Labourer*, *Times Literary Supplement*, 19 June 1917; R. H. Tawney, *Equality*, preface to the 1938 edn (new edn 1964), p. 27. For a more thorough discussion of Tawney's thought see J. M. Winter (ed.), *History and Society. Essays by R. H. Tawney* (1978), pp. 1–40.

10 I put it this way because the answer is more obviously a theory about democracy than explicitly about the class struggle. Thus it might be more exact to say that this theory has been, for social democrats, the functional equivalent of the theory of the class struggle for socialists.

11 Hobhouse, *The Labour Movement* (1893), pp. 3–4; *ibid.*, 3rd edn (1912), p. 22.

12 For this distinction see Peter Clarke, *Liberals and Social Democrats* (Cambridge, 1978), pp. 4–5.

13 Durbin, *The Politics of Democratic Socialism*, p. 329.

14 Quoted in Paul Smith (ed.), *Lord Salisbury on Politics* (Cambridge, 1972), pp. 26, 33.

15 This was Sidney Webb's expression in *Fabian Essays in Socialism*, ed. Bernard Shaw, pp. 59–61.

16 Churchill, *Liberalism and the Social Problem*, pp. 167–8, 361–2.

17 Hobhouse, *The Labour Movement*, 3rd edn, p. 125; Hobson, *The Crisis of Liberalism* (1909; reprinted, ed. P. F. Clarke, Brighton, 1974), p. 190; Tawney, *Equality*, p. 202. There are some suggestive comments on the asymmetry of Hobhouse's conception of progress in S. Collini, *Liberalism and Sociology* (Cambridge, 1979), pp. 145–6.

18 Hobson, *The Crisis of Liberalism*, p. 180; Durbin, *The Politics of Democratic Socialism*, pp. 215–16. Durbin was much influenced by Reginald Bassett whose book, *The Essentials of Parliamentary Democracy* (1935), was a reaction against the anti-parliamentary rhetoric of the Socialist League; see A. W. Wright, *G. D. H. Cole and Socialist Democracy* (Oxford, 1979), p. 171, on this debate.

19 Tawney, *Equality*, p. 201.

20 See the section of 'The Revolutionist's Handbook' headed 'The Political Need for the Superman', *Man and Superman*, Penguin edn (Harmondsworth, 1946 and reprints), p. 227. On the élitist challenge from social psychology see R. Soffer, *Ethics and Society in England* (1978), ch. 11.

21 Hobson, *The Crisis of Liberalism*, p. 189; 'The General Election: a Sociological Interpretation', *Sociological Review*, III (1910), pp. 114, 116–17, for the quotations in this and the next paragraph. There are some percipient reflections on this style of analysis in R. Hofstadter, *The Age of Reform* (1955; vintage edn, New York, 1960), p. 19.

22 E. P. Thompson, *The Poverty of Theory* (1978), pp. 29, 33, 360–1, 377, 264, 332, 364–5.

23 Cole was making a similar point when he spoke of 'two fundamental cleavages in

Socialist thought – the cleavage between revolutionaries and reformists, and the cleavage between centralisers and federalists'. See Wright, *G. D. H. Cole and Socialist Democracy*, pp. 137–8.

24 J. A. Hobson and H. D. Lloyd, *The Swiss Democracy* (1908), pp. 225, 251. I take moral populism to be Hobson's characteristic position and rational utilitarianism to be Durbin's; my point is that this particular argument is not open to Durbin's specific dissent from Hobson's tendency to identify 'democracy' in itself with social justice; see Durbin, *The Politics of Democratic Socialism*, pp. 235–6.

25 Tawney, *Equality*, p. 200; Foot, *Aneurin Bevan*, vol. II (1973), p. 631.

26 Thompson, *The Poverty of Theory*, pp. 29, 363.

27 *The Labour Movement*, 1st edn (1893), pp. 27–8, 48; these passages reprinted 3rd edn (1912), pp. 55–6, 84–5, with the addition of the new passage, p. 81.

28 P. Williams, *Hugh Gaitskell* (1979), p. 383; J. Morgan (ed.), *The Backbench Diaries of Richard Crossman* (1981), p. 459. Crossman saw the force of the historical analogy, writing at the time of Suez: 'Radicalism – the kind of Radicalism which made Byron fight for the Greeks and Lloyd George pro-Boer – is now relatively rare and predominantly middle-class. That is why Nye's instincts in this crisis have really been much more pro-Government than pro-Nasser.' (*Ibid.*, p. 517). He was therefore unmoved by Gaitskell's declaration: 'And what's so wonderful, Dick, is that we are morally in the right.' (*Ibid.*, p. 549). On the significance of the Boer War issue see Clarke, *Liberals and Social Democrats*, ch. 3.

29 Foot, *Aneurin Bevan*, II, pp. 383, 413.

30 See V. L. Allen, *Trade Union Leadership* (1957), p. 153.

31 Williams, *Hugh Gaitskell*, p. 343; Morgan (ed.), *The Backbench Diaries*, pp. 409–10; Williams, *Hugh Gaitskell*, pp. 593, 619.

32 Morgan (ed.), *The Backbench Diaries*, pp. 769–70. I have given a fuller account of the diaries as a source for developments in the Labour party in this period in 'Crossman and Social Democracy', *London Review of Books*, 16–29 April 1981, pp. 8–10.

2. Keir Hardie and the *Labour Leader*, 1893–1903

1 H. M. Pelling, *Origins of the Labour Party*, 2nd edn (1965), esp. pp. 193–8.

2 P. Hollis, *The Pauper Press* (1970).

3 A. J. Lee, *The Origins of the Popular Press in England 1855–1914* (1976), pp. 72ff. A valuable contribution to our knowledge of the press of the Independent Labour party (ILP). See also two articles by D. Hopkin, 'The Membership of the ILP 1904–10: a Spatial and Occupational Analysis', *International Review of Social History*, xx, 2 (1975), pp. 175–98 and 'Local Newspapers and the Independent Labour Party 1893–1906', *Bulletin of the Society for the Study of Labour History* no. 28 (1974), pp. 28–37.

4 G. D. H. Cole, *James Keir Hardie* (1941).

5 K. O. Morgan, *Keir Hardie: Radical and Socialist* (1975), pp. 138ff.

6 T. Carlyle, *Sartor Resartus* (1831), p. 201.

7 F. Reid, *Keir Hardie. The Making of a Socialist* (1978), p. 139.

8 See *Labour Leader*, 23 and 30 Aug., 25 Oct., 1 Nov. 1902.

9 Thus H. T. Samuel was 'Marxian'; Mrs Bream Pearce was 'Lily Bell' and David Lowe was 'Tricotrin'. D. Lowe, *From Pit to Parliament* (1923), p. 42.

10 *Glasgow Evening Times* and *Glasgow Evening News*, 14 Jan. 1896. There is a brief account of this episode in I. McLean, *Keir Hardie* (1975), p. 74.

11 T. Schults, *Crusader in Babylon* (Lincoln, Nebraska, 1960).

12 *Labour Leader*, 1 Feb. 1896.

13 *Ibid.*, 1 Feb. 1896.

14 *Ibid.*, 1 Feb. 1896.

15 *Ibid.*, 8 Feb. 1896.

16 *Ibid.*, 8 and 15 Feb. 1896.

17 *Ibid.*, 8 and 15 Feb. 1896.

18 *Ibid.*, 29 Feb. 1896.

19 *Ibid.*, 29 Feb. 1896.

20 *Ibid.*, 8 and 29 Feb. 1896.

21 *Ibid.*, 29 Feb. 1896.

22 *Ibid.*, 8 Feb. 1896.

23 *Ibid.*, 8 Feb. 1896.

24 *Ibid.*, 8 Feb. 1896.

25 H. C. Rowe, *The Boggarthole Contest* (Glasgow, 1900). See also *Manchester Guardian* and *Manchester Courier*, May–Aug. 1896.

26 S. D. Simon, *A Century of City Government: Manchester, 1838–1938* (1938), p. 310.

27 See letter in *Manchester Guardian*, 11 June 1896.

28 Confirmed by S. Davies, *North Country Bred* (1968).

29 *Manchester Guardian*, 11 June 1896.

30 *Ibid.*, 23 May 1896.

31 *Ibid.*, 25 June 1896.

32 *Ibid.*, 15 June 1896.

33 *Ibid.*, 15 June 1896.

34 *Ibid.*, 15 June 1896.

35 *Ibid.*, 23 July 1896.

36 *Ibid.*, 23 July 1896.

37 *Ibid.*, 23 July 1896 and see T. Woollerton, *The Labour Movement in Manchester and Salford* (Manchester, 1960).

38 *Manchester Guardian*, 6 Aug. 1896.

39 Simon, *Century of City Government*, p. 310. See *Labour Leader*, 16 Jan. 1897.

40 *Labour Leader*, 17 April 1897.

41 *Ibid.*, 19 Sept. 1897.

42 Independent Labour party, minutes of the National Administrative Council, 1893–1900 (British Library of Political and Economic Science).

43 *Labour Leader*, 18 March to 15 July 1899.

44 *Glasgow Evening Times*, 14 June 1899.

45 *Ibid.*, 30 June 1899.

46 *Ibid.*, 29 June 1899; and see leading article of 22 June 1899.

47 *Ibid.*, 22 June 1899.

48 *Ibid.*, 22 June 1899.

49 *Ibid.*, 5 July 1899.
50 *Glasgow Evening Times*, 19 June 1899.
51 E.g. *Labour Leader*, 29 Feb. 1897, 17 Dec. 1898, 11 Nov. 1899.
52 Lee, *The Orgins of the Popular Press in England 1855–1914*, pp. 73ff.
53 *Labour Leader*, 11 May 1899. For examples of illustrations see the issue of 1 Jan. 1898 for a drawing of Colonel Dyer of the Engineering Employers Federation, and of 10 July 1897 for a sketch of the Southampton ILP Club.
54 E.g. *ibid.*, 27 May 1899, for an interview with Winston Churchill.
55 *Ibid.*, 18 March 1898.
56 *Ibid.*, 24 July 1897.
57 *Ibid.*, 28 March 1896.
58 *Ibid.*, Nov. 1893.
59 *Ibid.*, 28 April, 5 and 12 May 1894.
60 *Ibid.*, 5 Feb. 1898.
61 Morgan, *Keir Hardie*, pp. 138, 141, gives 13,000, but see Glasier ms. diary, 25 Aug. 1905. (Diary in the possession of Mr Malcolm Glasier.)
62 Hardie to Lowe, 2 Jan. 1899, in Lowe, *From Pit to Parliament*, p. 164.
63 *Labour Leader*, 31 March 1894.
64 *Ibid.*, 5 Jan. 1895.
65 *Ibid.*, Dec. 1893.
66 *Ibid.*, 3 Oct. 1898.
67 *Ibid.*, Feb. 1893.
68 *Mr J. Keir Hardie v. The Scottish Labour Literature Society* (Glasgow, 1895), p. 1.
69 *Ibid.*, p. 1.
70 *Ibid.*, p. 7. For Pearce see Reid, *Keir Hardie*.
71 *Labour Leader*, 17 Aug. 1895.
72 Lowe, *From Pit to Parliament, p. 44.*
73 *Mr. Keir Hardie v. The Literature Society*, pp. 7ff.
74 *Labour Leader*, 15 Nov. 1895.
75 *Ibid.*, 17 Aug. 1895.
76 *Ibid.*, Nov. 1893.
77 For T. D. Benson's subsidies see Glasier ms. diary, 10 and 15 May 1904.
78 Reid, *Keir Hardie*, pp. 133ff.
79 *Labour Leader*, 10 Aug. 1894, 17 Aug. to 7 Dec. 1895.
80 *Ibid*, 11 April 1896.
81 *Ibid.*, 25 April 1896.
82 *Ibid.*, 7 Aug. 1897.
83 *Ibid.*, 6 March 1897.
84 *Ibid.*, 29 Aug., 11 Sept. 1896.
85 *Ibid.*, 21 March 1896. See 28 March, 9 May 1896, 6 Feb. 1897 and 12 Feb. 1898.
86 *Ibid.*, 9 Jan. 1897, 19 Feb. 1898.
87 *Ibid.*, 19 Sept. 1897.
88 Morgan, *Keir Hardie*, pp. 105ff.
89 E.g. *Labour Leader*, 29 Dec. 1896.
90 *Ibid.*, 4 Jan. 1896.

91 *Ibid.*, e.g. 11 June, 28 Nov. 1896, 13 Nov. 1896, 13 Nov. 1897. See R. Gregory, *The Miners in British Politics 1906–1914* (1968).
92 *Labour Leader*, 21 March 1896, 4 April 1896.
93 F. Bealey and H. M. Pelling, *Labour and Politics, 1900–1906* (1958).
94 *Labour Leader*, 20 Jan. 1900.
95 *Ibid.*, 20 Jan. 1900.
96 *Ibid.*, 10 Feb., 24 Sept. 1898.
97 *Ibid.*, 10 Feb., 24 Sept. 1898.
98 Reid, *Keir Hardie*, pp. 171ff.
99 *Labour Leader*, 17 Nov. 1897, 12 May 1898, 3 July 1898.
100 J. Keir Hardie and J. R. MacDonald, 'The ILP Programme', *Nineteenth Century*, XLV, 1 (1899), pp. 20ff.
101 *Ibid.*, and *Labour Leader*, 31 July 1897, 14 May, 8 Oct., 26 Nov. 1898.
102 *Labour Leader*, e.g. 21 Feb. 1903.
103 Independent Labour party, minutes of the National Administrative Council, 8 April 1898.
104 *Labour Leader*, 8 Sept. 1900
105 Glasier to Hardie, 26 Feb. 1902; Hardie to Glasier, 18 May 1903. Glasier correspondence, ILP Archive (Brit. Lib. of Pol. and Econ. Sci.).
106 Glasier to Hardie, 25 Jan. 1902. Glasier correspondence.
107 J. R. MacDonald to Glasier, 24 Jan. 1903. Glasier correspondence.
108 Hardie to Glasier, 18 May 1903. Glasier correspondence.
109 Hardie to Glasier, 12 Oct. 1903. Glasier correspondence. See Glasier ms. diary, 11 Nov. 1903.
110 Glasier ms. diary, 30, 31 Dec. 1903, 22 Jan. 1904.

3. Winston Churchill and the working class, 1900–14

1 L. Masterman, *C. F. G. Masterman: A Biography* (1939), p. 165.
2 R. Rhodes James, *Churchill: A Study in Failure 1900–1939* (Harmondsworth, 1973), p. 44.
3 R. Hyam, 'Winston Churchill Before 1914', *Historical Journal*, XII (1969), p. 168.
4 H. Pelling, *Winston Churchill* (1974), p. 644.
5 *Winston Churchill: Memoirs and Tributes Broadcast by the BBC* (1965), p. 47.
6 R. Rhodes James (ed.), *Winston S. Churchill: His Complete Speeches Vol III 1914–1922* (New York, 1974), p. 2685, speech of 3 March 1919.
7 R. Rhodes James (ed.), *Winston S. Churchill: His Complete Speeches Vol. I 1897–1908* (New York, 1974), p. 43, speech of 28 June 1899.
8 Lord Rosebery, *Lord Randolph Churchill* (1906), p. 136.
9 Randolph S. Churchill, *Winston S. Churchill Vol I: Youth 1874–1900* (1966), p. 318.
10 Rhodes James (ed.), *Speeches Vol. I*, p. 35, speech of 26 June 1899.
11 F. Woods (ed.), *Young Winston's Wars* (1972), p. 220.
12 Randolph S. Churchill, *Winston S. Churchill Vol II: Young Statesman 1901–1914* (1967), pp. 31–2.
13 Randolph S. Churchill, *Winston S. Churchill: Companion Vol II Part 1 1901–7* (1969), pp. 105–11.

14 J. B. Atkins (ed.), *National Physical Training: An open Debate* (1904), pp. 70–1.
15 Randolph S. Churchill, *Companion Vol II Part 1*, p. 72.
16 Winston S. Churchill, *Thoughts and Adventures* (1932), p. 54.
17 Winston S. Churchill, *Lord Randolph Churchill* (1951 edn), p. 211.
18 Winston S. Churchill, *Savrola* (1957 edn), Ch. x; Winston S. Churchill, *Lord Randolph Churchill*, p. 215.
19 Winston S. Churchill, *Lord Randolph Churchill*, p. 742.
20 Rhodes James (ed.), *Speeches Vol I*, pp. 397–8, speech of 28 Dec. 1904.
21 Quoted in G. R. Searle, *The Quest for National Efficiency* (Oxford, 1971), p. 248.
22 Rhodes James (ed.), *Speeches Vol I*, p. 517, speech of 19 Dec. 1905.
23 *Ibid.*, p. 669, speech of 6 Aug. 1906; Randolph S. Churchill, *Companion Vol II Part I*, p. 574.
24 Quoted in J. Grigg, *Lloyd George: The People's Champion 1902–1911* (1978), p. 156.
25 Rhodes James (ed.), *Speeches Vol I*, p. 676.
26 Pelling, *Churchill*, pp. 104–5.
27 Rhodes James (ed.), *Speeches Vol I*, p. 675, speech of 11 Oct. 1906.
28 *Ibid.*, p. 812, speech of 25 June 1907.
29 R. Rhodes James (ed.), *Winston S. Churchill: His Complete Speeches Vol II 1908–1913* (New York, 1974), p. 1321, speech of 4 Sept. 1909.
30 *Ibid.*, p. 1334, speech of 16 Oct. 1909.
31 Randolph S. Churchill, *Winston S. Churchill: Companion Vol II Part 2 1907–11* (1969), p. 934.
32 Rhodes James (ed.), *Complete Speeches Vol II*, p. 1072, speech of 20 July 1908.
33 Winston S. Churchill, *My Early Life* (1944 edn), p. 141.
34 Rhodes James (ed.), *Complete Speeches Vol I*, pp. 383–4, speech of 11 Nov. 1906; pp. 673–4, speech of 11 Oct. 1906; p. 1030, speech of 4 May 1908.
35 R. Page Arnot, *The Miners: A History of the Miners Federation of Great Britain 1889–1910* (1949), pp. 139–41, 197; R. Page Arnot, *South Wales Miners* (1967), pp. 135–6.
36 On Churchill's patronage of trade unionists see E. Halévy, *The Rule of Democracy 1905–1914* (1961 edn), p. 446.
37 P. F. Clarke, *Lancashire and the New Liberalism* (Cambridge, 1971); P. F. Clarke, *Liberals and Social Democrats* (Cambridge, 1978); R. Davidson, 'Sir Hubert Llewellyn Smith and Labour Policy 1886–1916' (Univ. of Cambridge PhD thesis, 1971) and the same author's 'Llewellyn Smith, the Labour Department and Government Growth 1886–1909', in G. Sutherland (ed.), *Studies in the Growth of Nineteenth Century Government* (1972), pp. 227–62; M. Freeden, *The New Liberalism* (Oxford, 1978); J. Harris, *Unemployment and Politics* (Oxford, 1972) and her *William Beveridge* (Oxford, 1977); B. B. Gilbert, *The Evolution of National Insurance in Great Britain* (1966).
38 Freeden, *The New Liberalism*, pp. 160–2; Clarke, *Liberals and Social Democrats*, pp. 116–17.
39 Compare Churchill's speech of 11 Oct. 1906, referred to previously, with a speech by Lloyd George on the same day: David Lloyd George, *Better Times* (1910), pp. 30–6.

40 Webb, *Our Partnership* (1948), p. 269, diary entry for 8 July 1903; p. 404, diary entry for 11 March 1908.
41 *The Nation*, 7 March 1908, pp. 812–13; Randolph S. Churchill, *Winston S. Churchill Vol II*, pp. 240–1.
42 Davidson, 'Sir Hubert Llewellyn Smith and Labour Policy', pp. 251–2.
43 Gilbert, *The Evolution of National Insurance*, pp. 272–3; Harris, *Unemployment and Politics*, p. 304.
44 Davidson, 'Sir Hubert Llewellyn Smith and Labour Policy', p. 262.
45 Hyam, 'Winston Churchill Before 1914', p. 168.
46 Rhodes James (ed.), *Complete Speeches Vol I*, p. 1034, speech of 4 May 1908.
47 *Ibid.*, p. 954, speech of 14 April 1908.
48 *Ibid.*, p. 30, speech of 31 Oct. 1898.
49 *Ibid.*, pp. 862–3, speech of 18 Jan. 1908.
50 L. Masterman, *C. F. G. Masterman* (1939), pp. 136–7; Grigg, *Lloyd George*, p. 178.
51 Randolph S. Churchill, *Companion Vol II Part 2*, pp. 904–5, 909.
52 Rhodes James (ed.), *Collected Speeches Vol II*, pp. 1284, 1288, two speeches of 17 July 1909.
53 C. Hazlehurst, 'Introduction', in Winston S. Churchill, *The People's Rights* (1970), p. 13.
54 My account of Tonypandy is based mainly on D. Smith, 'Tonypandy 1910: Definitions of Community', *Past and Present*, no. 87 (May 1980), pp. 158–84; and *Colliery Strike Disturbances in South Wales*, Parliamentary Papers 1911, LXIV, Cd 5568.
55 Page Arnot, *South Wales Miners*, pp. 187–8.
56 *Colliery Strike Disturbances*, p. 5.
57 *House of Commons Debates (Hansard)*, 5th ser., xx, 24 Nov. 1910, col. 409.
58 *Colliery Strike Disturbances*, p. 48.
59 Smith, 'Tonypandy', p. 160.
60 *Hansard*, 5th ser., xx, 20 Nov. 1910; xxi, 7 Feb. 1911; xxii, 6 March 1911.
61 Pelling, *Churchill*, p. 137.
62 Randolph S. Churchill, *Companion Vol II Part 2*, pp. 1095, 1098, 1273; Rhodes James (ed.), *Collected Speeches Vol II*, pp. 1860, 1865.
63 C. J. Wrigley, *David Lloyd George and the British Labour Movement* (Brighton, 1976), p. 62; Randolph S. Churchill, *Companion Vol II Part 2*, p. 1264.
64 Randolph S. Churchill, *Companion Vol II Part 2*, p. 1113.
65 B. Tillett, *Memories and Reflections* (1931), pp. 243–4.
66 Randolph S. Churchill, *Companion Vol II Part 2*, p. 1114.
67 *Times*, 23 Aug. 1911, p. 8.
68 Randolph S. Churchill, *Winston S. Churchill Vol II*, pp. 383–4.
69 *Times*, 21 Aug. 1911, p. 6.
70 Wrigley, *Lloyd George*, pp. 62–5.
71 *Times*, 16 Aug. 1911, p. 7.
72 Rhodes James (ed.), *Collected Speeches Vol II*, pp. 1878–9, speech of 3 Oct. 1911.
73 Randolph S. Churchill, *Companion Vol. II Part 2*, pp. 1271–2; Sir A. Fitzroy, *Memoirs*, 2 vols. (n.d.), ii, p. 462.

74 For criticisms by MacDonald and Hardie, *Hansard*, 5th ser., xxix, 22 Aug. 1911, cols. 2296–8, 2335–7.
75 Masterman, *C. F. G. Masterman*, p. 208.
76 Randolph S. Churchill, *Companion Vol II Part 2*, pp. 1247–8.
77 Rhodes James (ed.), *Collected Speeches Vol II*, p. 1917, speech of 1 March 1912.
78 *Ibid.*, p. 1880, speech of 3 Oct. 1911.
79 *Ibid.*, p. 1825, speech of 30 May 1911.
80 Sir Peter Gretton, *Former Naval Person: Winston Churchill and the Royal Navy* (1968), pp. 97–8.

4. Expectations born to death: local Labour party expansion in the 1920s

1 MacDonald to Ponsonby, 1 Nov. 1921, Ponsonby Papers, fo. 668 (Bodleian Library, Oxford).
2 Ray Stannard Baker, *American Chronicle* (New York, 1945), p. 345; Lady Algernon Gordon Lennox, *Diary of Lord Bertie of Thame, 1914–1918* (1924), pp. 264–5, reporting J. H. Thomas.
3 The alternative vote was a single transferable vote system which was deleted from the Representation of the People Bill of 1918.
4 C. P. Scott Diary, 3–5 Feb. 1918. BM Add. MS 50904 (British Library, London).
5 *Forward*, 30 March 1918; Baker, *American Chronicle*, p. 332.
6 *Labour Party Conference Report*, June 1918, pp. 31–44; *Times*, 29 June 1918.
7 R. H. Tawney's phrase in 'The Choice Before the Labour Party', reprinted in his collection *The Attack* (1953), p. 57; cf. Henderson's comment, *Labour Party Conference Report*, January 1918, pp. 98–9.
8 C. Howard, 'Henderson, MacDonald and Leadership in the Labour Party, 1914–1922' (Univ. of Cambridge PhD thesis, 1978), pp. 202–22.
9 *Birmingham Post*, 3 March 1919; J. H. Thomas, *When Labour Rules* (1920); L. Woolf, *Downhill All the Way* (1970), pp. 37–8.
10 J. Paton, *Left Turn!* (1936), pp. 111–12.
11 Spen Valley (polling day, December 1919; result declared, January 1920) set the seal on a number of encouraging Labour by-election performances at Swansea East, Bothwell, Widnes, St Albans and Bromley; see M. Cowling, *The Impact of Labour* (Cambridge, 1971), pp. 1–2.
12 H. Drinkwater in *Labour Organizer*, Dec. 1921; cf. H. Morrison in *London Labour Chronicle*, July 1919.
13 G. R. Shepherd in *Labour Organizer*, June 1921.
14 *London Labour Chronicle*, Nov. 1919, March 1920, April 1922.
15 The whole of this section is argued in greater depth in my 1978 Cambridge PhD thesis, 'Henderson, MacDonald and Leadership in the Labour Party', pp. 182–252.
16 Howard, 'Henderson, MacDonald and Leadership in the Labour Party', pp. 182–222.
17 L. J. MacFarlane, 'Hands of Russia. British Labour and the Russo–Polish War, 1920', *Past and Present*, no. 38 (1967), pp. 126–52 gives a comprehensive account of the Councils though MacFarlane was unable to use the Councils of Action file at the Labour party Library; cf. S. R. Graubard, *British Labour and the Russian*

Revolution, 1917–1924 (1956), pp. 83–114; S. White, 'Soviets in Britain', *International Review of Social History*, XIX, 2 (1974), pp. 165–93. For the unemployed movements, W. Hannington, *Unemployed Struggles* (1936).

18 Hannington, *Unemployed Struggles*, pp. 22–5; *Labour Leader*, 15 Dec. 1921; *Justice*, 15 Dec. 1921; *Cotton Factory Times*, 16 Dec. 1921. Although the *Communist* claimed that British Communist party members were operating within local Councils of Action at Bethnal Green, Paisley, Ashton-under-Lyne and Coatbridge there were few signs of any significant revolutionary activity outside South Wales and Coventry. Even those Scotland Yard agents looking for the slightest signs of 'sovietization' failed to find any: L. J. MacFarlane, *The British Communist Party* (1966), p. 73; Cabinet Papers, 1830, 1848, 1862, 2027, Sept.–Oct. 1920, CAB 24/111, 24/112, 24/118 (Public Record Office, London) (hereafter PRO CAB); M. Phillips to Middleton, n.d., Labour party Files CA/GEN/570 (Labour party Library, London).

19 In 1916 Easter week made little impression on British Labour; in 1918 the extension of conscription to Ireland was opposed with stunning inadequacy while the party conference of June 1918 would do no more than make a vague commitment to Home Rule all round: J. D. Clarkson, *Labour and Nationalism in Ireland* (New York, 1925), pp. 408–10.

20 A Labour deputation which included William Adamson, the Parliamentary Labour party (PLP) Chairman, and Arthur Henderson did travel to assess the British régime in Ireland in February 1920, but no action followed: *Labour Party Conference Report*, 1920, pp. 6–7.

21 The Labour National Executive Council (NEC) had refused to listen to suggestions from Irish representatives in Stockport that it should pledge a future Labour government to recognition of the Irish Republic and withdrawal of British forces. The Irish promptly ran William O'Brien of the Irish TUC and he secured enough votes to give the Coalition an easy victory: Labour party NEC Minutes, 10 March, 20 April 1920 (Labour party Library, London); *Labour Party Conference Report*, 1920, pp. 6–7.

22 Cabinet Paper, 319, 10 Dec. 1919, PRO CAB 24/95; Clarkson, *Labour and Nationalism in Ireland*, pp. 413–14.

23 Cabinet Papers 429, 1129, 9 Jan., 22 April 1920, PRO CAB 24/96, 24/104.

24 Cabinet Paper 1281, 13 May 1920, PRO CAB 24/105; North-East District Council of Action Circulars, Nov. 1920, Jan. 1921 and J. S. Middleton to Grainger, 15 Dec. 1920, Labour party Files, CA/GEN/1113, 1114, 727.

25 T. Johnston, quoted in Clarkson, *Labour and Nationalism in Ireland*, p. 414.

26 Rioting in Belfast in August 1920 was followed by the Balbriggan reprisals and the first Irish 'bloody Sunday'. After November there were concerted demands for Council of Action intervention in Ireland and, equally importantly, Asquith and Grey declared themselves in favour of Dominion Home Rule.

27 The Commission spent two weeks in Ireland; it was given an extensive tour of the south by Thomas Johnston and at one stage Henderson interviewed Arthur Griffith. The resultant report was written by Arthur Greenwood. *Report of the Labour Commission of Inquiry into the Present Situation in Ireland* (1920), pp. 1–7; F. Brockway, *Socialism Over Sixty Years* (1946), p. 172. Brockway had access to the now-destroyed diary of F. W. Jowett when writing his account.

28 C. L. Mowat, 'The Irish Question in British Politics 1916–22', in T. Desmond Williams (ed.), *The Irish Struggle 1916–22* (1966), p. 147; D. G. Boyce, *Englishmen and Irish Troubles* (1972), pp. 62–3; M. Bondfield, *A Life's Work* (1949), p. 188.

29 I. S. MacLean, 'The Labour Movement in Clydeside Politics' (Univ. of Oxford DPhil thesis, 1971), pp. 298–9. In an early post-war test of Irish Catholic opinion, the Glasgow Education Authority elections of 1919, many Catholic second preferences were given to Labour while James Maxton was the only Labour candidate without some Catholic assistance: *Forward*, 19 April 1919.

30 Cabinet Paper 343, 23 Dec. 1919, PRO CAB 24/95.

31 C. R. Attlee, *As It Happened* (1954), p. 45; Liverpool Waterloo Labour party to Middleton (n.d. ? Nov. 1920), Labour party Files CA/GEN/710.

32 *South Wales News*, 7 Nov. 1922; *Forward*, 7 Feb. 1920; F. S. L. Lyons, *John Dillon* (1968), pp. 460, 471–5. O'Connor was not opposed by Labour in Liverpool Scotland and after his death a mutually-acceptable successor was found in an Irish member of the Labour party.

33 H. J. Hanham, *Scottish Nationalism* (1969), pp. 140–1; J. Hunter, 'The Gaelic Connection: the Highlands, Ireland and Nationalism 1873–1922', *Scottish Historical Review*, LIV (1975), pp. 200–4.

34 F. A. Iremonger, *William Temple* (1948), pp. 220–40; W. Temple, 'The Life and Liberty Movement', *Contemporary Review*, CXIII (1918), pp. 161–8; J. M. Winter, *Socialism and the Challenge of War* (1974), pp. 171–5; S. Mews, 'The Churches', in M. Morris (ed.), *The General Strike* (Harmondsworth, 1976), pp. 319–21.

35 *The Times*, 21 March 1919.

36 P. R. Shorter, 'Political Change in the East Midlands' (Univ. of Cambridge PhD thesis, 1975), p. 36.

37 Bradford Trades and Labour Council, *Annual Report*, 1921; cf. H. Pelling, *The Origins of the Labour Party* (1954), pp. 134–5.

38 Gloucester Trades Council and Labour party, Minute Book (Gloucester County Record Office) [hereafter CRO], 10 Oct., 14 Nov. 1927 and Executive Minutes, 7 Sept. 1927.

39 Cardiff Trades and Labour Council, *Year Book*, 1922; *Yorkshire Post*, 13 Nov. 1922.

40 Cabinet Papers 319, 462, 18 Dec. 1919, 15 Jan. 1920, PRO CAB 24/95, 24/96. Noel still retains the notoriety gained by his flying of the red flag and Irish tricolour above Thaxted church.

41 *Memorial Presented to James Ramsay MacDonald, 13 March 1923*, copies in Baldwin Papers, vol. 42 (University Library, Cambridge) and in Labour party NEC Minutes, March 1923; *Daily Express*, 13 March 1923.

42 C. G. Lang, 'Labour's Challenge to the Churches', *Labour Magazine*, April 1923.

43 *Labour Organizer*, Oct. 1923; quotation from R. Blythe, *Akenfield* (Harmondsworth, 1972), p. 109; *Ludlow Advertiser and Craven Arms Gazette*, 14 April 1923, reporting P. F. Pollard (Workers' Union); J. J. Dodd, *If Labour Wins* (1922), pp. 22, 56–7.

44 D. Marquand, *Ramsay MacDonald* (1977), p. 307; G. K. A. Bell, *Randall Davidson: Archbishop of Canterbury* (1952), pp. 1251–3. D. Morse-Boycott, *They Shine Like Stars* (1947), pp. 285–7; *Church Times*, 1 Aug., 10 Oct. 1924.

45 *Church Times*, 17 and 24 Oct. 1924.

46 R. Groves, *Sharpen the Sickle* (1949), pp. 164–5; F. E. Green, *A History of the English Agricultural Labourers 1870–1920* (1920), pp. 298–9; TUC, *Annual Report*, 1918, p. 154.

47 *Labour Magazine*, Jan. 1924. In Norfolk and East Anglia the farm vote was larger than in any other region: M. Kinnear, *The British Voter* (1967), pp. 119–21.

48 Groves, *Sharpen the Sickle*, pp. 169–225; R. Hyman, *The Workers' Union* (Oxford, 1971), pp. 147–9.

49 *Yorkshire Post*, 27 Nov. 1923; National Union of Railwaymen, *Proceedings and Reports*, 1917 (accounts to Dec. 1917); A. Fox, *History of the National Union of Boot and Shoe Operatives* (Oxford, 1958), pp. 376–7; Groves, *Sharpen the Sickle*, p. 127.

50 R. McKibbin, *The Evolution of the Labour Party 1910–1924* (Oxford, 1974), pp. 154–5.

51 Cambridgeshire Labour party, Minute Book, 10, 23 Nov., 1, 28 Dec. 1918, 14, 28 Oct. 1922 (Cambs. Record Office); PP, XVIII, 1924 (2).

52 Groves, *Sharpen the Sickle*, p. 129; G. Hodgkinson, *Sent to Coventry* (1970), p. 101.

53 Cambridge Trades and Labour Council, Minute Books (Cambs. Record Office), 1919–45, *passim*; G. Hodgkinson, *Sent to Coventry*, p. 106.

54 Peterborough Labour party, Minute Book (Peterborough Library), 7 Dec. 1918, 18 March 1923. Donaldson's wife, Louise, was vice-chairman of the Peterborough party in 1923.

55 Cambridgeshire Labour party, Minute Book, 17 Nov. 1923, notes by Hon. Mrs H. B. Pease included with Minute Book.

56 *Yorkshire Post*, 26 Nov. 1923; *Lincolnshire Chronicle*, 24 Nov. 1922. For Buxton: MacDonald to Brown, 10 Feb. 1926, MacDonald Papers, 7/27 (PRO, London). Royce was a former Tory candidate who had made a fortune in South Africa: C. W. Ould, *W. S. Royce* (1925). Hugh Dalton found that publicans were of great use to him in the Maidstone hop-growing areas: Dalton Diary, 22 Aug. 1922 (British Library of Political and Economic Science).

57 Cambridgeshire Labour party, Minute Book, 1927–31, *passim*; correspondence concerning agent's salary and selection of candidate, March–June 1930, Cambs. Labour party records, 416/21; Peterborough Labour party, Minute Book, 1923–26, *passim*; Gloucester Trades and Labour Council, Minute Book, 1920–31, *passim*.

58 Labour party NEC Minutes, 22 Nov. 1926; S. Gee, 'The Problem of the Rural Constituencies', *Labour Organizer*, Oct. 1923; Peterborough Labour party, Minute Book, 8 Feb. 1925. For Suffolk, Suffolk Federation of Trades Councils and Labour Representation Committees, Minute Book (Suffolk CRO), 12 March 1922.

59 Labour party NEC Minutes, 22 Nov. 1926.

60 Howard, 'Henderson, MacDonald and Leadership in the Labour Party', pp. 263–5.

61 Lord Ernle in *The Times*, 19 Dec. 1921: as R. E. Prothero he had been President of the Board of Agriculture, 1916–19.

62 C. P. Hughes Papers (Eastern Counties Liberal Federation, Cambridge), *Report of*

Annual Meeting, 1923, containing speech by S. Cope-Morgan; S. L. Bensusan, 'Labour and Agriculture', *Fortnightly Review*, CXII (1922), p. 937.

63 G. T. Garratt, *Agriculture and the Labour Party* (1929), pp. 5–7; cf. F.M.L. Thompson, *English Landed Society in the Nineteenth Century* (1963), pp. 327–45.

64 *House of Commons Debates (Hansard)*, 5th ser., CLIX, 5 Dec. 1922, cols. 1635, 1657–8.

65 H. B. Pointing, 'The Agricultural Prospect', *Labour Magazine*, March 1922.

66 Labour party NEC Minutes, Feb. 1925 to 22 Nov. 1926, passim.

67 Independent Labour party, *A Socialist Policy for Agriculture* (1924). This document was heavily influenced by J. A. Hobson and E. F. Wise.

68 *Labour Organizer*, Jan. 1925; G. T. Garratt, *The Farmer and the Labour Party* (1927), pp. 3–4.

69 *Liberal Magazine*, Oct. 1921.

70 M. Pallister, *The Orange-Box* (1925), p. 55.

71 MacDonald was unwilling to give up Aberavon to fight Woolwich in 1921 and he took care to ensure that he would be able to return to South Wales at a general election: MacDonald Diary, 28–31 Jan., 5, 6 Feb. 1921, MacDonald Papers, 8/1.

72 I. H. Thomas to MacDonald, 31 Aug. 1919, MacDonald Papers, 7/20; taped interview with Glyn Williams (Bridgend), 22 April 1976; taped interview with T. Nicholas (Neath), 16 May 1974 (South Wales Miners' Library).

73 *South Wales News*, 7, 10, 11 Nov. 1922, 27 Oct. 1924; see *Western Mail*, 3, 14 Nov. 1922.

74 *South Wales News*, 11 Nov. 1922; J. Griffiths, *Pages From Memory* (1969), pp. 51–2.

75 Taped interview with Glyn Williams, 22 April 1976; taped interview with Glyn Williams, 21 May 1974 (South Wales Miners' Library).

76 Arthur Pearson (Pontypridd) to the author, 17 June 1976.

77 Aberavon Constituency Labour party, Organizer's Report, Jan. 1926, MacDonald Papers, 7/27.

78 J. MacNair, *James Maxton: Beloved Rebel* (1955), p. 97.

79 For the scarcity of active party workers in Doncaster, K. Teanby, 'Leftism in the Doncaster Labour Party 1921–26', *Bulletin of the Society for the Study of Labour History*, no. 39 (1979), p. 11. MacDonald's difficulties in Aberavon can clearly be seen from his papers, 7/28 but Marquand, *Ramsay MacDonald*, pp. 397–8, 481–3 provides a good summary.

80 J. Rees to R. Rosenberg, 15 Aug. 1927, MacDonald Papers, 7/28; Marquand, *Ramsay MacDonald*, pp. 481–3; Sheila Lochhead to the author, 18 Aug. 1975; *Western Mail*, 20 April 1927.

81 B. Hindess, *The Decline of Working-class Politics* (1971).

82 *Labour Organizer*, Nov. 1922.

83 *Labour Organizer*, Sept. 1922. This idea seems to have been consciously modelled on the activities of the German SDP, for which see E. Wertheimer, *Portrait of the Labour Party* (1929), p. 210

84 Labour party NEC Minutes, 12 June 1919; *Labour Organizer*, Jan., April 1921. Will Henderson, who was Arthur's son, was a publicity officer at party headquarters, Eccleston Square.

85 *Llanelly Labour News*, 14 Oct. 1924; Pontypridd Trades and Labour Council, Minute Book (Pontypridd Library), 15 Jan. 1919 to 10 Nov. 1924, *passim*.
86 *Labour Organizer*, June, July 1921.
87 Labour party NEC Minutes, 15 Jan. 1925.
88 *London Labour Chronicle*, May 1921; *Llanelly Labour News*, 3 April 1926.
89 *Labour Organizer*, Jan. 1924.
90 Labour party NEC Minutes, 15 Jan. 1925; *Labour Organizer*, March 1925.
91 Howard, 'Henderson, MacDonald and Leadership in the Labour Party', pp. 330–4 contains extensive though not exhaustive checklists of the Labour party press (that is, publications by organized groups affiliated to the Labour party) in circulation in 1921 and 1927–28. Revolutionary journals, pit or factory papers and trade union journals were not included in these lists.
92 *Labour Organizer*, July-Aug. 1921, April 1922, 1927–28, *passim*.
93 *Labour Organizer*, Oct. 1921.
94 Labour NEC Minutes, 26 Jan. 1926; *Labour Organizer*, April 1924, Aug. 1925.
95 Hertfordshire Labour Federation, Minute Book (Herts. CRO), 1932–34, *passim*.
96 G. R. Shepherd, 'A Task for Today', *Labour Organizer*, Feb. 1928. Shepherd became National Agent in 1928.
97 *Labour Organizer*, Sept. 1922; A. H. Birch, *Small-Town Politics* (Oxford, 1959), p. 63.
98 J. Jones, *Unfinished Journey* (1937), pp. 212–16.
99 Wertheimer, *Portrait of the Labour Party*, pp. 209–10; J. P. Nettl, 'The German Social Democratic Party 1890–1914 as a Political Model', *Past and Present*, no. 30 (1965), pp. 65–95.
100 *Labour Organizer*, June 1923, Oct.–Nov. 1925, Feb., March 1925.
101 Beatrice Webb, Ms Diary, 19 May 1930, Passfield Papers (British Library of Political and Economic Science).
102 See Birch, *Small-Town Politics*, p. 71; B. Hindess, *The Decline of Working-Class Politics*, pp. 17–29; J. Rowett, 'Sheffield Under Labour Control', *Bulletin of the Society for the Study of Labour History*, no. 39 (1979), p. 13.
103 Shorter, *Political Change*, p. 173; K. W. D. Rolf, 'Tories, Tariffs and Elections: the West Midlands in English Politics, 1918–35' (Univ. of Cambridge PhD thesis, 1974), pp. 116–17; Hindess, *The Decline of Working Class Politics*, p. 12.
104 Shorter, *Political Change*, p. 138n.; see F. Pethick-Lawrence, *Fate Has Been Kind* (1943), p. 128; Hodgkinson, *Sent to Coventry*, p. 80.
105 Margaret Bondfield could not have been alone in diverting the focus of her energies from the ILP to her union: Bondfield, *A Life's Work*, pp. 246–7. The influence of the war, the Russian revolution (and graduates of the Central Labour College) should also be borne in mind.
106 J. Brown to MacDonald, 5 and 17 Aug. 1927 and J. Rees to Rosenberg, 15 Aug. 1927, MacDonald Papers, 7/28; my taped interview with Glyn Williams, 22 April 1976.
107 For the importance of having free time during the working day, K. Richardson, *Twentieth Century Coventry* (1972), p. 201. For Griffiths, see his *Pages From Memory*, pp. 44, 49–52 and Llanelli Constituency party, Minute Book (Dyfed CRO), 1921–26, *passim*; for Mansfield, Peterborough Labour party, Minute

Book, 1918–29, *passim* and *Peterborough Advertiser*, 7 Dec. 1918; for Hodgkinson, his *Sent to Coventry, passim* and Richardson, *op. cit.*, pp. 201–5; for Taylor, Lord Taylor of Mansfield to the author, 4 April 1981.

108 Richardson, *Twentieth Century Coventry*, p. 201; Taylor of Mansfield to the author, 4 April 1981.

109 For Barnsley, Trevor Lindley, 'The Barnsley Labour Party 1918 to 1945', *Bulletin of the Society for the Study of Labour History*, no. 39 (1979), pp. 10–11; for Llanelli, Griffiths, *Pages From Memory*, pp. 44–52, *passim*; for Doncaster, Teanby, 'Leftism in the Doncaster Labour Party, 1921–26', p. 11; for Cambridge, Cambridge Labour Party, Minute Book, 1918–45, *passim*; for Cambridgeshire, Cambridgeshire Labour party, Minute Book, 1918–39, *passim*; for Wolverhampton, G. W. Jones, *Borough Politics* (1969), p. 170; for the Rhondda I have relied on oral tradition substantiated by Hywel Francis & David Smith, *The Fed: a History of the South Wales Miners in the Twentieth Century* (1980), p. 16.

110 Hodgkinson, *Sent to Coventry*, p. 106.

111 *Labour Party Bulletin*, I (1921), p. 19; F. Brockway, *Bermondsey Story* (1949), pp. 86–92; see H. Morrison, *Labour in Power and Labour Not in Power* (1922); Rowett, 'Sheffield Under Labour Control', p. 13.

112 B. Donoughue and G. W. Jones, *Herbert Morrison* (1973), pp. 47–8.

113 Pontypridd Trades and Labour Council, Minute Book (Pontypridd Central Library), 15 May 1922.

114 Pontypridd Trades and Labour Council, Minute Book, 15 Oct. 1923 and 25 Sept. 1922; Gloucester Trades Council and Labour party, Minute Book, 10 Sept. 1928; Jones, *Borough Politics*, pp. 166–7.

115 *Forward*, 22 Nov. 1919.

116 Beatrice Webb's description, reported in Dalton Diary, 20 July 1928.

117 J. McGovern, *Neither Fear Nor Favour* (1960), p. 64; T. Bell, *Pioneering Days* (1941), p. 34; Paton, *Left Turn!*, pp. 146–50.

118 *Llais Llafur* (Ystalyfera), 25 Nov. 1922.

119 M. Foot, *Aneurin Bevan 1897–1945*, 2 vols. (1962), i, pp. 84–5.

120 Foot, *Bevan*, ch. 3, *passim*.

121 See R. Skidelsky, *Oswald Mosley* (1975), pp. 151–4.

122 Gloucester Trades Council and Labour party, Minute Book 1922–31, *passim* and Executive Minutes, 16 Nov. 1928.

123 Suffolk Federation of Trades Councils and Labour Representation Committees, Minute Book (Suffolk CRO), 12 Dec. 1920, 31 Dec. 1921 and 31 Dec. 1922.

5. Post-war reconstruction in Wales, 1918 and 1945

1 H. Pelling, 'Taylor's England', *Past and Present*, no. 33 (1966), pp. 149–58, especially p. 150.

2 Most notably 'Wales and the Boer War', *Welsh History Review*, IV, 4 (1969).

3 H. Pelling, *Social Geography of British Elections, 1885–1910* (1967), chap. 21–4.

4 H. Pelling, *Popular Politics and Society in Late Victorian Britain* (1968), pp. 111–13.

5 K. O. Morgan, 'Peace Movements in Wales, 1899–1945', *Welsh History Review*, X, 3 (1981), pp. 398–430.

6 A. Bevan, *Why Not Trust the Tories?* (1944), pp. 79ff.

7 See particularly, J. Morris in *Y Beirniad*, Oct. 1914, pp. 217–24 and Oct. 1915, pp. 191–205; W. M. Edwards, *Cymru*, Feb. 1915 and editorial notes in that journal, from Nov. 1914 onwards.

8 A. Horner, *Incorrigible Rebel* (1960), pp. 182–3.

9 K. O. Morgan, *Consensus and Disunity* (Oxford, 1979), pp. 39–41.

10 In the 1922 general election, R. Hopkin Morris (Independent Liberal) defeated Ernest Evans (National Liberal), formerly Lloyd George's private secretary, in Cardiganshire; E. W. Evans to J. Herbert Lewis, 13 Jan. 1920, Herbert Lewis papers (National Library of Wales).

11 P. Addison, *The Road to 1945* (1975), pp. 270–8.

12 *Labour Voice*, 7 Dec. 1918. In this speech at Treboeth, Williams urged that Germany should pay the maximum in war indemnities. V. Hartshorn, *ibid.*, 28 Dec. 1918, expresses his strong support for Lloyd George's coalition.

13 R. Merfyn Jones, *The North Wales Quarrymen, 1874–1922* (Cardiff, 1981), pp. 320–1.

14 Notable among them were the poet Thomas Parry-Williams, whose academic preferment at Aberystwyth in 1920 had been endangered because of his wartime pacifism, and the literary critic, G. J. Williams. Gruffydd himself was staunchly anti-militarist: see his *Hen Atgofion* (Aberystwyth, 1936).

15 W. W. Craik, *The Central Labour College* (1964), pp. 112–25.

16 Morgan, *Consensus and Disunity*, ch. 4.

17 R. Earwicker, 'Miners' Medical Services before the First World War: the South Wales Coalfield', *Llafur*, iii, 2 (1981), pp. 39–52.

18 Bevan, *Why not Trust the Tories?*, pp. 24–6.

19 Ministry of Health, *Report of the Committee of Inquiry into the Anti-Tuberculosis Services in Wales and Monmouthshire* (1939).

20 See E. Jones, 'A Study of the Influence of Central Institutions on the Development of Secondary Education in Wales, 1944–49' (University of Wales: University College of Swansea PhD thesis, 1979).

21 D. Smith and H. Francis, *The Fed* (1980), pp. 429–30.

22 W. G. V. Balchin (ed.), *Swansea and its Region* (Swansea, 1971), p. 188. These developments were largely in the Penlan area.

23 R. Lowe, 'The Failure of Consensus in Britain: the National Industrial Conference, 1919–1921', *Historical Journal*, xxi, 3 (1978), pp. 649–76.

24 *The Times*, 1 Sept. 1920; *South Wales Daily News*, 1 Sept. 1920, 4 Nov. 1920. South Wales was the only major district to vote against a return to work in November 1920.

25 *House of Commons Debates (Hansard)*, 5th ser., cxix, 18 Aug. 1919, col. 2096.

26 See *South Wales Daily News*, 31 Dec. 1921 for V. Hartshorn's article 'The Coming Storm in the Coal Trade'. Also see P. Stead, 'Vernon Hartshorn: Miners' Agent and Cabinet Minister', in S. Williams (ed.), *Glamorgan Historian*, vi (1969), pp. 83–94.

27 M. G. Woodhouse, 'Rank and File Movements among the Miners of South Wales, 1910–1926' (Univ. of Oxford D.Phil. thesis, 1970).

28 D. Smith, 'The Struggle against Company Unionism in the South Wales Coalfield, 1926–1939', *Welsh History Review*, vi, 3 (1973), pp. 354–78. For an excellent study

of one community, see R. L. Williams, 'Aberdare in 1926' (University of Wales, University College of Swansea MA thesis, 1981).

29 Parliamentary Deputation on Unemployment in Wales, 1946, PREM 8/272 (Public Record Office, London). Unemployment in Wales, which had been only 15,000 in June 1945 had risen to 66,300 (9 per cent of the insured labour force) by June 1946. Thereafter the government's advance building programme trading estates and other measures had a positive effect.

30 *National Coal Board: Annual Report, 1951*, Parliamentary Papers, 1951–52, VIII, (190), p. 95.

31 H. Francis, 'Welsh Miners and the Spanish Civil War', *Journal of Contemporary History*, v, 3 (1970).

32 *First Interim Report of Welsh Advisory Council* (1943), pp. 111ff and materials in James Griffiths Papers, C1/2.

33 Report by Morrison, 23 Jan. 1946, 'The Administration of Wales and Monmouthshire', CP (46) 21, CAB 129/6 (Public Record Office, London) (hereafter PRO CAB); correspondence between Morrison and Griffiths, Oct. 1946, Griffiths Papers, C/2/6–11.

34 Note by Griffiths on 'The Area Boards covering Wales under the Electricity Bill', 17 Dec. 1946, CP (46), 462, PRO CAB 129/15.

35 Cabinet conclusions 15 Oct. 1948, PRO CAB/13; E. L. Gibson, 'A Study of the Council for Wales and Monmouthshire' (University of Wales, University College of Wales, Aberystwyth MA thesis, 1968).

36 Meeting of Organization Sub-committee of National Executive Committee (NEC), 15 Jan. 1947, Labour party NEC Minutes, 22 Jan. 1947 (Labour party archives, Walworth Road). Cf. R. I. McKibbin, *The Evolution of the Labour Party, 1910–1924* (Oxford, 1976), pp. 167–70.

37 Correspondence between Attlee and Welsh Labour MPs, 1946, Morgan Phillips Papers, GS/9/2 (Labour party archives). Also see Attlee to Goronwy Roberts, 31 July 1946, *ibid.*, GS/9. (I am indebted to Henry Pelling for the latter reference.)

38 For some intemperate and ill-informed comments which argue the contrary view, see L. Abse, *Spectator*, 29 May 1981.

39 I am grateful to Peter Stead for some helpful comments on this article.

6. Imperialism and the Labour government of 1945–51

1 Labour party, *Report of the Annual Conference 1945*, p. 115.

2 R. Palme Dutt, *Britain's Crisis of Empire* (1949), ch. 15.

3 G. Padmore, *Africa, Britain's Third Empire* (1949), pp. 9f, 12.

4 F. W. S. Craig, *British General Election Manifestos, 1900–1974* (1975 edn), p. 159.

5 D. Goldsworthy, *Colonial Issues in British Politics, 1945–1961* (Oxford, 1971), p. 23.

6 P. S. Gupta, *Imperialism and the British Labour Movement, 1914–1964* (1975), pp. 275–348.

7 R. Robinson, 'Andrew Cohen and the Transfer of Power in Tropical Africa', in W. H. Morris-Jones and G. Fischer (eds.), *Decolonization and After* (1980), pp. 50, 61–3.

8 Craig, *British General Election Manifestos*, p. 131.
9 DO (46)40, 13 Mar. 1946, para. 6, Cabinet Papers, 131/2 (Public Record Office, London) (hereafter PRO CAB).
10 See below, note 75.
11 DO (46) 1st and 5th meetings, PRO CAB 131/1.
12 DO (46) 5th meeting, 15 Feb. 1946, esp. p. 2, PRO CAB 131/1.
13 DO (46) 8th meeting, 18 Mar. 1946, p. 2, PRO CAB.
14 DO (46) 7th meeting, 8 Mar. 1946, p. 10, PRO CAB 131/1; DO (46) 27 for Attlee's views, PRO CAB 131/2.
15 DO (46) 40, Annex, 13 March 1946, PRO CAB 131/2.
16 *Ibid.*, para. 15.
17 DO (46) 10th meeting, 5 April 1946, PRO CAB 131/1.
18 DO (47)27 Annex 2, PRO CAB 131/4; also discussion on this on 26 March 1947 in DO (47) 9th meeting, minute 4, PRO CAB 131/5.
19 This is discussed in section III.
20 The main sources for the Indian developments are the volumes on the transfer of power edited by Professor Nicholas Mansergh. P N. S. Mansergh and P. Moon (eds.), *Transfer of Power* (hereafter *TOP*), 12 vols. (1970–80).
21 War Office Papers, 32/12313, para. 149 (Public Record Office, London) (hereafter WO).
22 See appreciation of the situation by the Indian Commander-in-Chief Claude Auchinleck, 24 Nov. 1945, *TOP*, VII, document 256; K. S. Himatsinghji to Auchinleck, 19 Nov. 1945, Auchinleck papers, MUL 1113 (John Rylands Library, Manchester).
23 Note by J. A. Thorne, 5 April 1946, *TOP*, VII, document 60.
24 C. Markovits, 'Indian Business and the Congress Provincial Governments 1937–39', *Modern Asian Studies*, xv (1981), pp. 487–526.
25 'Talks with Sir Evan Jenkins about the Situation in India, 27 Nov. 1945'. Prime Minister's Private Office Papers, 8/58 (Public Record Office, London) (hereafter PREM).
26 Gupta, *Imperialism and the British Labour Movement*, pp. 272ff.
27 *TOP*, VII, documents 87, 120.
28 *Ibid.*, document 85.
29 The evolution of the government's attitudes on the war costs and sterling balances can be seen in *TOP*, II, documents 375, 379, 751, 773, 780. For Churchill's views, Churchill to Linlithgow, 24 Sept. 1942, in *TOP*, III, document 25.
30 *TOP*, VI, documents 169, 186; *TOP*, VII, document 85.
31 *TOP*, VII, documents 86, 105.
32 *Ibid.*, documents 86, 105; also see Auchinleck, 'Military Implications of Pakistan' (Top Secret), 24 April 1947, Auchinleck Papers, MUL 1224.
33 *TOP*, VII, document 455, pp. 817ff. British troops in India were anxious to go home. Auchinleck wrote in his report for the year up to May 1946: 'The morale of British troops remained high . . . although service in India continued to be unpopular and questions of release and repatriation were topics of interest to the exclusion of all else.' WO 32/12314.
34 *TOP*, IX, documents 236, 243, 432.

35 On this see D. Potter, 'Manpower Shortage and the End of Colonialism: the Case of the ICS', *Modern Asian Studies*, VII (1973); T. H. Beaglehole, 'From Rulers to Servants: the ICS and the British Demission of Power in India', *Modern Asian Studies*, XI (1977).

36 CP (47)20, para. 15, PRO CAB 129/16 (hereafter specific Cabinet papers are referred to as CP).

37 CM 10(47)2, 13(47) 1, PRO CAB 128/9.

38 Montgomery to Alexander, 9 April 1947; Alexander to Montgomery, 11 April 1947, kept as annexures to CM 35(47)5, PRO CAB 128/9.

39 'India(Misc.)–Andaman & Nicobar Islands', PREM 8/574. This contains all the papers from 27 Feb. to 8 July 1947. See, in particular, Viceroy to Secretary of State, 21 June 1947. Also see Attlee's comments in Cabinet, CM 57(47)4, 26 June 1947, PRO CAB 128/10.

40 R. J. Moore, 'Mountbatten, India, and the Commonwealth', *Journal of Commonwealth and Comparative Politics*, XIX (1981), pp. 12–19.

41 Auchinleck to Geoffrey Scoone, 15 Sept. 1947, Auchinleck Papers, MUL 1259; Mountbatten to Auchinleck, 26 Sept. 1947, Auchinleck Papers, MUL 1260. Two years later, Philip Noel-Baker (Secretary of State for Commonwealth Relations) regretted that the Kashmir dispute had prevented the two countries from playing any part in Commonwealth defence plans. A hankering after the former part played by the Indian empire in British strategy is revealed in the following: 'should they settle their differences they are likely to be the only two members of the Commonwealth who are in a position to put reasonably equipped and trained forces into the field at short notice'. 'Defence Burdens and the Commonwealth', 30 Dec. 1949, by Noel-Barker, DO (49) 89, PRO CAB 131/7.

42 This was pointed out by the Chief of Air Staff, Lord Tedder, at a Cabinet meeting to discuss the Ceylonese demand for dominion status, CM 44(47)2, PRO CAB 128/9.

43 CP (45)130, 132 and 138, PRO CAB 129/1; CP (45)244, PRO CAB 129/3; CM 27(45)2, 30(45)3 and 46(45)4, PRO CAB 128/1.

44 CM 44(47)2, PRO CAB 128/9.

45 CP (47)171, PRO CAB 129/19; CM 51(47)4, PRO CAB 128/10.

46 The minister was Patrick Gordon-Walker. CP (48)91, PRO CAB 129/26.

47 CP (47)221, PRO CAB 129/20; DO (47)68, paras. 15 and 19, PRO CAB 131/4; CM 65(47)2, 67(47)2, 69(47)2 and 78(47)3, PRO CAB 128/10.

48 DO (47)68, para. 19, PRO CAB 131/4.

49 CP (48)61, PRO CAB 129/25.

50 For earlier fears see Gupta, *Imperialism and the British Labour Movement*, pp. 42–3, 217–20, 236ff; for post-war position, LP (DI) (46)72, PRO CAB 132/22. This shows that the only 'development area' in Lancashire with an unemployment rate of 5.9 per cent was the mining area of south Lancashire, not the cotton districts. See also Dalton's remarks at the Cabinet on 4 Feb. 1947, CM 16(47)2, PRO CAB 128/9.

51 For Australia, the joint paper by Lord Addison and G. A. Isaacs, CP (47) 67, PRO CAB 129/17, and also CM 26(47)6, PRO CAB 128/9. For Kenya, Goldsworthy, *Colonial Issues*, p. 141.

52 PREM 8/458; also see CM 78(46)7, PRO CAB 128/6. In order to facilitate good relations with Iraq, Bevin was anxious to find a place where this minority (who had fled to Iraq from Asia Minor at the time of the collapse of the Ottoman Empire and the emergence of modern Turkey) could be settled.
53 This is discussed in section V.
54 'Overseas Investment Policy, 1932–43', Treasury Papers, 236/173 (Public Record Office, London) (hereafter T).
55 CP (47)35, dated 8 Jan. 1947, PRO CAB 129/16.
56 CM 50(45), PRO CAB 128/4.
57 Only three Labour MPs (Norman Smith, R. R. Stokes and Stanley Evans) supported early day motions of this nature along with Conservative backbenchers in November and December 1945 (data from House of Commons Library).
58 CP (49) 188, para. 8, 12 Sept. 1949, PRO CAB 129/36.
59 *Ibid.*, para. 6.
60 CP (47)260, PRO CAB 129/21.
61 CP (47)35, PRO CAB 129/16; also see Cabinet Minutes of 28 Jan. 1947, CM 13(47)2, PRO CAB 128/9.
62 CP (47) 167, by Dalton, 28 May 1947, PRO CAB 129/19.
63 The Ministry of Food presented its problems at a number of Cabinet meetings. CM 30(47)5, 33(47)5, 39(47)5, PRO CAB 128/9; CM 56(47)2, PRO CAB 128/10.
64 Gupta, *Imperialism and the British Labour Movement*, pp. 314–15 needs revision in the light of these new pieces of evidence.
65 For the drafts of the Economic Survey, CP (47)19, PRO CAB 129/16; for the Creech Jones–Attlee correspondence on 26 March 1947, PREM 8/457.
66 CP (47) 175, PRO CAB 129/19.
67 CP (47) 242, 23 Aug. 1947, PRO CAB 129/20. Thomas mentioned that Creech Jones had discussed the memo. with Bevin before forwarding it.
68 CM 68(47), afternoon session, 1 Aug. 1947; CM 69(47)2 on 5 Aug. 1947, PRO CAB 128/10.
69 CM 77(47)2, PRO CAB 128/10.
70 CP (47)245 and 266, PRO CAB 129/21.
71 CM 77(47)1 and 79(47)5, PRO CAB 128/10.
72 CM 83(47)7, PRO CAB 128/10; also see CP (47)242, PRO CAB 129/20 and CM 74(47)2, PRO CAB 128/10 for discussions on the sale prospects of Malayan rubber.
73 An early day motion sponsored by the Labour MP R. W. G. Mackay and five other members from all parties on 13 March 1948 was signed by sixty-four backbench MPs on the first day (thirty-seven of them Labour). By 27 April the number of signatures had increased to 170 (of which about eighty-two of them were those of Labour MPs). (Data from the House of Commons Library.)
74 The phrase quoted is from a joint memo. by Bevin and Cripps on European economic cooperation, 6 March 1948, CP (48)75, PRO CAB 129/25.
75 CP (48)6, 4 Jan. 1948, PRO CAB 129/23. Also see the Cabinet minute on this and related memoranda, CM 2(48)5, PRO CAB 128/12.
76 Gupta, *Imperialism and the British Labour Movement*, pp. 276–9.
77 EPC (48)35, covering note by Plowden, para. 9; text of report, para. 44, PRO CAB 134/217.

78 Lord Addison to Mackenzie King, 9 April 1948, Addison papers, Box 137, folder 'Various Personal Letters' (Bodleian Library, Oxford).
79 Memo. by Listowel on internal office arrangements (n.d. but from content and provenance sometime in 1948), Creech Jones Papers, MSS Brit. Emp. s. 332, ACJ 54/2, fo. 10 (Bodleian Library, Oxford).
80 Herbert Morrison to Attlee, 20 June 1949, PREM 8/977.
81 CM 53(47)5, 16 June 1947, PRO CAB 128/10.
82 Minute by Creech Jones, 3 July 1948, Colonial Office Papers, 537/3031 (Public Record Office, London) (hereafter CO).
83 CM 20(48)2, PRO CAB 128/12.
84 Robert Scott (acting governor) to A. Creech Jones, 30 Oct. 1947, CO 96/795/31312 of 1948.
85 *Ibid.*, marginal comment, signature illegible.
86 CP (48) 7, PRO CAB 129/23.
87 When Bevin heard that the Colonial Office was planning to requisition the Shaftesbury Hotel to accommodate, apart from Colonial Service trainees, Colonial students, he strongly opposed it because it was too near King Street, the headquarters of the British Communist party. Minute by Creech Jones, n.d. but around July 1948, CO 537/2585, items nos. 10 and 11.
88 Robinson, 'Andrew Cohen and the Transfer of Power in Tropical Africa', pp. 60–7; also see J. W. Cell, 'On the Eve of Decolonization: the Colonial Office Plans for the Transfer of Power in Africa, 1947', *Journal of Imperial and Commonwealth History*, VIII (1980), esp. pp. 247–9; on Nigeria, see R. D. Pearce, 'Governors, Nationalists and Constitutions in Nigeria, 1935–51', *Journal of Imperial and Commonwealth History*, IX (1981), pp. 289–307.
89 CP (48) 193, para. 8, 30 July 1948, PRO CAB 129/29.
90 CP (48) 237, PRO CAB 129/30.
91 EPC(48) 35th meeting, 9 Nov. 1948, minute 4, PRO CAB 134/216. The quotation is at p. 6.
92 EPC(48)34, PRO CAB 134/217; also see EPC(48) 23rd meeting, minute 2, PRO CAB 134/216.
93 'Investment of Foreign Capital in the Colonies', EPC(49)74, 5 July 1949, kept with PREM 8/977; also see no. 303, 'Interdepartmental Committee on US Investment in the Sterling Area (Nov.–Dec. 1949)', PRO CAB 130/56.
94 'Draft to Cabinet of American Aid in Colonial Development', n.d., but sometime in 1949, Creech Jones Papers, ACJ 54/3, fo. 3.
95 Harold Wilson referred to the danger of British solvency being threatened 'by the continuance of unrequited exports on anything like the present scale!' CP (49) 179, para. 8, PRO CAB 129/36.
96 In the file on the colonial sterling balances, one Treasury official was impressed by the case for the colonies as presented by Sir Sidney Caine, but Dalton was not. See note on minute by SDW dated 30 July 1946. Dalton added (9 Aug. 1946): 'We must not admit – till a very late stage if at all – that any sterling creditor can make no adjustments.' T 236/51.
97 For Malaya, see M. Rudner, 'Financial Policies in Post-war Malaya: the Fiscal and Monetary Measures of Liberation and Reconstruction', *Journal of Imperial and*

Commonwealth History, III (1975), pp. 323–48. For India's tendency to run a deficit see references in CP (48) 35, para. 4 and annex A, PRO CAB 129/24; CP (48) 161 para. 11, PRO CAB 129/28; CP (49) 27, para. 57, PRO CAB 129/32.

 98 CP (49)58, PRO CAB 129/33; CM 17(49)1, PRO CAB 128/15.
 99 CP (49) 58, annex, para. 18, PRO CAB 129/33.
100 CP (47) 213, PRO CAB 129/20; CM 70(47)7, PRO CAB 128/10.
101 Commonwealth Finance Ministers' Conference, EMM(49) 10th meeting, 16 July 1949, p. 53, PREM 8/975.
102 EPC(49)79, appendix 2, 9 July 1949; Creech Jones's despatch to all colonies, 4 July 1949. All kept in PREM 8/975.
103 EMM(49) meeting on 15 July 1949, at p. 33, PREM 8/975.
104 CM 6(48) 5, PRO CAB 128/12. During drafting of the economic survey of 1949 it was suggested that the Colonial account could be presented separately to show the steady expansion of colonial exports and their contribution to the balance of payments. Cripps thought that to separate the figures 'might have an unfortunate effect on public opinion in the United States'. CM 16(49)4, PRO CAB 128/13. Cripps was evidently afraid of a renewed American attack on Imperial preference and a demand for convertibility.
105 CP (49)108, para. 16, PRO CAB 129/36.
106 Gupta, *Imperialism and the British Labour Movement*, pp. 262–3.
107 A. J. Stockwell, 'Colonial Planning during World War II: the Case of Malaya', *Journal of Imperial and Commonwealth History*, II (1974), p. 339.
108 Gupta, *Imperialism and the British Labour Movement*, pp. 262–330.
109 The standard work for the insurgency is A. Short, *The Communist Insurrection in Malaya, 1948–60* (1975).
110 J. D. V. Allen, *The Malayan Union* (New Haven, 1967), p. 19; M. R. Stenson, *Industrial Conflict in Malaya* (1970), pp. 128–32.
111 A. R. Stockwell, 'The Formation and First Years of the United Malay National Organization (UMNO), 1946–48', *Modern Asian Studies*, XI (1977), pp. 494ff.
112 Rudner, 'Financial Policies in Post-War Malaya', pp. 325–7.
113 C(46) 1st meeting, Colonial Affairs Committee, 7 Jan. 1946, PRO CAB 134/52.
114 Minutes of Governors' Conference, 20 Aug. 1946, CO 537/1596; 'Visit of Capt. Gammans and Col. Rees-Williams to Malaya', CO 537/1594; 'Malayan Policy', CP(46)439, PRO CAB 129/15; MSS and typed drafts of CP(46)439 in Creech Jones Papers, ACJ 57/2, item 1; C(46) 3rd meeting, 2 Dec. 1946, PRO CAB 134/52.
115 CP (46) 439, PRO CAB 129/15, annexure, para. 7, and covering note by Addison; also see Creech Jones–Edward Gent correspondence from Jan. to Sept. 1946, with the minister insisting that the basic principle of common citizenship must not be flouted. CO 537/1542.
116 Stockwell, 'The Formation and First Years of UMNO', p. 479; also the sources cited in note 114 above.
117 The material is available in CO 537/1567 and CO 537/2148.
118 Governors' conference, 19 Jan. 1947, CO 537/2165, item 7; Creech Jones to Gent, 4 Jan. 1947, sent with Attlee's approval, CO 537/1567, fo. 14.
119 CO 537/2150, fos. 1, 3.
120 CO 537/2175, fo. 1.

121 CP (47) 187, PRO CAB 128/19.
122 CO 537/3670.
123 CP (49)52, para. 8(d), PRO CAB 129/33; CP (50)75, paras. 6 and 7, PRO CAB 129/39.
124 CP (49)52 para. 9, PRO CAB 129/33.
125 Sir H. Gurney to Creech Jones, 12 Jan. 1950, Creech Jones Papers, ACJ 57/2, item 6.
126 CM 37(50)1, 19 June 1950, PRO CAB 128/17.
127 CP (47)16, Annex E and F, PRO CAB 129/16; CM 1(47)4, PRO CAB 128/9.
128 CP (50)138 para. 12, 26 June 1950, PRO CAB 129/40.
129 See section I.
130 CO 537/5348 is a typical file of the joint defence organization.
131 CO 537/2516.
132 L. Berger, *Labour, Race, and Colonial Rule: the Copperbelt from 1921 to Independence* (Oxford, 1974), pp. 97–9.
133 The average rate of Afrikaner immigration to Northern Rhodesia in the pre-war years of 1937–39 was 45 per cent of all immigrants; in the years 1946–49 it was 49 per cent. CO 537/5896. For Cohen's views on the recent British immigrants, see minute, 12 Oct. 1948 in CO 537/3608.
134 Note by Cohen, 11 June 1946, CO 537/1518.
135 CO 537/1224, item 6, pp. 3ff.
136 CM 51(47)3, PRO CAB 128/10.
137 Minutes by Orde-Browne, 25 Jan. 1946, and by Cohen, 25 Jan. 1946, CO 537/1510.
138 Berger, *Labour, Race, and Colonial Rule*, pp. 88–92.
139 *Ibid.*, pp. 100–09.
140 Correspondence between Rita Hinden and Creech Jones between 25 May and 30 Nov. 1948, Fabian Colonial Bureau Papers, 26/1, fos. 86–90 (Bodleian Library, Oxford).
141 Berger, *Labour, Race, and Colonial Rule*, p. 114.
142 Minute by Lambert, 9 Oct. 1950, and by J. Dugdale, CO 537/5896.
143 CO 537/5923, item 38, 10 Oct. 1950.
144 CM 30(50)6, 11 May 1950, PRO CAB 128/17; CP (50)171, 17 July 1950, PRO CAB 129/41.
145 CP (50)171, para. 14, PRO CAB 129/41.
146 Note by Creech Jones, n. d. but around Aug.–Sept. 1947, CO 797/164, item 3.
147 CO 797/164, items 6 and 12.
148 Item 38, Meeting between Creech Jones and a Northern Rhodesian group, CO 537/3608.
149 Minute by Creech Jones (Top Secret), 8 Oct. 1948, CO 537/3608.
150 *Ibid.*, another minute, n.d.
151 *Ibid.*, minute by Cohen, 12 Oct. 1948.
152 Labour party, International Department, Commonwealth Affairs Sub-committee, meeting on 18 Nov. 1947, and connected papers. Noel-Baker Papers, NBKR 2/70, fos. 7–8 (Churchill College, Cambridge).
153 D. A. Low and A. Smith (eds.), *History of East Africa*, 3 vols. (Oxford, 1976), III, pp. 12–15, 53–5, 112–28.

154 P. Mitchell to Creech Jones, 16 Sept. 1948, Creech Jones Papers, ACJ 55/4, item 5; also see his despatch of 30 May 1947, quoted in Cell, 'On the Eve of Decolonization', pp. 252–5.
155 J. Murray-Brown, *Kenyatta* (1972), pp. 227–39.
156 CO 537/5884, items 5, 7, 8, 9, 17, 91.
157 Low and Smith (eds.), *History of East Africa*, II, pp. 125–6.
158 CM 47(49)8, PRO CAB 128/14.
159 CP (50)36, PRO CAB 129/38, annexure, 'Report of Judicial Inquiry'.
160 CM 3(50)1, PRO CAB 128/17.
161 CM 11(50)7, PRO CAB 128/17.
162 CM 62(50)4, PRO CAB 128/18.
163 Sir E. Baring to Secretary of State, Commonwealth Relations Office, 24 March 1950, para. 28, Board of Trade Papers 11/4441, item 12 (Public Record Office, London).
164 CO 537/5884, item 31.
165 *Ibid.*, item 56 for meeting with Huggins; items 69 and 70 for meetings with Welensky.
166 A. Creech Jones to Sir A. Vincent, 10 Aug. 1949, Creech Jones Papers, ACJ 7/4, fo. 74.
167 Memo. on 'Relations of the two Rhodesias and Nyasaland', 9 May 1950, by Cohen and Lambert, CO 537/5884.
168 CO 537/5887, item 134, for Griffiths' remarks on 20 Sept. 1950, but the special reference to consulting Africans was watered down at the request of the governor of Northern Rhodesia. *Ibid.*, item 140.
169 All the relevant papers are in CO 537/5923 and PREM 8/1113; also see CP (50) 270, PRO CAB 129/43; CM 76(50)1, PRO CAB 128/18.
170 Gupta, *Imperialism and the British Labour Movement*, p. 269.
171 CM 65(48)3, PRO CAB 128/13.
172 CP (48) 7, para. 43, PRO CAB 129/23.
173 C. W. G. Greenidge to George Hall, 6 Nov. 1945, CO 537/1224.
174 Minute by Listowell, 9 April 1948, CO 537/2588.
175 Creech Jones minuted on 25 May 1948 that the aim was laudable but education rather than legislation would solve the problem, CO 537/1224.
176 Letter to Attlee, dated 16 June 1948, from J. D. Murray, C. F. Grey, James Harrison, Frank Mcleavey, R. W. G. Mackay, T. Reid, Louis Tolley, T. J. Brooks, J. R. Leslie, Percy Holman and Meredith P. Titterington, Home Office Papers, 213/244 (Public Record Office, London) (hereafter HO).
177 EPC(48), 23rd meeting, 15 June 1948, PREM 8/827.
178 'Who organised this incursion?' Attlee to Creech Jones, 16 June 1948, PREM 8/827.
179 For the draft reply, HO 213/244; also see A. H. Poynton to T. Hutson, 6 July 1948, in the same file for Creech Jones' role.
180 Note by Attlee, 20 June 1948, PREM 8/827.
181 Memo. by Havard, 15 Feb. 1949, HO 213/869.
182 T. I. K. Lloyd to Sir Frank Newton, 11 Oct. 1948, HO 213/716; CO memo. on St Helena and on 'Unemployment in The West Indies'.

183 The files of this working party are HO 213/716 and HO 213/868.
184 HO 213/869.
185 HO 213/716, item 3, a ten-page report by the Ministry of Labour.
186 HO 213/868, paras. 13–16 of the report.
187 Minutes by W. S. Murrie, 23 June 1949, and by Kenneth Younger, HO 213/870; note by J. E. Thomas of the Colonial Office, 8 Oct. 1949.
188 CO 537/4273.
189 CM 13(50)7, PRO CAB 128/17.
190 CM 37(50)2, PRO CAB 128/17.
191 Dr Goldsworthy (*Colonial Issues*, pp. 156ff) says that 106 Labour MPs signed it. An inspection of the House of Commons register showed that ninety-seven signed it on 26 Feb. 1951, and another fifteen on 27 Feb. 1951.
192 J. Morris, *Farewell the Trumpets: an Imperial Retreat* (1978), p. 497.

7. Work and hobbies in Britain, 1880–1950

1 R. W. Emerson, *English Traits* (1856), p. 89.
2 *Report of the Tariff Commission*, vol. 4 (*The Engineering Industries*) (1909), para. 403.
3 R. H. Best, W. J. Davis and C. Perks, *Brassworkers of Berlin and Birmingham: A Comparison* (1910), p. 23.
4 See *Report of the Royal Commission on Technical Instruction*, Parliamentary Papers (PP), 1884, xxix, C 3981, p. 519.
5 C. B. Hawkins, *Norwich: A Social Study* (1910), pp. 311–12.
6 M. E. Loane, *An Englishman's Castle* (1909), p. 35.
7 A. Shadwell, *Industrial Efficiency*, 2 vols. (1906), i, p. 29, ii, pp. 252–306.
8 J. Cohen, 'The Ideas of Work and Play', *British Journal of Sociology*, v (1953), pp. 318–21.
9 See particularly, Shadwell, *Industrial Efficiency*, ii, pp. 455–63.
10 *Hobbies*, i (Oct. 1895).
11 C. E. B. Russell, *Manchester Boys* (Manchester, 1913), p. 4.
12 Hawkins, *Norwich*, pp. 310–15.
13 M. Phillips, *The Young Industrial Worker* (1922), pp. 18–19.
14 J. G. Leigh, 'What do the Masses Read?', *Economic Review,* xiv, 2 (1904), pp. 171–2.
15 I have discussed this elsewhere. See R. McKibbin, 'Working Class Gambling in Britain, 1880–1939', *Past and Present*, no. 82 (1979), p. 169. Certain kinds of betting clearly meet these criteria and I have argued the case for betting as a hobby in there. For that reason I have excluded it from this essay.
16 For details, see J. C. Loudon, *An Encyclopaedia of Gardening* (1834), pp. 350, 353, 1036, 1227. The weavers of Lancashire, Spitalfields and the west of Scotland were famous florists and they were largely responsible for the development of auriculars. It is said that Gertrude Jekyll, wife of the great gardener William Robinson, designed her first garden for a factory operative in Rochdale 'who wanted his plot to contain as many variety of plants as could be contained within its confines'. M. Hadfield, *A History of British Gardening* (1979), pp. 353–4.
17 Emerson, *English Traits*, p. 61.

18 J. Dumazedier, *Sociology of Leisure* (Amsterdam and New York, 1974), p. 57.
19 T. H. S. Escott, *England: Its People, Polity and Pursuits*, 2 vols. (1885), II, pp. 417–18.
20 Escott, *England*, II, pp. 423–4.
21 Royal Commission on Labour (1891–94), PP, 1892, xxxv, C 6795, *Minutes of Evidence*, QQ7880–1 at p. 1032.
22 *Hobbies*, 11 Jan. 1896.
23 E. Dückershoff ('A German Coal Miner'), *How the English Workman Lives* (1899), p. 33.
24 R. A. Bray, 'The Boy and the Family', in E. J. Urwick (ed.), *Studies of Boy Life in Our Cities* (1904), pp. 72–3.
25 E. Hyams and E. Smith, *English Cottage Gardens* (1970), p. 163.
26 *The Land: The Report of the Land Enquiry Committee*, 2 vols. (1914), II, pp. 131–3.
27 F. A. Talbot, 'Those Amazing Allotments', *The World's Work* (1919), pp. 130–3.
28 Royal Commission on Labour, PP, 1892, xxxv, C 6795, *Minutes of Evidence*, QQ7580–3 at pp. 305–8.
29 *Report of a Departmental Committee of Inquiry into Allotments*, PP, 1968–69, xxxiii, Cmd 4166, p. 178.
30 *Ibid.*, p. 178.
31 N. Dennis, F. Henriques and C. Slaughter, *Coal is our Life* (1956), p. 167.
32 M. E. Loane, *From Their Point of View* (1908), p. 39.
33 See p. 142.
34 See McKibbin, 'Working Class Gambling', pp. 151–60.
35 Hawkins, *Norwich*, pp. 313–16.
36 Dückershoff, *How the English Workman Lives*, p. 67.
37 Russell, *Manchester Boys*, p. 56. For the only scholarly study of the social development of football, see Tony Mason, *Association Football and English Society 1863–1915* (Brighton, 1980), pp. 222–42 particularly.
38 A. Freeman, *Boy Life and Labour* (1914), pp. 151–2.
39 A. Paterson, *Across the Bridges* (1911), pp. 144–5.
40 Freeman, *Boy Life and Labour*, pp. 60–1.
41 A. Williams, *Life in a Railway Factory* (1915), p. 287.
42 F. Zweig, *The British Worker* (Harmondsworth, 1952), p. 124.
43 Freeman, *Boy Life and Labour*, p. 112.
44 H. Durant, *The Problem of Leisure* (1938), pp. 84–5 fn.
45 Zweig, *The British Worker*, pp. 97–8.
46 For the most comprehensive, though not always the most comprehensible account of Marx's attitudes, see P. Naville, *De l'Aliénation à la Jouissance* (Paris, 1957), pp. 130–60.
47 N. Anderson, *Man's Work and Leisure* (Leiden, 1974), p. 11.
48 G. Friedmann, *The Anatomy of Work* (1961), p. 110 particularly, and this chapter, p. 143.
49 See pp. 145–6.
50 Royal Commission on Labour, PP, 1893–4, xxxiv, C 6894, *Minutes of Evidence*, QQ25, 751–3 at p. 188.

51 Royal Commission on Labour, PP, 1892, xxxv, C 6708, *Minutes of Evidence*, QQ7682–4 at pp. 305–8.
52 Williams, *Life in a Railway Factory*, pp. 38–9.
53 *Ibid.*, p. 49.
54 Dennis *et al.*, p. 73.
55 Williams, *Life in a Railway Factory*, p. 52.
56 Dückershoff, *How the English Workman Lives*, p. 60.
57 G. v. Schulze-Gävernitz, *The Cotton Trade in England and on the Continent* (1895), pp. 138–9.
58 See here the interesting observations in O. Banks, *The Attitudes of Steelworkers to Technical Change* (Liverpool, 1960), pp. 124–5.
   It should be emphasised, however, that although our hypothetical situation specified that 500 men would be out of a job as a result of the new machinery, most of the men rejected the idea that this was necessarily a corollary of technical change. It was the firm conviction of the majority that displaced workers could always be found something to do in the firm . . .
59 Shadwell, *Industrial Efficiency*, ii, pp. 73–5.
60 Zweig, *The British Worker*, p. 111.
61 M. Viteles, *The Science of Work* (1934), pp. 322–9.
62 Williams, *Life in a Railway Factory*, pp. 79–81.
63 M. Cohen, *What Nobody told the Foreman* (1953), p. 3.
64 Royal Commission on Labour, PP, 1892, xxxiv, C 6708, *Minutes of Evidence*, QQ5904, 6061–73 at pp. 324–30.
65 Dennis *et al.*, p. 30.
66 P. de Rousiers, *The Labour Question in Britain* (1896), p. 6.
67 Dückershoff, *How the English Workman Lives*, p. 19.
68 Mass Observation, *War Factory: A Report* (1943), pp. 78–9.
69 Williams, *Life in a Railway Factory*, p. 267.
70 P. Göhre, *Three Months in a Workshop* (1895), pp. 78–9.
71 R. Brown, P. Brannen, J. Cousins and M. Samphier, 'Leisure in Work', in M. A. Smith, S. Parker and C. S. Smith (eds.), *Leisure and Society in Britain* (1973), p. 107.
72 Williams, *Life in a Railway Factory*, pp. 292–3.
73 See the sensitive discussion of this in Durant, *The Problem of Leisure*, pp. 4–5.
74 S. de Grazia, *Of Time Work and Leisure* (New York, 1962), p. 425.
75 Zweig, *The British Worker*, p. 113.
76 A. Wylie, *Labour, Leisure and Luxury* (1884), p. 19.
77 de Rousiers, *The Labour Question in Britain*, p. 5.
78 For an assessment of the evidence see P. Stearns, *Lives of Labour* (1975) pp. 219–235.
79 Stearns, *Lives of Labour*, p. 233.
80 Royal Commission on Labour, PP, 1893–4, xxxiv, C 6894, *Minutes of Evidence*, QQ31120–2.
81 See p. 134.
82 S. Parker, *The Future of Work and Leisure* (1972), pp. 47–9.
83 For the best statement of this position, see Friedmann, *The Anatomy of Work*, pp. 110ff.
84 Zweig, *The British Worker*, p. 153.

85 Williams, *Life in a Railway Factory*, pp. 38–9.

86 Florence, Lady Bell, *At the Works* (1911), pp. 209–29.

87 See also P. Willmott and M. Young: 'The hobby of a sound engineer of Islington, hi-fi, was evident from the speakers we heard in every room.' *The Symmetrical Family* (Harmondsworth, 1980), pp. 219–20.

88 F. E. Green, 'The Allotment Movement', *Contemporary Review*, cxiv (1918), p. 90.

89 A. Tilgher, *Work* (1931), pp. 184–5.

90 D. Caradog Jones (ed.), *The Social Survey of Merseyside*, 3 vols. (1934), ii, p. 276.

91 Young and Willmott, *The Symmetrical Family*, p. 223.

92 Zweig, *The British Worker*, p. 150; Banks, *Attitudes of Steelworkers*, pp. 32–3. See also F. Zweig, *Men in the Pits* (1948), p. 104.

93 J. Mott, 'Miners, Weavers and Pigeon Racing' in Smith *et al.* (eds.), *Leisure and Society in Britain*, pp. 93–4; Hawkins, *Norwich*, pp. 314–15.

94 Russell, *Manchester Boys*, pp. 63–4.

95 Royal Commission on Labour, PP, 1892, xxxv, C 6795, *Minutes of Evidence*, Q7686 at p. 308.

96 Jackson, *Working-Class Community* (Harmondsworth, 1972), p. 31.

97 R. Q. Gray, 'Religion, Culture and Social Class in Late Nineteenth and Early Twentieth Century Edinburgh', in G. Crossick (ed.), *The Lower Middle Class in Britain, 1870–1914* (1977), p. 149.

98 Paterson, *Across the Bridges*, pp. 97–8.

99 See Stearns, *Lives of Labour*, pp. 216–17; for the apprenticeship system see the excellent discussion in C. More, *Skill and the English Working Class, 1870–1914* (1980), pp. 41–93, 215–20.

100 See the use of the word and its context in W. G. Ward, *Seven Night's Discussion. Capital and Labour* (Nottingham, 1872), p. 33.

101 Zweig, *The British Worker*, p. 93.

8. Credit and thrift and the British working class, 1870–1939

1 F. Engels, *The Condition of the Working-Class in England*. Preface to the First German Edition. (Moscow, 1977), p. 13.

2 This question is dealt with tangentially by Gareth Stedman Jones in his study of casual labour in London, and briefly by James Treble in his recent work on poverty. See: G. Stedman Jones, *Outcast London* (Oxford, 1971) *passim*; J. H. Treble, *Urban Poverty in Britain* (1979), esp. pp. 130–9.

3 Among these invaluable institutional histories are: A. Bonner, *British Co-operation* (revised edn. Manchester, 1970); H. Oliver Horne, *A History of Savings Banks* (Oxford, 1947); D. Morrah, *A History of Industrial Life Assurance* (1955).

4 These percentages are the estimates given in C. H. Feinstein, *Statistical Tables of National Income, Expenditure and Output of the UK 1855–1965* (Cambridge, 1976), Table 57.

5 Vividly portrayed by Walter Greenwood in *Love on the Dole* (1933).

6 B. S. Rowntree, *Poverty and Progress* (1941), pp. 155–171. H. Tout, *The Standard of Living in Bristol* (Bristol, 1938). See especially the life-cycle poverty graph on the front cover.

7 Royal Commission on the Aged Poor, Parliamentary Papers (PP), 1895, xiv, C 7684. See especially *Report*, pp. xii–xiii, civ–cviii for statistics which show about 30 per cent of the population aged over sixty-five to be dependent on Poor Relief.

8 B. S. Rowntree, *How the Labourer Lives* (1913), pp. 307–9.

9 There are over 100 Charity Organisation Society case papers relevant to the period covered by this paper deposited with the Greater London Council Record Office, County Hall.

10 C. Booth, *Life and Labour of the People in London*, 17 vols. (1886–1903); H. Llewellyn Smith, *New Survey of London Life and Labour*, 3 vols. (1930); D. Caradog Jones, *Social Survey of Merseyside*, 3 vols. (1934); P. Ford, *Work and Wealth in a Modern Part: An Economic Survey of Southampton* (1934); A. L. Bowley and A. R. Burnett-Hurst, *Livelihood and Poverty* (1915); B. S. Rowntree, *Poverty: A Study of Town Life* (1901), *Poverty and Progress* (1941); H. Tout, *The Standard of Living in Bristol* (1938).

11 E. W. Brabrook, *Provident Societies and Industrial Welfare* (1898); *Institutions for Thrift: Two Lectures . . .* (1905).

12 Royal Commission on Friendly and Benefit Building Societies. *First Report*, PP, 1871, xxv, C 452, QQ3537, 5258–60, 5497, 5628–31, 6686–9, 7728–9, 8198–202.

13 G. Routh, *Occupation and Pay in Great Britain, 1906–1960* (Cambridge, 1965), pp. 4–5.

14 *Ibid.*, p. 57.

15 Policy registers of the Royal Standard Benefit Society, Greater London Council Record Office, A/RSB/34. The figure for clerks' membership comes from a 25 per cent sample of 1,759 policies entered in Register No. 8 between March 1876 and August 1899.

16 Registers of the membership of the Blackburn Philanthropic Friendly Collecting Society at the date of the Certificate of Incorporation, 2 Sept. 1913. (Liverpool City Library, uncatalogued.) The occupation of members is taken from a 5 per cent sample of the 7,580 Preston members and the 10,400 Bolton members. The work of the society was confined almost wholly to Lancashire.

17 The entrance fee was 3s 6d, the monthly subscription 2s 6d. See: J. Cox, *Royal Standard Benefit Society. The History of the Society During the One Hundred Years of its Existence 1828–1928, with part II (1929–1966) by A. C. W. Mell* (1967), p. 3.

18 The case papers are those from Area 1, boxes 1–7, and Area 4, boxes 1 and 7, which contain the necessary details of occupation and financial standing.

19 Routh, *Occupation and Pay*, p. 104.

20 G. Crossick, *The Lower Middle Class in Britain, 1870–1914* (1977), pp. 25–6.

21 The Hire Traders Protection Association (later the Hire Purchase Trade Association) was founded in 1891, but it concerned itself solely with formal hire-purchase retailing. See the Report of the Committee on Consumer Credit, PP, 1971, Cmnd 4596, p. 43.

22 L. Davies, *Co-operation in Poor Neighbourhoods* (Manchester, 1899), p. 10.
23 C. Booth, *Life and Labour of the People in London*, 1st ser., vol. 1 (1892), p. 46.
24 F. Bullen, *Confessions of a Tradesman* (1908), pp. 159–60.
25 *Pall Mall Gazette*, 6 Feb. 1879, cited in Stedman Jones, *Outcast London*, p. 50.
26 Women's Co-operative Guild, *The Extension of Co-operation to the Poor* (Manchester, 1902), pp. 19–20.
27 F. Bell, *At the Works* (1907), p. 70.
28 W. H. Whitelock, 'Industrial Credit and Imprisonment for Debt', *Economic Journal*, XXIV (1914), p. 34.
29 See Davies, *Co-operation in Poor Neighbourhoods*, p. 11; Bell, *At the Works*, pp. 82–3. For the rare sympathetic view see J. Greenwood, *Low Life Deeps* (1876), pp. 257–66, and E. S. Watkins, *Credit Buying* (1939), p. 71.
30 R. Roberts, *The Classic Slum* (Hardmondsworth, 1973), pp. 32–3.
31 H. Gosling, *Up and Down Stream* (1927), quoted in G. Crossick, *An Artisan Elite in Victorian Society* (1978), p. 63.
32 H. Bosanquet, *Rich and Poor* (2nd edn, 1898), p. 89.
33 The number of local societies advancing credit to members is listed in the Returns of Industrial and Provident Societies. See *Annual Report of the Chief Registrar of Friendly Societies*, from 1886 to 1911.
34 *Co-operative Congress Annual Report*, Statistical Appendices for 1921 and 1922.
35 E. C. Warren, *Credit Dealing* (1939), pp. 14–15.
36 Roberts, *The Classic Slum*, pp. 228–9.
37 The 1938 Hire-Purchase Act spawned a number of books on the subject. Some, like those by Warren and Watkins, explain the working of the Act, while others, like that by Aylmer Vallance, roundly condemn the whole idea of credit purchase. A. Vallance, *Hire Purchase* (1939).
38 *Supplement to the 24th Report of the Commissioners of the Inland Revenue*, PP, 1881, XXIX, C 2979, p. 46; *5th Report of Customs and Excise*, PP, 1914, XVII, Cd 7574, p. 62.
39 *Select Committee on Pawnbrokers*, PP, 1870, VIII (377), Appendix 14.
40 C. A. Cuthbert Keeson, 'Pawnbroking London', in G. R. Sims (ed.), *Living London* (1902), II, p. 37.
41 Bosanquet, *Rich and Poor*, p. 99.
42 A. Newton, *Years of Change* (1974), p. 23.
43 C. Grant, *Farthing Bundles* (c. 1931), p. 98.
44 Davies, *Co-operation in Poor Neighbourhoods*, p. 13. *Select Committee on the Pawnbrokers Bill*, PP, 1872, XII (288), Q460.
45 See: Bell, *At the Works*, pp. 82–3; Bosanquet, *Rich and Poor*, p. 89; Davies, *Co-operation in Poor Neighbourhoods*, p. 11; *Select Committee on Pawnbrokers*, 1870, QQ4547–50.
46 J. Greenwood, *Low Life Deeps*, p. 261.
47 *Select Committee on Pawnbrokers*, 1870, QQ313–14.
48 *Select Committee on Pawnbrokers Bill*, 1872, Q379. COS, *Report on the Best Means of Dealing with Exceptional Distress* (1886), Q1192.
49 *Porcupine*, 21 May 1864, p. 60.
50 *Select Committee on Pawnbrokers*, 1870, Q3527. See also Q81.

51 *Ibid.*, Q402. See also QQ960, 1073, 3778, 4464.
52 Roberts, *The Classic Slum*, p. 25. The Pilgrim Trust, *Men Without Work* (Cambridge, 1938), p. 124.
53 *The Pawnbroker's Gazette and Trade Circular*, 22 Jan. 1898, p. 57.
54 Roberts, *The Classic Slum*, p. 32.
55 Stedman Jones, *Outcast London*, p. 49.
56 S. A. Barnett, 'Thrift in the Home', in COS, *Thrift Manual* (1908), p. 20.
57 There is, however, a reference to working-class 'saving . . . in the shape of additions to household furniture' in the Minority Report signed by Dunraven *et al.* of the Royal Commission on the Depression of Trade and Industry, *Report*, PP, 1886, XXIII, C 4893, p. xlv.
58 M. Douglas and Baron Isherwood, *The World of Goods: Towards an Anthropology of Consumption* (1979), pp. 141–3.
59 The Pawnbrokers Act, 1872 35/36 Vict c. 93.
60 *Select Committee on Pawnbrokers*, 1870, Q695. C. Bundy and D. Healy, 'Aspects of Urban Poverty', *Oral History*, VI (1978), pp. 90–1.
61 *Pawnbrokers' Gazette*, 1 Jan. 1897, p. 12.
62 *Select Committee on Pawnbrokers*, 1870, Q1023.
63 An indicator of default is the number of small debt cases filed at the county courts. In 1913, for example, there were 1,172,189 for sums under £20. *Judicial Statistics, Civil*, PP, 1938–39, XXV, Cmd 6135, p. 46. In his account of industrial credit, Whitelock estimated that 'the proportion of cases where the ordinary trader has to issue process varies from 5 per cent. to 12 per cent. of his credit transactions, whilst in money-lending cases the proportion varies from 15 per cent to 20 per cent'. *Economic Journal*, XXIV (1914), p. 37.
64 For example, see evidence given to the Royal Commission on the Aged Poor which is summarized in Edwin Cannan, 'The Stigma of Pauperism', *Economic Review*, V (1895).
65 Bell, *At the Works*, pp. 124–5.
66 I. H. Mitchell, 'Thrift and Trade Unions', *Thrift Manual*, p. 66.
67 Mrs Pember Reeves, *Round About a Pound a Week* (1913), p. 72; Grant, *Farthing Bundles*, p. 90; S. Dark, 'London Thrift', in Sims (ed.), *Living London*, II, pp. 257–8.
68 This was certainly found to be the case among some poor families surveyed in New York in 1960. See D. Caplovitz, *The Poor Pay More* (New York, 1963). He found that (p. 97)

> some family heads felt that it was easier to buy on credit than to save and pay cash. They made it plain that they were referring to the discipline required for advance saving. This they found difficult to achieve. Faced with many day-to-day demands upon their resources, they found it hard to build up substantial reserves. For them credit provided a system of enforced savings with the discipline imposed from without.

69 *Select Committee on Friendly Societies*, PP, 1888, XII (389), Q57.
70 Annual Returns of the Liverpool Victoria Friendly Society, Friendly Society Papers, FS 16/57 (Public Record Office, London) (hereafter FS).
71 Only two of the major societies or companies appear to have kept records of their early policies. These are the Britannic Assurance Company, which has in its Birmingham headquarters policy registers dating back almost to the formation of the

company in 1866, and the Royal London Mutual Insurance Company, which has kept all the original proposal forms from the early years of this century.

72 Royal Commission on Friendly and Benefit Building Societies. *Report of the Assistant Commissioners for Cheshire, Derbyshire, etc.*, PP, 1874, XXIII, part II, C 996, p. 106. There are some examples also in the COS case papers. Area 1, box 5, case 26/59. Life insurance for out-of-work casual labourer, wife and eight children: 2s 8d per week to the London and Manchester, 7d to the Prudential. Area 1, box 6, case 31/582. Life insurance for a widow: 3d per week to the Prudential, 6d to the Manchester and Liverpool.

73 Figures for industrial assurance companies are taken from the appropriate part of successive editions of the *Statistical Abstract* from 1886, and from the *Report of the Industrial Assurance Commissioner for 1937*, PP, 1937–38, XII (163), pp. 46–7. The total number of industrial assurance company policies in force before 1905 is not stated in the official returns, so an estimate has been made based on the statistics given in the *Prudential Assurance Company Annual Reports*. Figures for friendly collecting societies are taken from the *Reports of the Chief Registrar of Friendly Societies*. These refer only to registered societies, but it is known that a number of local unregistered societies existed. The only statistics we have on unregistered membership come from Rowntree's second poverty survey of York. In 1938, the registered friendly society membership in York was 17,305, and the membership of non-registered clubs was estimated at 14,000. See B. S. Rowntree, *Poverty and Progress*, pp. 208–10. This tallies with E. W. Brabrook's estimate 'that the extent of the unregistered societies was as large as that of the registered societies'. Royal Commission on the Aged Poor, *Report*, PP, 1895, XV, C 7684, II, Q11,039.

74 Grant, *Farthing Bundles*, p. 105.

75 Rowntree, *Poverty and Progress*, p. 213.

76 J. Hilton, *Rich Man, Poor Man* (1944), p. 106.

77 *Select Committee on Friendly Societies Act, 1875*, PP, 1889, x (304), Appendix 5; Annual Returns of the Royal Liver Friendly Society. FS 16/38.

78 *Porcupine*, 21 Sept. 1861, p. 294.

79 J. Edward Squire, 'Thrift and Health', *Thrift Manual*, p. 46.

80 Review by Bosanquet of Mrs Pember Reeves' *Round About a Pound a Week*, *Economic Journal*, XXIV (1914), p. 110.

81 *Porcupine*, 7 Aug. 1869, p. 175.

82 Rowntree, *Poverty and Progress*, p. 212.

83 Pilgrim Trust, *Men Without Work*, pp. 183–4.

84 *Ibid.*, p. 184.

85 *Report of the Registrar of Friendly Societies for 1880. Part II (B)*, PP, 1883, LXVIII (212–I), pp. 1118–19. *75th Statistical Abstract*, PP, 1931–32, XXIV, Cmd 3991, p. 223. *22nd Abstract of Labour Statistics*, PP, 1936–37, XXVI, Cmd 5556, pp. 160–1.

86 Royal Commission on Friendly and Benefit Building Societies, *2nd Report Part II*, PP, 1872, XXVI, C 514–I, QQ13,573–4. See also QQ2,415, 8,557, 10,992, 11,428.

87 B. B. Gilbert, *The Evolution of National Insurance in Great Britain* (1966), p. 166. The contrasting ratios of occupations of members of the Royal Standard Benefit

Society and the Blackburn Philanthropic Friendly Collecting Society given above lend weight to this view.

88 For the Royal Liver figure: Royal Commission on Friendly and Benefit Building Societies, *2nd Report, Part II*, Q1437. For the Oddfellows figure: *Oddfellows Quarterly Report*, April 1892, pp. 50–3.
89 Crossick, *An Artisan Elite in Victorian Society*, particularly ch. 9.
90 *Select Committee on National Provident Insurance*, PP, 1884–85, x (270), Q1455.
91 *House of Commons Debates, (Hansard)*, 4th ser., cxc, cols. 568–9, 15 June 1908.
92 H. Bosanquet, *The Strength of the People* (1902), p. 241.
93 H. Oliver Horne, *A History of Savings Banks* (Oxford, 1947). Appendices II and III, pp. 386–92.
94 *Ibid.*, p. 232.
95 *61st Statistical Abstract*, PP, 1914–16, LXXVI, Cd 7636, pp. 366–7.
96 *43rd Annual Report of the Postmaster General*, PP, 1897, XXIV, C 8586, p. 14. See also P. H. J. H. Gosden, *Self-Help* (1973), pp. 239–40.
97 S. Dark, 'London Thrift', in Sims (ed.), *Living London*, II, p. 255.
98 *75th Statistical Abstract*, 1931–2, p. 220.
99 *Ibid.*, *83rd Statistical Abstract*, PP, 1939–40, x, Cmd 6232, p. 268.
100 E. J. Cleary, *The Building Society Movement* (1965), pp. 184–91.
101 The Abbey Road Building Society statistics are from Cleary, *The Building Society Movement*, p. 189. The money deflator is from the retail price index given in Feinstein, *Statistical Tables of National Income, Expenditure and Output of the UK 1855–1965*, Table 65.
102 J. S. Duesenberry, *Income, Saving and the Theory of Consumer Behaviour* (Cambridge, Mass. 1949), p. 28.
103 Pilgrim Trust, *Men Without Work*, p. 189.
104 See Douglas and Isherwood, *The World of Goods*, pp. 74–6 for their explanation of this term.
105 Duesenberry, *Income, Saving and the Theory of Consumer Behaviour*, p. 33.
106 For examples of such views see: Bosanquet, *Rich and Poor*, pp. 99–100; Nurse Loane, *The Common Growth* (1911), p. 105. The quotation is from S. Meacham, *A Life Apart* (1977), p. 198.

9. Intelligent artisans and aristocrats of labour: the essays of Thomas Wright

1 E. J. Hobsbawm, 'The Labour Aristocracy in Nineteenth Century Britain', collected in *Labouring Men* (1964), pp. 272–315.
2 E. J. Hobsbawm, 'Trends in the British Labour Movement Since 1850', *Labouring Men*, pp. 316–43, though see his 'Lenin and the "Aristocracy of Labour" ', in *Revolutionaries* (1973), pp. 121–9 for an interesting reconsideration.
3 R. Q. Gray, *The Labour Aristocracy in Victorian Edinburgh* (Oxford, 1976); G. Crossick, *An Artisan Elite in Victorian Society* (1978).
4 This had just previously been forcefully restated in J. Foster, *Class Struggle and the Industrial Revolution* (1974).
5 See also G. Crossick, 'The Labour Aristocracy and its Values: a Study of Mid-Victorian Kentish London', *Victorian Studies*, XIX (1976), pp. 301–28.

6 H. Pelling, 'The Concept of the Labour Aristocracy', in *Popular Politics and Society in Late Victorian Britain* (1968), pp. 37–61.

7 G. Stedman Jones, *Outcast London* (Oxford, 1971); S. Price, 'Rivetters' Earnings in Clyde Shipbuilding 1889–1913', *Scottish Economic and Social History*, I (1981), pp. 42–65; and, especially interesting in relation to the rest of this essay, the use of oral material in E. Roberts, 'Working-class Standards of Living in Barrow and Lancaster, 1890–1914', *Economic History Review*, 2nd ser., xxx (1977), pp. 306–21.

8 Pelling, 'Labour Aristocracy', pp. 52–5, a point partly conceded in E. J. Hobsbawm, 'The Artistocracy of Labour Reconsidered', *Proceedings of the Seventh International Economic History Congress* (Edinburgh, 1978), pp. 457–66, especially 460–1.

9 Pelling, 'Labour Aristocracy', pp. 41–52; G. Stedman Jones, 'Class Struggle and the Industrial Revolution', *New Left Review*, no. 90 (1975), pp. 35–69.

10 G. Stedman Jones, 'Working-class Culture and Working-class Politics in London, 1870–1900: Notes on the Remaking of a Working Class', *Journal of Social History*, VII (1974), pp. 460–508. For another interesting approach to the problem, see P. Bailey, ' "Will the Real Bill Banks Please Stand Up?" Towards a Role Analysis of Mid-Victorian Working Class Respectability', *Journal of Social History*, XII (1979), pp. 336–53. I am grateful to David Crew for letting me see his unpublished paper 'Some Suggestions for Analysing the Structure and Culture of the Working Class in Europe, 1870–1914', which contains many perceptive remarks on the role of women in maintaining a 'respectable' life-style, and on the differences between generations, themes which are further pursued below.

11 P. Joyce, *Work, Society and Politics* (Brighton, 1980); K. McClelland, 'A Politics of the Labour Aristocracy?', *Bulletin of the Society for the Study of Labour History*, no. 40 (1980), pp. 8–9.

12 See the comments by Hobsbawm and Gray in *Bulletin of the Society for the Study of Labour History*, no. 40 (1980) pp. 6–8, and R. Gray, *The Aristocracy of Labour in Victorian Britain* (1981).

13 A Journeyman Engineer, *Some Habits and Customs of the Working Classes* (1867); The Journeyman Engineer, *The Great Unwashed* (1868); Thomas Wright, *Our New Masters* (1873).

14 See, for example: J. Hinton, *The First Shop Stewards' Movement* (1973), pp. 95–6; P. Bailey, *Leisure and Class in Victorian England* (1978), pp. 85–6, 90–2. I am indebted to Joyce Bellamy of the *Dictionary of Labour Biography* for sending me all the information on Wright that she has been able to compile.

15 R. Lowe (Viscount Sherbrooke), *Speeches and Letters on Reform* (1867), especially pp. 49, 74.

16 W. E. Gladstone, *Speeches on Parliamentary Reform in 1866* (1866), especially pp. 27–31, 315–36; *Essays on Reform* (1867); L. Levi, *Wages and Earnings of the Working Classes* (1867); J. M. Ludlow and L. Jones, *Progress of the Working Classes 1832–1867* (1867); R. D. Baxter, *The National Income* (1868).

17 Crossick, *An Artisan Elite*, pp. 127–8. The notion of a 'labour aristocracy' has a slightly different history from that of an 'upper stratum', tending to be used much more in debates about trade unionism. M. A. Shepherd, 'The Origins and Incidence of the Term "Labour Aristocracy" ', *Bulletin of the Society for the Study of Labour History*, no. 37 (1978), pp. 51–67.

18 Wright, *Our New Masters*, pp. 5–6. This procedure is most obvious in the introductory chapter, 'The Emergence of the Labour Aristocracy', in F. B. Smith, *The Making of the Second Reform Act* (Cambridge, 1966), pp. 8–14. Clearly the full-length studies of the subject have involved more sophisticated techniques and a wider range of sources, but this procedure is still evident and this particular quotation appears in Hobsbawm, 'The Labour Aristocracy', p. 275, R. Harrison, *Before the Socialists* (1965), p. 28 and Stedman Jones, *Outcast London*, p. 338. For other uses of Wright see Gray, *The Labour Aristocracy*, pp. 137–9, 143 and Crossick, *An Artisan Elite*, pp. 145, 154, 156.

19 Wright, *The Great Unwashed*, pp. 2–3, see also more generally pp. 1–4; *Habits and Customs*, pp. v–vi, 83; and *Our New Masters*, pp. vi, vii, 5.

20 Wright, *The Great Unwashed*, pp. 21, 22, 22–5, 19.

21 In an interesting passage in *Habits and Customs* (p. 3) Wright remarks that

> . . . it would be doing both the working classes and those who take an interest in their welfare a service if some admirer would favour the world with a plain definition of what an intelligent artisan really is. The phrase 'intelligent artisan', like many other well-sounding stock phrases, is somewhat vague, and may mean a variety of things, and have different meanings to different people.

He suggests four groups to whom the phrase might refer: (a) skilled workers, (b) skilled workers with 'a natural shrewdness of character', (c) skilled workers who were moderately well-read and thought for themselves and (d) any workers who took an interest in politics, especially the Reform movement. In the essay 'Working Men', Wright's use of the phrase combines (b) and (d) with the emphasis more on 'natural shrewdness' than on any particular definition of skill.

22 Wright, *The Great Unwashed,* pp. 15, 14–21.

23 For more detailed critiques of the educational system see the essays 'The Working Man's Education' in Wright, *Habits and Customs*, pp. 1–28 and 'Working Class Education and Mis-education' in Wright, *Our New Masters*, pp. 110–38.

24 Wright, *The Great Unwashed*, p. 7.

25 *Ibid.*, pp. 6, 7, 10, 20.

26 *Ibid.*, p. 10.

27 *Ibid.*, p. 11.

28 Wright, *Habits and Customs*, p. 4. In this quotation Wright means the phrase 'intelligent artisans' to be understood in sense (c) in note 21 above.

29 Wright, *Our New Masters*, p. 5.

30 *Ibid.*, p. 6, see also p. 283.

31 *Ibid.*, p. 6.

32 Wright, *Habits and Customs*, p. 258. Interestingly enough, this paragraph is referred to in Smith, *Second Reform Act*, pp. 9–10, as evidence for the social pretensions of the 'labour aristocracy': 'There is a certain understood dignity and exclusiveness of caste pertaining to the artisan class which every individual of it is practically compelled to respect and support. A mechanic when out of employment can scarcely take work as a labourer, even if it is offered to him . . . .' However, to cut off the quotation at this point is to shift the emphasis of the passage away from the objective constraints of restrictive practices in the workplace towards an alleged subjective sense of superiority.

33 Wright, *Our New Masters*, pp. 6, 124, 117.

34 *Ibid.*, pp. 9–10, 12, 72–5, 346–7, 350.

35 *Ibid.*, pp. 12–14, 350.

36 *Ibid.*, p. 300.

37 *Ibid.*, pp. 306–9; see also Wright, *The Great Unwashed*, pp. 103–4, and the essay 'Tramps and Tramping', pp. 256–83.

38 For his most systematic account of the trade cycle, see Wright, *Our New Masters*, pp. 43–6 and for other comments see Wright, *Habits and Customs*, pp. 257–9 and Wright, *The Great Unwashed*, pp. 246, 250–3. Like Marx, *Capital*, 3 vols. (1974), I, pp. 625–7, Wright was particularly struck by the sufferings of the highly skilled during the 1866–67 slump in the Thames shipbuilding industry, Wright, *Our New Masters*, p. 44 note. He also frequently emphasized that fluctuations in employment led not only to immediate poverty but also to an absence of any simple correspondence between earnings and standards of living, as debts had to be paid off, furniture and clothes redeemed from the pawnshop etc. Wright, *The Great Unwashed*, pp. 204, 252–3; Wright, *Our New Masters*, pp. 59, 260.

39 Wright, *Our New Masters*, pp. 44, 43.

40 *Ibid.*, p. 242.

41 Wright, *The Great Unwashed*, p. 32.

42 Wright noted that it was customary for skilled men to marry at the same time as they completed their apprenticeships, and while increases in labour mobility and industrial fluctuation had made this inadvisable, the men concerned were slow to change their habits. Some of them had sufficient savings and regularity of employment to avoid disaster but 'Thousands and tens of thousands of artisans marry when they are provided in none of these respects, and commencing their married lives in poverty, continue and end them in the same condition'. Wright, *The Great Unwashed*, p. 47.

43 *Ibid.*, p. 31.

44 Wright, *Habits and Customs*, pp. 71–5, 94–6, 189–90, 223–7.

45 Wright, *Our New Masters*, p. 361.

46 *Ibid.*, pp. 49–50.

47 Wright, *The Great Unwashed*, p. 25.

48 *Ibid.*, pp. 37–8; Wright, *Habits and Customs*, pp. 206, 239–40; Wright, *Our New Masters*, pp. 375–7.

49 Wright, *Habits and Customs*, p. 117.

50 Wright, *The Great Unwashed*, p. 254; Wright, *Habits and Customs*, p. 194.

51 Wright, *Habits and Customs*, pp. 118–19.

52 *Ibid.*, p. 118.

53 *Ibid.*, pp. 119–24.

54 *Ibid.*, pp. 124, 240, 254; Wright, *Our New Masters*, pp. 7–-1, 163.

55 Wright, *The Great Unwashed*, p. 5.

56 Pelling, 'Labour Aristocracy', p. 57.

57 Wright, *Our New Masters*, pp. 15–17.

58 *Ibid.*, p. 18.

59 *Ibid.*, pp. 18–21.

60 *Ibid.*, pp. 21–4, 232.

61 *Ibid.*, p. 23.

62 *Ibid.*, passim.

63 Wright, *Habits and Customs*, p. 35.
64 Wright, *Our New Masters*, pp. 66–7, 101–3.
65 *Ibid.*, p. 103.
66 *Ibid.*, p. 4 and Wright, *The Great Unwashed*, pp. viii, 205.
67 Wright, *Our New Masters*, p. 64, see also p. 216.
68 *Ibid.*, p. 75, see also pp. 282–3.
69 *Ibid.*, p. 25.

10. Anglo-Marxism and working-class education

1 On Hyndman and Anglo-Marxism, see C. Tsuzuki, *H. M. Hyndman and British Socialism* (Oxford, 1961), p. 276 and *passim*.
2 *'Plebs' Magazine*, i, 1 (1909).
3 *The Story of Ruskin College* (Oxford, 1949), p. 15.
4 W. W. Craik, *The Central Labour College* (1964), p. 79.
5 *Ibid.*, p. 53.
6 Plebs League, *The Burning Question of Education* (Oxford, 1909), p. 15.
7 J. P. M. Millar, *The Labour College Movement* (1979), p. 11.
8 Plebs League, *The Burning Question of Education*, p. 20.
9 D. Hird, *From Brute to Brother, a Clarion pamphlet* (n.d.), *passim*.
10 *'Plebs' Magazine*, i, 8, 10, 11 (1909), esp. pp. 171, 244.
11 *'Plebs' Magazine*, v, 5 (1913), p. 117.
12 *Justice*, 2 March 1912.
13 H. Pelling, *A History of British Trade Unionism* (1963), p. 139.
14 N. Ablett *et al.*, *The Miners' Next Step* (Tonypandy, 1912), pp. 8, 17, 19, 29.
15 Millar, *Labour College Movement*, p. 20.
16 *Ibid.*, p. 26. J. F. and W. Horrabin, *Working-class Education* (1924), p. 36.
17 Craik, *Central Labour College*, p. 133.
18 F. Brockway, *Inside the Left* (1947), p. 137.
19 Millar, *Labour College Movement*, pp. 43, 66.
20 Craik, *Central Labour College*, p. 130.
21 W. Kendall, *The Revolutionary Movement in Britain 1900–21* (1969), p. 240.
22 H. Pelling, *The British Communist Party. A Historical Profile* (1958), p. 6.
23 *Communist International*, 5 Sept. 1919, quoted in *Call*, 22 April 1920.
24 *Call*, 15 July 1920.
25 *Call*, 1 April, 6 May 1920.
26 Craik, *Central Labour College*, p. 125.
27 Millar, *Labour College Movement*, p. 80.
28 *Plebs*, x, 1 (1918), pp. 8–9; *Plebs*, x, 2 (1918) pp. 30–4.
29 *Plebs*, xi, 2 (1919), p. 29.
30 *Plebs*, xi, 3 (1919), pp. 40–1.
31 *Plebs*, xi, 8 (1919), pp. 117–18.
32 *Plebs*, xi, 5 (1919), p. 75.
33 *Plebs*, xi, 8 (1919), pp. 120–1.
34 *Call*, 5 June 1919.
35 *Call*, 11 Sept. 1919.

36 *Plebs*, xii, 1 (1920), p. 3.
37 *Plebs*, xii, 2 (1920), p. 30.
38 J. T. Murphy, *New Horizons* (1941), p. 117.
39 W. Gallacher, *Revolt on the Clyde* (1949), pp. 250–3.
40 Pelling, *The British Communist Party*, p. 18.
41 *Plebs*, xv, 4 (1923), pp. 154–6.
42 *Plebs*, xv, 5 (1923), pp. 200–1.
43 *Plebs*, xv, 8 (1923), pp. 364–5.
44 Millar, *Labour College Movement*, p. 87.
45 *Ibid.*, p. 87.
46 *Plebs*, xvii, 3 (1925), pp. 167.
47 *Plebs*, xvii, 7 (1925), pp. 287–8.
48 *Plebs*, xvii, 8 (1925), pp. 301–12.
49 Millar, *Labour College Movement*, p. 44.
50 Craik, *Central Labour College*, pp. 141–3.
51 *Plebs*, xxi, 2 (1929), p. 46.
52 Millar, *Labour College Movement*, p. 99.
53 Quoted in Millar, *Labour College Movement*, p. 102.
54 Ibid., pp. 106, 120, 125.
55 *Plebs,* xviii, 6 (1926), pp. 208–13.
56 Quoted in *Plebs*, xx, 2 (1928), p. 26.
57 *Sunday Worker*, 8 Jan. 1928.
58 *Plebs*, xx, 2 (1928), p. 26.
59 *Plebs*, xxiii, 8 (1931), pp. 171–3; xxiii, 11 (1931), pp. 247, 249.
60 *Plebs*, xxiii, 8 (1931), p. 174.
61 Millar, *Labour College Movement*, p. 113.
62 *Plebs*, xxv, 3 (1933), p. 61.
63 *Plebs*, xxvii, 1 (1935), p. 7. Millar's book says almost nothing about this aspect of the history of the NCLC.
64 Millar, *Labour College Movement*, pp. 131–2.
65 *Plebs*, xxxvii, 9 (1945), p. 105.
66 Millar, *Labour College Movement*, p. 249.

11. Did British workers want the welfare state? G. D. H. Cole's Survey of 1942

1 B. B. Gilbert, *The Evolution of National Insurance. The Origins of the Welfare State* (1966), pp. 25–6; J. R. Hay, *The Origins of the Liberal Welfare Reforms 1906–1914* (1970), p. 25.
2 H. Pelling, 'The Working Class and the Origins of the Welfare State', *Popular Politics and Society in Late Victorian Britain* (1968), pp. 1–18.
3 J. R. Hay, *Origins of Liberal Welfare Reforms*, p. 28; J. Hinton, *The First Shop Stewards' Movement* (1973), ch. 1; J. Harris, *Unemployment and Politics* (Oxford, 1972), pp. 289–91, 317–18.
4 P. Thane, 'The Working Class and State Welfare 1880–1914', *Bulletin of the Society for the Study of Labour History*, no. 31 (1975).
5 G. D. N. Worsick, 'Cole and Oxford 1938–1958', in A. Briggs and J. Saville (eds.),

Essays in Labour History (1960), I, pp. 29–33; G. D. H. Cole Papers, B3/4/C, Box
I (Nuffield College, Oxford) Nuffield College Social Reconstruction Survey
Report, 26 May 1942, The original questionnaires, local reports, and Cole's digest
of information received are preserved in several hundred files and boxes in Nuffield College Library. The following summary is based on this material, except
where otherwise indicated.

6 Nuffield College Social Reconstruction Survey Report, 26 May 1942, p. 12.
7 Nuffield College Social Reconstruction Survey, 6th Progress Report, Jan. 1942,
   G. D. H. Cole Papers, B3/4/C, Box I.
8 Nuffield College Social Reconstruction Survey, Conference of Chief Local Investigators, 7 Feb. 1942, G. D. H. Cole Papers, B3/4/C, Box I.
9 Nuffield College Social Reconstruction Survey, 8th Progress Report, June 1942,
   G. D. H. Cole Papers, B/3/4/C, Box I.
10 Nuffield College Social Reconstruction Survey, local reports from South Wales,
   Manchester and Oxford.
11 Cole's claim was somewhat disingenuous since, as was inevitably the case with
   such a survey, the findings had to be processed before they could be used at all.
   Cole's digest of answers to questionnaires survives in the papers of the Nuffield
   College Social Reconstruction Survey, LG(10) (1) and LG(17) (2).
12 Memoranda on 'National Health Insurance', 5 June 1942: 'Pensions', 'The Assistance Board' and 'Public Assistance', 19 June 1942; 'Workmen's Compensation',
   22 June 1942. Cabinet Papers, 87/80 (Public Record Office, London) (hereafter
   PRO CAB).
13 The exceptions came almost exclusively from rural and mining areas of Scotland.
   Miners interviewed in Lothian and Fife gave 'a series of unsolicited testimonials
   expressive of sincere gratitude and satisfaction regarding doctors' services' (local
   report from Edinburgh).
14 In the twenty-seven regions covered by the Survey, local investigators reported
   that in nineteen panel service was thought to be inferior to private medicine, two
   reported no perceived difference, and six were non-committal.
15 Local report from Edinburgh.
16 This was mentioned as a major problem in all but three of the twenty-six areas.
17 Delay before benefits were paid lasted an average of 3 weeks in all approved
   societies, in the Prudential, 6 weeks.
18 Under existing arrangements, maternity benefit consisted simply of a lump sum of
   40s, paid to Insured women who had made a minimum of twenty-six contributions.
19 The three groups were those receiving pensions under (a) the Old Age Pensions
   Act 1908, (b) the Widows', Orphans' and Old Age Contributory Pensions Act of
   1925, and (c) the Old Age and Widows' Pensions Act 1940.
20 Local Report from Bristol.
21 Nuffield College Reconstruction Survey, report on Matters Relating to Pensions
   and Public Assistance not covered in the Separate Questions.
22 Local report from South Wales.
23 *Ibid.*
24 The TUC pressing for a totally separate system of workmen's compensation paid
   for solely by employers – the one point on which they differed fundamentally from

Beveridge's 'comprehensive' insurance proposals. Trades Union Congress Replies to Queries submitted by Sir William Beveridge, 3 April 1942, PRO CAB 87/79.

25 Social Insurance Committee, Minutes of Evidence, 24 June 1942, PRO CAB 87/78.

26 Note by Sir George Reid on the Report of the Nuffield College Social Reconstruction Survey so far as it relates to Pensioners and the work of the Assistance Board, 10 June 1942, PRO CAB 87/80.

27 Nuffield College Social Reconstruction Survey, 8th Progress Report, June 1942, G. D. H. Cole Papers, B3/4/F.

28 Nuffield College Social Reconstruction Survey, Investigators' Conference, 20 Sept. 1942, G. D. H. Cole Papers, B3/4/F.

12. Images of the working class since 1930

1 A. Willener, *Images de la Societé et Classes Sociales* (Paris, 1957); S. Ossowski, *Class Structure in the Social Consciousness* (1963); E. Bott, *Family and Social Network* (1957); D. Lockwood, 'Sources of Variation in Working-class Images of Society', *Sociological Review*, xiv, 3 (1966), pp. 249–67; J. H. Goldthorpe, D. Lockwood, F. Bechhofer and J. Platt, *The Affluent Worker in the Class Structure* (1969); and M. Bulmer (ed.), *Working Class Images of Society* (1975).

2 Goldthorpe *et al.*, *The Affluent Worker*, p. 147.

3 J. Westergaard and H. Resler, *Class in a Capitalist Society: A Study of Contemporary Britain* (1975), p. 29.

4 *Ibid.*, p. 29.

5 W. G. Runciman, *Social Science and Political Theory* (1960), p. 138.

6 Bott, *Family and Social Network*, p. 163, cited by Lockwood, *Sociological Review*, xiv, 3 (1966), p. 249.

7 D. V. Glass, 'Introduction', in D. V. Glass (ed.), *Social Mobility in Britain* (1954),
In a society divided into a series of 'estates', the rank, privileges and contents of these 'estates' being defined by law, there should theoretically be no problem in identifying the position of an individual in the social hierarchy. But in contemporary society, the different levels are not so specified and the criteria chosen must reflect a *customary* rather than a legal structure [my italics].

8 See e.g. *ibid.*, pp. 5–6; I. Reid, *Social Class Differences in Britain* (1977).

9 Sir H. Llewellyn Smith (ed.) *The New Survey of London Life and Labour*, 6 vols. (1932–34), iii (1932), p. 105.

10 *Ibid.*, vi (1934), p. 153.

11 *Ibid.*, ii, p. 416, vi, p. 153.

12 *Ibid.*, iii Appendix 1, p. 416.

13 *Ibid.*, vi, p. 153.

14 D. Caradog Jones, *The Social Survey of Merseyside*, 3 vols. (1934).

15 *Ibid.*, i, p. 310.

16 E. Wight Bakke, *The Unemployed Man: A Social Study* (1933), Preface by Sir Hubert Llewellyn Smith.

17 Ministry of Reconstruction, *Housing in England and Wales: A Memorandum by the Advisory Housing Panel on the Emergency Problem (1918)*, p. 7.

18 *House of Commons Debates (Hansard)*, 5th ser., ccxxxvii, 17 April 1930, col. 3079.

19 15 & 16 Geo. V, ch. 14, 5th Schedule; 26 Geo. VI and 1 Edw. VIII, ch. 51, 11th Schedule.

20 Ministry of Labour, *Report of the Unemployment Insurance Statutory Committee on Remuneration Limit for Insurance of Non-Manual Workers* (1936), pp. 7–8.

21 *Ibid.*, p. 15.

22 *Report of the Committee on Holidays With Pay*, Parliamentary Papers, 1937–38, xii, Cmd 5724, pp. 48, 65.

23 *Ibid.*, pp. 48, 65.

24 M. Cohen, *I Was One of the Unemployed* (1945; 1978 edn), p. 40.

25 Charles Fiske to Bess Fiske, 5 May 1925. Fiske Letters (British Library of Political and Economic Science).

26 H. L. Beales and R. S. Lambert, *Memoirs of the Unemployed* (1933), pp. 165, 166.

27 *Ibid.*, pp. 116, 119.

28 *Ibid.*, p. 76.

29 Quoted in M. Bragg, *Speak for England* (1976), p. 203.

30 A. Giddens, *The Class Structure of Advanced Societies* (1973), p. 111.

31 Bakke, *The Unemployed Man*, p. 11.

32 See for example *Railway Review*, 26 Feb. 1937.

33 Beales and Lambert, *Memoirs of the Unemployed*, p. 208.

34 Bakke, *The Unemployed Man*, p. 12.

35 Most recently to hand is this comment (dating from the beginning of the war) of a miner to his son: 'This row of houses is the best part of Cecil Street. All good workers . . . .' T. Wakefield, *Forties' Child* (1980), pp. 2–3.

36 Kean to A. V. Sugden, 3 Nov. 1930, Wallpaper Workers' Union Papers, MSS 39W B8 (Modern Records Centre, University of Warwick).

37 Stacey, *Tradition and Change: A Study of Banbury* (1960), p. 153.

38 G. A. W. Tomlinson, *Coal-Miner* (1937), pp. 92–3.

39 Beales and Lambert, *Memoirs of the Unemployed*, p. 228.

40 *Ibid.*, pp. 183, 189.

41 *Listener*, 13 Oct. 1938.

42 Guild of Insurance Officials, General Purposes Committee Minutes, 1 Dec. 1933; speech delivered by Major H. L. Nathan MP, at London Branch Annual Meeting, 15 March 1932 (Modern Records Centre, University of Warwick, MSS 79).

43 See M. Green, *Children of the Sun* (1977), p. 230.

44 Hugh Dalton's Diaries, 17 Sept. 1938, Dalton Papers (British Library of Political and Economic Science).

45 H. Montgomery Hyde, *Baldwin: The Unexpected Prime Minister* (1973), p. 434.

46 J. Richards, 'Gracie Fields: The Lancashire Brittania', *Focus on Film*, no. 34 (1979), p. 34.

47 W. Brierley, *Means Test Man* (1935), p. 219.

48 W. Greenwood, *Love on the Dole* (1933), pp. 13–15.

49 *Ibid.*, pp. 9–10.

50 A. M. Carr-Saunders and D. Caradog Jones, *A Survey of the Social Structure of England and Wales* (1937), p. 66.

51 Gareth Stedman Jones, 'Working-class Culture and Working-class Politics in

London 1870–1900: Notes on the Remaking of a Working Class', *Journal of Social History*, VII (1974), p. 493.

52 Brierley, *Means Test Man*, pp. 21–2.

53 Greenwood, *Love on the Dole*, p. 337.

54 P. Wilmott, *Growing Up in a London Village: Family Life between the Wars* (1979), p. 30.

55 Vivienne Hall Diary, 4 Sept. 1939 (Imperial War Museum, London).

56 *The Times*, 8 July 1943.

57 Chuter Ede Diary, 5 Aug. 1941, British Library Add. MS 59690 (British Library, London).

58 *Ibid.*, 16 Oct. 1941, Add. MS 59691.

59 *Ibid.*, 21 Oct. 1941, Add. MS 59691.

60 *Reynold's News*, 11 July 1943.

61 Chuter Ede Diary, 11 July 1943, Add. MS 59696.

62 See Marwick, *Class: Image and Reality* (1980), chapter 11.

63 L. J. Carr and J. E. Sterner, *Willow Run: A Study of Industrialisation and Cultural Inadequacy* (1952), p. 89.

64 See for example M. Stacey, *Tradition and Change*; University of Liverpool Department of Social Science, *The Dock Worker* (1954); N. Dennis, F. Henrickes, C. Slaughter, *Coal is our Life: An Analysis of a Yorkshire Mining Community* (1956); R. Lewis and A. Maude, *The English Middle Classes* (1949); C. Bell, *Middle Class Families* (1968); Mass Observation, 'The London Middle Class Housewife and her Food Problems' and 'The London Middle Class Housewife and her Expenditure', Mass Observation Archives, file 3073 (University of Sussex).

65 Glass, *Social Mobility in Britain*, p. 3.

66 W. G. Runciman, *Relative Deprivation and Social Justice* (1966), p. 77.

67 University of Liverpool Social Science Department, *Neighbourhood and Community: An Enquiry into Social Relationships on Housing Estates in Liverpool and Sheffield* (1954), pp. 68–9.

68 The British Gallup Poll table is in G. H. Gallup, *The Gallup International Public Opinion Polls: Great Britain 1937–1975* (1976), vol. 1, 1973–1964, p. 172 (March 1948); the French and American ones were brought together by N. Rogoff, 'Social Stratification in France and in the United States', *American Journal of Sociology*, LVIII (1953), p. 349.

69 F. M. Martin, 'Some Subjective Aspects of Social Stratification', in D. V. Glass (ed.), *Social Mobility in Britain*, p. 58.

70 A. Marwick, *Class*, pp. 294–5.

71 Written by Bryan Forbes, produced by Richard Attenborough and Bryan Forbes and directed by Guy Green. The 'book of the film', *The Angry Silence: A Novel from the Screenplay of B. Forbes* by John F. Burke was published in 1961.

72 B. Forbes (i.e. J. T. Clarke), *Notes for a Life* (1974), p. 280.

73 A. Sillitoe, *Saturday Night and Sunday Morning* (1958); the film, directed by Karel Reisz, was released in 1960.

74 Sillitoe, *Saturday Night and Sunday Morning*, 'Heritage of Literature Series' (1968), pp. x, xii, 222.

75 Goldthorpe *et al.*, *The Affluent Worker*; Marwick, p. 316.

76 See R. P. Coleman and L. Rainwater, *Social Standing in America: New Dimensions of Class* (1978), p. 45: 'The class label they seem to prefer for themselves is *working class*; this is especially popular with men, who take a measure of pride in its evocation of hard work and physical effort even while it suggests that on the job "we take orders, not give them".'

77 Goldthorpe *et al.*, *The Affluent Worker*, pp. 69–77; H. Beynon, *Working for Ford* (1973), pp. 118, 121, 125.

78 Letter dated 4 March 1968 in Etheridge Papers, MS 202 (Modern Records Centre, University of Warwick).

79 See, e.g. *The Times*, correspondence columns 3, 9 and 15 Dec. 1976, 9 May 1977; *Evening Standard*, 10–14 Sept. 1979; *Sunday Telegraph*, 7 and 14 Oct. 1979.

80 See J. Goldthorpe, *Social Mobility and Class Structure in Modern Britain* (1980).

81 Stacey, *Tradition and Change*, pp. 14ff, pp. 160ff; R. Dahrendorf, *Conflict after Class* (1967); Goldthorpe, *Social Mobility and Class Structure*, pp. 40–6, *passim*.

82 See the survey material in R. Scase, 'English and Swedish Concepts of Class', in F. Parkin (ed.), *The Social Analysis of Class Structure* (1974), pp. 149–77.

13. Unemployment, nutrition and infant mortality in Britain, 1920–50

For advice on this paper, thanks are due to Sir Dugald Baird, Volker Berghahn, Peter Clarke, Jo Garcia, Ann Oakley, Jim Oeppen and Henry Pelling.

1 M. H. Brenner, 'Fetal, Infant, and Maternal Mortality during Periods of Economic Instability', *International Journal of Health Services*, III (1973), p. 155.

2 See the citation of Brenner's work in the recent report of a working party of the Department of Health and Social Security, *Inequalities in Health* (1980).

3 R. C. O. Matthews, 'Why has Britain had Full Employment since the War?', *Economic Journal*, LXXVIII (1968), pp. 555–69.

4 D. Seers, *The Levelling of Incomes since 1938* (1950).

5 Brenner, 'Economic Instability', p. 153.

6 W. I. B. Beveridge, *Influenza* (1977).

7 T. McKeown, *The Modern Rise of Population* (1976). The advice of Ann Oakley was particularly helpful on this point.

8 J. M. Winter, 'The Impact of the First World War on Civilian Health in Britain', *Economic History Review*, 2nd ser., XXX (1977), pp. 487–508.

9 J. A. Heady, C. F. Stevens, C. Daly and J. N. Morris, 'Social and Biological Factors in Infant Mortality. IV. The Independent Effects of Social Class, Region, the Mother's Age, and her Parity', *Lancet*, 5 March 1955.

10 J. N. Morris and R. N. Titmuss, 'Health and Social Change: I. – the Recent History of Rheumatic Heart Disease', *Medical Officer*, 26 Aug., 2, 9 Sept. 1944.

11 S. C. Rogers and J. A. C. Weatherall, 'Anencephalus, Spina Bifida and Congenital Hydrocephalus. England and Wales 1964–1972', *Office of Population Census and Surveys. Studies in Medical and Population Subjects*, 32 (1976).

12 J. Boyd Orr, *Food, Health and Income* (1937), pp. 24–5 and *The Impact of the War on Civilian Consumption in the United Kingdom, the United States, and Canada* (1945), pp. 26–31.

13 This point has already been made with reference to Brenner's work. See S. V. Kasl, 'Mortality and the Business Cycle: Some Questions about Research Strategies when Utilizing Macro-social and Ecological Data', *American Journal of Public Health*, LXIX (1979), pp. 784–8, and the same author's comment in J. E. Barrett *et al., Stress and Mental Disorder* (New York, 1979), pp. 217–18.

14 O. D. Anderson, *Time Series Analysis and Forecasting. The Box-Jenkins Approach* (1975). Thanks are due to Jim Oeppen of the SSRC Cambridge Group for the History of Population and Social Structure for statistical help on this and other points.

15 Firm conclusions cannot be drawn, though, since the Box–Jenkins approach requires a time series of at least fifty years. Pre-1920 measurements of unemployment rates are thereby introduced, which vitiates comparisons.

16 A full report of the findings of the analysis of variance will be published by Dr Brian Benson and the author.

17 R. N. Titmuss, *Problems of Social Policy* (1950), ch. 25.

18 *On the State of the Public Health during Six Years of War* (1946), p. 42.

19 Sir L. Parsons, 'The War in Britain: an Experiment in Social Pediatrics', *Birmingham Medical Review*, XV, 3 (1947), pp. 125–38. I am grateful to Dr Robert Dare for having drawn my attention to this article.

20 Seers, *The Levelling of Incomes*, chaps. 1–2.

21 M. Olson, *The Economics of the Wartime Shortage* (Durham, North Carolina, 1960).

22 Royal College of Obstetricians and Gynaecologists, *Maternity in Great Britain* (1948).

23 J. M. Winter, 'Military Fitness and Public Health in Britain During the First World War', *Journal of Contemporary History*, XV (1980), pp. 211–44.

24 Titmuss, *Problems of Social Policy*, p. 530.

25 This help could backfire if council housing rents were too high. See G. C. M. M'Gonigle, 'Poverty, Nutrition, and Public Health', *Proceedings of the Royal Society of Medicine*, XXVI (1933), I, pp. 677–87.

26 C. A. Smith, 'Effects of Wartime Starvation in Holland on Pregnancy and its Products', *American Journal of Obstetrics and Gynacology*, LIII (1947), pp. 599–608.

27 Z. Stein, M. Susser, G. Saenger and F. Morolla, *Famine and Human Development. The Dutch Hunger Winter of 1944–45* (Oxford, 1975). The only exception, which is interesting for our purposes, is a disproportionately high incidence of central nervous system disorders detected during medical examination of recruits who were born during the 'hunger winter'.

28 J. B. de V. Weit, 'The Assessment of the Growth of Schoolchildren with Special Reference to Secular Changes', *British Journal of Nutrition*, XI (1952), pp. 19–33.

29 N. Scrimshaw, C. Taylor and J. Gordon, *Interactions of Nutrition and Infection* (New York, 1968).

30 D. Baird, 'The Epidemiology of Low Birth Weight: Changes in Incidence in Aberdeen 1948–72', *Journal of Biosocial Science*, VI (1974), pp. 323–41. D. Baird, 'The Interplay of Changes in Society, Reproductive Habits, and Obstetric Practice in

Scotland Between 1922 and 1972', *British Journal of Preventive and Social Medicine*, xxix (1975), pp. 135–46.

31 D. Baird, 'Epidemiology of Congenital Malformations of the Central Nervous System in (a) Aberdeen and (b) Scotland', *Journal of Biosocial Science*, vi (1974), pp. 113–37. D. Baird, 'The Changing Pattern of Human Reproduction in Scotland, 1928–72', *Journal of Biosocial Science*, vii (1975), pp. 77–97.

32 D. Baird, 'Environment and Reproduction', *British Journal of Obstetrics and Gynaecology*, lxxxviii (1980), pp. 1057–67.

33 On cohort effects, the literature is enormous. See W. O. Kermack, A. G. McKendrick and P. L. McKinlay, 'Death-rates in Great Britain and Sweden. Some General Regularities and their Significance', *Lancet*, 31 March 1934; J. N. Morris and J. A. Heady, 'Social and Biological Factors in Infant Mortality. V. Mortality in Relation to the Father's Occupation', *Lancet*, 12 March 1955. On the specific subject of this essay, see Titmuss, *Problems of Social Policy*, p. 538: 'But just as the advances of one generation may show their full effects through the lives of succeeding generations so, too, may the retreats.'

Index